Visible Now

VISIBLE NOW

Blacks in Private Schools

*Edited by DIANA T. SLAUGHTER
and DEBORAH J. JOHNSON*

Foreword by James P. Comer

Contributions in Afro-American
and African Studies, Number 116

GREENWOOD PRESS
New York • Westport, Connecticut • London

Library of Congress Cataloging-in-Publication Data

Visible now : Blacks in private schools / edited by Diana T. Slaughter
and Deborah J. Johnson.
      p.   cm. — (Contributions in Afro-American and African
studies, ISSN 0069-9624 ; no. 116)
   Bibliography: p.
   Includes index.
   ISBN 0-313-25926-7 (lib. bdg. : alk. paper)
   1. Afro-American children—Education.   2. Private schools—United
States.   I. Slaughter, Diana T.   II. Johnson, Deborah J. (Deborah
Jean), 1958-   .   III. Series.
LC2731.V57 1988
371′.02′0973—dc19   88-10236

British Library Cataloguing in Publication Data is available.

Library of Congress Catalog Card Number: 88-10236
ISBN: 0-313-25926-7
ISSN: 0069-9624

First published in 1988

Greenwood Press, Inc.
88 Post Road West, Westport, Connecticut 06881

Printed in the United States of America

The paper used in this book complies with the
Permanent Paper Standard issued by the National
Information Standards Organization (Z39.48-1984).

10 9 8 7 6 5 4 3 2 1

TO OUR PARENTS

The late John I. Slaughter
and Gwendolyn M. Armstead
and great-grandmother, Bertha B. Alexander

Lois and Richard Johnson
and grandmother, Mildred Vaughn

Contents

Figure and Tables

FIGURE

TABLES

Foreword
James P. Comer

Black students in independent schools are "Visible Now." But probably because slightly more than 90 percent of all Black students remain in public schools, researchers have paid little attention to the process and outcomes of independent school education for the students, their parents, and their schools. In so doing we have been ignoring a valuable source of information and insights which can be applied to the education of Blacks students in public as well as private schools. There is an urgent need for such information and insights.

A number of people are concerned that our educational systems are not giving students the kind of experiences that will enable our country to maintain a democratic political system in the face of massive scientific and technological changes. Also, the Carnegie Forum on Education and the Economy[1] recently pointed out that without significantly improving the education of American children our nation will be hard-pressed to compete with other industrialized nations in the very near future. A similar concern was recently expressed by business leaders through a report of the Committee for Economic Development.[2]

Black Americans, who currently make up a little over 10 percent of the labor force will make up about 25 percent of the work force in the very near future. But a disproportionate number of Black children are living in families most adversely affected by difficult conditions in the past and, in turn, are being under prepared for school success and the future.

Black children in independent schools are generally succeeding. Who are these children? In which ways are their parents the same or different from parents of children in public schools? Which independent schools are succeeding, why, and at what price? These and many other questions need and receive attention in this pioneering and timely book. A backward glance should be useful in considering the findings and implications of this work, I will briefly review the historical antecedents of the problems for which this book provides helpful insights and suggestions.

The effects of the undereducation of Blacks were masked until shortly after World War II. Prior to that time Black heads of households worked in the basement of the American economy first as slaves and then largely as agricultural and industrial laborers and domestics. But they worked, obtaining the many psychosocial benefits we now understand that working provides such as organization, purpose, a sense of adequacy, and belonging. Many were part of small-town and rural subcultures that provided support and nurturance to children and families alike, even though unfair and repressive laws limited social and economic opportunities. Many were enmeshed in rich religious subcultures with social networks that offered protection against the most adverse effects of social and economic oppression.

Because of the protective factors inherent in small-town culture and those created by Black families and their social networks, most Black families functioned reasonably well until the 1950s. In fact only 22 percent of Black families were single-parent families as late as the 1950s, a statistic that is now 50 percent. And most Black communities were reasonably safe.

But because Blacks were denied political, economic, and social power, public policy permitted massive undereducation of the Black community through World War II. As late as the 1940s, four to eight times as much money was spent on the education of a White child as that of a Black in the eight states that held 80 percent of the Black population. The disparity was as great as twenty-five times in areas that were disproportionately Black. The same situation existed in higher education. In fact, as late as the mid-1960s, one half the endowment of Harvard was equal to that of the combined endowment of two prestigious White women's colleges and was more than that of all of the more than one-hundred Black colleges put together.

After World War II, education became the ticket for admission to adequately paying jobs and economic and technological developments began to dramatically and permanently change the nature of American life--including families, neighborhoods, and schools. Sociocultural protective factors were weakened and adequate income became more necessary to maintain well-functioning families. Given the transfer from generation to generation of attitudes, values, and customs, families educated and participating in the mainstream of society prior to World War II had the best opportunity to function in a way that would enable them to prepare their children to function well in the changed conditions of society after the 1950s. Blacks most excluded from participation in the mainstream of society and denied adequate education were most vulnerable.

Many Black families were able to maintain their sociocultural supports in urban, especially industrial, settings. These were usually the families who were most successful prior to the 1950s. But given the massive rural to urban movement of Blacks around the 1940s, their extreme undereducation prior to the 1940s, and continued racial discrimination, many families that had once functioned reasonably well in rural situations began to function less well. Also in order to participate in the economic and social mainstream, many of the most successful families--among all groups--began to reduce their size. This occurred less often among families functioning least well.

Undereducation, racial abuse, and exclusion from the economic mainstream put many Black families under excessive stress and decreased their ability to prepare their children for school, which, in turn, reduced their children's future opportunity to participate in the economic and social mainstream. Public policy in the area of education has not facilitated an adjustment on the part of public schools to meet the needs of such children and families. The low level of achievement and high level of behavior problems which now occur in public schools serving such youngsters and their families have led to the abandonment of public schools by many Black and White parents who are conscious of the critical link between adequate education, employment, and the quality of life their children can experience in the future.

After school segregation became illegal, much research, public policy, and program innovation efforts centered on issues related to this major social change, and concern about low-income Black children led to such concepts as cultural deprivation and the culturally disadvantaged--with limited benefits. Perhaps the magnitude and sensitivity of the racial issue obscured the fact that poor children from all groups underachieved in public schools, while, at the same time, similar children succeeded in independent schools. Indeed, only recently has the organization and management, staff preparation, and focus on content and methods rather than child development in public schools been considered as a source of their limited success and failure. A focus on Black children in independent schools is not only a window on the people involved and racial issues, but also an opportunity to observe the effects of different structures, attitudes, and relationships in these schools as opposed to public schools.

This book provides valuable clues to the needs, wants, and wishes of parents and students in independent schools. It will help independent schools understand and better meet the needs of Blacks students. But an equally important contribution will be the attention the book brings to the greater success of Blacks students in independent schools and the factors involved that hold important implications for public schools. If we can put to use the findings from this study, and future studies that this work may stimulate, we may well provide the nation with the kind of future citizens and work force it needs to move successfully to and through the twenty-first century.

As the editors and authors indicate, however, implicitly and explicitly, there are no quick and easy answers, and much more work needs to be done. But they have tapped into a neglected and potentially rich vein of useful information needed to support Black education, quality education for all, and the needs of the nation.

NOTES

1. Carnegie Forum on Education and the Economy, <u>A Nation Prepared: Teachers for the 21st Century</u>. Report of the Task Force on Teaching as a Profession (New York: Carnegie Corporation of New York, 437 Madison Avenue 10022, 1986).

2. Research and Policy Committee of the Committee for Economic Development, <u>Children in Need: Investment Strategies for the Educationally Disadvantaged</u> (New York: 477 Madison Ave, 10022, 1987).

Acknowledgments

When a book is successfully completed, many institutions and persons must share the credit. This book is no exception. We owe, of course, a special debt of gratitude to all our contributors, for their unfailing enthusiasm and support. They were prompt in responding to our queries and conscientious in taking our editorial suggestions very seriously.

Throughout, Dean David Wiley and support staff at the School of Education and Social Policy, Northwestern University, contributed beneficially. With the backing of the Dean's office, financial assistance was obtained from the Northwestern University Research Committee. In the final phases of work on the manuscript, release time was provided to Diana Slaughter for its completion.

Three School of Education and Social Policy support staff should be cited. A very warm debt of gratitude to both Sarah Adams and Irene Hutchison, whose loyalty, perseverence, and mere presence were often the glue that kept the office together. The volume itself can be credited to the many, many hours of typing and proofing logged by Irene. We also appreciate the impromptu typing of letters and related documents by Joan LeBuhn. Finally, at the end, Lorrie Odom of Howard University came through for us; thanks.

This book was completed while Deborah Johnson was engaged in postdoctoral study under the auspices of the University of California President's Office. In particular, we wish to thank her host department within the University, Afro-American Studies, for providing some of the necessary resources.

We benefitted from the thoughtful guidance of Greenwood Press. The technical assistance from Loomis Mayer and Susan Baker was especially appreciated.

Last, but not least, our colleagues and friends in education and child development, as well as Black studies, have always made all such efforts worthwhile because they keep us mindful of the real purpose of the product: *to benefit the children.*

DTS
DJJ

Visible Now

1
Introduction and Overview
Diana T. Slaughter and Deborah J. Johnson

Education professionals assume that both families and schools play significant roles in childhood learning and development, because both primary institutions engage in child socialization.[1] Both institutions are responsible for transmitting the culture and history of the broader community to children, and for ensuring that the children, as adults, are capable of contributing positively and productively to society. Achievement in school is largely the result of successful socialization for achievement. The child's "significant others" (e. g. , parents, teachers), as well as the "generalized other" or culture within which the child lives, greatly impact achievement aspirations, motivations, and performance.

Sara Lightfoot reports that, stemming from their own childhood experiences, both teachers and parents have images and stereotypes of one another which shape their views of what schooling is, and ought to be, for the children in their care.[2] She also reports that William Waller expressed similar views nearly fifty years earlier.[3] Both authors have emphasized that the attitudes and beliefs of parents and educators about schooling have been shaped in a sociocultural and historical context, indeed a community context, in which the families and schools are themselves embedded.

Black Americans have experienced continuing crises around the education of their children. Lightfoot points to a history in which the children of slaves were, by national and local policy, to be kept uneducated and illiterate.[4] Further, in northern states, where slavery was abolished prior to the Civil War and Reconstruction, Black children were initially legally forbidden to attend schools with White children. Public dollars were not, without the repeated struggles of Black parents and communities, allocated even for the "separate but equal" education of Black children. Even today, once allocated, educational dollars are rarely distributed equitably. Desegregation efforts, initially pursued by Black parents and communities to ensure that Black children would have equal access to quality education, have been systematically resisted and thwarted by White communities in all regions of the country.[5] In short, as many others in addition to Lightfoot have suggested, Black Americans have long had a "crisis of confidence" relative to the benefits of public education for their children.[6] Although the majority of Black Americans favor public education, many express continuing concern about the contributions of public schools to their children's learning and development. It is not surprising to learn, therefore, that many Black families, particularly middle-income families with the ability and willingness to pay tuition at the elementary and secondary school levels, have recently been exploring a variety of options, including nonpublic ones, for educating their children.   Evidence to date suggests that Black students, generally, are achieving in private schools.[7]

Although the percentage of Black students attending nonpublic schools is small, the number of children actually affected is impressive. For example, according to a 1981 report of the National Center for Educational Statistics, about 7.3 percent of all Black elementary school students attended nonpublic schools, most of whom attended religiously affiliated schools (6.2 percent). This means that about 270,000 Black elementary school children attended nonpublic schools in 1979, and indications are that this number has not significantly decreased.

In fact, since 1970, increasing percentages of Black students have enrolled in nonpublic schools in diverse, though predominantly urban, regions of the nation.[8] Between 1967 and 1977, Black private elementary school enrollment increased as a percentage of the total enrollment in this category from 3.7 to 5.5 percent. Enrollment in private elementary schools was estimated at 214,000 in 1977, 263,384 in 1979, and, even with the financial problems many Black families can be assumed to be having in the 1980s, in 1984 the enrollment of Black children ages 6-13 years was estimated to be 247,506.[9]

Schneider and Slaughter have reported how these figures are arrayed according to school network: sectarian, independent elite, and independent alternative. Regarding sectarian schools, in 1980 the total Black elementary enrollment in church-related schools was estimated at 207,494.   The overwhelming majority of these students attended Catholic schools. In the case of independent elite schools, typically members of the National Association of Independent Schools (NAIS), the total Black enrollment (including secondary school enrollment, which is largest) was estimated in 1984 at 14,355, about 4.2 percent of the total population in these schools. Comparable statistics for independent alternative schools are not available. There are over 250 such schools specifically established for minority students throughout the nation, probably averaging fifty or more students per school. In addition, Black elementary school students attend racially mixed independent alternative schools. Between the two types of schools, probably about 30,000 Black children are enrolled.[10]

Black family income was surprisingly similar in 1984 for families with children in public and nonpublic elementary schools. Among private-school families, although the modal family income in 1984 was between $25,000 and $34,999, nearly 25 percent of the sending Black families reported incomes of less than $10,000. A similar modal family income was reported for public-school families, but in that instance, nearly 45 percent of the sending Black families reported incomes of less than $10,000. The two groups of Black families differ most dramatically in the proportions of children living in families below, rather than at or above, the poverty line.[11]

Many Black parents shuttle their children back and forth between public and private schools, depending upon perceptions of the child's current needs and the family's immediate life-style. In these cases, the enrollment patterns of Black school children are but reflections of the changing life-styles experienced by many middle-income Black families. For other Black families, private schooling may be perceived as the best hope their child has of receiving a quality education, as they define it, given their current residential location. Black parents may seek to empower themselves, particularly with reference to leaving their children a "legacy" of successful school achievement, by using private schooling.

Black families have a tradition of sending their children to private schools, typically to predominantly Black private schools. More recent trends include increased attendance at these schools and racially mixed private schools. These trends have been observed in each of the three primary networks previously discussed. Private schools have their own reasons for encouraging desegregation. As racial and ethnic populations become increasingly non-White in American cities and national demographic data predict proportionate increases in the number of non-White children, many urban schools may simply seek to assure enrollment. Others may perceive themselves to be facilitating the efforts of Black families to empower themselves, this time through desegregation.

There are theoretical and research issues associated with the increased visibility of Blacks in private schools, and there are also practical and policy concerns. The contributors to this volume attempt to bring these issues and concerns into focus by systematically addressing them for the first time in the history of American education. Before presenting a brief overview of the issues and concerns and outlining the organization of this volume, more background to our involvement in the area of Black education is indicated.

BACKGROUND

In the spring of 1979, one of the editors, Diana Slaughter, was contacted at Northwestern University by the National Institute of Mental Health (NIMH) and invited to submit a research proposal on Black students' experiences in independent alternative schools. Once submitted to NIMH, the proposal was judged more appropriate for review by the National Institute of Education (NIE). A revised proposal was submitted to NIE with a collaborator, Barbara Schneider, Education Faculty member in Administration and Policy Studies in February, 1982. Dr. Schneider had a demonstrable history of interest in private schools, particularly private elite schools. With this collaboration, schools identified with two networks in the overall private school arena were included in the study.[12] Further, a school from the parochial network was also included because this is the type of school attended by the majority of Black private school students, and research into contrasting types of private elementary schools seemed especially important to conduct if the full spectrum of experiences of Black children and parents with these schools was to be tapped.

When the second editor, Deborah Johnson, began doctoral studies with Slaughter in October, 1983, in the Human Development and Social Policy Program, the Slaughter and Schneider study had just begun a few months earlier. Pilot research for Johnson's independent study of Black parents and their children attending predominantly Black private schools was conducted with data from the Slaughter and Schneider study. The editors expect that this research will contribute to the literature on the education of Black children, both by describing the achievement socialization contexts in which significant numbers of Black children are today learning and developing, and by characterizing the special resiliencies and vulnerabilities of the Black children and parents participating in these contexts.

FOCUS

This volume reports some findings from the earlier Slaughter and Schneider, and Johnson studies (see chapters 15-16), but primarily takes advantage of the breadth of contacts made during that research with persons in the diverse private school networks, including academicians, administrators, and parent communities, to offer multiple perspectives on the educational issues and concerns facing Black families with children in private schools.

Throughout the volume, the emphasis is upon relations between Black families and schools, rather than, for example, parent-teacher or teacher-child relations. Existing educational research has neglected family-school relations. The result has been that individual difference parameters have been studied, but the contextual information needed to assist in interpreting these parameters has been largely absent. As Bronfenbrenner would probably say, the "microsystemic level of analysis" has been emphasized to the neglect of "mesosystemic" factors.[13]

Black children, as all children, carry the cultures of their communities and families into their schools. Successful academic achievement socialization of the children, therefore, is dependent upon cooperative relations between families and schools. This volume examines societal and social factors which, in the past and at present, promote and inhibit close ties between Black families and the private schools attended by many children.

This perspective also has practical significance if one agrees, as we do, with the late Ron Edmonds' premise that school reform or school improvement is likely to be most effectively accomplished at the schoolwide (or district-wide), rather than teacher or parent, level.[14] Although we agree with Edmonds that one indirect, but powerful, influence of the home is contingent upon the schools' reaction to children's home backgrounds, we differ from him in that we also emphasize that Black communities, families, and parents have played, and continue to play, highly significant roles in their children's achievement development. Given available research data, the younger the children, the more likely this is to be true.[15] Family influence is particularly evident among Blacks who send their children to nonpublic elementary schools because the parents are clearly exercising options and making sacrifices on behalf of their children. However, we believe that other research, including some of our own, indicates that, for better or worse, the influence is no less in the case of parents whose children attend public schools.[16]

ORGANIZATION

In parts 1-3, family-school relations in each of three private school networks--elite, Catholic, and alternative--are discussed from a variety of perspectives, some theoretical, some practical, and some highly personal (e.g., chapter 2). Some chapters report research findings (chapters 3-4, 8-13) while others stress interventions supportive of Black family-school relations (chapters 2, 5-7). Parts

4-5 focus on research and policy issues, respectively, in the arena of family-school relations which appear to transcend school type. At this writing, research appears to be primarily focused on Black parents' goals and expectations regarding private schools, for their children (chapters 14-16). More general discussions of private school policies in relation to Blacks emphasize interpretations of Black community and parent opinions (see chapters 11, 17-18).

Our understanding of the preliminary issues and concerns to be raised by persons extremely knowledgeable about Black families and children in private schools was that most are generic to any serious discussion of the education of young Black children generally. For example, chapters discuss desegregation, parent involvement, parental educational goals and expectations, parental racial socialization, community and/or schoolwide support systems for students, culturally sensitive schools, and family choice among educational options. Consequently, when we decided to invite discussants of selected chapters, as well as of the entire volume, we felt unencumbered in our decisionmaking. All but one of our educational researchers have primarily written about public schools.[17]

However, each discussant is considered an expert in one or more of the primary topics of the chapters under consideration. The invited commentaries are designed to stimulate dialogue between the other contributors and their readers, and to further orient the entire volume toward contemporary aspects of Black education generally.

Clearly, there is considerable research and theorizing to be done in reference to family-school relations in private, and probably also public, schools. In the epilogue, we discuss the implications of the reports presented in earlier chapters about the recent experiences of Black families in private schools for reconceptualizing Black family-school relations. Hopefully, this volume will stimulate additional efforts.

NOTES

1. See, for example, Robert Hess and Susan Holloway, "Family and School as Educational Institutions," in Ross Parke, ed., Review of Child Development Research (Chicago: University of Chicago Press, 1985), vol. 7, pp. 179-222; and James P. Comer, School Power: Implications of an Intervention Project (New York: Free Press, 1980).

2. Sara Lightfoot, Worlds Apart: Relationships between Families and Schools (New York: Basic Books, 1978).

3. William Waller, Sociology of Teaching (New York: Wiley, 1932).

4. Lightfoot, Worlds Apart.

5. See, for example, Diane Ravitch, The Troubled Crusade: American Education, 1945-1980 (New York: Basic Books, 1983); and Ray Rist, The Invisible Children: School Integration in American Society (Cambridge, Mass.: Harvard University Press, 1978).

6. See Kenneth Clark, Dark Ghetto (New York: Harper, 1965); Diana T. Slaughter, "Alienation of Afro-American Children: Curriculum and Evaluation in American Schools," in Edgar G. Epps, ed., Cultural Pluralism (Berkeley: McCutchan, 1974), pp. 144-174; John Ogbu, The Next Generation: An Ethnography of Education in an Urban Neighborhood (New York: Academic Press, 1974); and the Winter, 1987, issue of the Journal of Negro Education (Slaughter and Epps, eds.) for twenty years of comment on similar issues.

7. See, for example, James S. Coleman, Thomas Hoffer, and Sally Kilgore, High School Achievement: Public, Catholic, and Private Schools Compared (New York: Basic Books, 1982); Thomas Hoffer, Andrew Greeley, and James S. Coleman, "Achievement Growth in Public and Catholic Schools," Sociology of Education, 58 (April 1985): 74-97; see also Congressional Budget Office, Trends in Educational Achievement (Washington, D. C.: Government Printing Office, April 1986), p. 82. This report takes a more conservative view of student achievement in private secondary schools, and also indicates that little is known in this area, even today, at a national level. Data seem more accessible at the secondary, rather than elementary level.

8. National Center for Educational Statistics, United States Department of Commerce, Bureau of the Census. Condition of Education (Washington, D. C.: Government Printing Office, 1979, 1980, 1981).

9. Barbara L. Schneider and Diana T. Slaughter, "Educational Choice for Blacks in Urban Private Elementary Schools," in Thomas James and Henry Levin, eds., Comparing Public and Private Schools (London: Falmer Press, 1988), vol. 1, pp. 294-310; see also Diana T. Slaughter and Barbara L. Schneider, Newcomers: Blacks in Private Schools. ERIC, 1986 (ED 274 768 and ED 274 769).

10. Ibid.

11. Ibid.

12. Slaughter and Schneider, <u>Newcomers</u>.

13. Urie Bronfenbrenner, <u>The Ecology of Human Development</u> (Cambridge, Mass.: Harvard University Press, 1979).

14. Ron Edmonds, "The Last Obstacle to Equity in Education: Social Class," <u>Theory Into Practice</u> 20, no. 4 (1981): 269-272.

15. Diana T. Slaughter and Edgar G. Epps, "The Home Environment and Academic Achievement of Black American Children and Youth," <u>Journal of Negro Education</u> 56 (Winter 1987): 3-22.

16. See, for example, Reginald Clark, <u>Family Life and School Achievement: Why Poor Children Succeed or Fail</u> (Chicago: University of Chicago Press, 1983); and Slaughter and Epps, "Home Environment."

17. Thomas Hoffer is an exception because of his collaboration on a pioneering study of private secondary schools, many of which serve low-income and minority students.

Part 1
Independent Schools with
Black Children

Independent schools with the lowest percentages of Black students are most likely to be private elite schools. These schools typically enjoy considerable academic and social prestige in their home communities, have few, if any, ethnic minority teachers, and began to voluntarily desegregate in the 1960s out of a sense of administrative commitment to the civil rights goals of the broader American society. During that era, and since then, Black students and their families have increasingly participated in these institutions, as have Black faculty. These families are a vanguard group, breaking tradition in the Black community in their decision to send their children to a predominantly White private elite institution. The following chapters give an accounting of some of the historical background, discuss the special needs of participating Black students and parents, and most importantly raise the question of how academic excellence can be combined with healthy racial identity formation in the course of these Black children's development. Importantly, whereas Blacks were the most visible ethnic minority group in these schools initially, today the number of Blacks is slightly less than the number of Asian-American students, and Hispanics have been substantially increasing their numbers. Blacks have, apparently, not only expanded an educational option for themselves, but have been the forerunners of such an option for other minority groups.

Professor Brookins, an expert in Black child development whose child attends a private elite school in the South, begins chapter 2 by describing the experiences of herself, her husband, and their son with private education. She outlines the decisionmaking process by which the family chose private education, pointing to the particularly poor quality of public education, in her view, in the state of Mississippi. She also analyzes perceived costs and benefits to this decision: specifically, the risk of losing leadership opportunities and healthy identity development in the pursuit of a high-quality academic education. Brookins also describes personal intervention in the school environment, acting herself as a concerned parent on behalf of her son and other Black children.

In chapter 3, Speede-Franklin, formerly Director of Information Services and Minority Affairs at the National Association of Independent Schools (NAIS), attempts to dispel several myths about ethnic minority students in independent elite schools. Recruited students frequently suffer the burdens of these myths within the independent school communities. In support of her arguments, she summarizes the findings of the 1985 Bell market research study commissioned by NAIS to address policy and practice implications for stabilizing minority enrollment and sustaining meaningful diversity in such schools. The research survey included a socioeconomic profile of Black and other ethnic minority families in the schools, key factors influencing choices of independent schools, and parental recommendations for enhancing the independent school experience. Speede-Franklin reminds us that at present, Asian-Americans are the largest ethnic minority group in independent elite schools, and that the emphasis on diversity should include attention to socioeconomic diversity.

Chapter 4 by Griffin and Johnson presents the history of A Better Chance, Inc.--its mission, organizational structure, and current functions with regard to private elite school communities. The upbeat chapter also summarizes research documented on the career choices in math and science made by A Better Chance alumni over the past twenty years since the special community-focused intervention program was initially supported by the Rockefeller Foundation. The authors believe that significant numbers of these Black students, in contrast to nonparticipating Black students, chose math and science careers following participation in the program.

In chapter 5, Patterson, Executive Director of the Black Student Fund (BSF), an organization responsible for placing and retaining Black students in southeastern private elite schools since the mid-1960s, describes the BSF program, contrasting the model it presents with that of the Baltimore Project for Black Students and the Richmond Black Student Foundation, two offspring of the parent BSF. Like the historical information provided by Griffin and Johnson, Patterson's discussion illuminates why most predominantly White independent schools with Black children tend to be private elite schools. Patterson points out that as the goals of the Black civil rights movement changed, so too did the goals and expectations of many of the Black parents who had children in independent schools. The schools also responded to the reduced commitment to civil rights observed in American society in the seventies, though not as negatively as they might have. These issues are considered in the context of student recruitment and maintenance of enrollment, as well as the quality of Black student campus life.

In chapter 6, Royal discusses the needs of Black children and youth in these independent schools for academic and social support from administrators and faculty. She profiles the various phases of Black family and student involvement in independent schools and points to a variety of forms that student support can assume during these phases. She emphasizes that both ethnic minority and majority students need to experience Black and other ethnic minority adult role models in positions of authority. She describes one program, currently implemented by herself at one independent school which, in its focus on contacts with African nations, is designed to inform and enrich all students and ensure that Black students in these schools maintain a positive Black identity.

Chapter 7 by Oyemade and Williams describes the efforts of parents at one private elite school to ensure that attending Black children and youth develop positive racial identities. Both authors stress the importance of Black parent involvement in independent schools for all facets of children's learning and development. However, as a parent of a Black child in the school and an expert in Black child development, Oyemade had a special interest in ensuring that a quality program for positive Black parental involvement was established at her child's school.

2
Making the Honor Roll: A Black Parent's Perspective on Private Education
Geraldine Kearse Brookins

It is the 1983 closing day ceremony at the Brookover Day School, a private, elite, Episcopalian school in Jackson, Mississippi. The children in pre-kindergarten through fourth grade are seated on the floor of the gymnasium. The "graduating" fourth graders are all dressed in white and seated in chairs near the podium. The proud parents line the bleachers and walls to form a sea of supporting spectators. Following each grade group's rendering of a poem and song that typify its progress in learning for the year, the principal indicates that she will, with the help of some lower school students, announce the winners of various awards. These awards include the winner of the school spelling bee, recognition for participation in the Safety Patrol and Student Council, recipients of male/female citizens of the year, and recipients of overall High Honors and Honors. Following the announcements, each fourth grader receives a certificate indicating that he or she has completed all requirements for the lower school.

On the surface, these activities appear to be appropriate, if a little lengthy, for "graduation exercises" in an elementary or lower school. However, for a Black parent, a number of questions emerges. Why is it that all of the student presenters of the awards are White? This task requires no special talent, except to be able to hear since the principal whispers the recipients' names to the child. Why, also, are all of the Student Council members White? Does this imply something about leadership capabilities, starting even in the first grade? Finally, of the third and fourth graders, why is there only one Black child receiving honors? Surely, in this state where education and academic achievement take a backseat to a number of mundane issues, White children can't have a monopoly on intelligence or academic ability.

I look around the audience and see a number of Black parents. I peruse the pre-kindergarten through fourth graders and estimate that Blacks comprise about eight percent of the student body. I also notice a few Black third graders seeming to anticipate their names being called for honors, only to find them skipped as the presenter moved along alphabetically. I left with my questions and my son, who was then in kindergarten, vowing to make an appointment with the principal the following week.

During the meeting I express my dismay and total disapproval of the manner in which the closing ceremonies were handled with regard to Black children. The principal replied by pointing out that race was never an issue since the students were "all of God's children." I responded by noting that my child was one of God's Black children and I wanted him recognized as such. While still not representative of the Black student composition, all subsequent closing ceremonies have had Black participation.

The above provides a backdrop to this chapter, which is essentially a discussion of the author's role in making decisions regarding her child's education and the perceived compromises resulting from those decisions. Following this, there is a brief discussion of the educational climate in a Deep South state and how that climate influences decisions regarding public or private education for some Black parents.

PUBLIC VERSUS PRIVATE: ASSETS AND LIABILITIES IN A CHANGING EDUCATIONAL CLIMATE

Public Education: Policy and Practice

Upon moving to Mississippi in 1975, I discovered that there was no compulsory school attendance. Mississippi at one time had a compulsory attendance law that was not strictly adhered to, in part due to the vestiges of an agrarian economy within the state and thus a dependency on unskilled labor during planting and reaping times. However, in 1955, when integration seemed certain to be the law of the land, the state attendance laws were changed to facilitate the status quo, in particular Blacks and Whites not attending school together. There were a few Whites who went against the tide and continued to support the public schools during that transition period. Mainly, however, the lack of a compulsory attendance policy legally allowed and supported a massive exodus of Whites from the public school system to rapidly developed private educational entities; or in some cases, parents decided to keep their children home and teach them themselves.

Since we had no compulsory attendance, it is of note that while most states began collecting drop-out data for students around the ages of fourteen to sixteen, we had similar data for children entering and leaving the first grade. In spite of the fact that there were pockets of excellence across the state within the public school system, this policy of not requiring children to attend school set a tone regarding the significance of education that rang throughout the state. Such a posture on education was not without dire consequences. In 1979 Mississippi had 59 dropouts per 100 graduating high school seniors. The state ranks 50th with a per capita income of $8,098. Noteworthy is the fact that while Mississippi is the poorest state in the nation, we spend 25 percent more state money per capita on highways than welfare and health.[1] In 1982-83, an average of $1,906 per student, the lowest in the South, was spent on education.[2] These statistics and related others placed the state in a position of being less able to attract industry and other new enterprises that might bolster the economy and thus the quality of life for the state's residents. This says nothing of the truncated life options for many of its youth.

In 1980, Governor Winter promised that there would be sweeping changes for the education of our children. Accordingly, the governor and his staff worked diligently to have the Education Reform Act passed in the Mississippi. With provisions such as kindergartens in all school districts by 1986-87, reading aides in each first through third grade classroom, and compulsory attendance for ages six through thirteen, by 1989, the Education Reform Act was signed into law in 1982. In spite of the merits of this law, there were many detractors who were afraid that compulsory attendance would take away the rights of parents to choose how to educate their children. The provision for kindergartens in all school districts by 1986-87 was challenged as a waste of money; that is, kindergarten was viewed merely as public babysitting that the State could ill-afford.

As a professor who had taught developmental psychology courses in the higher education system in the state and had seen first-hand both the benefits and drawbacks of the earlier policies that had driven the educational system, I was even more concerned as a parent with a child about to enter into the arena of formal education. Having been educated in a public school system from kindergarten through twelfth grade, I felt comfortable with public education and had no personal experience with private education with the exception of studying private preschools. What I saw operating in the public education system in Mississippi, however, caused some concern for me.

My son was born September 2, 1976. The date that would have made him eligible for first grade attendance was September 1, 1976. Since there were no provisions for exceptions to that rule, my child would have to begin first grade at the age of seven. This would not have been a problem except that my being a working mother had necessitated his having been in some sort of school setting since the age of two. As expected, he had basically mastered a number of the requisites for first grade by age five. It was incumbent upon me and his father to find an educational setting that would continue to challenge him academically and socially. We thought we had found such a setting in Brookover Day School. We knew about the school because my husband's niece and nephews had attended the school some years earlier. In fact, they were among the first Black students to attend. In spite of its reputation regarding integration, we still had some concerns because the school was predominantly White and had a reputation for being elitist. The next section will focus briefly on the history of Brookover Day School regarding its orientation toward integration and quality education

Private Education: Viable Options?

With increasing costs for private and public higher education, many Black middle-class parents such as myself tend to believe that a "front-loaded" investment (i.e., private elementary and secondary education) may increase the probability of our children gaining admission to a quality undergraduate institution with a scholarship. On a less long-term, pragmatic basis, many parents send their children to Brookover Day School because of its reputation for quality education and small student-to-teacher ratios. Important in the decisionmaking process is the reputation Brookover Day School has regarding integration. While most independent or private schools were established in order to bypass the mandate of integration, Brookover was one of a few independent schools across the South that took steps towards being a leader in the integration of private schools.[3]

Brookover Day School actually followed the lead of its church. In the early 1960s James Meredith's attempt to register at the University of Mississippi not only fanned the coals of hatred but also raised the consciousness of a number of people. With the leadership of the Episcopalian bishop, a group of ministers, bishops, and laymen formed a Committee of Concern whose purpose was to restore the fifty-five churches that had been burned down within the state and influence other Christians to preach against violence and for civil rights.[4]

The Episcopalian cathedral was one of the few places in Jackson where Blacks and Whites could meet together. Indeed, during the early sixties the cathedral held integrated "kneel-ins" in prayerful search to answers regarding the strife of the civil rights movement. These church leaders felt that they were abrogating their responsibilities if they did not also take the lead in responding to desegregation in a manner that was coincident with their religious beliefs.

Even though Brookover Day School had never had a policy of racial discrimination, it had also never actively sought Black student participation in this segregated city. However, when school administrators and board members approached various individuals within the Black community about student participation in the school, the reputation of the cathedral facilitated Black acceptance of the school. Thus, the first Black student to attend Brookover Day School began matriculation in the 1966-67 academic year.

With this introduction of Blacks to Brookover Day School came an educational option beyond parochial and public education for Black parents to consider for their children. I am of the belief that it is important to have an array of options both within settings as well as across settings in order to facilitate a more appropriate "student-environment fit." Black parents who could afford it and who thought their children would benefit from a private educational setting, sought out Brookover Day School with both enthusiasm and caution. Caution, in some ways, is probably more evident in the mid-eighties than it was during the mid-to-late-sixties, the possible reasons for which are discussed at the conclusion of this chapter. What follows is my perception of what Black students gain and lose by their matriculation at Brookover.

Academic Achievement: At Whose Expense?

As noted earlier, Brookover Day School has an excellent academic reputation within the state. It also has a reputation for its role in educational integration and non-discriminatory practices. It is because of these two reputed distinctions, I think, that until recently, parents, administrators, and teachers were reluctant to address some serious concerns regarding the total development of Black children at the school. The ethos of the school is that all children are creations of God and no distinctions are made as regards race or creed. The reality is that Brookover Day School is enmeshed within the context of a southern city that is still very much racially segregated, even as we approach 1990. As such, the teachers, parents, and students are products of this divided society. While children might interact with each other in school as dictated by the parameters of instruction, for the most part, their lives after school do not intersect.

In spite of the fact that the school has been integrated in terms of students for twenty years, there is not even a handful of Black teachers on the faculty. When I brought this to the attention of one of the school administrators, the response was that the school policy was to hire teachers with independent school experience and many Black teachers were without such experience!

Most of the Black children attending Brookover Day School are good to gifted students. While, in some cases there are reasons related to ego investment on the part of the parents regarding their children's attendance at Brookover, I doubt seriously that many parents would spend the kind of tuition money required if they did not think their children were capable of meeting the academic rigors of the curriculum. It thus appears that more Black children than there are should be cited for academic honors throughout the year. This discrepancy evokes two possible interpretations: the children's achievement performance was influenced by the lack of similarity between themselves and recognized authority figures;[5] or, unconscious stereotypes regarding Black students intervened in the course assessment process. In either case, the potential for erosion of self-esteem for these children increases with each succeeding year of attendance. This potential erosion process is exacerbated by the virtual lack of concomitant opportunities to experience and develop leadership skills.

Diana Slaughter and Barbara Schneider (1986) reported on the (sociometric) peer status of the Black children in the four desegregated private schools they studied.[6] In three of those schools, the Black population ranged from 28-50 percent of the student body. In these schools, Black students were reported to be involved, active participants in most school activities. Further, the peer status of the Black students was largely determined by the number of votes received from Black peers. In one school, Black students were less actively involved; at this elite school, Black students constituted 6 percent of the student body. At Brookover, a similar situation prevails. Black students constitute less than 10 percent of the student body. I believe that a majority of the Black students at Brookover Day School do not view themselves, or are not viewed by peers and instructors, as full and equal citizens. Consequently, I am concerned about the long-term developmental implications for these youngsters.

If these Black students represent an important segment of the potential leadership of the Black community, how can they assume effective leadership roles if their experiences in an important socializing setting during a critical developmental period accrues marginal status to them? As a parent I have tried to think carefully about the balance between academic achievement and other qualities and attributes necessary for a Black child to become a competent, contributing adult. As Elsie Moore notes, we know so little about these qualities and attributes.[7] We do know that academic competence at the expense of social and emotional health is unlikely to accrue quality to the life of the individual or the community in which he or she resides.

CONCLUSION

I have attempted to underscore some of the issues and concerns regarding the decision to send our child to a private school. As has been indicated, we are not totally comfortable with that decision, and I think we as parents weigh the pros and cons on an ongoing basis. In other chapters in this volume there are discussions about parental decisionmaking regarding private schools and their children that are based on empirical findings. I conclude by speculating about the contextual fabric that holds the interweave of reasons why Black parents are sending their children to private schools, using my personal and professional experiences as the basis for discussion.

With few exceptions, the Black children who attend Brookover Day School come from middle-class homes. Their parents represent the traditional middle-class occupations--doctors, lawyers, academicians, businesspeople, etc.--with modern configurations, namely dual-career rather than dual-earner couples.[8] In many instances, these individuals are "first-generation" college graduates and represent racial and community pride and progress. Some parents recognize the that American society no longer pays heed to the equal opportunity laws that were enacted and thus, they more aggressively pursue quality education for their children as a potential guarantee against the rising tide of retrenchment regarding civil rights. It should be noted that many of these parents "came of age" in the sixties within this southern city and expect to enjoy and have their children enjoy the full benefits of the gains made during that time. They also recognize that their children will have to compete within a sphere where the competition becomes increasingly keen and resources diminish. As such, their expectations and aspirations for their children seem to go beyond those of their middle-class forebears. At the same time, the middle-class parents of Brookover Day School seem to be less willing to have their children attend a prestigious school without the students having the benefit of full participation and acknowledgement of their individual and group uniqueness.

With this duality of purpose, quality education and acknowledgment of individual and group heritage, comes a potential tension between the Black parents and those in charge of guarding the goals and heritage of the school. Each year as the Black children approach adolescence with its attendant social manifestations, the number of students leaving to find comfort in numbers and "sameness" increases. Some enter the public school system; others try the parochial schools that offer somewhat more ethnic heterogeneity among the student bodies, but not necessarily anything substantially different regarding faculty racial composition.

These events underscore the problems Black parents have regarding the education of their children. Few parents dispute the quality and potential benefits of the curriculum and enrichment activities at Brookover. Many however, express dismay that they have no real options regarding the total development of their children within educational settings. Others experience conflict between providing the best academic foundation for their children and being responsive to the children's other psychosocial developmental needs as the children progress through the life course. They often rationalize the decision to follow the wishes of their children by noting that the early years is the time for building a firm educational foundation. Many parents would rather err on the side of educational content than feel remiss in providing the ill-defined foundation for the development of those other elusive qualities and attributes necessary for competent adult functioning.

NOTES

1. Department of Commerce, <u>Statistical Abstract of the United States, 1982-1983</u> (Washington, D. C.: Government Printing Office, 1983); see also Commission of Children and Youth, <u>The Status of Children in Mississippi</u> (Jackson, Miss.: Governor's Office of Federal State Programs, 1985).

2. Mississippi Department of Education, <u>Data Report</u> (Jackson, Miss.: State Department of Education, 1983).

3. Zebulon V. Wilson, <u>They Took Their Stand: The Integration of Southern Private Schools</u> (Atlanta, Ga.: Mid-South Association of Independent Schools, 1983).

4. Ibid; see also James Meredith, <u>Three Years in Mississippi</u> (Bloomington: Indiana University Press, 1966).

5. Margaret B. Spencer, "Racial Variations in Achievement Prediction: The School as a Conduit for Macro-Structural Cultural Tension," in Harriette P. McAdoo and John L. McAdoo, eds.,<u>Black Children: Social Educational and Parental Environments</u> (Beverly Hills, Calif.: Sage, 1985), pp. 85-112.

6. Diana T. Slaughter and Barbara L. Schneider, <u>Newcomers:</u> <u>Blacks in Private Schools</u> ERIC, 1986 (ED 274 768 and ED 274 769).

7. Elsie G. Moore, "Ethnicity as a Variable in Child Development,"   in Margaret B. Spencer, Geraldine K. Brookins, and Walter R. Allen, eds., <u>Beginnings: The Social</u> <u>and Affective Development of Black Children</u> (Hillsdale, N.J.: Lawrence Erlbaum, 1985), pp. 101-116.

8. Geraldine K. Brookins, "<u>Dual Career Black Parents:</u> <u>Aspirations</u> <u>and Expectations for Child Development</u>" (Manuscript in progress).

3
Ethnic Diversity: Patterns and Implications of Minorities in Independent Schools

Wanda A. Speede-Franklin

Over the past twenty-five years, researchers, educational administrators, school personnel, parents, and students have debated the impact of efforts to desegregate private schools. The motivations, process, and impact of desegregation in independent schools are discussed in this chapter.

Independent schools are a subset of approximately 900 private, precollegiate educational institutions which are members of the National Association of independent Schools, Inc. (NAIS) headquartered in Boston, Massachusetts. Total private school enrollment, which includes the independent and parochial sectors, accounts for nearly 13 percent of overall U.S. elementary and secondary school enrollment. NAIS active member schools comprise approximately 3 percent of all private elementary and secondary schools in the United States, and enroll approximately 350,000 students, accounting for less than 1 percent of total precollegiate enrollment.[1]

Because of their historical role in educating the gentry of American society these predominantly White institutions are commonly referred to as "elite private schools"--a label which carries the image of academic, financial, and social inaccessibility for the masses of students.[2] Interestingly, NAIS membership requirements defy such an image. NAIS member schools are nonprofit, tax-exempt organizations which subscribe to principles and policies of nondiscrimination. They are approved by a recognized evaluation process, maintain fiscal independence from government and church entities, and are governed by independent boards of trustees, directors, or advisors. Independent schools widely perceive themselves as institutions which stress public service, emphasize social responsibility, actively promote a multicultural and multiracial environment, and strive to build a diverse and pluralistic student body.

Given this self-perception, I examine the development of desegregation in independent schools, consider the profile of Black and other minority families who patronize independent schools, and outline policy concerns and recommendations for stabilizing minority enrollment and managing diversity effectively in order to maximize its benefit to all members of the school community.

DESEGREATION: RACIAL DIVERSITY IN INDEPENDENT SCHOOLS

An exhaustive discussion of the history of minority student enrollment in predominantly White independent schools is beyond the scope of this chapter. However, it is interesting to note that the presence of Black students on independent school campuses predates the early, systematic recruitment initiatives of the mid-twentieth century. In his 1963 monograph entitled <u>Negro Students in Independent Schools</u>, David Mallery states that "...schools reported spectacular examples of Negro students whose morale and abilities worked to make possible their winning top scholastic honors, merit scholarships, student elections and top leadership positions, and moving on the leading colleges."[3] Mallery cites an early example reported by Arthur W. Kiendl, then head of Mt. Hermon School:

> You might be interested to know a little bit about the first Negro boy, who came in 1886. He was Thomas N. Baker, born in slavery, and honored by Yale University in 1903 by having a Ph.D. conferred upon him. He came to Mt. Hermon from Hampton Institute; after graduating from here in 1889 he received an A.B. degree from Boston University in 1893 where he was valedictorian of his class. Subsequently he attended Yale Divinity School and was ordained into the Christian ministry. We have others who have gone on to spectacular careers.[4]

Obviously, Thomas Baker was an absolute token as the only Black student enrolled in the school at the time. By the 1950s a small number of independent schools had achieved some measure of desegregation, but the small number of Black students still constituted token representation. If a young man were not the only Black student in his school, then he was most probably the only one in his class.

Three basic imperatives led to the campaign to recruit significant numbers of Blacks and other minorities to independent schools between 1955 and 1980. First, there was the moral imperative based upon the notion of *noblesse oblige*, which suggests that the privileged class is morally obligated to alleviate conditions of poverty through charitable gestures toward the poor and so-called disadvantaged. Contemporary interpretations of this social phenomenon extend the obligations of the privileged class beyond simple provisions for basic human needs such as food, clothing, and shelter, to a commitment to mitigate the underlying conditions of inequality, injustice, and poverty. The assurance of quality education for minorities was widely perceived as a key opportunity to address the broader social problem of inequality.

The second major imperative which instigated the development of efforts to recruit minority students to independent schools was economic. Certainly the Supreme Court decision on <u>Brown</u> in 1954, coupled with federal civil rights laws of the 1960s and consequent judicial support, compelled all educational sectors to respond to the systematic exclusion of minorities in educational and employment mainstreams of society. However, the 1970s ushered in concern and controversy over the enforcement of IRS regulations on compliance with racially nondiscriminatory policies for tax-exempt educational organizations. While many schools were already acting on moral grounds, recalcitrants faced the lurking threat of losing tax-exempt status. Such a threat would mean the financial collapse of many independent schools.[5]

More recently, the demographic reality of America's school-aged population presents a third imperative to improve the ability of independent schools to attract and retain minority students. When enrollment dips and the traditional population of independent school patrons diminishes, minorities represent a potential market for maintenance, stability, or expansion. Minority enrollment in independent schools grew at a rate of 13.1 percent, or four times the rate of total student enrollment from 1980-81 through 1983-84. As a whole, the minority category has continued to show impressive gains throughout the 1980s. In 1980-81, minorities comprised 8.4 percent of total enrollment, while in 1986-87 they constituted 11.2 percent.[6]

RACE AND SOCIAL CLASS BIASES IN EARLY SCHOOL DESEGREGATION EFFORTS

The altruistic intentions of independent schools afforded some minorities highly marketable education credentials; however, these individuals and their communities paid a high price. The minority recruitment process has too often involved an emotional and psychological detachment of student from home and community. A few of the brightest and most talented minority students were selected from among a narrow group of public and parochial schools and labelled "reasonable risks." Many arguments have been presented to rationalize these early overtures. Some believed that only the most talented minority students could survive the rigors of the academic experience. Mallery further notes that others sought and admitted only the most dazzling of minority students "supposedly to give impressive examples of the capacity of the race--a kind of unnecessary defensive posture."[7]

A narrow commitment to identify and develop an academic elite among minorities was widely accepted by most of the minority student recruitment programs. National, regional, and local programs such as A Better Chance, Prep For Prep of New York, and the Black Student Fund of Washington, D.C.,   had a significant impact upon minority enrollment in the 1960s and 1970s. With the exception of the Black Student Fund, most programs identified, screened, placed, and tracked the progress of minority students who were classified as gifted and talented. The academic records of these students notwithstanding, many programs required these youngsters to participate in remediation programs in preparation for independent school matriculation. In effect, intensive remediation of gifted and talented minority students implied that even the best minority student was somehow inadequate to compete in the independent school setting.

Another bias was the widespread perception that dramatic socioeconomic differences existed between Black and White students in independent schools. To be sure, many Black students were from low-income, inner-city backgrounds and their White counterparts were largely wealthy. However, even as early as 1970, over 45 percent of the minority families whose children attended NAIS member schools received no financial aid; and at that time, Black students comprised a full 92 percent of the minority population. Often, Black children from financially able families were treated as if they were poor and impoverished.

I think the misperceived poverty of Black students attending independent schools was as much the result of ignorance as it was of deliberate design. Admissions officers entered the Black community as scouts, but because of their limited exposure they could not recognize the subtle forms of middle-class status in the largely Black impoverished inner city. Moveover, they had been sent to identify the culturally disadvantaged academic superstar--a student who was by definition poor--and in so doing, often overlooked the indicators of middle-class attitudes and aspirations among these students and their families.

Despite the presence of middle-class Black students, misperceptions about socioeconomic background fueled stereotypes that all Blacks were poor and all Whites were rich. The assumption that Black students were overwhelmingly dependent upon heavy financial aid stigmatized them, and created a false sense of entitlement among their White counterparts. Moreover, rather than validate the cultural richness of the communities from which these early Black students emerged, schools often viewed home communities as educationally unsupportive and indifferent. Some assumed that these students' talents and abilities were exceptional and scarce in what they considered the larger, culturally bankrupt Black community. Many independent school educators appeared to believe the students needed to be salvaged from the entrenched pathologies of the inner city. There was little commitment to a cultural exchange. The message was clear: Black students were there to change and differences were to be abandoned and overcome if the students were to be successful.

DIVERSITY IN INDEPENDENT SCHOOLS: CONTEMPORARY ISSUES

Significant shifts have occurred in the quest for diversity in independent schools. Over the past twenty years, schools have broadened their minority focus to include Asian, Hispanic and Native Americans as well as African Americans (see table 3.1).

Table 3.1

Minority Student Enrollment in Independent Schools:

Selected Years from 1967 through 1987

	African American	Hispanic American	Asian American	Native American	% of Total Enrollment
1967	3,720	NA	NA	NA	NA
1970	7,617	575	NA	139	4.0*
1972	9,629	1,610	1,581	159	6.3*
1974	9,023	1,969	2,500	158	6.2*
1976	10,851	3,124	3,051	183	6.8
1978	11,150	3,501	4,132	202	7.0
1980	11,883	5,297	5,717	324	8.8
1982	12,649	5,117	8,945	294	9.1
1984	13,215	5,120	11,240	425	9.6
1986	14,355	5,464	13,802	382	10.7
1987	15,096	5,709	15,193	347	11.2

Source: NAIS Minority Group Survey: 1969-70 and Preliminary Report on Minority Student Enrollment and Minority Teachers in NAIS Member Schools, 1975-76 prepared by William L. Dandridge; and NAIS Spring Statistical Reports for selected years between 1972 and 1987.

Asterisks indicate rough percentages based on approximate total enrollment figures.

The first significant trend relates to the relative proportion of minority subgroups over time. In 1980, Asian American students became the second largest minority group. By 1987, Asian American student enrollment surpassed African American enrollment, making the former the largest single minority student group in independent schools. For many administrators, the term minority had previously been synonymous with Black; however, given the numerical shift between Black and Asian American students, such an anachronistic connotation certainly demanded reconsideration.

A second statistical trend occurred by the 1980s and has changed the nature of concern about minorities in independent schools. Minorities were perceived historically as nearly fully dependent upon financial aid. A 1969-70 NAIS survey on minorities indicated that 53.5 percent of minority students then enrolled were on financial aid. The report concluded,

> Despite the uncertainty of some of the figures above, including as they do a number of estimates, it is clear that the enrollment of minority students carries with it the necessity to provide a disproportionate share of the financial aid budget and a substantially higher-than-average grant in individual cases, which of course is not the least bit surprising. And for many schools the ability to increase their enrollment of minority group students is obviously closely related to their ability to increase their financial resources.[8]

By 1983, 33.1 percent or one third, of all minority students received financial aid. They received a proportionately low 24.8 percent of all financial aid dollars, compared to the 33 percent of total aid dollars they had received in 1969-70.[9] Of the 36,000 minority students enrolled in 1987, minority recruitment programs were responsible for placing less than 10 percent. The balance of families pursued and exercised the independent school option on their own volition. Many minority families are applying to several schools and selecting among options, rather than being selected or chosen themselves by minority recruitment programs and school admissions officers. The rules to the admission game have changed to favor these families.

Despite recently published statistics which demonstrate new trends in minority representation, the perceptions of independent school professionals have not changed. For example, minority parents report that recruitment tactics frequently reflect a paternalism inappropriate for this new, paying population. To address these concerns and command the attention of independent schools, NAIS commissioned a study of minority families in independent schools in 1985. The study, entitled A National Market Study of Minority Families in Independent Schools, was conducted by Bell Associates, Inc., of Cambridge, Massachusetts.[10] It was designed to determine an accurate profile of African American, Hispanic American, and Asian American families in independent schools and to ascertain key factors which influenced these families' decision to choose independent schools over other educational options.

The Bell study included focus groups held with parents who had considered enrolling their youngsters in independent schools, parents with youngsters currently enrolled, and recent graduates of independent schools. The study also included a national telephone survey of a random sample of minority and White parents and selected students enrolled in independent schools. The questionnaire included queries about family background, factors influencing parental choice of independent schools, costs and benefits, and perceived areas for improvement of independent education.

African Americans, Asian Americans, Hispanic Americans, and Whites comprised 31, 27, 6, and 34 percent of the respondents respectively, while 2 percent were designated in the "other" category for a total of 1,042 respondents. Over 52 percent of the survey respondents earned between $30,000 and $100,000 in annual income; fewer than 25 percent earned less than $30,000; and nearly 30 percent reported annual incomes greater than $100,000. Nearly 80 percent of the respondents were married, and 85 percent owned their own homes. Less than 10 percent of the respondents had completed only high school, and 51 percent had pursued some graduate study.

Financial aid was received by 18 percent of the respondents. Only 25 percent of the respondents had applied for financial aid. Of those who did apply, 69 percent were satisfied with the amount receive. The report notes that "overall, it is clear that only a small number of our parent respondents are in a position where aid is needed to meet tuition expenses...When the information was examined by race, proportionately more Hispanics were receiving aid. Blacks were second, while proportionately fewer Asians received aid. Further, remembering that the number of respondents borrowing loans was small, proportionately more Blacks were borrowing and proportionately fewer Hispanics were borrowing."[11]

For all of the ethnic minority subgroups of Bell study, quality of education and the reputation of the school for academics ranked first among factors influencing choice. Other significant factors included class size and the perception that attendance at an independent school would positively influence a student's admission to college.

The Bell study allows significant observations about all of the ethnic minority groups surveyed. However, this chapter focuses upon the concerns and recommendations of Black parent respondents. The study indicated that Black parents felt the strongest about improving the receptivity and attractiveness of independent schools by recruiting minority teachers and administrators more vigorously and implementing a multicultural curriculum. The focus groups indicated that among minority parents who were more affluent and did not require financial aid, some dismissed the independent school option when a high-quality public school with a Black principal presented an alternative. The study further indicated that "Black and Asian parents are particularly dissatisfied with the curriculum insofar as it meets the needs of their children regarding representation of their cultural history and backgrounds."[12]

Among Black parents who participated in the focus groups and had explored but chose not to enroll their youngsters in independent schools, concern was expressed that only a limited number of slots was available for Black students in many independent schools, irrespective of the families' ability to pay. Further, they stated that in an effort to actively market the merits of the school to these families, schools stressed how the family would be fortunate to be accepted by the school. This approach was perceived as offensive and patronizing--particularly to affluent Black and Hispanic families. The report clearly notes that affluent minority families have options in high-quality urban/suburban public schools and that families are exercising those options. Some families absorb the cost of tuition at out-of-area public schools in order to benefit from greater minority staff representation, a multicultural curriculum, and opportunities for greater socialization with other minority youngsters. Finally, even the more affluent respondents expressed concern that independent schools should continue to promote accessibility by maintaining and increasing financial assistance to those in need. It is in the best interest of all families of color to support accessibility in order to ensure greater social and educational options for their youngsters.

CONCLUSIONS AND IMPLICATIONS

Over the past twenty years, the image and composition of elite private schools have changed. The ability to pay is no longer the single factor determining admission and enrollment. For years, school administrators have argued that limited financial aid resources can restrain their ability to achieve meaningful diversity. In fact, the dollar amount of financial aid awarded by independent schools continues to grow despite the reduced demand of minorities for such aid.[13]

A fully paying minority population eases the burden on schools to absorb large amounts of financial aid. However, as the class character of minorities in independent schools skews in the direction of the affluent, the quality and value of the desegregated experience weakens.   A system which serves an upper-class enclave of people of different shades--all of whom can pay--or a system that serves only the very poor and most wealthy, will not ensure the pluralistic ideal for which independent schools strive.

The contemporary reality of minorities in independent schools thrusts to the forefront the latent issue of class.   Early documentation suggests that the social status of some Black families minimized racial stigmatization and facilitated their swift acceptance into the independent school world:

> John F. Gummere, head of the William Penn Charter School, in Philadelphia, notes that the school's first Negro student, entering in kindergarten, was the grandson of a president of a distinguished Negro university and the son of educated, professional people. The one or two people who objected to the arrival of a Negro child seemed to be silenced when they heard about his background. Dr. Gummere and other school heads have found perhaps surprising changes of attitude on the part of a few objecting parents and alumni when a Negro student turns out to have parents of some special kind of professional or social distinction. This reveals a kind of social class prejudice as a good deal stronger, in this case, than race prejudice, a fact which complicates the problem but also helps reveal it.[14]

However comfortable and convenient class homogeneity may appear, recent gentrification of the minority population in independent schools, whether contrived or natural, threatens to seriously undermine the diversity which many schools have begun to work so hard to achieve.

During the next decade, independent schools will be compelled to examine the ethnic and socioeconomic character of the minorities they serve. They must deliberately fashion a plan which defines optimal diversity along racial, ethnic, and social class lines and specifies goals, objectives, and processes for achieving them. At the same time, schools must tend to the expectations and concerns of a broad range of parents of color as expressed in the Bell study. Systematic advances in developing multicultural curricula as well as recruiting, supporting, and advancing teachers and administrators of color will ensure that these families choose independent schools over other viable educational options.   They must ensure implementation of in-service training designed to reeducate the faculty and administration about the benefit which diversity brings to White members of the school community.   Schools must articulate clearly their expectations of staff in promoting diversity, reducing prejudice, and creating an atmosphere of mutual respect. Furthermore, schools must examine and broaden their notion of the "qualified minority." Students of color should represent the same range of academic talent, interest, and potential as their White counterparts; and teachers of color in independent schools should demonstrate adequate preparation--no more, no less.

Finally, schools must face their responsibility for potentially encouraging the wholesale abandonment of the Black community by Black professionals. Until schools celebrate rather than supplant the cultural experiences of Black and other minorities, such abandonment remains an imminent risk of school desegregation.

It is important to comprehend the nature of abandonment by well-educated and credentialed Black professionals because it is precisely these individuals who may influence the future of the Black community. One should not underestimate the impact of independent schools on the development of public, civic, and corporate leadership among Americans. NAIS knows that a staggering majority of independent school graduates go on to complete college and graduate school and enter the most influential professions and careers in business, medicine, law, journalism, and public service. Black students from independent schools are amassing a similar track record of achievement and influence. While contemporary Black leaders predominantly emanate from public and parochial schools and historically Black colleges, this trend is likely to change by the turn of the century. Growing numbers of Black students identified as gifted, talented, and possessing leadership potential are passing through the doors of independent schools and predominantly White colleges. In their passage, they gain access to current and future power brokers in political circles and corporate suites. They will either choose to negotiate the future of the Black community or, in choosing not to, will deflect that responsibility elsewhere.

NOTES

1. National Center for Educational Statistics, <u>Private Elementary and Secondary Education, 1983</u>" (Washington, D.C.: Government Printing Office, December 1984).

2. For a historical analysis of the development of nonpublic education, see Otto F. Kraushaar, <u>American Nonpublic Schools</u> (Baltimore: Johns Hopkins University Press, 1972).

3. David Mallery, <u>Negro Students in Independent Schools</u> (Boston: National Association of Independent Schools, 1963), p. 50.

4. Ibid.

5.   Kraushaar, <u>American Nonpublic Schools</u>, pp. 256-61.

6.   See <u>Fall 1984 NAIS Statistical Supplement and Spring 1987 NAIS Statistics</u> (Boston: National Association of Independent Schools, 1984, 1987).

7.   Mallery, <u>Negro Students</u>, p. 49.

8.   <u>Minority Group Survey, 1969-70</u> (Boston: National Association of Independent Schools, 1970), p. 3.

9.   <u>Fall 1984 NAIS Statistical Supplement</u>, p. 4.

10. For brevity's sake, I have summarized some key findings of the study. For a copy of the executive summary of <u>A National Market Study of Minority Families in Independent Schools</u>, write to the Office of Minority Affairs, National Association of Independent Schools, 18 Tremont Street, Boston, MA 02108. The author was authorized by Alan Bell, President of Bell Associates, Inc., to use excerpts from the text of the Bell report in this paper.

11. Alan Bell, <u>A National Market Study of Minority Families in Independent Schools</u>,(Cambridge, Mass: Bell Associates, Inc., 1985), p. 25.

12. Ibid, p. 121.

13. <u>Spring 1987 NAIS Statistics</u> (Boston,: National Association of Independent Schools, 1987), p. 3.

14. Mallery, <u>Negro Students</u>, pp. 18-19.

4

Making a Difference For a New Generation: The ABC Story

Judith Berry Griffin and Sylvia Johnson

> It must be borne in mind that the tragedy in life doesn't lie
> in not reaching your goal. The tragedy lies in having no
> goal to reach. It isn't a calamity to die with dreams
> unfilled, but it is a calamity not to dream. It is not a
> disaster to be unable to capture your ideal, but it is a
> disaster to have no ideal to capture. It is not a disgrace not
> to reach the stars, but it is a disgrace to have no stars to
> reach for. Not failure, but low aim, is sin.
>
> Benjamin E. Mays[1]

The story of A Better Chance, Inc., (ABC)--its mission and its
accomplishments over the past quarter century--can be viewed from
two perspectives. One is evocative, anecdotal, subjective, and
inspiring. It is a story about parents who dare to dream that their
children will grow up to "be somebody." It is a story about
schools whose administrators heeded a moral (if not pragmatic)
imperative to recognize the multicultural aspect of America and to
end the exclusion of minority children from all that a privileged
education makes possible. It is about people of all races,
backgrounds, and vocations who generously contribute their time,
energy, knowledge, and financial support to a cause which has
always attracted its share of detractors.

It is a story about thousands of children who eagerly grasp the
opportunities offered, and who regularly demand, expect, and
finally achieve for themselves--contrary to reasoned
predictions--the very highest levels of success. And it is about the
thousands of dedicated volunteers who, year after year, continue to
seek these children out, believe in their abilities and determination,
and so continue to encourage, cajole, argue, plead, and demand on
their behalf.

On the other hand, the ABC story is factual, quantifiable, and technically precise. It is a systematic, standardized process of assessment and selection which is clearly and demonstrably effective, even as each season's methods and results are scrutinized and refinements are developed.

The first chapters of the story began to unfold in 1964, when forty-nine talented boys, thirteen to fourteen years old, were offered scholarships to attend twenty-three of the country's leading independent preparatory schools. The story has spun on for twenty-five years, embellished by memorable domestic and financial crises and the mounting achievements (and occasional misadventures) of some 6,500 graduates attending up to 175 member schools across the country.

Since those beginning years, new chapters have been added to the ABC story when time and resources have permitted. Compiled through an arduous process of collection, recording, and interpretation of data, they have detailed the characteristics, behaviors, successes, and failures of a disparate group of subjects united by a profound common experience. And as each chapter is completed, additional questions are posed and new demands made for additional data and interpretation.

These two perspectives on the brief (to date) but turbulent lifetime of A Better Chance differ only in the language used to describe them. Woven together as warp and woof, they create a fabric vividly patterned with successes. But within the pattern also lies a double challenge.

The first is to provide those left out of the American dream a better chance to make the most of every educational opportunity; a better chance to choose how they wish to spend their working lives; a better chance to make the most meaningful contributions of which they are capable.

The second challenge, equally daunting, is to provide those for whom the American dream was fashioned a better chance to create, through broadened friendships and fresh empathies, a future colored by the bright dreams and contributions of us all. The measure of ABC's success, then, is the extent to which this twin charge is fulfilled.

THE BEGINNINGS OF A BETTER CHANCE, INC.

The idea which was to become ABC was born at Dartmouth College in 1963. Dartmouth, among several other colleges, was concerned about increasing its number of Black students. It was thought that one way to do so was to seek high school students with excellent potential and provide them a summer of intensive academic work, thus paving the way for college entrance and easing what would undoubtedly be a difficult academic and social transition. This pilot program was given the name "Project ABC: A Better Chance."

Meanwhile, the heads of some of the country's leading independent boarding schools were advancing a similar plan to recruit Black students through a project called "Independent Schools Talent Search" (ISTS). Joining forces, ABC and ISTS (which would eventually formally merge to become A Better Chance, Inc.) worked out the plan that resulted in the enrollment in the group of prep schools of approximately fifty boys. Their admission was made contingent upon their successful completion of Project ABC on the Dartmouth campus.

Funding was garnered from private sources and from the federal government, which was eager to find workable ideas to fund through its anti-poverty programs.[2] A goal for the fledgling program was agreed upon: it would, it was hoped, "substantially increase the number of well-educated minority people who can assume positions of responsibility and leadership in American society." And this goal has remained constant through the years, although varying methods of effecting it have been employed, refined, or discarded.

Significant changes occurred as the program struggled to take wing. Girls' boarding schools were added to the roster of member schools. Day schools were included. In the late 1960s, ABC's unique Public School Programs (PSPs) were introduced. Funded and organized entirely by local volunteers who live in the community in which the program operates, the PSP experience is modeled after the boarding school concept. ABC students, who attend the local high school, live in a community-sponsored "ABC House" staffed by local volunteers and paid resident directors who live on site.

THE PROCESS: ABC AT WORK

The basic activity of ABC, recruiting and placing students, has remained standard, although refinements continue to be made. Ably assisted by a network of some 3,000 volunteers across the country, the ABC staff distributes 15,000 applications each fall and works with upwards of 400 "feeder schools" to identify promising students and encourage them to apply. A lengthy application must be completed, including short-answer questions as well as an essay assignment. Also required are transcripts and teacher recommendations. Applicants are asked to take the SSAT (Secondary School Admission Test) and are interviewed, in person, by ABC staff and/or volunteers.

Once the returned applications are processed by the staff, approximately 1,300 are selected for further evaluation. These 1,300 are eventually narrowed down to a pool of about 700 active applicants, whom ABC staff believes would be successful matriculants if places were available for them at member schools. The actual number of these places is limited by available scholarship dollars, school size and location, and other factors.

As a final step, these 700 applications are read and rated by a committee of ABC staff, which carefully matches and refers each student to two or more member schools. The schools make final admission decisions, and the ABC staff continues to work with admissions offices until the summer, by which time places have been found for approximately 350 students, most of whom will be offered full scholarships by the accepting schools. It is a difficult, complex, task, but the care with which it is undertaken is reflected in students' remarkably low attrition rate (6 percent in recent years).[3]

A staff alumni affairs officer confronts the formidable task of keeping track of the whereabouts, occupations, and interests of ABC's highly mobile graduates. And a research initiative will, it is hoped, provide enough information to add several new chapters to the ABC story.

CAREER OPTIONS AND LIFE CHOICES OF ABC GRADUATES

To complete this 25-year-old tapestry, the factual and quantifiable perspective on ABC is also needed, and it requires a more formal approach--one based on hard data, carefully collected and soundly analyzed. The organization has long been committed to developing a research program which would document student and alumni achievement. Recently it has been enabled to undertake the sustained effort such a program requires. In 1982, a generous research grant made it possible to examine the effects of ABC's intervention more systematically.[4]

The school experience, generally, is a primary intervention. ABC intervenes actively and specifically by moving children from their local schools to others that might provide a stronger program. Making more high-quality school experiences pivotal in the lives of minority children, particularly among those children whose daily experiences may expose them to negative interventions, has the potential of increasing the number of students flowing vigorously through the academic pipeline. How could the effects of this intervention be more formally examined? This was the task facing the research team which was assembled in 1982.

It had become a familiar finding from national surveys that when measureable academic indicators are compared--high school grades and test scores, proportions of students graduating from high school and enrolling in college--Black and Hispanic students as a group fall below non-minority students.   Such gross comparisons across groups mask the large variability in performance within groups. There are many achieving minority children. There can be many more achieving minority children. One way to ensure this increase is to identify factors that positively affect minority performance and see that they become part of more of these childrens' lives.

There certainly are many such factors. There are undoubtedly many interventions that have worked--home-based, community-based--operating steadily over the years. But many children have missed, and are still missing, these positive interventions.

Focus of the Survey of ABC Alumni

Within the overall goal of extending life choices, a focus on the study of the career options selected by ABC graduates seemed a good starting point for the research efforts. In examining the effectiveness of the kinds of experiences to which students were exposed as a result of their contact with ABC, it also seemed important to examine how useful that experience had been in broadening career options and assisting in the choice of a meaningful and satisfying career.

It was further decided to focus initially on the proportions of graduates choosing mathematics and science careers. Many research studies had shown that the proportions of Blacks and Hispanics entering technical and scientific careers lagged well behind that of non-minorities. The question, then, became: had the ABC experience enabled those students interested in mathematics and science careers to choose those careers if they wished to do so?

To gather the information needed to provide an answer, a comprehensive survey instrument was assembled and mailed to all ABC graduates with known addresses. It was designed to assess a broad range of characteristics that the research literature suggested was related to career choice in science and mathematics among minorities and women. Information was requested from ABC alumni on their educational backgrounds and experiences, school grades and academic abilities, family relationships, personal values, attitudes, and goals. They were asked about the process of their choice of both a college major and a career. If they had made changes in these choices along the way, they were asked to describe when and why.

It seemed reasonable that the graduates' school experiences had prepared them to choose an academic specialty and a subsequent career from a position of strength, rather than to elect one from a limited range of competencies. The secondary schools which they had attended had offered and even required this preparation of their students, and counselors and advisors had encouraged them to take more background work.

Additionally, it seemed reasonable that a study of ABC graduates should allow a look beyond the many studies which reported that Black and Hispanic youth did not choose math and science careers because of insufficient high school preparation. Now the task was to find out what happens when young people do have the necessary preparation for a wide range of career choices. From a position of strength, to what majors and career fields do they move, and why?

Background to the ABC Survey

The concept of "career choice" is relatively new among minorities living in the United States. As Blacks pursued educational opportunities after the Civil War and during this century, even those with college and university degrees have found themselves limited to the traditional professions of teaching, law, medicine, the clergy, and social service, or consigned to service jobs such as postal worker or pullman porter, with no middle ground. Biased hiring and recruitment practices and limited availability of educational opportunities established and perpetuated this situation. Personal and family values also encouraged Blacks to seek careers in "helping" professions, rather than in more technical areas.

The result of all this attention was not encouraging. Blacks represented 11.1 percent of the U.S. Population in 1970, but less than 2 percent of those employed in engineering and physics in 1973. The figures for Black women, and women in general, were also low. The rate of their participation in advanced high school mathematics and science courses did not offer much hope for immediately improving these figures. An accelerated national effort in the mid 1970s was directed at increasing the participation of Blacks, women, and ethnic minorities in science and mathematics-related fields.

These efforts, focused primarily on the field of engineering, had two purposes: to increase the interest of minority students in mathematics and science, and to retain minority candidates in undergraduate math, science, and engineering courses. Despite individual successes, many of these programs suffered from low enrollment and high attrition rates. In 1980, the National Science Foundation again found Blacks constituting only 1.6 percent of the science and engineering work force.

These problems of enrollment and attrition have redirected attention to the high school years, and have generated interest in the factors leading both to the selection and maintenance of careers in science and mathematics. From this focus has emerged the importance of personal and environmental factors as they have affected the development of career choice.

Minorities who have dropped out of math and science programs in college report as a major reason for their decisions inadequate preparation for their college course work. Yet, from this information, it is not possible to tell whether their dropping out is actually caused by low ability or by poor academic preparation. Since students with weaker preparation in mathematics and science also will not score as well on aptitude or achievement tests, they may not be inclined to take advanced work in high school and may easily accept counsel that urges alternate curriculum and career choices.

Test scores for ABC students generally had been below average when they entered ABC member schools. ABC had given these young people wider opportunities, but it was important to know more precisely what career choices these talented students made, and what had influenced them to do so.

Findings of the ABC Survey

As the information from more than 800 responding ABC alumni who had graduated from secondary schools between 1967 and 1981 was compiled, a picture of their backgrounds began to take shape.   To begin the analysis, each set of background characteristics was summarized, and the relationship of that set to the careers chosen by the group was examined. The strategy, then, was to collect those characteristics within each set that seemed to show the greatest relationship to career choice, compile them, and then determine which of these factors told the most about whether or not students were likely to choose a career related to science or mathematics.

The emerging picture showed a group that was slightly over half (55 percent) male. Just over three quarters (76 percent) were Black, 11 percent were Hispanic, 6 percent were White and 3 percent each were from Native American and Asian backgrounds.

These young people came from relatively large working-class and lower middle-class families, and had gone well beyond the median educational level of their parents (10.2 years for fathers and 11.7 for mothers). Half lived with both parents while growing up, and a quarter lived with their mothers. The remaining quarter lived with a parent and stepparent, grandparents, or in extended family arrangements. Most indicated that had societal circumstances been more favorable, their own parents would have chosen to pursue professional careers or to establish their own businesses.

In terms of personal characteristics these alumni exhibited positive self-concepts, were more oriented toward persons than things, were sociable, and showed strong task orientation and perseverance. They tended to accept personal responsibility for their successes and their failures.

The personal values they rated most important involved relationships with people in large and small groups. These included participation in community leadership, working with people, and being close to parents and relatives. Vocational stability and marriage and family were next, followed by high income and community admiration. Also of importance was inner-oriented, original, and creative activity.

The secondary school backgrounds of slightly over half of the group included advanced mathematics and science courses, while 43 percent took advanced courses in English, foreign languages, or social sciences. Most of the students taking advanced courses took them in several areas, and those doing well in the advanced mathematics and science courses tended also to do well in advanced courses in other areas.

Responses to questions asked about their high school course offerings and about the academic atmosphere of the schools showed that both graduates with positive opinions about the math and science offerings and those who reported a strong academic atmosphere in their schools tended to major in mathematics and science. These students also tended to choose related careers.

Students were also asked to rate their abilities in several areas. As a group, they rated themselves from "above average" to "top 10 percent" on the abilities of critical thinking, leadership, and drive to achieve. Ratings assigned to science and mathematics ability fell between "average" and "above average." Those who described themselves as higher in mathematics and science ability tended to choose careers in these areas.

One set of open-ended questions examined the influences of elementary and high school teachers.[5] The long responses were rich and varied, with many positive statements related to academic growth, development of values, and development of an emerging sense of personal competency. Among those students reporting that a math or science teacher had the greatest influence on them in elementary or high school, 55 percent had enrolled in advanced mathematics or science in high school and by the time they were college seniors, 39 percent of the males and 28 percent of the females were headed for careers in math or science.

Parental values were also related to the choice of a math or science career. The alumni who said that their parents had encouraged them to study math and science tended to choose science and math-based careers, as did those who said that their mothers believed strongly in the development of individual talents without regard to traditional sex roles. This latter point was true for both male and female alumni.

Once the major content areas in the instrument had been examined, and factors related to the choice of a scientific or technical career had been identified, the next task was ready to be undertaken. This task was to rank these factors, determining among all of the information collected from graduates which pieces were most useful in predicting the choice of a career in math or science.

When all of the major factors were examined, they showed that the choice of a career in science or mathematics was most related to the following:

o   self-perceived ability

o   choice of a math or science teacher as most influential

o   perception of the quality of the high school mathematics curriculum

o   enrollment in advanced math courses in high school

o   self-perceived leadership and critical thinking ability

o   perception of the academic atmosphere of the high school.

One of this study's most significant findings was that the proportion of ABC graduates choosing math and science-related careers was the same as many studies report for the proportion choosing math and science careers nationally (25 percent). This finding was true for both the total ABC graduate sample as well as for the sample of Black students considered separately. Thus, given a high school background that allows one to choose from a variety of majors, ABC alumni are as likely to choose a math or science career as are non-minority students.

Summary and Conclusion

Twenty-five years after A Better Chance began its work, there are still negative differences between Black and White students in the indices of academic performance listed earlier, i.e., high school grades, test scores, and proportions of students graduating from high schools and enrolling in college, But, for the sizable number of students ABC has been able to reach, a critical area of endeavor has been equalized. In a remarkably brief period of time, it has been possible for ABC students to build the personal enablers for choosing careers in science and math, if they care to, to the same degree as non-minority students. ABC has made this difference by providing the opportunities and experiences that students apparently need to maximize their abilities.

In addition to providing useful information about the experience provided by the ABC intervention, these findings clearly commend a specific course of action. If progress is to be made, and it must, toward assuring Black and other minority students their long-sought and rightful opportunities to select personally satisfying careers, and thereby make the most meaningful societal contributions of which they are capable, then two complementary areas need attention.

o   High school students need to be actively and consistently encouraged and enabled to take advanced science and mathematics courses.

o   High school students need to be actively and consistently encouraged and enabled to see themselves as able to achieve in science and mathematics.

It should be noted that the study's findings also demonstrated that superior performance alone is probably not enough to develop students' perceptions of superior ability.   It cannot be overemphasized how crucial both teacher encouragement and personal interest are in developing positive perception of oneself as a capable learner.

The interest among minorities in people-oriented careers has been widely documented. The implications of this interest for career choice, however, may be misunderstood by minority students themselves, who may not understand that not all engineers and scientists are isolated in labs and over drawing boards. Students need to be taught early that many of these professions deeply involve management and other people-related skills as well as a technical academic background, and pay salaries commensurate with such training.

Medicine, scientific communications, and science teaching are just a few areas requiring both "people skills" and scientific background. Many able youngsters opting for social service careers could also make meaningful contributions to the welfare of their clients by managing technical facilities in a humanistic way. Minority students need to be advised, also from an early age, that people-orientation and a personally satisfying technical career are not mutually exclusive options.

AFTERWORD

Like other organizations with comparable goals, A Better Chance finds itself at the end of the 1980s adjusting to a decidedly unfriendly political and economic environment for supporting and encouraging its mission. There is much less interest in--and correspondingly fewer dollars available for--issues of equity. Are not Black students far more visible on independent school and college campuses than they were twenty-five years ago? Ought not schools be more able, by now, to recruit and welcome minority students with greater confidence and less disquiet? And so, inevitably, the question arises; what is ABC's relevance to today's world?

The answer is not hard to find. Since 1981, Blacks have been rapidly losing ground in the struggle for equality, and nowhere is this more evident, or frightening, than in the areas of education. Despite some notable exceptions, public schools in the nation's cities are palpably distressed. Enrollment of Blacks in colleges and graduate schools is depressed as financial aid has become generally more scarce. Outbreaks of violence against Black students are becoming increasingly common on college campuses.

At the same time, demographic information warns that like no other before it, the decade of the 1980s is critical to America's future. American society must increasingly come to rely upon the productivity of its young people, the majority of whom will soon be non-White. If they are to live full, productive lives, then a commitment must be made to making quality education available to all of them, no matter where they live, what their social or economic background, or what their race. To do anything less will jeopardize our system of government, our national economy, and our hopes for the future. In short, it would threaten our survival as a nation. In such a climate, A Better Chance is needed more than ever.

But for an organization which demands so deep a commitment from so many dedicated supporters, it is insufficient to merely rest on the knowledge that there exists a need for its services. The more critical judgment is to examine the extent to which its activities are addressing and meeting that need. Has, and is, ABC in fact increasing "the number of well-educated minority people who can assume positions of responsibility and leadership in American society?"

Apart from the research results on the long-term career patterns of ABC graduates, there is much informal, anecdotal verification that ABC's intervention has been--and remains--extraordinarily effective and positive. Independent schools, nationwide, continue to seek membership. Colleges and potential employers eagerly recruit ABC alumni. Volunteers continue to provide time and energy. Corporations and foundations continue their support. Students steadily strive to reach the highest standards of excellence.

Across the country, ABC's alumni, gradually coming of age, continue to distinguish themselves. One is appointed treasurer of a major city. Another reports, as a cover story for the major news magazine which employs him, the story of his life, beginning with his ABC experience.

Letters and telephone calls are received--from an investment banker, a city councilman, a clinical psychologist, a Rhodes scholar, a clerk for a federal judge. Several ABC alumni now serve as trustees of their schools as well as on ABC's national board of directors, and several also serve on the staff of ABC's national office. During one week, two gifts of $1,000 arrive from alumni, and one gift of $100, an academic prize awarded to, and then contributed by, a graduating ABC senior. And then, there are the voices of the students and graduates themselves:

> I look forward to an education that will not prepare me for the world as it is, but an education that will show me the way to make the world a better place for myself and others. I thank ABC for allowing me the opportunity to see the many aspects of my world and for showing me the avenues that will lead me to a fulfilling and satisfying future of responsible leadership.
> Alumnus
> The Colorado Springs School 1985

> I felt I could be comfortable and achieve anywhere, anytime, and in any company.
> Alumnus
> Phillips Academy 1970

> My experience through ABC has allowed me to dream and, what is more important, to believe that my dreams are attainable. I can do anything I want to do, and while one

may be hard put to call that a skill, it is indeed a
prerequisite for any great leader.
Alumna
The Master's School 1984

I know now that you can never learn enough or too
much, and I thank you, A Better Chance, for helping me
with all my heart. I love you.
Special Program Participant
Newark, NJ 1986

NOTES

1. Benjamin E. Mays, Quotable Quotes. (New York: Vantage
   Press, 1983). Dr. Mays was the former president of
   Morehouse College, Atlanta, Ga.

2. By 1979, government funding had altogether disappeared.
   Although the organization worked valiantly to replace these
   funds from private sources, it was simply impossible to do so.
   As a consequence, the tuition stipends paid by ABC to its
   member schools, which this funding had made possible, were
   reduced, and finally discontinued in 1984.

3. The types and levels of support ABC can offer its students,
   member schools, and volunteers must, again, be influenced by
   the priorities of its donors. Various summer programs have
   been instituted, primarily to introduce students to career and
   educational options. Through the Member College Program,
   for example, seniors are provided information to assist them in
   making college decisions.
       Programs to encourage academic excellence in younger,
   non-ABC students have also taken place. Besides providing
   valuable services to students and school systems, these
   programs increase the numbers of potential ABC applicants,
   and share with the broader community some of what has been
   learned over the years about the aspirations, needs, and
   motivations of gifted, disadvantaged minority students.

4. S.T. Johnson and S.E. Prom, Science and Mathematics Career
   Choice Among Talented Minority Graduates of A Better
   Chance, Inc. (Boston: A Better Chance, Inc., Final Report to
   the Ford Foundation, January 1984).

5. S.T. Johnson and S. Prom-Jackson, "The Memorable Teacher:
   Implications for Teacher Selection," Journal of Negro
   Education 55 (1986): 272-283.

5
Promoting Independent School Enrollment in the Southeast: Three Organizational Efforts

Barbara Patterson

The struggle to effectively integrate the independent schools of Washington, D.C., Maryland, and Virginia began in 1964, two years following James Meredith's enrollment in the University of Mississippi and one year after A. Philip Randolph, John Lewis of SNCC, Bayard Rustin, and Dr. Martin Luther King, Jr., led the March on Washington to demonstrate support for congressional passage of the Civil Rights Act. First, the integration effort focused on persuading schools to enroll Black children. Then the task became recruiting, assisting families in the application process, raising funds to meet the constantly rising costs of tuition, and finally, providing a broad base of support for the young people who remained a small minority in these schools.

Over the past twenty-four years since its founding in 1964, the Black Student Fund (BSF) has taken primary responsibility for initiating and maintaining Black presence and participation in the Washington area schools. It has acted as a model for the process in Baltimore, Maryland, and Richmond, Virginia. The BSF has maintained chronological files on students enrolled in the independent schools and statistics on admissions and enrollment patterns. The presence of this data leaves the BSF in the extraordinary position of being able to chart the history and progress of this program, changing trends in the area of independent school integration, and issues and approaches to a variety of problems which have arisen over time.

In the early 1960s, the most salient issue was integration: the enrollment in the independent schools of a few Blacks (the pioneers) who were superior students, and presumed capable of adjusting to an elite White environment. The 1970s--the second decade for the Black Student Fund--brought fundraising problems as tuitions began to increase significantly, and the problem of maintaining interest in this program while beginning to raise race-related concerns with the schools. The 1980s present what appear to be even more difficult problems.

In spite of consistent efforts, the Black population in the independent schools has remained stagnant at 9-10 percent for the past ten years. In a city such as Washington, D. C., where the Black population is over 70 percent and 95 percent of the students in the public schools are Black, a 10 percent Black enrollment is nowhere near enough to create a school environment which begins to reflect the realities of the community. Attendance at these schools is now clearly affected by racial concerns raised by a more affluent and informed Black population. Issues such as an integrated curriculum, the number of Black teachers and administrators, and covert and overt racial biases among students and teachers must be addressed if there is to be equal treatment for the Black students in these schools. Assessment of the school environment, review and analysis of school policies, practices, and basic philosophies, and evaluation of the educational experience for Black students are all important in determining why the average of 10 percent does not increase and to developing strategies for increasing Black enrollment and improving the Black experience in independent schools.

Although the need to increase Black enrollment in independent schools is nationwide, approaches and procedures to the problem vary according to the location of the communities and the philosophies, mores, and financial positions of the majority population in the schools. Procedures must be adjusted not only on a regional or statewide basis, but often in response to the unique conditions in the town or city where the school is located and from which the children are recruited.

THE BLACK STUDENT FUND: WASHINGTON, D. C.

In 1964, when the Negro Student Fund was established as a charitable trust in Washington, D.C., the environment was ripe for change and the politics of the community supported that change. In the decade following the 1954 Supreme Court decision in Brown vs. the Board of Education, the civil rights movement had been created. In 1956 the buses in Montgomery, Alabama, were desegregated following a year-long, nonviolent boycott which overtly began when Rosa Parks refused to give up her seat on a public bus at the end of a long day. President Eisenhower had sent federal troops to Little Rock, Arkansas, in 1957 to protect the first Black students to enroll in Little Rock's Central High School. In 1963, Medgar Evers, Mississippi NAACP field secretary, was assassinated; 250,000 people gathered in Washington D. C., heard

Dr. Martin Luther King, Jr. deliver his "I Have a Dream" speech; and in 1965, Malcolm X was assassinated. It was time for Whites to take direct action to demonstrate their belief in and support for inclusiveness and the growing body of civil rights court decisions and legislation. Even in this atmosphere, however, change came slowly.

The Black Student Fund was begun by a group of prominent citizens whose children attended local independent schools. Mark Schlefer, a local lawyer, was joined by Lydia Katzenbach, wife of Nicholas Katzenbach, deputy attorney general in the Kennedy administration, and two other independent school parents, Lee Bird and Alison MacLean, in forming the organization which became known as the Negro Student Fund. The original board of trustees consisted of these four, another White, newspaper publisher Walter Ridder, and two Blacks, Burma Whitted, vice-president of the Consolidated Parent Group, Inc., and Louis Martin, a newspaper editor from Chicago who was vice-chairman of the Democratic National Committee and one of the highest-ranking Blacks in the Kennedy and Johnson administrations.

Speaking on the occasion of the 20th anniversary of the BSF, Mark Schlefer had this to say about the goals of the founders of the Black Student Fund, "I guess we were concerned both from a moral and ethical point of view, and also from the point of view of the education of our children, who we felt should be educated with Black children. We thought there ought to be an integrated school environment for our children and for the children of the Black community." It was with this social justice agenda, which remains central to the current BSF philosophy, that the original group of parents approached eight schools to state their goal and their belief in its correctness.

At this time, Black students in most independent schools were from diplomatic families from the Third World. They constituted less than one percent of the student population. There was no financial aid available, so the newly formed Negro Student Fund raised funds to ensure that the families of the first eight students could meet tuition costs. In 1964 the tuition at leading independent schools in the city was just under $1,000; in 1974, it had reached $2,500; in 1984, it was $6,500; and today it is over $7,500.

Still, within twelve years, by 1976, fifty schools had become "Black Student Fund Participating Schools" and the Black population had increased to 10 percent of the student body in these schools. Scholarship aid progams were established in the schools and it was even thought that the BSF might not be necessary much into the future. The Black students, rather than including only high achievers, now included slightly above average and average students, as well as students from established professional families and those who lived in poverty.

With the 1970s came a new struggle to raise money for tuitions. Whereas in the late sixties donors were in abundance, now it became increasingly difficult to raise funds to send Black children to independent schools. Most schools had a few Black faces, and, to many, integration seemed to have been accomplished. This was clearly not true. The population in Washington, D. C., in this decade was at least 70 percent Black, yet the independent schools were barely maintaining a 10 percent Black population. These were hard times, not only for the BSF, but for the Black students in the schools.

Throughout the seventies and into the eighties, the political climate changed and progress slowed dramatically. In 1978, the Supreme Court had declared the use of rigid quota systems unconstitutional in the Bakke decision, thus threatening affirmative action programs which had been established to open educational and employment opportunities to minorities. Although the court reaffirmed court-ordered school busing in the following year, it did so on a divided vote. In 1982, the president had opposed reauthorization of the Voting Rights Act of 1965, and congress had reauthorized that act only after lengthy debate. Perhaps the schools, against the backdrop of a changed political climate, felt they had done enough. Black parents, now more aware of and concerned about the particular needs of their children in an integrated environment, were not so quick to rush to the schools. Therefore, although BSF recruitment efforts increased, the enrollment of Black students in the schools did not rise above 10 percent.

With the opening of the eighties, the notion that these students would be assimilated needed to be examined. The students had not been assimilated; neither their parents nor the BSF were necessarily interested in having them be assimilated. Further, the professional staffs in the schools were not equipped to meet the needs of Black students as Blacks. In the face of rhetoric, but little substantive change, Black parents in the eighties discovered that the schools, which wanted Black children, had only a rigorous academic education to offer their children. They could not offer an education in a racially balanced environment, meet the needs of people in a minority situation, or provide Black teachers and administrators to bridge the gap. These problems, coupled with tuition fees, led Black parents to question the value of this experience for their children.

The Black Student Fund, concerned about racial problems within the schools and about the absence of Black professionals on staff, began to evaluate schools and make recommendations, suggesting Black books to integrate and improve the school libraries, and asking schools to review their American history courses. In response to specific concerns articulated by the BSF, the schools expressed a commitment to diversity and multicultural education and a desire to be sensitive to students in minority situations. Still, the number of Black students admitted did not change, nor did the curriculum or the number of Black faculty.

Because the BSF remained committed to increasing the Black population in these schools and believed that it was important to reduce the negative effects of racial bias on the students, the BSF staff began a Teacher Recruitment Program in 1980 designed to locate and refer Black teachers to the schools. When the program began, less than 2 percent of the professional staffs in the schools were Black. The educational philosophies, racial and gender mixes, and grade levels of the fifty participating schools varied widely. Most had either one or no Black faculty members. In six years, the BSF was able to raise the percentage to 5 percent, but only after determined effort on the part of the BSF staff, its board of trustees, and some committed headmasters who actively supported the BSF. Much like the effort in 1964, this effort required persistence.

Just as the participating schools continuously stated that they wanted Black students, they said they were anxious to hire Black teachers. The results do not adequately substantiate the stated commitment. On the other hand, there are many schools who consistently demonstrate their commitment in all areas of diversity. These key schools help to provide models for the others. Of the forty-eight BSF schools surveyed in 1986, fifteen have Black populations of over 10 percent and six over 20 percent. A few have one or two Black administrators and fifteen have more than 5 percent Black faculty.

Since 1982, the number of BSF student referrals has averaged 400 a year, and the acceptance rate for these children has been 25-45 percent, depending on the year. This is a high percentage in a geographical region where independent schools accept approximately one in six applicants. Still, with a relatively constant and high referral and acceptance rate, there had been no significant increase in the Black population in the schools since 1976. Therefore, by the mid-1980s, this phenomenon led the BSF to begin assessing Black dropout rates on the annual survey of the participating schools. We have learned that some Black families try independent schools for a few years and withdraw their children for reasons that include social and racial isolation, transportation problems, a drain on the family income, and racial bias that is negatively affecting their children's ability to achieve.

Increasing the enrollment of Blacks in largely White schools is necessary, both for social justice and the large commitment to global education. However, the BSF believes that the needs of Black children are a priority and that integrating should not take place at the expense of the Black child. The programs of the BSF are therefore designed to support the Black students in the schools while increasing their numbers.

Often there is an imbalance in opportunity for the children that is created by wealth. Black children, like any other children, occasionally have problems with particular subjects. In many of these schools, parents can afford to hire highly qualified, professional tutors to assist their children when they have difficulty. Middle and low-income families struggling to meet tuition costs do not have extra funds to meet this need. Thus, these students may struggle in class with no extra help or, at times, receive student tutoring, which is inadequate when compared with the assistance provided by professional tutors. In high-powered academic schools, students who fall behind often can not catch up. Their grades suffer, their self-confidence is damaged, and the independent school experience becomes a frustration. So the problem has become not only recruitment and acceptance, but providing support for these students so that they remain in the system successfully.

The BSF staff arranges and, when necessary, pays for professional tutoring for those students who encounter temporary academic difficulty. Support counseling is done by the staff, who serve as a sounding board for student concerns, fears, and frustrations and help them develop strategies for coping. Intervention between students and schools can involve attending a parent-teacher conference with parents who feel they need additional support, responding to calls from students who feel they have a problem they can not solve alone, and meeting with parents and students on racial bias issues. The BSF staff often meets with school administrators to discuss issues; it provides careful documentation of problems in the schools and works with the schools to correct negative situations. These efforts have proven worthwhile. Most often, schools respond quickly to racial issues and make adjustments. Sometimes, it has taken two or three years to eliminate racial bias on the part of a teacher or school or change a process that is discriminatory. Still, with persistence, the BSF has ultimately been successful in supporting Black students in these difficult circumstances and in effecting change in the schools. Over the past five years, BSF students have dropped out of school at a lower percentage rate than any others, regardless of race or economic background.

As we approach the 1990s, Black parents have again begun to show an interest in the independent schools for several reasons. Some want to ensure that their child will attend a good college. Others prefer something different from the public schools and believe that the opportunities far outweigh the problems. Finally, some want to do as their professional peers do--send their children to highly selective, academically accelerated schools. Attendance at the BSF School Fair, known nationally for its size, indicates many

Black families are actively investigating independent school education. In recent years, approximately seventy schools and 800 to 1,000 parents have participated in this event annually.

In 1987, Blacks are visible in most independent schools in the Washington D. C., metropolitan area. They are visible in the classrooms as students and teachers; some are in administration and some are members of the school board of trustees. Black material is in every school library in the area. Issues of diversity and multicultural education are discussed at all levels of independent school education. Curricula are being integrated and most schools are, again, actively seeking increased Black enrollment. Financial aid totaling over $2 million was distributed to Black families in 1987, and, although Black enrollment has not risen above 10 percent, it has not decreased. Black parents are more aware of their educational options. Clearly, the work is in its second stage, where the focus is on making the quality of life better for Blacks in the schools.

Black Student Fund students who have graduated since 1964 have achieved. Survey statistics gathered by BSF in 1987 are informative. Of those 96.3 percent entering college, 36 percent are still in college, 10.1 percent have dropped out, and 49.1 percent have graduated from college (4.7 percent of the college entrants could not be interviewed). We located 160 of the 165 college graduates. Of these, ninety-seven (60.6 percent) entered graduate school. Thirty-eight (39.1 percent) are still in graduate school. Of the fifty-nine (60.8 percent) who have completed graduate school, twenty-eight received Masters degrees and forty-three received Doctoral level degrees. Of our former students, 63 percent live and work in the Washington, D. C., Metropolitan area.

THE BALTIMORE PROJECT FOR BLACK CHILDREN

The Baltimore Project was established by the Black Student Fund in 1982 in response to a request by the heads of four Baltimore private schools who wanted to increase the number of Black students and faculty in their schools. The leadership in this effort was taken by the headmistress of a Baltimore girls' school, and the effort began as a pilot. It was designed differently from the BSF in two basic ways. First, the original members of the board of the Baltimore Project were all heads of schools, rather than parents and community people. Secondly, the schools initiated the project, requesting support from the Black Student Fund, rather than being approached by an organization seeking to integrate the schools. The schools provided the financial support for administration of the Baltimore Project, which had no financial aid program of its own. Its primary purpose was to recruit and refer students to member schools.

The school heads retained the Black Student Fund as a consultant in the establishment of the program in Baltimore, paying it an administration fee which the BSF used to hire a project coordinator, who operated under BSF supervision.   This arrangement guaranteed autonomy from the school heads for the Baltimore Project coordinator and allowed the freedom necessary for the Baltimore Project to follow the BSF procedure of evaluating each school and making recommendations for change, thus ensuring that it, too, would be an advocate for the children.

In spite of the similarity of goals and procedures, there were other fundamental differences between these two programs. The Baltimore Project was established in a quite different political climate, and Baltimore is different from Washington D. C., in important ways. The Baltimore population is 55 percent Black. The public schools are viewed as stronger, and there is not the sense of competition with the independent schools for good students. Whereas there are currently forty-eight participating independent schools in Washington, D. C., there are only eleven in Baltimore. Under these circumstances, it is possible for the Baltimore Project to directly visit and recruit students from the public and parochial systems.

In 1985, the formal relationship between the Black Student Fund and the project in Baltimore ended, and the project coordinator became executive director of the independent Baltimore Project. By 1986, it had grown into a viable and self-sufficient program whose board included community members as well as school heads. Sources of funding now include individuals and foundations in the Baltimore community as well as the schools themselves. There is an increased number of applicants and acceptances.

THE RICHMOND BLACK STUDENT FOUNDATION

Established in 1984, the Richmond Black Student Foundation more closely resembles the Black Student Fund in its organizational structure. The initiative for its establishment was taken by a public relations officer in a national corporation located in Richmond, Virginia. That corporation had made a grant to the Black Student Fund, and the officer asked the BSF to assist in organizing a comparable program in Richmond, Virginia. He contacted school heads in the city and arranged a meeting with the executive directors of both the BSF and Baltimore Project. This group spent several weeks reviewing and evaluating the situation in Richmond and selecting a board of trustees. Once this was accomplished, the Richmond board hired an executive director who spent two months in the BSF office learning the program. From 1984 until 1986, the BSF served as a consultant to the Richmond Foundation.

Student recruitment proved to be difficult in Richmond. Although Blacks represent 51 percent of the city's population, Black parents wondered about the motivation behind the program and resisted the project out of concern that their children would be tokens in the schools. Established in the entirely different political climate of the eighties, initially it had difficulty raising money in the community. However, building on the BSF experience, the foundation developed a program of outreach and managed to recruit students who were accepted and funded by the six participating schools and the foundation itself. In 1984, there were less than 5 percent Black students in the participating independent schools. In 1986-87, twenty-eight students entered the eight member schools, and financial aid for these students came to over $50,000, provided mostly by the schools. The program remains in need of more corporate and foundation support if it is to become financially stable.

CONCLUSION

The Black Student Fund is the longest-surviving program of its kind. It has met the challenges of each decade and grown largely because of its determined, talented, integrated, and powerful board of trustees. Its basic mission has remained the same--integration of the independent schools.

In the Washington, D. C., metropolitan area, Baltimore, and Richmond, and in every school involved with the BSF, it is clear that committed, sensitive admissions directors who are determined to create integrated and economically diverse student bodies are the most important people in developing effective programs in the schools. Strong admissions directors not only affect enrollment, they influence the tone of their schools.

The achievement belongs to the students and their parents. They have in many cases entered a foreign environment, and dealt with overt and covert racial bias, social isolation, and incredible academic demands. They have been and still are the pioneers who take opportunity and use it to their advantage. In 1987, Black students are visible not only in the classrooms, but also on athletic teams, and in debate clubs, school newspapers, chorus, school plays, the yearly list of Merit Achievement Scholars, and at Oxford as Rhodes scholars. Black enrollment should increase as Blacks begin to play more significant roles in the schools and second generations return to their parents' alma mater. As schools become more adept at meeting the needs of diversity and adjust their philosophies and goals, the advantages for all students will be obvious.

Many schools have grown in their acceptance of Black students; some are able to define and implement diversity. They are not merely adding Black bodies to White classrooms, but are recognizing the value in exchanging ideas and perspectives among people of different cultures and races. They realize that the mix is an educational advantage for White children who will have to communicate in a multiracial world.

Awareness issues must be continuously addressed. Equality in education, not the mere increase in numbers, will be a determining factor in continuing Black support for independent schools. School administrators will need to hire faculty who believe in the value of multiracial experiences and who are relatively free of racial bias. Middle-income families and upwardly mobile families will need to make the financial sacrifice and students must continue to be highly motivated and goal-oriented to meet the academic demands on their time and intellect.

Independent school education can be a fulfilling experience for some students, but will never be the answer for all students. Black parents must recognize this fact and seek the best school for each child, whether independent, public, or parochial. Independent schools are not a panacea; they are, in fact, like most American institutions, a vehicle that some can use to move toward success and others will find to be a serious deterrent. For Black children, the most critical long-range problem is that no education is excellent if it permanently damages the child's self-esteem, self-confidence, racial pride, or cultural values.

6
Support Systems for Students of Color in Independent Schools
Cathy L. Royal

The importance of role models and support services on independent school campuses is vital for the education of all students and critical for the emotional well-being of many students of color. Many of the children who enroll in these institutions are pioneers who need organized systems of support. They are the first members of their families who have ventured into the world of New England boarding schools or private day schools that require rigorous academic vigor and demanding extracurricular schedules. The surroundings are new, the expectations are different and the child is living away from home, for the first time, at an early age. Support services should not be misunderstood to mean remedial services or assistance for emotional problems exclusively. There is a need for these services on any campus and they should not be limited to a special segment of the population. Support services for students of color on independent school campuses should include these services, as well as providing a network of activities and people who are sensitive and aware of the needs of students from Black, Asian, or Hispanic backgrounds. Any strong support program should be available to all students of the community, but also allow clear guidelines about the nature and purpose of the program. This allows access by various members of the community, but also provides for ownership by the students of color.

Support services should include a designated person(s) who has direct and frequent contact with key administrators who are responsible for the policies and guidelines that affect all aspects of a student's career. Support programs should also include ways for the students to interact and gain greater viability throughout the larger campus community. Programs should be continuous and display the involvement of the non-White student body in the school. The programs should also provide the entire community with a sense of the history of the non-White population, both as it relates to the school's history and to the history of the world at large.

The answer to the question why such programs are needed is that all too often the school community fails to acknowledge the contributions and significance of students of color on their campuses. Many times, classroom curricula exclude the contributions of Black, Asian, or Hispanic heroes in the literature or study of a historical information. Campuses in the 1980s are still bastions of White Anglo-Saxon culture. This makes it extremely vital for support programs to be in operation on private school campuses. It is also crucial for the school to actively seek faculty and support staff from non-White communities. A support program that does not involve adults of color is deficient. Adult role models are necessary for the education of all students and adults in the community. Role models provide the White student with an opportunity to interact with adults of color in authoritative roles and allows the student of color a member of his community who can assist with the link between his ethnic background and the new environment.

This chapter highlights, through case studies and examples, the reasons why it is important for all independent schools to begin to examine the procedures and services they provide for their non-White and ethnic populations. It also describes the types of social supports that have been found to be most useful to Black and other minority students in independent schools. As independent schools begin to examine their demographic, admissions, and attrition data on non-White students, many will come to the conclusion that if they are going to remain strong, competitive academic institutions they must be able to provide both the middle-class and working-class non-White student with an environment that allows them to achieve and flourish.

BLACK STUDENT RECRUITMENT TO INDEPENDENT SCHOOLS

Throughout U.S. history there have been educational institutions that have as their goal the education of the young men and women who will become the leaders of this country and the world. Until very recently these schools have not admitted students of color in great   numbers.[1]   The fact that the schools were all or predominantly White was a direct result of the effects of discrimination, segregation, and stereotypes that fostered the belief that Black males were intellectually inferior and that "private education" was for the academically superior only. In the historical overview of independent schools it should be noted that these educational institutions were tuition based, and therefore, many academically strong middle, and working-class students were excluded because of their inability to meet the tuition requirements.

In the late 1960s, after the consciousness-raising of the civil rights movement and the destruction and frustration of the urban riots, both led by Black communities nationwide, independent schools began to reexamine their admissions standards and procedures. Several of the oldest and most prestigious of these schools helped to establish the new recruitment policies that had lead to the increased presence of students of color in private school populations.[2] Programs that were established called for increased recruitment in nontraditional areas, increased scholarship budgets for low and middle-income families, and the recruitment of teachers of color to the then, and still, predominantly White, male faculties. The schools instructed their recruiters to select the "best and brightest" youngsters from the Black communities and admit them to their schools. In urban public schools around the country, guidance counselors, principals, and coaches were approached by private schools to identify qualified "minority students" to their admissions officers for possible admission to preparatory school, affectionately known as "prep school."

For the most part the programs were successful. Black families responded with cautious enthusiasm. Independent schools began to see an increase in the number of Black students on their campuses, and working-class Black communities began to discuss the possibilities of sending children off to "boarding school." As the New England prep schools began to make inroads in the Black community, so did independent day schools. The independent day schools had not been a part of the first wave of tuition-paying schools to tap the resources of the non-White community, but they quickly took advantage of the inroads created and began to accept more Black applicants.

With the programs in place and the momentum high, both the school communities and the Black communities were alive with the excitement of having discovered a new frontier. Black students headed off to preparatory and day schools with excitement and anticipation. Students and parents prepared themselves for what they hoped would be one of the keystones in their lives. They were not disappointed. The prep schools were prepared for the arrival of their new charges with details worked out concerning schedules, housing, athletics, and student orientations. All systems seemed to be working fine. Not until some students began to get into academic or disciplinary trouble did concerns begin to be voiced about the shortcomings or oversights of "minority recruitment." Black students were electing not to return to school, were being placed on academic probation, and were finding themselves involved with discipline and behavior problems.[3]

Both the schools and the families were quite concerned about the status of the children involved. After six years, as statistics became available on the retention and graduation rate for the first large wave of minority students, a clearer picture was available concerning the full impact of minority recruitment on schools and families. It became clear that there was a vital need for the schools to do more than simply admit students of color. Schools needed to adjust their environments and curricula to reflect the plurality of society and the cultural differences of their school population.[4] Stereotypical explanations were given as reasons for a Black student's poor performance with no acknowledgement of the difficulties of adjusting to the school's unfriendly, often even hostile, environment. According to these stereotypical beliefs Blacks were academically inferior to White students, Black males were good for school athletic teams; but in the classroom they were a disappointment, and all Black children were on scholarship. Many schools did examine their programs and how they could alter circumstances to assist non-White students in their pursuit of academic credentials, but the stereotypes and misconceptions continued. They were present in the dormitories, classrooms, dining halls, in social settings, and on the coaching fields. Black students felt the isolation of being away from home, of being Black in an all-White setting, and of having rigorous academic pressures. The problems increased as the percentage of non-White adult role models remained negligible. There simply were no adult Blacks on the school campuses. The number of Black students on independent school campuses was increasing, but the proportionate number of Black adults was not. The prep school campus was, and still can be, a lonely place for young adolescents without a strong network of support systems at their disposal. The campuses of predominantly White schools can be especially difficult for students of color without curricula that recognize the contributions of Blacks and other peoples of color in world history.

COMMUNITY OUTREACH AND AWARENESS PROGRAMS

Parents who are well-informed about the educational options available for their child are in a better position to provide the support needed by that child once a school is selected. Delores Friedman, in the chapter on private schools in Education Handbook for Black Families, urges parents to shop carefully for a school that will provide the educational program best suited to their needs.[5] One way that schools can provide this information is through community outreach programs. These are programs that provide a variety of services regarding independent school education to the community as part of a school's recruitment and retention program.

The outreach program allows parents to familiarize themselves with the school and its representative while they are making decisions about their child's education. Representatives from schools often set up informal gatherings for interested parents and students at various times during the year. During these sessions parents are encouraged to ask questions about the enrollment and admissions process, academic expectations, and financial assistance and other offerings that schools provide for their students. This is not a recruitment venture, but a community service. This is part of the support services that begin before the student arrives on the campus. In an outreach session, information is provided about the importance of strong academic preparation, how schools conduct their selection process, what schools look for in a "strong candidate," and how parents can begin to prepare their child to become a competitive candidate if they decide that they, parents and child, wish to continue pursuing independent education. Schools who offer this service are aware that parents are a crucial part of the decision to attend an independent school. The more schools can "demystify" independent education, the more successful recruitment efforts will be in non-White communities.

Through the outreach program, parents and community leaders decide to encourage students to attend the hosting school, but this should not be the main purpose of an outreach program. If host schools enter into the program with the idea that their non-White student enrollment will increase dramatically through these efforts, there will be serious disappointment for all involved. In structuring a community outreach and awareness program, school administrators must be willing to listen to the suggestions and concerns of the non-White communities. It is not enough to send a representative to the community; community suggestions must be implemented if the school's credibility is to remand intact. Schools must be willing to open their campus to community leaders and parents. The outreach program should contain opportunities for parents or members of the community to experience the environment firsthand without making a firm commitment to become a part of the institution. This experience empowers parents and is particularly important for families with little discretionary income, or experience with independent education. The schools are thus perceived by the students and their families as places that are willing to support them through the unfamiliar and sometimes difficult decisionmaking process surrounding school selections. For parents and students with more knowledge, but limited experience with independent education, the ability to visit and tour the campus supplies them with more information as they make their decisions.

Traditional independent-school families are frequently involved with the school through identifying prospective students from their communities, working with the parents' league to raise money for the school, or assisting teachers and administrators with special projects. These same opportunities should be provided, and encouraged, for non-White parents through the community outreach program. When community leaders, parents, and other professionals are asked to participate in the school community, it provides the school with the optimum reciprocal relationship--the school has increased visibility in the non-White community and members of the minority community are visible and active on the school campus. White students have the opportunity to see people of color in equitable relationships with the school and other White adults. All parties profit, but the outreach program is only as strong as the faculty members who implement it. Schools must be careful to select outreach representatives who are sensitive to and aware of the needs of the community they are serving.

When several schools join together to provide outreach programs for communities, they must be very clear about guidelines. All parties involved must be committed to the program and understand that the services are for the community, and not totally for their individual institutions. Joint programs are difficult, but can be quite beneficial if executed properly. There are many services that can be shared through joint outreach programs. Schools can provide mini-workshops on test-taking, the significance of test results, how to apply to an independent school, and how to select a school for each individual child.

When Phillips Academy and Brooks schools began to present workshops for parents in Detroit and Chicago, the interest in their schools among Black and Hispanic parents increased noticeably. Parents and community leaders began to discuss the possibilities of enrolling their children in these schools. Parents began to request information from the spokespersons regarding testing, admissions timetables, and early preparation for students.[6] Once community leaders knew that the program would be continuous, they took responsibility for its success and began to critically evaluate the program and provide input concerning ways to improve its format. The communities viewed this effort as a joint project and they wanted it to succeed. Outreach programs can do much to eliminate the initial problems that families encounter when dealing with prep schools by providing families and communities with the information they need concerning the strengths and differences of various types of schools. The crucial components in an outreach program are that it be consistent, ongoing and provide solid information and service to the community.

ADULT ROLE MODELS

Once students arrive on campus the support services become more student-directed. The presence of non-White adults is crucial.

Students need to see adults of color in positions of authority within this new environment. It is also as important for the White student to interact with people of color as it is for the non-White student. White students are affected by their relationships with non-White adults and these experiences carry over into their relationships with non-White students.   Dormitory tensions can be reduced significantly if there are adults of color active in these settings. Often students from predominantly White communities have never had to deal with authority figures that are not White. Non-White role models assures that the school environment provides an opportunity for both students and adults to work with adults from diverse cultural and economic experiences.

Recruitment and retention of non-White faculty members is the best expression of commitment to a diverse school climate. Faculties and administrations that reflect representation from diverse ethnic communities assure students and parents that the school   acknowledges the value of multicultural education. Role models must be persons who are concerned with the education and the welfare of students of color. It is not enough for faculty members to be present in the minority community. It is necessary for them to be allowed to take an active part in the development of services for non-White students. Support services must identify faculty members of color who are committed to maintaining cultural identity and assisting students with the dilemmas they may be facing in a predominantly White environment. Administrators are needed on campus to implement any support programs. It is impossible for a faculty member with a full academic load to also function as advisor or counselor to students of color and maintain a strong presence in the classroom. However, both types of roles are needed.

When faculty members of color are questioned about their careers in independent schools, an overwhelming consensus establishes the fact that they are often called upon to act as counselor, teacher, coach, mentor, and representative for their race or ethnic group. When the New England Minority Affairs Committee (NEMAC), an organization of Black and Hispanic teachers and administrators, met in January of 1987, their key agenda item was how to develop a broader support system for the students of color on their campuses and in the New England area. The members of NEMAC work closely with the non-White students on their campuses. They are also painfully aware of the need for more role models on the campus and for the recruitment of Black or Hispanic administrators. NEMAC members have called for the immediate and aggressive recruitment of minority administrators for independent school campuses.

In recent interviews with minority students for school campuses, Gregory Pennington, an A Better Chance alumni, reported that the students were calling for a larger representation of

Black, and Hispanic teachers and adults.[7]   The question was asked, "What can be done to help minorities be successful?" The recurring response was more exposure to minority role models. When Black and Hispanic students of the class of 1985 assessed their careers at Phillips Academy in an open letter to the faculty, they were quite definite in their assertion that their lives would have been less stressful and lonely if they had had more adults of color on campus. The graduates called for the establishment of a position on the faculty of Minority Counselor who would be responsible for the development of programs and support for students of color at Andover.[8] These students were not critical of their White teachers, but very aware that there is a need for people of color on White campuses.

That there is a need for role models on predominantly White campuses is also underscored by Black mental health professionals. Dr. Carlotta Miles, a Washington, D. C., psychologist, in an address to parents and faculty at the Park School, spoke about the "crisis of self-hatred" that students often experience when they are placed in environments that are devoid of identity models. She underscored the fact that when children are in environments where there are "no Black faces," except those of the custodial staff, they very often experience feelings of race hatred and isolation.[9] These feelings of self-hatred and isolation are very damaging for all children of color, but they are most serious for children in the elementary grades, for they do not have the coping skills of older children and are often unable to communicate their feelings to their parents. Role models on campus can counteract the effects of being in an environment where all the visible signs, and many of the subliminal messages, indicate that White skin is the most valued, and that White students are the most highly accepted.

Many independent schools have begun to address the need for support persons on campus by establishing "Minority Affairs" counselors or committees. These persons are responsible for working directly with students to eliminate some of the problems of isolation and culture shock that students might experience when placed in new circumstances. Minority Counselors often work with parents, faculty and alumni, and community leaders to identify the best possible ways for the school and the students to change the climate of the campus. They should have the budget and freedom to create programs, either tutorial or social, that will enhance student experiences. Counselors should be allowed to interface with discipline committees and academic counselors on the behalf of students of color. Counselors are available to the students for confidential advising and support. When this system is in place students have the option of discussing their concerns and problems with a person they can feel confident is working on their behalf. The discipline and academic systems on a campus need not, and should not, be altered for the student of color. However, the inclusion of the counselor as an ombudsman for the student makes possible early intervention before most problems become critical.

Case studies of schools that have established Minority Affairs officers on a permanent basis indicate that students of color respond well to having a clearly identified person at their disposal. One such testimony relates to a student at a very prestigious New England boarding school. Dionne came to the school from a large inner-city public school. She had been an outstanding student in her previous school and was excited about coming to "New England Prep." However, Dionne soon found her experience to be less than joyful; she found it difficult to make friends and began to receive poor grades in most of her courses. She was, by her own definition, "depressed and discouraged." To make matters worse, thefts in the dormitory were occurring and she was being accused. Dionne wanted to go home, but she also wanted to remain at school; a lot was riding on her graduating from New England Prep. Things continued to worsen as the school year progressed. The faculty "red-flagged" Dionne at the middle of the school year and she was asked to visit the Minority Affairs officer. She did so reluctantly but continued to return after her first visit.

As the term progressed, Dionne was able to open up to the counselor and identified some of the problems that were troubling her. Dionne's ability to share her frustrations with a person of color, who had both the time and skill to offer assistance, prevented her from getting into serious academic trouble. The counselor obtained confidential and sensitive information which she was able to screen and interpret for the faculty as they made decisions about Dionne's standing at New England Prep. Dionne remained at school, cleared her reputation in the dormitory, and improved her academic standing by the end of her freshman year. The work of the counselor was facilitated by a faculty that was aware and supportive of the role of the Minority Affairs officer.

The support of a counselor is needed not only by students in difficulty, but many times by students who are growing and questioning their place in an all-White environment. These students can be served by having role models and confidants on campus just as much as the student who is experiencing some form of difficulty. It is cruical for schools to recognize that it is equally important for students who are doing well academically to have support services as it is for students who are not, because all students undergo personal social development.

Carlos was having a great experience academically at "Anycity Country Day," where he was an honor student and chairman of the Afro-Latin Student Society. He saw his future as bright and promising. Still Carlos felt uncomfortable in many of his classes when students made references to the economic plight of Blacks or

Puerto-Ricans from his neighborhood. Carlos was weary of explaining what it meant to be Black and/or Hispanic to his peers. He was also beginning to feel the tension of traveling between two worlds, that of his low-income neighborhood and that of his prep school. Carlos was finding himself in one of the situations that Edward Smith describes in Black Students in Interracial Schools, and which W. E. B. DuBois termed "double consciousness, the sense of always looking at one's self though the eyes of others. One ever feels his two-ness."[10] Carlos was able to seek the advice of the Minority Counselor at his school, who was able to assist Carlos in identifying the reasons for his discomfort with his situation. The counselor had been in similar situations as a student and later faculty member at predominantly White schools. Carlos and the counselor were able to discuss the pros and cons of the school climate and the need to remain in touch with the people in Carlos' neighborhood. Carlos told his counselor and friend upon graduation that he might have dropped out of school if he had not had him to talk to, the pressure of living in two worlds on a daily basis had begun to close in on him! There are many reasons why minority faculty are important on preparatory school campuses, but the overriding reason is clearly the presence of minority students who need role models to use in building a strong, positive, personal identity.

SPECIAL CULTURAL PROGRAMS

William S. McKersie, formerly of Northfield Mount Hermon, addressed the issue of curriculum and multicultural education in his article "The Seeds of Dignity," in which he observed that schools do not reflect a diverse or multicultural curriculum. The curricula of most preparatory schools are quite Eurocentric and traditional.[11] Schools are often reluctant to change their history syllabus, or their English reading list because of their Eurocentric view of the world. American History is not reflective of the contributions of non-White Americans and little attention is given to the achievements of Blacks and other people of color in the fields of science or mathematics. The school climate, both physically and in the textbook, is often predominantly White and male.

Support programs can offset this deficiency by providing the schools with lecture series and projects that regularly bring people of color to the campus. It is the responsibility of every teacher and administrator to support these programs when they are offered. Students of color should be allowed to play a primary role in developing special programs for the school community. Their involvement provides opportunities for them to assume leadership roles within the student community and gives them increased opportunities to interface with professionals from their ethnic background. Phillips Academy has for several years provided its entire community with opportunities to experience and participate in several celebrations of ethnic life and culture. Each year, students plan and execute two cultural weekends, Latin Arts Weekend and Black Arts Weekend. The events are organized by the students and include speakers, entertainment, and student presentations. The Office of Minority Counseling assists the students with organization and planning, but the responsibility for the weekends rests with the students. The events are open to the school community and the public. The students also organize and develop several lecture series for the school during each school year. Support and financial backing for these programs comes from various departments on campus. One program may be under-written by the English department chairman and another co-sponsored through the History department or the school Chaplain.

Brooks School, Milton Academy, and Phillips Exeter all sponsor orientation programs for new minority students. These programs are offered as part of the schools' support services for students of color. During the programs, students are not only exposed to a sampling of the school's daily schedule, they are given the opportunity to hear guest lecturers discuss the significance of cultural identity at a predominantly White school and other issues that previous non-White students have indicated would have been helpful to them during their school careers. Careful reviews of policies and school codes are also done at this time. Students who have been through these orientations feel that they not only helped them to adjust to their new surroundings quickly, but that it was an excellent way to establish new friendships.

Special programs do not relieve a school of its responsibility to present a multicultural academic program to its student body, but it is one way to offset the omissions that are currently present in independent school curricula. As part of support services or the Minority Affairs Office, some schools have established programs that provide students with opportunities to speak out about their experiences at predominantly White schools. Students have formed Black Awareness Coalitions or Black/Hispanic Student Alliances which help them to maintain a cultural identity and support system. These organizations plan social and cultural programs for the students themselves and for the larger community. Through these organizations students discuss a variety of issues such as their heritage, stereotypic images of people of color, omissions in their curricula concerning the contributions of various ethnic groups, the pros and cons of interracial dating and Black male-female relationships.

Students from several New England schools took this idea a step further in 1985 and formed the New England Afro-Latin Student Alliance (NEALSA), an organization that was created to support students in the New England area who attend private boarding and day schools. With the support of NEMAC the students successfully plan regional conferences that include keynote speakers from business and industry, workshops for new students, and college counseling for juniors and seniors. At the regional conference held in the spring of 1987, students addressed the issue of attending predominantly Black colleges. They were responding to requests by members to have more information about Black colleges since all too often their schools offered little information on these schools.

When there is an established office of Minority Affairs and a committed budget for special programs to be generated out of that office, the possibilities for curriculum enhancement are tremendous. The Dakar Project is an example of this. The Dakar Project takes volunteers from Phillips Academy to Dakar, Senegal, in West Africa for a community service project on Goree Island. Goree Island is the site of the exportation of more than 16 million slaves to the new world. Students who are selected for the project, through a school-wide essay competition, must participate in a nine-week lecture series on Africa and African contributions to the world, including the impact of slavery on Africa and America, prior to departing for Senegal. The project is open to all students, but it is sponsored by the Office of Minority Counseling. Students are required to prepare presentations for the larger school community once they return from Senegal, including submitting essays to the PALAS, a student publication, which was dedicated to the Dakar Project this year. It is made clear from the onset that the project is a work and study project. Students are required to fundraise to underwrite the cost of the trip and each student must commit to organizing at least one event for the project. The project was so successful that the students going to Senegal this year have elected to invite the president of Phillips Exeter's Afro-Exonian Society to participate in the project this year, with aspirations of including more Exonians next year.[12]

SUMMARY AND CONCLUSIONS

Independent School campuses have changed a great deal since Black students arrived on their campuses through major recruitment efforts in the 1960s. But for the students of color on independent school campuses in the 1980s the changes appear to be negligible. Students feel the isolation of being the only student of color in their class or dormitory, and they still discuss the impact of going through their academic careers without experiencing a single Black teacher. The need for support services, both academic and social, is very clear from college campuses concerning the same feelings of isolation and alienation.[13] If students on predominantly White college campuses are having difficulty with these problems, it is easy to understand why adolescents on private school campuses are in distress.

Multicultural education is necessary for students of all races, and support for multicultural education must come from the administrations of private schools. Support services provide students with the coping tools that are needed to counteract the subliminal message that "White is right." Students are at risk on private school campuses if the curriculum does not address the contributions of non-White ethnic groups and the school does not work actively to eliminate the intentional or unintentional perpetuation of stereotypes and racism on their campuses. "To carry on a curriculum or school climate that...ignores or belittles diversity will prevent students from developing as fully as they might" is how McKersie states the justification for creating a climate that is multicultural and supportive of students from diverse backgrounds, both ethnically and economically.[14]

The independent school of the 1990s can be a very different place from the preparatory school of the last 200 years.[15] The schools now have at their disposal twenty-five years of experience and student testimony to assist them in restructuring the total school environment so that it will be hospitable to a multiethnic population. The administration of the 1990s will also have to reflect a more diversified group of individuals. Significant changes must occur if Black, Hispanic, and Asian students from all economic levels are to be able to achieve successful academic preparation from these institutions. Support services provide the entire school community with clear and consistent programs to educate all segments of the community concerning the cultural diversity that is present when Black, Hispanic, and Asian students attend predominantly White schools.

The programs should not begin when the student has been admitted to school; there should be programs actively involved with the early identification of talented youngsters. Communities should be involved with the schools in long-range planning for the recruitment and retention of youngsters. Support programs should assist parents with informed, educated presentations concerning various educational choices for their child. Recruitment plans should include key community-based organizations in the identification and selection of independent school candidates. Support programs that are reciprocal have the strongest chances for success. Programs that work with the local public schools on projects other than student recruitment are most successful in developing strong relationships that benefit all parties. Public schools and private schools can work together to provide the academic and curriculum information that is needed to assure student success in any academic environment.   When the independent school works closely with public school and community educational leaders there is a better understanding between both parties. It is the responsibility of the school to extend itself to non-White communities.

Prep schools, since they are not hampered by complex bureaucratic mandates, have the ability to structure their school climate and curriculum to reflect a sincere commitment to the retention of non-White students. The need for programs to be in place before students arrive on campus has already been discussed. Recruiters from independent schools should be constantly in touch with leaders in the non-White community. Through this network independent schools can structure community education programs that assist parents and educators in gaining a more thorough understanding of independent education. By utilizing an existing network a school can expand and solidify its reputation in a community without considerable added financial expense. The community leaders who are interested in quality education would be willing to assist their residents with acquiring more options for its youth.

Support services and role models provide the initial steps that are needed for schools to become multicultural and open to a diverse student body. It should not be the problem of the student to accommodate and or assimilate into the schools' traditional culture. Schools are capable of providing an excellent education while accommodating the cultural differences of a multiethnic student body. The establishment of support services and the aggressive recruitment of non-White faculty members are the first steps in the long journey private schools must undertake to be truly representative of the diversity that is found in their student population and in America.

NOTES

1. Benjamin Snyder, William Walters, and William Dandridge, Minority Affairs Report. Boston: National Association of Independent Schools, 1978).

2. Gregory Pennington, "The Minority Student Experience in Predominantly White High Schools" (Report for Whitney M. Young Foundation and A Better Chance, Inc., 1983. Available from author of this chapter).

3. Joseph Ford, "Evaluation of Secondary School Support Services" (Paper presented at the National Association of Independent Schools Conference, February 1985).

4. Ibid.

5. Delores Lowe Friedman, Education Handbook for Black Families: Educating Your Child from Preschool to College. (Garden City, New York: Anchor Press - Doubleday, 1980).

6. Y. Rae Jones and Gwen Winston, "Brooks/Andover Recruitment Evaluation" Unpublished manuscript, 1985.

7. Pennington, "Minority Student Experience."

8. Sidney Smith and the Black seniors of Andover, "Farewell Letter to Phillips Academy Faculty," June 1985. The author has a copy of this open letter.

9. Carlotta Miles, "Minority Students at Independent Schools." Taped address to Park School parents, April 1986.

10. Edward Smith, Black Students in Interracial Schools: A Guide for Students, Teachers, and Parents (Garrett Park, Maryland: Garrett Park Press, 1980); and W. E. B. DuBois, The Souls of Black Folks (Greenwich, Conn.: Fawcett, 1961).

11. William S. McKersie, "The Seeds of Dignity," Independent School (Fall 1986): 53-61.

12. The Afro-Exonian Society is the Black and Hispanic student organization at Phillips Exeter Academy in Exeter, New Hampshire.

13. Brent Staples, "The Dwindling Black Presence on Campus," New York Times Magazine, April 27, 1986, 46-62.

14. McKersie, "Seeds of Dignity."

15. Ibid.

7

A Social Experiment in Action: An Analysis of Black Parent Involvement in an Urban Private School

Ura Jean Oyemade and Robert D. Williams

A generation of Blacks has now experienced upward mobility as a result of opportunities realized through the Civil Rights Act of 1964. This new generation of Black families is firmly committed to the idea that education is the key to higher achievement for their children. They know that education makes it possible to escape poverty. Although this view was questioned by some social scientists shortly after the civil rights program began, Black families remain convinced, because of their experience, that education is the best strategy to ensure future success.[1]

Education for today's children is even more essential because our society is becoming increasingly complex. Greater levels of knowledge are needed for individuals to contribute productively to the world's economy. Therefore, most Black families are seeking to ensure their children's achievement by providing education, networking contacts, and social skills that will enable them to profit from every available opportunity.[2]

For these Black families, success is not limited only to higher educational achievement. Success also means that their children will have strong self-concepts, positive racial identities, strong leadership skills, outstanding moral character, and a sense of social responsibility for their community.

This chapter will focus on one important element in this formula for success: Black parents want their children to be educated in well-equipped, desegregated schools. These experiences are expected to help eliminate feelings of racial inferiority and uncertainty that are still cultivated by some elements in American society. If Black students maintain their ethnic identity and effectively interact and compete with

Whites daily, adult Blacks will be prepared to compete with their White counterparts and still feel comfortable with their own identity as a Black person.

THE LEGACY OF DESEGREGATION: DILEMMAS FOR BLACK PARENTS

In the aftermath of desegregation, Black parents have the choice of a variety of educational settings that will help them reach their goals for their children. Neighborhood public schools, magnet schools (i.e., specialized public schools that recruit students from a larger area), parochial schools, private independent schools, and alternative schools (i.e., schools designed to address the special needs of Black children) are available in most urban and suburban areas. The characteristics of each of these types of schools need to be examined closely when Black parents select the best settings for their children.

Desegregation was initially viewed as a way to enhance the personality growth, social development, and educational achievement of Black children. However, only limited success in reaching these goals has been documented.[3] In fact, desegregation has had negative consequences for many Black students. Why? Black children feel a sense of powerlessness in many desegregated settings. They may be made to feel they are part of a marginal culture. Teachers and programs may fail to support Black children's ethnic identity, and in doing so children's academic self-confidence is reduced, their expectations for achievement are lowered, and they lose their motivation. Black children in desegregated settings may be exposed daily to racial prejudice. All of these factors can lead to feelings of anxiety and less than optimal performance in school.[4]

These characteristics, found in most public schools, are magnified in independent schools that generally enroll smaller numbers of minority students. In addition, Black children and parents may perceive a lack of control in an independent school. Greater socioeconomic differences are common and Black children are usually isolated from their own community. Few independent schools have an abundant number of minority teachers or administrators.[5] Moreover, in private schools, racism may be more covert, although it is often camouflaged by the facade of a liberal, color-blind attitude. As a result of all these factors, independent schools may also lead to negative experiences for Black students and their parents.

On the other hand, if high educational achievement is considered, Black parents may tend to favor the independent school. Students in private and Catholic high schools consistently outperform public school students.[6] Low pupil-teacher ratio, more individualized instruction, more selective competition, stronger academic programs, superior facilities, fewer disciplinary problems, and reduced exposure to social problems such as drugs may all help to account for these higher levels of achievement.

When Black parents choose a private school, therefore, children not only receive a better education, but the school gives Black children daily opportunities to compete effectively with some of the most academically superior White children. These experiences will undoubtedly give Black adults an edge in feeling comfortable when competing with Whites in college and at work.

Faced with the conflict of the risks of negative social development versus the opportunity for a superior education, Black parents who send their children to private schools have found it necessary to develop mechanisms to help them, and their children, minimize the drawbacks of the independent school experience. Two strategies are commonly used:

1. Parents may select schools with administrations that are sensitive to minority concerns and which have made a conscious effort to reduce the negative effects on minority students.

2. Parents may initiate involvement in the school to further enhance sensitivity to minority concerns and to promote the development of their children.

Many parents will undoubtedly employ both strategies. Their efforts are likely to be more effective because a sensitive administration in a private school may institute changes more easily than the administration in more bureaucratic public schools.

PARENT INVOLVEMENT: THE CASE OF SIDWELL FRIENDS SCHOOL

Active parent involvement is indeed one of the most important factors in a child's success in school.[7] For example:

> When parents are actively involved with the school instructional program, there is a greater likelihood of the student becoming academically successful. As parental visits to the school are made, knowledge about the student is increased. With this knowledge, parents are better able to assist the school in helping the student to the fullest. Without this knowledge, parents and teachers may be at cross purposes, or may each deal with the young person in ignorance of the other setting.[8]

Parents can get involved in many ways. At a minimum, it may entail simply talking to their children about their school experiences. Parents may also talk with teachers or administrators, help with projects, participate in PTA or related organizations, and otherwise become more fully involved in the life of the school. In the course of this involvement, parents often become part of informal or formal networks that are created as opinions are expressed. These networks may serve as the origin of groups who bring issues before administrators and school boards.

In chapter 14, Nancy Arnez and Faustine Jones-Wilson discuss the reasons for parental choice of private schools in the greater Washington, D. C, area, and they stress the importance of Black parent involvement for children's effective use of today's schools. In this chapter, we now turn to a closer look at how Black parents in one independent school in the city used these parent involvement strategies to increase the quality of education for their children.

School History

Quakers have sponsored schools since the earliest days of their society, in part to share with their children the particular spiritual illumination that led them to the Society of Friends, and in part because their religious convictions persuaded them to endorse a form of schooling somewhat different from what was the norm. The private school under consideration is located in the nation's capital and was established in 1883 as a Friends School. At the time, there were forty-five White and eleven "colored" schools, as well as tutors, small private academic establishments, and Catholic high schools in the city. Located in a prime residential area, the school became prestigious and for decades drew students from the diplomatic corps, military, congress, government, and other influential families.

In 1888, the Meeting divested itself of the school, allowing the headmaster to operate it as a proprietary institution. It was incorporated as a nonprofit organization in 1934 as a "school that strives in a quiet way to develop in its pupils a high regard for ideas of simplicity."[9] Its charter required that the Board of Trustees be composed of a majority of Friends, thus assuring that the Friends Meeting maintained a strong role in the school. Still respected for its high academic standards, the school strives to "offer an education of uncommon excellence to a diverse group of academically talented students within a Quaker setting."[10]

In the mid-1950s, following the Brown vs. Board of Education ruling, the Meeting was challenged by the community and the moral climate of the nation itself to reconsider its segregationist policy. Until that time, most Quakers had accepted the idea of "separate but equal" education for Blacks, and the School's Board of Trustees, led by people raised in the South, was reluctant to change its policy. A major concern was the need to provide an environment in which children "would associate with other young people whom they might freely invite to their home[s] and in which their acquaintances and future husbands and wives were suitable from the standpoint of race and morals.

Thus it was not until January 1956, after several years of debate, that the Board of Trustees adopted a policy of "one-grade-a-year integration of admissions and to open the kindergarten to qualified Negro applicants in the fall of 1956."[12] As a result of this decision, a few parents, including Senator James O. Eastland of Mississippi, chose to take their children elsewhere, but many others were waiting to take their places.[13]

The decision to integrate was rather late in coming. Some independent schools in northern cities, such as Phillips Academy, Phillips Exeter, and Northfield Mount Hermon, had been admitting Blacks for nearly a century. In fact, some Friends schools had had Black students for at least twenty years.[14] Moreover, although the school began its one-grade-a-year admissions policy in 1956, it was not until 1963, fully a decade after the Supreme Court decision, that the policy was liberalized to admit Blacks to all grades.

At about the same time, in March 1964, contributions to a Black Student Fund were solicited from individuals to help low-income Blacks attend the school on either partial or full scholarship. During the early years of integration, Black children were recruited by the Black Student Fund or were enrolled by parents who selected the school because of its reputation and educational standards. Few efforts were instituted to recruit more affluent Blacks from the large Black professional population in the city. Since the 1963 decision to integrate, enrollment in the Upper School has increased from thirteen Black students (less than 5 percent) to 121 Black students (12.5 percent) in 1975 and 158 Black students (15.5 percent) in 1986.

How Blacks Perceive the School

For the most part, Black families associated with the school since 1963 have felt positively about their experiences with it.

Initial Perceptions. The Black students enrolled in the first years after integration apparently did not perceive the curriculum to be any more rigorous than those to which they were accustomed. However, Black children were outnumbered and automatically felt like outsiders because of their race. Blatant discrimination and hostility were absent, but discrimination manifested itself in more subtle ways. For example, stereotypes were typically found in assignments for dramatic roles, in discussions of slavery, and in attribution of athletic ability.

Many Black children enrolled in the school felt isolated and estranged from their community and friends.[15] There was little emphasis on multicultural education, although individual instructors did introduce students to Black authors, including Langston Hughes and Richard Wright. Many Black graduates from these early years developed feelings of marginality--they were unable to identify with either Blacks or Whites. As a result, their adjustment may have been hampered later in life.

Parents of Black children enrolled in the school sensed that teachers held lower expectations for Black students than Whites. They noted that if Black students made B's, their teachers seemed to indicate that this was fine. Generally, it was felt that the faculty did not motivate Blacks to work harder to improve or get A's. Because of this attitude, parents became especially vigilant in monitoring teacher interactions with children.

These observations are consistent with those of Pamela C. Rubovits and Martin L. Maehr who found in one study that the gifted Black students were given the least attention, the least praise, and the most criticism when compared to White children and non-gifted Black children.[16] They suggest that White teachers may deal with bright, verbal Black children by shutting them out of classroom interactions.

More Recent Issues. Despite the increase in the number of Black students from 1963 to 1975, many of the same issues lingered for Blacks at the school. Although there were few instances of overt prejudice among students, parents, or faculty, some faculty and students did make racial slurs and insults. Three stereotypes were common--that Blacks were less academically talented, that all Blacks were from low-income families and thus received financial aid, and that Black students were good athletes.

Many Blacks noted that the school attempted to disregard their culture by subscribing to the color-blind theory, which was inconsistent with the reality of American society. Black students continued to feel isolated. The few who were enrolled tended to be sprinkled throughout the grades. When Martin Luther King, Jr. or other Black culture topics were discussed, teachers and students always seemed to look to the one Black student in the class for direction. Few attempts were made to incorporate Black arts into the curriculum. Plays were supposedly cast without regard to color. Under these conditions, Black students were only infrequently chosen for parts. Therefore, most Black students had to go elsewhere to obtain experience in the arts.

A number of parents continued to remark that teachers' expectations seemed to be lower for Black students and that it appeared that more Blacks were tracked at less demanding levels. They expressed deep concern about Black children's self-concept. Children who entered the school at younger ages were seen as especially vulnerable to the cumulative effects of these covert indications of racism. Parents were concerned, for example, that teachers might unconsciously, because of their lack of understanding of Black culture or subconscious stereotyping, fail to reinforce Black children's achievements, thus making children feel insecure in the classroom.

Additionally, because it appeared that teachers had lower expectations for Black children, as the years went by parents feared that their children would gradually fall behind the White children, although everyone had entered on an equal level. Indeed, Black teachers observed that Black children who entered the school during the Middle School years exhibited more self-confidence and "arrogance" and as a result appeared to thrive.

In an effort to encourage interaction of students outside of school, the Lower School faculty encouraged the exchange of home visits and instituted a rule that when invitations to parties were issued in the school, all children in the class were to be invited. Nonetheless, Black parents tended to sense that White parents were reluctant to have their children visit neighborhoods outside of their predominantly White communities. In an attempt to foster simplicity and reduce class distinctions, there was also an effort to reduce the ostentatious display of wealth by discouraging parties for school events from being held in the homes of very wealthy families.

At the same time, the school expressed concern about the tendency of Black children to socialize more with other Black children during the Middle and Upper School years. Such behavior is a reflection of the natural tendency for early adolescents to move toward "in groups" and should therefore be interpreted as reflecting a positive identity with their race, not as prejudice or rejection of White children. This identification and interaction is particularly important because, as noted earlier, many of the Black children in the school felt somewhat ostracized by their neighborhood friends.[17]

Parents of Black males were especially sensitive to what they perceived was differential treatment of their sons. Especially in the Lower and Middle Schools, White female teachers apparently found it difficult to relate to and understand the behaviors of Black males. Outspoken children were often perceived as too aggressive or emotionally immature. Quiet males were seen as withdrawn. Therefore, teachers were unable to deal effectively with these young men, a real loss because nurturing teachers are so important to young children.

These observations are consistent with research findings that suggest that of all groups of children, Black males are probably the most feared, the least likely to be identified with, and the least likely to be taught effectively.[18]

Similarly, in a study of the relationship of race-sex status to schooling experiences, Linda Grant found that Black males are privately rated lowest in education and ability by teachers, although they are most often praised.[19] These males have the least personal rapport with teachers and are the least likely to approach the teacher when they have difficulty in school. They are the group most often threatened by the teacher, sent to the principal or guidance counselor, and disciplined by calling in the parents.

Additionally, it has been found that Black girls receive significantly higher grades than Black males, a result consistent with the finding of a similar sex difference in Whites.[20]   When teachers are interviewed, they report that Black girls receive better conduct ratings and behave better (more passively?) than Black males.

At the same time, Black males are not without school success, and are most likely overrepresented in school athletic achievement. This further suggests that the "nonacademic but athletically gifted" stereotype of Black males may also condition school personnel to route Black males toward athletic activity at the possible expense of academics, both creating and reinforcing the stereotype.[21]

Another concern centered around teacher conferences, especially with single parents. Many Black parents tended to perceive a lack of communication during conferences, particularly if there were problems with the child. In most instances, unless the parent had clear documentation of the child's performance, teachers seemed reluctant to consider the parent's assessment or recommendations.

As time passed, it became clear that although Blacks attending the Friends school were extremely good students and were admitted to Ivy League colleges, their academic achievements were often realized at the expense of their overall self-esteem and leadership skills. The net result for many of these students was failure to realize their full leadership potential or to accomplish as much as their counterparts or their parents had, often with less prestigious credentials.

It is particularly important that Black children, males and females, have opportunities to develop self-confidence and leadership skills through the associations children normally build during their formative years at school. Whites have long had access to power and privileged positions and as a result may not have the high level of aspirations traditionally associated with Black students. In elite settings such as this school, there are many White students who can simply rely on their inheritance or connections to maintain their standard of living, and hence may be less motivated toward careers. Most Blacks, on the other hand, need to attend graduate school and devote themselves to careers.

Efforts to Minimize the Negative Aspects of the School
Parent Actions. Black parents have attempted to influence this Friends school environment primarily through informal group discussions. Distance and socioeconomic differences among parents make it difficult for parents to unite in formulating specific suggestions about how the school can improve for the benefit of Black children.

During the two and one-half decades since integration, two parent groups have been active outside the school. Both groups were formed to help alleviate some of the covert prejudice and to enrich the school environment. Many issues have surfaced. In brief, the groups have recommended that the school needs to:

o   Further promote the ethnic identity, self-concept, motivation, and leadership abilities of Black children

o   Hire more Black teachers to serve as role models

o   Recruit more minority students

o   Involve minority parents as resources to supplement children's education

o   Create an environment that fosters the interaction of Black children and parents

o   Enable Black parents to interact more fully in the school

o   Obtain more information on the effects of education for both Black and White children of comparable abilities in this and other settings

o   Increase discussion regarding children's experiences in the school

o   Expand Black parent involvement in all phases of school activities

Black parents agree that when these issues are addressed the school will be more truly integrated and, when combined with the already academically stimulating environment of the school, appropriate action will enable Black children to develop to their full potential.

In light of these concerns, Black parent groups met independently to discuss their strategies to achieve their goals. They agreed to pool their resources and to achieve many of the objectives outside of the school. Finally, they decided the issues raised should be discussed with the administration. Unfortunately, due to turnover in the parent group, the formal group meetings were eventually discontinued. Parents continued to meet informally, however.

Administrative Efforts.   After the decision was made to admit Black students to the school, the Board of Trustees and administrators demonstrated sensitivity to the needs of Black students and were concerned about their successful adjustment to school life. Black students were recruited through the Black Student Fund, and financial aid was made available through an annual fundraiser.

In the late 1970s, a Black Student Union was formed in the Upper School. Its purposes were to increase interaction within groups and to support and enhance the multicultural aspects of student life and the curriculum.

While these efforts indicated the administration's sensitivity to the special needs of Black students, it was not until issues had beeen raised by parents that the decision was made to devote considerable attention to the issue of racial diversity and the needs of Black students in the school.

Combined Parent and Administrative Efforts.   The administration was alerted to the concerns of Black parents after they met as a group. Presentations were then made by Black parents to the Board of Trustees and to the Parent Association in an effort to stimulate even greater responsiveness by the administration to the needs of racial minorities.   As a result, in 1986 a study that examined current conditions resulted in what is commonly called the Diversity Report.[22]

The report expresses an overwhelming responsiveness to Black parents' concerns. This responsiveness can be attributed to several factors, the most significant of which lies in the inherent Quaker philosophy of the school.

The Society of Friends has historically been strongly concerned with the need to provide equality of opportunity between the sexes and among races, cultures, and economic classes. Fundamental Quaker philosophy emphasizes the value of experiential learning. Certainly, learning experiences are greatly enhanced by the diversity of the student body.   Quaker philosophy also stresses the belief in "that of God in every man," which means learning to recognize and value what is special and good in each person. The Board of Trustees stated that this belief would be enhanced if students encountered diverse religions, nationalities, values, races, and economic conditions and if they learned to assess the meaning of such differences.

Finally, Quakers adhere to the belief that individuals have intrinsic value and worth regardless of extrinsic differences of race, color, creed, and economic status.

Thus, the foundations of a Quaker belief in the value of a diverse student body can be said to depend on a Quaker commitment to schools that are socially relevant, that provide environments for experiential learning and to teach students about spiritual worth of all people, irrespective of their overt identities.[23]

Based on all of these tenets, the Board of Trustees concluded that racial diversity was beneficial not only for Black children but for White children as well. A careful review of racial concerns was then conducted based on this philosophy, and several recommendations were made to implement strategies, including:

o   Evaluate the curriculum in all three divisions to determine whether it sufficiently represents the Black experience and culture

o   Review the arts program to evaluate whether content of the music and drama programs encourages Black students to participate and contributes to a supportive environment for Black students o   Determine the increase in the number of Black students needed to reduce the sense of isolation Black children feel in the classroom

o   Review class placement of Black students and develop guidelines for faculty to use in making placement decisions

o   As necessary, increase the number of Black faculty, ensuring other criteria are fully respected

o   Appoint a Black principal, ensuring other criteria are fully respected

o   Sensitize faculty, parents, and students to the existence of covert and overt racial prejudice in the school, enabling them to understand how it occurs and seeking their collaboration to eliminate it

o   Establish support of Black parents to share concerns and issues related to their children's experiences in the school

The Diversity Report was generally well-received by Black parents. Its recommendations coincided remarkably with the needs outlined in meetings of Black parents. Moreover, they were consistent with research findings regarding the conditions necessary for optimum integration of Black students into a predominantly White school setting.

If successfully implemented, the Board's recommendations could significantly improve the successful adjustment and performance of Black students. For example, an increased number of Black students would reduce the anxiety and feelings of social threat and isolation now experienced by minorities. The appointment of additional Black teachers and a Black principal, and establishing the Parents of Black Students organization, would enhance the sense of control of parents and students, thereby making them more at ease at the school.

A multicultural curriculum and integrated staff would support the ethnic identity of Black students while reducing feelings of cultural marginality. Seminars and other activities designed to improve sensitivity of teachers, students, and parents should enhance cross-racial contact and support positive racial attitudes while reducing stereotypical responses to Black students.

The study of class placements and teacher expectations for achievement of Black students should result in equal access to high quality programs and thus enhance the motivation, self-esteem, and academic confidence of Black students.

Finally, the acceptance of economic diversity should reduce feelings of deprivation formerly experienced by students from low-income families.

Effects of the <u>Diversity Report</u> on the School Community

When the <u>Diversity Report</u> was adopted and presented to the school community, reactions varied. While most Black parents were moved by the responsiveness of the school and felt positive about the report, many were skeptical of the administration's motives and commitment to the recommendations. Similar reactions were obtained from White parents, faculty, and students. The student newspaper, in what has come to be a standard response to desegregation, suggested that the increase in Black students and faculty would result in a watered-down curriculum.

Despite the criticism, steps were taken to implement the report. Black students were actively recruited. A Black counselor and a Black Assistant Principal were appointed. Sensitivity sessions were held for the faculty. Meetings were held with parents. The Parents of Black Students group was activated. The curriculum has been broadened to include multicultural concepts. For example, the Middle School parents assisted the Black students in producing a cultural musical for Black History Month.

Overall, there is a general feeling of greater sensitivity and recognition of cultural factors and their importance for the healthy development of children. Although the report has yet to be fully implemented, its success will depend on two important factors: continued commitment by the Board of Trustees and administration, and active participation by the Parents of Black Students. If true integration is to be achieved, Blacks must offer constant input and be ever vigilant in a supportive, nonthreatening manner. The Parents of Black Students can

o   Pinpoint, monitor, and propose solutions to problems affecting Black children

o   Identify and provide outside resources for help when warranted

o   Discuss past examples of disparate treatment

o   Serve as a resource to the school to enhance its multicultural aspects

o   Assess the effects of the school on children during and after attendance

o   Serve as a positive role model

o   Arrange career counseling, college visits, alumni discussions, and internships with Black professionals o   Create an environment that fosters the interaction of Black children

o   Expose Black students to the Black community in a positive manner, thereby enhancing their sense of social responsibility

General Effects of Desegregation

These experiences indicate that there are many related issues regarding desegregation that can affect the quality of life and education for minority students.

As Nancy H. St. John[24] points out, desegregation is a symbol of equality affirmed and powerlessness denied. Therefore, desegregation should increase Black students' personal sense of control over the environment while at the same time enhancing White parents' appreciation of democracy--If Black parents have some power to affect school policies, rather than being viewed as outsiders by students, faculty, and administrators. This sense of control could be even further realized if Blacks were in positions of control.

As we have seen, low expectations and weak self-esteem are interrelated. This school, for instance, is viewed as a high-status program. However, if Black students primarily are placed in lower-level tracks and activities, they may soon suffer a decrease in their feelings of self-worth. These children may well feel deprived. Morale will suffer if Black students are denied access to certain activities and honors. A positive environment for all students, on the other hand, could eliminate feelings of deprivation whenever and wherever possible.

Low expectations can also result in the phenomenon known as the self-fulfilling prophecy: children become what we expect them to be. Parents hold high expectations for children enrolled in a prestigious school such as this one. If the teachers do not hold similar expectations, and offer help when it is needed for success, children are caught in the conflict and may become anxious. Parents and teachers may need to meet to discuss how expectations could be raised for minority students.

Desegregation can also bring associations with peers who have favorable norms and attitudes. For this to happen, it is essential that racial desegregation means social class desegregation so that it does not result in official or unofficial within-school segregation. Most often, Black children who enter a desegregated setting are sociological strangers. The setting is unfamiliar and they are generally in the minority. These children may fear rejection or physical harm, depending on the community, the circumstances surrounding desegregation, individual ego strength, and their prior interracial experiences. Hubert M. Blalock, Jr. and Nancy H. St. John have stated that for minority children not to feel alone, a minimum of

15 percent of minority children is needed in a classroom.[25] We believe, given the diversity of geographical populations in this nation, every effort should be made to reach these goals and attenuate any adverse effects upon the minorities who are present when these goals cannot be met.

When Black children enter a desegregated private school setting, they have the opportunity for cross-racial evaluation, which can be highly informative and increase children's incentive to do well. Black children in interracial classrooms want to succeed and they soon learn that all Whites are not superior students. The level and pace of instruction may be more stimulating than in a public school if help is available, expectations are high, and instruction and evaluation are fair.[26]

Black children in a desegregated setting are expected to bridge two social worlds. Their loyalty to and identity with their own racial group may be weakened. Faced with a choice between separation and acculturation, children face estrangement from their own racial group and rejection by others--as well as confusion about their identity and resultant normlessness.

If we are to eliminate children's feelings of marginality in schools, we must remove racist overtones from the curriculum, provide multicultural education, and integrate the staff. Children must be free to assimilate both cultures and experience pluralism according to the needs of their minority group.[27]

NOTES

1. Christopher Jencks, Inequality: A Reassessment of the Effect of Family and Schooling in America (New York: Basic Books, 1972).

2. Diana T. Slaughter and Barbara L. Schneider, Newcomers: Blacks in Private Schools, ERIC, 1986. (ED 274 768 and ED 274 769).

3. See James S. Coleman et al. Equality of Educational Opportunity (Washington, D.C.: Government Printing Office, 1966); Nancy H. St. John, School Desegregation: Outcomes for Children (New York: Wiley, 1975); Alvis V. Adair, Desegregation: The Illusion of Black Progress (Lanham, Md.: University Press of America, 1984); and Harold Cruse, Plural But Equal (New York: William Morrow, 1987).

4. See St. John, School Desegregation: Outcomes for Children, and Irwin Katz, "Factors Influencing Negro Performance in the Desegregated School," in Martin Deutsch, Irwin Katz, and Arthur Jensen, eds., Social Class, Race and Psychological Development (New York: Holt, Rinehart and Winston, 1968), pp. 254-289.

5. Alan Bell, A National Market Study of Minority Families in Independent Schools (Cambridge, Mass.: Bell Associates, Inc., 1985).

6. James S. Coleman and Thomas Hoffer, Public and Private High Schools: The Impact of Communities (New York: Basic Books, 1987).

7. Ibid; and Reginald M. Clark, Family Life and School Achievement: Why Poor Black Children Succeed (Chicago: University of Chicago Press, 1983).

8. Clark, Family Life, p. 205.

9. William R. MacKaye and Mary Anne MacKaye, Mr. Sidwell's School. A Centennial History 1883-1983 (Washington, D.C.: Acropolis Books, 1983), p. 18.

10. Sidwell Friends Board of Trustees, "Diversity at the Sidwell Friends School" (Washington, D.C.: Unpublished report, 1986), p. 1.

11. MacKaye and MacKaye, Mr. Sidwell's School, pp. 168-169.

12. Ibid, p. 172.

13. Ibid.

14. David Mallery, Negro Students in Independent Schools (Boston: National Association of Independent Schools, December 1963).

15. David Nicholson, "One Student Remembers," Washington Post Education Review (April 5, 1987), p. 21.

16. Pamela C. Rubovits and Martin L. Maehr, "Teacher Expectations: A Special Problem for Black Children with White Teachers," in Mort L. Maehr and William M. Stallings, eds., Culture, Child, and School: Sociocultural Influences on Learning (Monterey, Calif: Brooks/Cole, 1975).

17. See Bell, A National Market Study.

18. Bruce Robert Hare and Louis A. Castenelle, Jr., "No Place To Run, No Place To Hide: Comparative Status and Future Prospects of Black Boys," in Margaret B. Spencer, Geraldine K. Brookins, and Walter R. Allen, eds., Beginnings: The Social and Affective Development of Black Children (Hillsdale, N.J.: Lawrence Erlbaum, 1985).

19. Linda Grant, "Black Females' 'Place' in Desegregated Class-rooms," Sociology of Education 57 (April 1984): 98-111.

20. Morris Rosenberg and Roberta G. Simmons, Black and White Self-Esteem: The Urban School Child (Washington, D.C.: American Sociological Association, 1971); Bruce Robert Hare, "Racial and Socioeconomic Variation in Preadolescent Area-Specific and General Self-Esteem," International Journal of Intercultural Relations 1, no. 3 (1977): 31-51; Eleanor Maccoby and Carol Jacklin, The Psychology of Sex Differences (Stanford: Stanford University Press, 1974).

21. J. H. Braddock, "Race, Sports and Social Mobility: A Critical Review," Sociology Symposium 30 (1980): 28-38.

22. See Sidwell Friends Board of Trustees, Diversity at the Sidwell Friends School.

23. Ibid, p. 4.

24. See St. John, School Desegregation: Outcomes for Children.

25. Hubert M. Blalock, Jr., Toward a Theory of Minority-Group Relations (New York: Wiley, 1967); also see St. John, School Desegregation: Outcomes for Children.

26. Ibid.

27. See Katz, "Factors Influencing Negro Performance."

Summary and Discussion
Edgar G. Epps

The authors of the chapters in the section that has focused on Blacks in independent schools address many of the same issues that have been the focus of research and discussion in forums on public school integration and racial integration of colleges and universities during the past three decades. Issues of access, recruitment, support, retention, racial composition of faculty, student loss of identity and self-esteem, and abandonment of the Black community have surfaced in those forums as they have in this volume. What that suggests to me is that Blacks attending independent schools face a set of conditions that permeates all traditionally White institutions in America today. Put simply, such institutions continue to reflect historical American values and beliefs, including racial stereotypes and prejudices. How such beliefs and their behavioral manifestations affect the social and academic development of Black children is the focus of all of the authors.

Brookins provides a poignant description of the type of decision-making process Black parents go through in choosing schools for their children. What is the quality of the local public schools? What other alternatives are available? What effect will being a minority in a mostly White school have on the self-image of the child? How will the racial climate affect the child's academic development? How will the child's social and emotional development be affected? What are the costs (financial, time, transportation, anxiety, etc.) and are they greater than the benefits? The parents finally engage in an overall cost-benefit analysis and decide that, all things considered, the benefits outweight the costs. As Brookins put it, "many parents would rather err on the side of (high quality) educational content."

Independent schools historically have been homogeneous in race and ethnicity as well as social class. In performing their perceived role of training the leadership class of the next generation, little consideration was given to ethnic or class diversity. Speede-Franklin provides an excellent overview of the strains and tensions encountered as these institutions attempted to expand their visions to include racial minorities and the poor among their future leaders. While there have been some successes, the overall progress has been extremely modest.

It is of interest to note that attempts to diversify selective institutions of higher education reflect patterns similar to those described here for preparatory schools. For example, the tendency of affluent White students to assume that all Black students live in inner-city ghettos and are in poor financial circumstances is mirrored on Ivy League college campuses and at other traditionally White institutions. The absence of multicultural curricular and social events also mirrors conditions at many traditionally White colleges and universities. In addition, the dramatic increase in enrollment of Asian Americans is reflected in freshman classes at many selective colleges and universities. Finally, the increasing presence of relatively affluent Black, Hispanic, and Asian American students on independent school campuses is also being seen at colleges and universities as financial aid becomes increasingly scarce and affirmative action efforts are weakened by lack of legal enforcement and an absence of moral commitment.

We might conclude from the analysis presented in chapter 3 that the search for ethnic diversity has succeeded with the influx of Asian American students (although no other group has reached demographic parity). However, the search for class diversity seems to be moving in the opposite direction toward an increase in class homogeneity.

The remaining papers in this section describe efforts to improve recruitment, expand access, increase retention, and provide more effective social and academic support for minority students at independent schools. The efforts of organizations such as ABC and BSF have been exemplary in helping to raise awareness of diversity issues among institutional staff, parents, and community leaders. The focus on the mutual benefits of working together to increase diversity on campuses and expand opportunities for minorities has found widespread support. The success of these efforts is demonstrated by increased, or at least stable, enrollments and outstanding achievements of graduates.

Research on the most effective predictors of institutional success in producing Black college graduates has consistently found that financial assistance and the availability of Black faculty are among the most important factors associated with institutional effectiveness. Other research has found social integration (as perceived by the student) to be a strong predictor of individual success. There appear to be similar trends in the studies of support systems reported in this volume. The schools that have been successful in recruiting Black faculty are also perceived to be most successful at recruiting and retaining Black students. The presence of Black faculty and students is associated with students' sense of acceptance and involvement in the life of the campus. As reported by Speede-Franklin, there has been a significant increase in the proportion of relatively affluent Blacks students at independent schools. This might be interpreted as an indication that the need for financial assistance is declining. However, it is precisely the pool of nonaffluent students that must be tapped if the size of the Black population on campuses is to increase from its present 10 percent. Thus, the availability of financial aid remains an important consideration.

Several authors express concern about the potential loss of talent to the Black community that may occur if the trend of Blacks attending independent schools continues and expands. On the one hand, the most ambitious and able students are lost to public schools, thereby depriving their Black peers of role models while at the same time reducing the possible influence of the parents in helping to improve public schools. While this is a genuine cause for concern, I would caution against proposals that would restrict the choices available to Black children and their parents. We live in a very competitive society and many Black parents want their children to have the kind of education that will prepare them for competition on an equal basis.

How well do independent schools prepare Black children for success in the "real world?" One answer to that question is provided in several of the preceding chapters. They go to college in record numbers and are quite successful; they attend graduate and professional schools and enter "nontraditional" majors and professions. We can assume that they will be successful in their careers as well. What we do not know is how well this type of racial interaction prepares them for their roles as spouses or parents. We do not know if rates of mental illness or social maladjustment are greater or less than among graduates of schools with larger minority populations. This is an area of research that needs careful study. We have some evidence that survivors who have successfully navigated the "seas of Whiteness" appear to have strong self-concepts, a strong sense of personal control, and a strong sense of racial identity.

What lessons from history can we bring to bear on the issue? W.E.B. DuBois was educated in practically all-White schools until he attended Fisk University. He also attended practically all-White graduate schools. Yet he became one of our most revered leaders. Many other Black leaders have returned to the Black community after having been educated in a White academy. Why should we expect less today? Some observers may argue that the leaders of yesterday might have remained in the White world if the White world has been willing to accept them. Such an observer may also conclude that the importance of race has declined to relative insignificance in the latter half of the twentieth century. Thus, many of the current generation of "integrated" students may opt for the mainstream and be permanently lost to the Black community. My own observations lead me to conclude that most of the young people educated in independent schools will return to the Black community and join in the struggle for racial equality for the same reason that Du Bois "came home." That reason is racial isolation and rejection today as it was during Du Bois' day. Until the significance of race declines to the point where it no longer affects life-chances, residential choices, and patterns of social relations, the talented Black person has few choices other than to join in the struggle for racial equality. A significant proportion of future Black leaders will arise from the ranks of independent school graduates. This would not occur if race did not matter; it will occur because the survival of racism in America continues to play such a large role in the lives of Black Americans.

Part 2
Catholic Schools and
Black Children

About 90 percent of Black private-school students attend Catholic schools, though only about 30 percent of these families are, in fact, Catholic. Unlike the independent elite schools, Catholic schools have long been an educational option for Black families. In the 1980s, we are witnessing an increased desire on the part of the Black families to use private schooling, particularly Catholic schools, at the same time that many Catholic administrators and laypersons are concerned that shrinking budgets necessitate increased numbers of school closings in neighborhoods, particularly inner-city neighborhoods, throughout the nation. The problem is exacerbated because, unlike many other participating ethnic groups, Black families tend not to be Catholic. In many communities, with the withering away of the parish, the schools are also lost. Given the years of quality educational services rendered to Black communities, the authors in this section are justifiably concerned about the future of Catholic schools in central cities.

In chapter 8, Franklin and McDonald present the historical background to African American participation in Catholic elementary and secondary schools. They point out that the Catholic Church in the United States has long had policies toward "ethnic parishes" and show how these policies relate to the present-day Black presence in urban Catholic schools. They additionally argue that, whether segregated or desegregated, Catholic schools have demonstrated their effective capacity to provide quality academic education to Black children. Primarily because of this demonstrated capability, Catholic schools as well as other quality private schools, should be supported by the Black community and the national polity in order to maintain them as a viable educational option to Blacks.

In chapter 9, Barnds summarizes some of the findings of the 1986 National Catholic Education Association Study. An administrator in the National Catholic Education office, she focuses on Black students from low-income families who attend Catholic high schools. Barnds points out that, in comparison with White and Hispanic students in low-income area high schools, Black children differ in a number of characteristics. Blacks, for example, are more likely to come from non-Catholic families, have a greater discrepancy between long-term expectations for themselves and immediate academic achievement, and show male-female differences in these expectations which favor
females. She emphasizes that more research on parent involvement is needed to better understand the obtained information on individual student characteristics.

In chapter 10, Bauch presents research data from her study of Black parent involvement in three different predominantly Black Catholic high schools serving lower-income urban communities. One school is coed and the other two are a boys' and girls' schools, respectively. After setting a rich descriptive context for each school, the author discusses her findings on parent participation in the three schools. Parent participation rates do not differ by family structure or whether or not the family is Catholic; however, the most highly involved parents in Church-related activities are two-parent non-Catholic families. Least involved are single-parent Catholic families. Participation was especially high in the coed school, also the one school of the three which was clearly college preparatory.

In chapter 11, Cibulka discusses central-city school closings of Catholic elementary and secondary schools. The author describes several different approaches to these school closings, which are expected to particularly affect disadvantaged ethnic minority youth. In the poor Black communities in which many of these youth reside, bishops have typically kept the schools open, rationalizing their decisions on the basis of need and the great demand for equality of access, despite the obvious economic and social inefficiently from a management perspective. Cibulka describes better and worse strategies for managing school closings in relation to local and neighboring communities when, regrettably, closings are mandated.

8
Blacks in Urban Catholic Schools in the United States: A Historical Perspective

V. P. Franklin and Edward B. McDonald

The Roman Catholic Church is the largest single body of Christians in the United States, with over 52 million adherents. The 1980 Census of Religious Bodies revealed that Catholics comprised 21 percent of the total U.S. population and 42.2 percent of the "religious adherents." Catholics of African descent or Black Catholics in the United States totaled 1,294,000 in 1984. This was about 2.4 percent of Catholics and 4.9 percent of the total Black population. As a Black religious grouping, Black Catholics are exceeded in number only by the African Methodist Episcopal Church, with its 2,210,000 adherents in 1980. Black church membership, however, is concentrated in Protestant denominations, with Black Catholics comprising an estimated 8-10 percent.[1]

Some Africans and African Americans were Roman Catholics from the colonial era, principally in Louisiana and Maryland; there were no extensive missionary activities until after the Civil War. The Mill Hill missionaries from England were charged with Negro work in the United States in 1871 and established their first parish at St. Francis Xavier's Church in Baltimore. Although pastoral letters concerning the plight of Blacks in the United States had been issued earlier, at the Third Plenary Council of Baltimore in 1884 the "Commission for Catholic Missions among the Colored People and the Indians" was formed and received support through a yearly national collection. In 1906 the Catholic Board for Mission Work among the Colored People was established particularly to assist the religious sisterhoods in developing their programs. However, despite these activities, the number of Black converts was small and there were only a few Black priests.[2]

This pattern began to change in the twentieth century, especially after World War II. The number of Black Catholics steadily rose from less than 100,000 in 1890 to over 750,000 in 1975, the greater part being added in the last twenty years. By 1984 the number reached almost 1,200,000, a 40-percent increase.[3] Moreover, this increase took place overwhelmingly in urban areas within the United States and included large numbers of adult conversions. The great migrations of the twentieth century brought larger and larger numbers of southern Blacks from Protestant backgrounds into contact with urban Catholic parishes and the parochial school systems.[4] Although it has been suggested that enhanced social status was the major reason for Black conversions in the North, there is a great deal of evidence that the perceived success of Roman Catholic schools in providing Black children with schooling superior to that provided by inner-city public schools was what attracted large numbers of urban Blacks to the Roman Catholic Church.[5]

CATHOLICS AND BLACK EDUCATION: AN ENDURING RELATIONSHIP

Historically and at present, the area of greatest activity of the Roman Catholic Church with regard to the Black population in the United States has been in the provision of schooling. The Catholic Church has provided schooling for Blacks at the elementary, secondary, and higher education levels as part of their overall missionary activities to the Black community.[6] The first Catholic parish school geared specifically for the education of students of African descent appears to have been the one opened by Rev. Jacques Nicolas de la Muraille in Baltimore in 1828, which laid the foundation for the organization of the Oblate Sisters of Providence. This was followed by the opening of Black Catholic schools in Charleston, Pittsburgh, Cincinnati, and Washington, D. C., by the end of the 1860s. The first seminary for the training of Black priests, St. Joseph's, was established in Baltimore by the Mill Hill missionaries in 1888. Sister Katherine Drexel of Philadelphia was instrumental in the founding of the Blessed Sacrament Sisters for Indians and Colored People in 1891. This group was responsible for the opening in 1915 of Xavier University in New Orleans as a Catholic institution of higher education for Blacks.[7]

The work of the Roman Catholic Church among African Americans in the United States expanded significantly between 1915 and 1965. For example, in 1890 it was estimated that there were twenty-seven Catholic priests working with Blacks in twenty-four churches. At that time there were about eighty-five small Black Catholic schools. In 1935 there were 243 priests in 210 churches ministering to about 229,000 Black Catholics. By

1965 there were about 800 priests in charge of 525 Black church congregations, 350 with schools, located overwhelmingly in urban areas.[8]   Although major changes have occurred since the official desegregation of Roman Catholic schooling in the late 1950s, it has been estimated that in the 1980s there are more than 400 predominantly Black Catholic schools in the United States.[9]

It appears likely that the civil rights movement of the 1950s and 1960s had a profound impact on race relations within the Roman Catholic Church and the increased visibility of Black Catholic congregations. There is still a need for a thorough assessment of the impact of the various civil rights campaigns upon practices in Roman Catholic churches, schools, and other institutions from the 1950s through the 1980s. Many Roman Catholic priests and nuns were personally involved in the civil rights struggles and campaigns of that volatile era. At the same time, however, some attempt should be made to determine whether the changes in the social and educational policies and practices of the Roman Catholic Church were the result of internal demands from Black Catholics and others, or were really the result of external forces generated by the civil rights movement and the larger society. Black and White Catholics contributed great energy and efforts to this important social movement, which ultimately challenged the moral commitments of Americans of all religious persuasions.[10]

Although race relations within the Roman Catholic Church needs further examination, there have been a few specialized studies of Blacks in urban Catholic schools. Researchers who have touched upon practices and conditions affecting African Americans in Catholic schools have emphasized (1) the impact of legal segregation (Jim Crow) upon Roman Catholic educational policies and practices historically, and (2) the academic success of Black children in urban Catholic schools, especially in comparison with the "academic failure" of Blacks in many urban public school systems. Throughout the nineteenth and early twentieth centuries, the major social interactions between African Americans and Roman Catholics took place in schools and other educational institutions opened specifically for the training of Black students.

CATHOLIC EDUCATION AND THE BLACK COMMUNITY IN THE NINETEENTH CENTURY

Although the vast majority of religious Blacks are non-Catholics, there is no intrinsic relationship between African Americans and Protestantism. The vast majority of people of African descent in the New World, especially in Central and South America, profess Catholicism. However, in the United States during the nineteenth century, Roman Catholic missionary activities among African

Americans were limited by racial and religious discrimination and persecution. Roman Catholics were often the victims of prejudice and discrimination, from the dominant Protestant majority and anti-Catholic riots took place in several northern cities, especially in the 1830s and 1840s. Thus Catholic missionary activities among enslaved and free Africans and African Americans were often sidetracked by anti-Catholic prejudices in society at large as well as anti-Black prejudices on the part of many Roman Catholic immigrants from Europe.[11]

Given the religious persecution in the early nineteenth century, many Roman Catholic bishops recognized the need to develop Catholic parish schools and parochial school systems. This "voluntary segregation" by the Catholic religious minority into separate schools was greatly influenced by the conditions for Catholics in the cities at large and particularly in the local public school system. In Milwaukee and St. Louis, for example, there was little friction between Protestants and Catholics over schooling, and Catholic parents sent their children to public schools where there were often Catholic teachers and administrators. In New York City, Boston, and Philadelphia the sizable Catholic minority exercised a great deal of influence over decisions affecting the public schools. However, in the face of renewed "anti-Catholic crusades" in the 1890s and early 1900s, many American Catholic bishops began to emphasize even more to immigrant and second-generation parents the importance of Catholic schooling for Catholic children. Their major fear was "leakage," the slow but steady erosion of the Catholic faith among immigrant Catholics in a Protestant-dominated society.[12]

One answer to the problem of leakage was the policy of establishing "national parishes" that reflected the language, rituals, celebrations, and beliefs of the major ethnic groups of Roman Catholic communicants. These national parishes represented a type of official segregation along cultural lines within the Roman Catholic Church in the United States. The practice allowed local parishes in American cities to provide "that little touch of home" to Irish, Italian, German, or Slovak immigrants and their families. There is evidence that the practice helped stem the leakage from Catholicism among European immigrant groups.[13]

Catholic school systems in cities where segregation was mandated by law, such as St. Louis, Baltimore, Washington, D.C., and New Orleans, opened separate Black Catholic elementary schools and secondary schools from the early decades of the nineteenth century. In northern cities, including Boston, New York, Philadelphia, and Chicago, predominantly Black parish schools developed much later in the wake of the twentieth-century migrations from the South. Ostensibly, the provision of Catholic schools for Blacks in nineteenth-century southern cities was part of the Church's overall missionary activities. In Washington, D.C., in 1818 a Roman Catholic priest, Father Elroy, began a Sabbath School for Blacks, where he taught "spelling, reading, writing and Christian doctrine."[14] In Charleston, South Carolina, in the 1850s Bishop John England authorized the opening of a school for Black boys and girls. With Emancipation and the end of the Civil War, Roman Catholic leaders at the Second Plenary Council at Baltimore in 1866 addressed the issue of the Church's response to the "sudden liberation of so large a multitude." In a pastoral letter, the council urged Roman Catholics in the name of "Christian charity and zeal" to provide "the most generous cooperation with the plans that may be adopted by the Bishops of the Dioceses...and extend to them [the freedpeople] that Christian education and moral restraint which they so much stand in need of."[15]

There is evidence that several Roman Catholic religious orders responded to the depressed postwar educational conditions for the freed people by establishing separate Black Catholic schools. The educational programs of the Mill Hill Fathers were assisted by the Fathers of the Holy Ghost in 1872, the Fathers of the Divine Word in 1906, and the African Mission Fathers in 1907. Among women's religious orders, the Franciscan Sisters (1881) and the Mission Helpers (1890) were active in Baltimore, while the Sister Servants of the Holy Ghost and Mary Immaculate (1893) and the Sisters of the Blessed Sacrament (1891) were successful in opening schools for Blacks in several southern cities.[16]

CATHOLIC EDUCATION AND THE BLACK COMMUNITY IN THE TWENTIETH CENTURY

The opening of separate Black Catholic schools had become official Church policy by the end of the nineteenth century and the maintenance of separate Black parish schools remained diocesan policy throughout the United States until the end of World War II. This educational policy was in keeping with Jim Crow laws in many southern states as well as the Roman Catholic Church's overall practice of supporting the establishment of ethnic or "national" parishes and schools. However, beginning in the late 1940s the Roman Catholic hierarchy was confronted with demands from militant Roman Catholics, Black and White, for the voluntary desegregation of parochial schools and other Catholic institutions. In St. Louis, in November 1944 Archbishop John Glennon was confronted by a demand from Black Catholic laity and several White priests for desegregation of Catholic parish schools. This same coalition of Black and White Catholics had been successful in gaining the desegregation of Webster College and St. Louis University. The group also gained equal treatment for students and graduates of St. Joseph's High School, a Black Catholic secondary institution, at citywide Catholic meetings and graduation ceremonies in 1943 and 1944. But Archbishop Glennon first responded to the group's request for integration of parish schools by noting that "the question regarding the admittance of colored children to our parochial Catholic schools is being studied and we hope that within due time a favorable solution to this important question would be reached."[17]   When pressed further, Glennon allowed desegregation to begin without publicity or fanfare with the Visitation Parish School in the fall of 1945. Upon the death of Archbishop Glennon in 1946, the formal desegregation of Catholic institutions in St. Louis was carried out by his successor, Bishop Joseph E. Ritter, in 1947 and 1948. Ritter had just completed the desegregation of Catholic schools in Indianapolis, Indiana, and vigorously pursued racial change in Catholic St. Louis.

Archbishop (later Cardinal) Patrick A. O'Boyle launched the desgregation of Roman Catholic facilities in Washington, D. C., in 1948, and Archbishop Joseph F. Rummel carried out the desegregation of Catholic schools and other institutions in New Orleans between 1949 and 1953. In San Antonio, Texas, in 1953 Archbishop Robert A. Lucey openly rebuked the continued practice of segregation in Catholic schools and quietly worked to bring about the desegregation of Catholic institutions in the city. After the Supreme Court's decision in Brown vs. Board of Education in 1954, declaring segregation in public education unconstitutional, the pace of Catholic school desegregation quickened and became part of official Church policy by the late 1950s.[18]

The largest Catholic school system in the United States is found in Chicago, and although there were no laws calling for the separation of Blacks and Whites in public or private schooling, the first separate Black parochial school, St. Monica's, was opened at Thirty-Fifth and State Streets by Father John Morris in 1913. The school lasted only one decade and was merged in 1923 with St. Elizabeth Parish School, another predominantly Black Catholic school on the South Side.[19]   Chicago's Black parishes and schools were not the result of the enforcement of segregation laws, as was the case in St. Louis, Washington, D.C., and New Orleans but more a consequence of George Cardinal Mundelein's policy of enforcing "parochialism." German, Slovak, Italian, and Black Catholics in Chicago should "stay in your own back yard," declared the powerful prelate, and his policy was to encourage the creation of national parishes. Despite sporadic protests against the "Jim Crow Catholic schools," by 1946 there were nine predominantly Black Catholic schools in Chicago, enrolling an estimated 3,500 students.[20]

In other northern cities, including Boston, Detroit, New York City, and Philadelphia, Black children were usually allowed to attend the Catholic diocesan schools in their neighborhoods. However, in Philadelphia, from as early as 1912 there were reports that the Saint Peter Claver Parish School was an all-Black school.

Moreover, this Catholic school served as a social center for the local Black community of South Philadelphia (as did the separate Black public schools) well into the 1950s.[21] In the state of New York, there were five separate Black Catholic schools in the 1920s, and twelve by the 1940s. These schools were located in Albany, Brooklyn, Buffalo, Manhattan, and other urban areas. Also by the 1940s, in Harlem there were at least five formerly Irish Catholic parish schools that had become all-Black.[22]

There are presently wide gaps in our knowledge of the history and development of Black Catholic schooling in urban America in the late nineteenth and twentieth centuries.[23] However, on the basis of available evidence we can discern some definite patterns. In both northern and southern cities separate Black Catholic schools were created by Roman Catholic diocesan policy, religious orders acting with diocesan approval, and by the transformation of previously predominantly White parish schools to all-Black schools. In the southern and border states, where segregation was mandated by law, diocesan policy was prescribed by legal statute. Following the Brown vs. Board of Education decision, Roman Catholic schools sometimes desegregated more rapidly than the public school systems.

In northern (and possibly western) cities, separate Black Catholic schools were not mandated by law, but were created as part of diocesan educational policy. By the 1960s, with the increase in the number of Blacks enrolled in urban Catholic schools, there was an increase in the number of all-Black or predominantly Black urban Catholic schools. However, the increase in the number of Blacks in urban Catholic schools was more a consequence of the deterioration of urban public school systems in the 1950s and 1960s than the result of missionary activities in the Black community by Roman Catholics.

By the 1950s, in many large cities Black parents were attracted to Roman Catholic schools because of the high quality of instruction available to their children. The overall deterioration of "inner-city" public schools was common knowledge among socially aware parents as well as urban educational researchers. Insufficient funding of large public school systems in general meant serious deficiencies in predominantly Black schools by the late 1950s, if not earlier. For many middle and working-class Black families, the public schools were "blackboard jungles" populated by poorly paid teachers with serious morale problems using often outdated and impractical materials in overcrowded classes. The public schools had to be avoided, and these families were willing to make great financial sacrifices to pay for what they considered to be better schooling.[24]

The general deterioration in the 1950s and 1960s of the quality of urban public schooling drove away thousands of middle and working-class parents, Black and White, who viewed the inner-city

Catholic schools as not too expensive alternatives for their children. Unfortunately, as the cost of maintaining parochial schools increased, the ability of Black parents to pay higher tuitions decreased, and some inner-city parish schools were closed before they were able to attract a sufficient number of financially able students. The general policy of Church officials became the provision (or retention) of Catholic schools "where parishes can pay for them." Many times, in order to keep from closing, inner-city parochial schools began admitting non-Catholics in larger numbers.[25]

This practice, however, touched off another debate within Roman Catholic circles about whether or not Catholic money and resources should be used for the training of non-Catholic children. Whereas the Church's pragmatists often pointed out that many inner-city parochial schools had become a drain on the diocese's financial resources, many Black Catholic leaders saw these schools as important outposts for attracting Black converts and argued that these schools should be considered part of the Roman Catholic Church's mission to the Black community.[26]

Black parents would be well-advised to support the preservation of Catholic parish schools in predominantly Black urban areas at reasonable costs. Numerous studies have concluded that in general the academic achievement levels for students and graduates of urban Catholic schools were consistently higher than those for their public school counterparts. This was the case even when Catholic school teachers were paid less than teachers in the public schools, and when student/teacher ratios were noticeably higher in the Catholic schools.[27] However, the reasons for and significance of the better performance by Catholic school students and graduates on standardized tests and other measures remains the subject of lively and ongoing debate among educational researchers.[28]

One issue within the debate over the effectiveness of public versus private schooling is the degree and amount of academic success for Black and other minority students enrolled in Catholic secondary and elementary schools, especially in the larger cities. Although there is very little historical data on the effectiveness of Catholic schooling for Black and other minority students, Andrew Greeley found in a 1980 study of Black and Hispanic students enrolled in Roman Catholic secondary schools that achievement levels were much higher than those for minority students in public high schools, even when family background characteristics, such as parental education and income, were taken into account.[29] However, Thomas Z. Keith looked at the achievement test scores of Black and Hispanic high school seniors enrolled in Catholic and public schools in the "first wave of the (1980) High School and Beyond longitudinal study" and found that when measures of student ability, such as reading comprehension skills, were taken into account, the apparent positive effect of Catholic schools was reduced, though still meaningful. Keith suggested that "greater homework demands" in the Catholic schools may partially account for the differences in the effects of schooling on achievement by Black and Hispanic high school students.[30]

With regard to Black and other minority students in Catholic elementary schools, the findings were similar. The most comprehensive study was commissioned in 1978 by the Catholic League for Religious and Civil Rights. This study included fifty-four private, mostly Catholic schools where Blacks accounted for 56 percent of the enrollment, Hispanics 31 percent, and Whites 8 percent. All the schools charged tuition, averaging $400 per year, and family income averaged $15,000 per year, with 15 percent of the families making less than $5,000 in 1978. These particular families were noticeably similar in public educational or Protestant religious background to their Black neighbors. However, one important factor distinguished this group of parents: "their desire for high quality education." According to one report, "analyses of the responses of parents showed that this factor outweighed all others, including religious beliefs." Although the schools were "overwhelmingly Catholic" in affiliation, "nearly one-third (31 percent) of the students were Protestant and 2 percent listed themselves as having no church affiliation. Among Black students, the proportion of non-Catholics was even higher; 53 percent of all Black students reported that they were Protestant."[31]

On a number of significant nonacademic measures, including frequency of student discipline and attendance problems and parent-teacher relations, these private Catholic schools appeared to be serving their minority clientele well. There were far fewer student discipline problems in the private schools, and parent-teacher relations were close and cooperative. This was understandable since these parents had invested great amounts of time and money in the decision to enroll their children in private school and were generally attentive to their investment. Teachers and administrators at urban Black Catholic schools often face enormous financial stresses, including frequent vandalism, high insurance premiums, and economic insecurities among the students. Often, these dedicated educators are sustained primarily by the spiritual support of working and middle-class Black parents committed to maintaining quality educational programs for their children.[32]

CONCLUSIONS AND EDUCATIONAL POLICY IMPLICATIONS

Recently, spokespersons for public education and the teacher's unions have leveled charges of elitism and racism at Catholic and other private schools. Some educational researchers have also suggested that the increase in the number of private schools in urban areas, especially Catholic schools, has added to the degree of segregation in urban public school systems. In the 1960s and 1970s national and local civil rights groups brought suits to desegregate urban public school systems in hopes of improving the quality of schooling available to minority children. At times, these groups argued that the Catholic schools absorbed (and thus benefitted from) the "White flight" from urban public schools following court-ordered desegregation.[33] However, defenders of the parochial school systems countered that urban Catholic schools have helped to stem White flight from inner-city areas by providing middle and working-class parents, Black and White, with a viable alternative to the increasingly inadequate urban public schools.[34]

What had generally been overlooked in this recent debate was the historical reality that there was a great deal of de jure and de facto segregation in urban Catholic schools in the United States throughout the twentieth century. As was mentioned, before the 1950s in Baltimore, St. Louis, New Orleans, Washington, D.C., and other southern and border cities, the opening of "Jim Crow Catholic schools" by religious orders or diocesan officials was in keeping with southern law and Roman Catholic policy and practice. In northern cities, such as Chicago and Philadelphia, separate Black Catholic parish schools also existed. These schools were associated with predominantly Black Roman Catholic congregations, but they were also sanctioned by diocesan authorities. Gradually, the number of Black Catholic parish schools increased as more and more non-Catholic children were enrolled by Black parents seeking quality education at minimal expense.

In the 1960s and 1970s, despite widespread campaigns for "quality integrated public schooling," many Black families in northern and southern cities believed that the quality of the schooling received by their children in separate Black or predominantly Black Catholic schools was higher than that available in the local "desegregated" public schools. At the same time, educational researchers demonstrated the positive effects of Catholic schooling upon poor and working-class minority student achievement at the elementary and secondary levels.

Important policy implications may be drawn from this historical and sociological evidence. Despite campaigns to end racial isolation and improve academic achievement levels for Black and other minority students in urban public schools, significant positive change has been elusive. If it can be determined that, historically, achievement levels for poor and working-class Black students in all-Black or desegregated Catholic schools were significantly higher than those for Black (and White) students in urban public schools, then it would suggest that greater federal or state support should be provided to Catholic and other private schools, segregated or desegregated, that produce high levels of academic achievement for Black and other minority students in urban America. In an urban environment cluttered by academic failure, these data suggest that financial resources should be made available to those educational institutions, public or private, that can produce academic success for poor and working-class Black children.

Historically and at present, Black Catholic schools have been considered "alternatives of excellence" to Black parents and children in the inner city. These schools and families deserve the support of religious, philanthropic, and governmental agencies in continuing and expanding their efforts to provide quality schooling for minority children in urban America.

NOTES

1. Frank S. Mead and Samuel S. Hill, Handbook of Denominations in the United States, New Eighth Edition (Nashville: Abington Press, 1985), pp. 164-69, 226-29;   Bernard Quinn et al., Churches and Church Membership in the United States 1980 (Atlanta, Ga.: National Council of Churches, 1982), Table 1, "Churches and Church Membership by Denomination, for the U.S.; 1980," pp. 1-8; "Black Catholics in the United States," in Felician Foy, ed., The Catholic Almanac,1987, (Huntington, Ind.:1987), pp. 480-81.

2. For extensive discussions of Blacks and Catholics in the U.S., see New Catholic Encyclopedia, vol. 10 (New York: McGraw Hill, 1967), Parts I-IV, pp. 299-314; John T. Gillard, Colored Catholics in the United States (Baltimore: Josephite Press, 1941), pp. 14-27; Edward J. Misch, "The Catholic Church and the Negro, 1865-1884," Integrated Education 12 (November-December, 1974): 36-40; Cyprian Davis, "Black Catholics in Nineteenth Century America," and William L. Portier, "John R. Slattery's Vision for the Evangelization of American Blacks," U.S. Catholic Historian 5, No. 1(1986): 1-44. This issue of U.S. Catholic Historian is devoted to "The Black Catholic Experience."

3. Josephite Pastoral Center, Statistical Profile of Black Catholics, 1984, (Washington, D. C.: Josephite Pastoral Center, n. d. Reprinted in Foy, Catholic Almanac, 1987, pp. 480-81.

4. Joe R. Feagin, "Black Catholics in the United States: An Exploratory Analysis," Sociological Analysis 29 (Winter 1968): 186-92.

5. The following sources emphasized higher status as the reason for Black conversions: Hart M. Nelsen and Lynda Dickson, "Attitudes of Black Catholics and Protestants: Evidence for Religious Identity," Sociological Analysis 33 (Fall 1972): 152-65; Larry L. Hunt and Janet G. Hunt, "A Religious Factor in Secular Achievement Among Blacks: The Case of Catholicism," Social Forces 53 (June 1975): 595-605; and "Black Catholicism and Occupational Status in Northern Cities," Social Science Quarterly 58 (March 1978): 657-70.

6. Harold A. Buetow, "The Underprivileged and Roman Catholic Education," Journal of Negro Education 40 (Fall 1971): 373-389.

7. Feagin, "Black Catholics," pp. 152-53; Gillard, Colored Catholics, pp. 17-24; Christopher Vecsey, "Black Catholics," Commonweal 104 (27 May 1977): 332-36; Cyprian Davis, "Black Catholics in America: A Historical Note," America 142 (2 May 1980): 376-78. For information on Xavier University, see Rita C. Bobowski, "Gert Town's Neighbor: Xavier University of Louisiana," American Education 11 (August-September 1976): 26-29; Edward P. St. John, A Study of Selected Developing Colleges and Universities-Case Study III: Xavier University (Washington, D. C.: Office of Education, 1977), pp. 2-37.

8. Statistics on the number of Black priests and Catholic schools from New Catholic Encyclopedia, vol. 10, "Negroes in the U.S.," pp. 310-14.

9. Special Edition, "The Black Experience in Catholic Education," Momentum 18 (February 1987): 7-30; see especially Bishop John H. Ricard, "Catholic Schools-Focal Point of Black Bishops Concerns," p. 4.

10. This issue is touched upon in J. P. Alston, L. T. Alston, and E. Warrick, "Black Catholics: Social and Cultural Characteristics," Journal of Black Studies 2 (December 1971): 245-255; and L. L. Hunt and J. G. Hunt, "Religious Affiliation and Militancy Among Urban Blacks: Some Catholic /Protestant Comparisons," Social Science Quarterly 57 (March 1977): 821-33. The civil rights movement served as the background for the creation of the Black Catholic movement; for discussion, see "Symposium: Black and Catholic," America 142 (29 March 1980): 256-277; however, there is need for a scholarly examination of Roman Catholicism and the civil rights movement in the U.S.

11. R. A. Billington, The Protestant Crusade, 1800-1860: A Study in the Origins of American Nativism (1938; reprint, New York: New York Times Books, 1976), pp. 45-56; M. J. Feldberg, The Philadelphia Riots of 1844: A Study of Ethnic Conflict (Westport, Conn.: Greenwood, 1975).

12. V. P. Franklin, "Ethos and Education: The Impact of Educational Activities on Minority Ethnic Identity in the United States," Review of Research in Education 10 (1983): 3-23.

13. Robert M. Linkh, American Catholicism and European Immigrants, 1900-1924 (New York: Center for Migration Studies, 1975) Dennis Clark, The Irish in Philadelphia: Ten Generations of Urban Experience (Philadelphia: Temple University Press, 1973), pp. 88-105; V. P. Franklin, "Continuity and Discontinuity in Black and Immigrant Minority Education: A Historical Assessment," in Diane Ravitch and Ronald Goodenow, eds., Educating an Urban People: The New York City Experience. (New York: Teachers College Press, 1981), pp. 44-66.

14. Special Report of the Commissioner of Education, District of Columbia, 1868 (1869; reprint, New York: Arno Press, 1969), pp. 217-19.

15. Harold A. Beutow, Of Singular Benefit: The Story of Catholic Education in the United States (New York: Macmillan, 1970), pp. 150-53; see also Peter Guilday, A History of the Councils of Baltimore, 1791-1884 (1932; reprint New York: Arno Press, 1969), pp. 195-96 220; Martin E. Marty, Modern American Religion: The Irony of It All, 1893-1919 (Chicago: University of Chicago Press, 1986), pp. 178-90.

16. Beutow, "Underprivileged," pp. 382-83.

17. Donald J. Kemper, "Catholic Integration in St. Louis, 1935-1947," Missouri Historical Review 73 (October 1978): 9-17.

18. Beutow, Of Singular Benefit, pp. 258-59, 278-79, 385.

19. Joseph J. McCarthy, "History of Black Catholic Education in Chicago, 1871-1971" (Ph.D. dissertation, Loyola University of Chicago, 1973), pp. 72-75.

20. Ibid, pp. 25-27 111; see also James W. Sanders, The Education of an Urban Minority: Catholics in Chicago, 1833-1965 (New York: Oxford University Press, 1977), pp. 207-14.

21. V. P. Franklin, The Education of Black Philadelphia: The Social and Educational History of a Minority Community: 1900-1950 (Philadelphia: University of Pennsylvania Press, 1979), pp. 97, 117-21.

22. Carleton Mabel, Black Education in New York State: From Colonial to Modern Times (Syracuse: Syracuse University Press, 1979), pp. 250-52.

23. The authors hope to fill this present gap in our information about Black Catholic schooling and education through a larger study of the education of Black Catholics. See also Edward B. McDonald, "Against All Odds: Saint Augustine High School, New Orleans, LA., 1951-1976" (Paper presented at History of Education Society Meeting, Teachers College, Columbia University, October 1987), pp. 1-15.

24. For information on the poor conditions in urban public schools in the 1950s and early 1960s, see U.S. Commission on Civil Rights, Civil Rights, U.S.A.: Public Schools, North and West (Washington, D. C.: Government Printing Office, 1964); and Civil Rights, U.S.A.: Public Schools, Southern States (Washington, D. C.: Government Printing Office, 1964).

25. National Office of Black Catholics (NOBC), "The Crisis of Catholic Education in the Black Community," Integrated Education   14 (November-December 1976): 14-17; Thomas Vitullo-Martin, Catholic Inner-City Schools: The Future (Washington, D. C.: U.S. Catholic Conference, 1979), pp. 3-15; and Genevieve Schillo, "Non-Catholics in Catholic Schools: A Challenge to Evangelization" (Paper presented at National Catholic Educational Association meeting, April 1980). Available through U.S. Department of Education ERIC.

26. NOBC, "Crisis of Catholic Education," p.15. The need for Roman Catholic missionary activities to the Black community is discussed by several of the contributors to the "Black and Catholic" special issue of America, 142 (29 March 1980): 256-277.

27. See, for example, J. L. Morrison and B. J. Hodgkins, "The Effectiveness of Catholic Education: A Comparative Analysis," Sociology of Education 44 (Winter 1971): 119-31; and "Social Change and Catholic Education," Education 98 (March-April 1978): 264-79l; G. F. Madeus and Roger Linnan, "The Outcome of Catholic Education?" School Review 81 (February 1973): 207-32; James Coleman, T. Hoffer, and S. Kilgore, "Cognitive Outcomes in Public and Private Schools," Sociology of Education 55 (April 1982): 65-76; and High School Achievement: Public, Catholic, and Private Schools Compared (New York: Basic Books, 1982).

28. For extended coverage of this debate, see Sociology of Education 55 (April 1982): 64-132, and 56 (October 1983): 157-221.

29. Andrew Greeley, Catholic High Schools and Minority Students (New Brunswick, N.J.: Transaction Books, 1982), pp. 73-88.

30. Thomas Z. Keith, "Academic Achievement of Minority Students Enrolled in Catholic and Public High Schools" (Ph.D. dissertation, Duke University, 1982), pp. 37-43; Thomas Z. Keith and Ellis B. Page, "Do Catholic High Schools Improve Minority Student Achievement?" American Educational Research Journal 22 (Fall 1985): 337-49.

31. Virgil C. Blum, "Private Elementary Education in the Inner City," Phi Delta Kappan 66 (May 1985): 644; see also Diana T. Slaughter and Barbara L. Schneider, Newcomers: Blacks in Private Schools ERIC, 1986 (ED 274 768 and ED 274 769).

32. NOBC, The Black Community, Dioceses and Diocesan School Systems (Washington, D. C.: National Office of Black Catholics, 1979), pp. 6-11; see also special section, "The Black Experience in Catholic Education," Momentum 18 (February 1987): 10-20; see especially William Harkins, "Higher Expectations in a Catholic Inner City High School," pp. 14-18.

33. James S. Coleman, "Racial Segregation in the Schools: New Research with New Policy Implications," Phi Delta Kappan 57 (October 1975): 75-78; Thomas Pettigrew and Robert L. Green, "School Desegregation in Large Cities," Harvard Educational Review 46 (February 1976): 1-53, and (May 1976): 216-33; R. G. Wegmann, "White Flight and School Resegregation," Phi Delta Kappan 58 (January 1977): 389-93; G. K. Cunningham and W. L. Husk, The Impact of

Court-Ordered Desegregation on Student Enrollment and Residential Patterns in Jefferson County (Louisville) Public School District (Washington, D. C.: National Institute of Education, 1979), pp. 1-16; Charles V. Willie, "Desegregation in Big City School System," Educational Forum 47 (Fall 1982): 82-96.

34. Greeley, Catholic High Schools, pp. 107-111; Diane Ravitch, The Troubled Crusade: American Education, 1945-1980 (New York: Basic Books, 1983), pp. 140-145. For an extended discussion of the impact of White flight on urban public and Catholic schools, see Gary Orfield, "White Flight Research," Educational Forum 40 (May 1976): 525-36.

9
Black Students in Low-Income Serving Catholic High Schools: An Overview of Findings from the 1986 National Catholic Educational Association Study

Mary Lynch Barnds

This chapter describes some of the findings of a comprehensive study which was reported in two parts: (1) Catholic High Schools: A National Portrait, and (2) Catholic High Schools: Their Impact on Low Income Students.[1] The study was conducted with a grant to the National Catholic Educational Association (NCEA).[2] The study built on previous research by collecting information to help define what Catholic schools are and do and establishing a baseline of information to help educators understand the present reality in Catholic high schools and monitor change in the future. The study also provided data for future research into how Catholic high schools are serving the educational mission of the Catholic Church, which is explicit about providing educational opportunity for the poor.[3]

The first part of the study reported survey returns from school principals. Principals of 1,464 Catholic high schools were invited to complete the survey; 910 (62 percent) returned the survey to NCEA. The 56-page survey instrument was developed to provide a national, composite view of the resources, programs, facilities, personnel, and policies of Catholic secondary schools.

The second part of the study addressed a number of significant, previously unanswered questions about Catholic high schools, especially concerning nonacademic effects. The data were drawn from principals, teachers, students, and field staff observation. Much of this discussion focuses on the findings of this part of the study relative to Black student outcomes in low-income serving (LIS) Catholic high schools. Behavioral outcomes measured in the study included those that characterize the purpose of Catholic schooling: values, religion, and life skills. This chapter summarizes findings from both parts of the larger study, particularly as these findings pertain to low-income Black high school students in comparison to low-income White and Hispanic high school students.

BACKGROUND

A primary purpose of the NCEA study was to address American Catholic bishops' commitment to provide educational opportunities and options for the poor. Therefore, it is important to briefly review the history of that commitment before describing the NCEA study.

The Catholic Church and Its Commitment to the Poor

As noted by Franklin and McDonald in the preceding chapter and by others, Catholic schools in the United States began their mission to serve the poor and disadvantaged during the mid-1850s.[4] Between 1880 and 1920 the number of Catholic parochial (affiliated with a parish) schools rose from 2,200 to 5,800 and the number of students from 400,000 to 1,700,000. Seventy-six of these schools were opened to serve poor Black families. Given the changing demography of cities throughout the Depression and second world war, Catholic schools have been credited with fostering economic improvement among second-generation immigrants.[5] In the latter half of the twentieth century, continuing demographic changes and Catholic school statistics indicate that the number of low-income students attending Catholic high schools increased during the 1970s at a time when the total number of Catholic schools declined.[6]

Description of NCEA Study

Recent research shows that Catholic high schools are serving a significant percentage of low-income students. James Coleman, Thomas Hoffer, and Sally Kilgore, who studied the academic performance of children from comparable socioeconomic and family backgrounds in public and private schools, and Greeley, who analyzed data from the High School and Beyond study, all document the effectiveness of Catholic high schools in promoting relatively strong academic performance among children from low-income families.[7]

Catholic High Schools: Their Impact on Low Income Students built on this and other previous research. Its specific objectives included: (1) comparing LIS high school attributes with those of other Catholic high schools; (2) describing low-income students' characteristics by family background, school attitudes and academic programs, academic achievement patterns, values, religious beliefs, and life skills; (3) exploring the degree to which student characteristics may vary as a function of family income, race or ethnicity (Black, Hispanic, White), grade, and sex; (4) describing the teachers who work in LIS Catholic high schools; (5) estimating the degree to which poor students, compared with other subgroups of students, gain after four years of Catholic high school in academic achievement, values, religion, and life skills; and (6) identifying factors which promote the desired student outcomes among poor students, comparing the effects of family background, student characteristics, and institutional variables.

In the study, schools were classified as LIS if more than 10 percent of their students came from families with annual incomes of less than $12,500. A subset of 106 LIS schools was studied in the second part of the study.   Certain characteristics of LIS Catholic high schools should be noted. First, not all LIS schools are alike. The same variety exists among them as among all Catholic high schools: some are large, some small, some growing, and some have declining enrollments. Second, not all students in LIS schools are from low-income families. An average of 13 percent of the students in LIS schools come from homes with estimated annual incomes of more than $30,000. A third characteristic of all LIS Catholic high schools is the high percentage of enrolled minority students. In LIS schools, 38 percent of the students are minority, as compared to 18 percent in all Catholic high schools. Of the minority students in the 106 LIS schools of the study, 22 percent (1,675) are Black . However, only 38 percent of the Black students in these schools are Catholic. In comparison, 90 percent of the Hispanic students and 92 percent of the White students are Catholic.

Student characteristics were examined in terms of four demographic characteristics: grade (9th and 12th), sex, race or ethnicity, (Black, Hispanic, White), and family income (very poor = VP, moderately poor = MP, and non-poor = NP). This discussion focuses chiefly on the Black students in the study; data on Hispanic and White students will be used only for comparative purposes (Data collected from other students, for example, Asian American or Native American, will not be discussed here).

DISTRIBUTION OF BLACK STUDENTS BY GRADE AND FAMILY INCOME

In the 9th grade, 59 percent of students are from a minority group, while in 12th grade, the minority enrollment falls to 52 percent. Black enrollment in LIS Catholic high schools, however, remains the same for 9th and 12th grade at 22 percent. Of these Blacks, 30 percent are very poor (VP = estimated annual family income of less than $12,500), 36 percent are moderately poor (MP = estimated annual family income between $12,500 and $20,000), and 34 percent are non-poor (NP = estimated annual family income greater than $20,000). Since the purpose of this study was to look at how Catholic high schools are serving poor students by first identifying schools that are serving large numbers of those who qualify as very poor or moderately poor, it is useful to examine family income distribution in all Catholic high schools as reported in the first part of the study.[8] Roughly a third of the students in all Catholic high schools surveyed (910 of 1,464 schools in 1983) live in families with annual incomes less than $20,000. Another third are in families with incomes between $20,000 and $30,000 and a third have family incomes over $30,000. The subset of 106 schools labeled LIS for the second part of the study followed this national average, with a slight edge for the very poor (34 percent).[9] At 30 percent, Black students were slightly underrepresented in the VP category.

In 1983-84, the average per-pupil cost for Catholic high schools was $1,783. That year, parents who chose Catholic high schools paid tuition, on average, which was $523 lower than per-pupil expenditures, or $1,230 per pupil.[10] For a family with income under $20,000 this represents a considerable sacrifice; 66 percent of Black families in this study are in that income category. Tuition payments cover about 60 percent of the expenses for the average Catholic high school.[11]

FAMILY COMPOSITION AND MATERNAL EMPLOYMENT

Black students are less likely than Hispanic or White students in LIS Catholic high schools to have both mother and father (natural, step, or adoptive) at home. Mothers are reported in 91 percent of Black families, while 57 percent report fathers in the home. Of Black students in LIS schools 90 percent report mothers employed outside the home. Mothers are reported in 94 percent of Hispanics homes, 70 percent working outside. Fathers are reported in 76 percent of Hispanic homes. White students reported 96 percent of mothers in the home, 74 percent working outside; 85 percent of fathers of White students are reported in the home. Presence of a mother at home does not vary by sex or income level in LIS Catholic high schools. The increased rate of parental employment may help to explain the relatively low level of involvement of parents in LIS schools, as reported by LIS principals in the first part of the study.[12] Overall, 78 percent of LIS students report maternal employment, which is much higher than that reported in the 1980 national census (55 percent).

STUDENT'S USE OF TIME

By the 12th grade, 60 percent of all students have some paid employment, the majority working less than 20 hours a week. Non-poor students are most likely to be employed (51 percent). The likelihood of employment is inversely related to family income: the lower the income, the less likely is the student to be employed. In LIS schools, 63 percent of all Black students, 64 percent of all Hispanic students, and 44 percent of all White students are unemployed.

Sports participation outside school hours involves more boys than girls. In comparison to Hispanics and Whites, Blacks participate most (16 percent with three or more sports).

Musical activities involve more Black than White students in LIS schools. Students who spend one to four hours a week on music represented: Blacks, 25 percent; Hispanics, 25 percent; and Whites, 17 percent. Of those who spend eleven or more hours a week on music, 7 percent are Black, 4 percent are Hispanic, and 5 percent are White. This could be explained by the large number of Black students in the study (36 percent) reporting affiliation with a Baptist church, presumably with a predominantly Black congregation, which might be more likely to engage youth in music performance than White or Hispanic Catholic congregations. Other in-school clubs and organizations involve 47 percent of Black students, 46 percent of Hispanic students, and 46 percent of White students.

Participation in non-school activities was reported by 62 percent of both Black and White students and 53 percent of Hispanics. Again, this could be explained by the predominant culture in the students' churches: Black Baptist churches may involve Black students more than Catholic churches in the United States involve Hispanics. Catholic churches reflect the predominant White culture, which could influence the numbers of Hispanic Catholic youth who report participation in non-school programs.

Among LIS school students, 15 percent report doing ten or more hours of homework a week, compared to 18 percent of all Catholic high school students. Black and Hispanic students report an increasing amount of time spent on homework between 9th and 12th grade; White 9th and 12th graders do about the same amount. On a seven-point scale ranging from "no homework is assigned" to "I do more than ten hours of homework a week," very poor Blacks have a mean score of 4.6, moderately poor Blacks 4.8, and non-poor Blacks 4.9. Mean scores for Hispanics are: VP = 5.0, MP = 4.9, and NP = 5.2. Mean scores for Whites are: VP = 5.1, MP = 5.1, and NP = 5.3.

Television viewing time reported for Blacks and Hispanics does not change when comparing 9th and 12th grades, but White 12th graders watch less television than White 9th graders.

It is interesting to compare how all Black, Hispanic, and White students in LIS schools report their use of out-of-school time:

o   White students are more likely than Blacks or Hispanics to have after school jobs

o   Black students are more likely than Whites to be involved in sports, Hispanics least likely

o   More Black students (10 percent more) than White students are involved in music; Hispanics fall midway between

o   Black, Hispanic, and White students are about equally involved in school organizations

o   Hispanic and Black students watch more television and do less homework than White students

Other interesting key findings show that girls in LIS schools report doing more homework and watching more television than do boys, and very poor students do less homework and watch more television than moderately poor or non-poor students. The study reports that 23 percent of Black, 15 percent of Hispanic and 13 percent of White students entering LIS Catholic high schools had no previous Catholic schooling. This may help to explain why homework among Blacks and Hispanics appears to increase between the 9th and 12th grades, while homework rates remain the same among White students, who may be more likely to understand, upon entrance, Catholic school expectations regarding homework.

EDUCATIONAL EXPECTATIONS

Students were asked to appraise their academic ability, present and future, and to report their parents' expectations for them. Among all students, 9th graders have higher expectations generally than 12th graders, except that 12th graders report that they are more likely to finish college than 9th graders. Among Black students, 26 percent rate their school ability as being "above or far above average"; 17 percent report having skipped or "cut" one or more day of school in the past month; and 82 percent say their chance of graduating from college is "excellent or good." Comparable figures for Whites are 34 percent, 14 percent, and 74 percent; for Hispanics the figures are 24 percent, 17 percent, and 77 percent.

Black students report lower grades than Whites or Hispanics, but report higher self-assessments on college ability, higher educational expectations, and higher parental expectations. Highest educational expectations of all are experienced by Black females. On a seven-point scale ranging from "I think I will drop out before I get a high school diploma" to "I think I will get an advanced degree after college (Ph.D., M.D. or law degree)," Black females have a mean score of 5.2, Black males 4.9. On a five-point scale, reporting student perceptions of their parents' expectations of them, Black females have a mean score of 3.9, Black males 3.7. Hispanic males report higher expectations from themselves and their parents than do Hispanic females. There is no reported difference between White males and females regarding their own or their parents' expectations for them.

Among Black 12th-grade students in LIS Catholic high schools, 71 percent report they are in an academic track in their school; 23 percent report being in a general track, and 6 percent report being in a vocational track. Among the very poor, Black students are more likely than White students to be in an academic track; in the non-poor group, the reverse is true. Hispanics and Whites are equally likely to be enrolled in academic programs in all income groups.

Black students are more likely than their Hispanic and White peers to meet national guidelines in science and math, less likely in social studies and English. It should be noted that the study surveyed courses in religion and the arts and that 76 percent of Blacks reported taking three or more years of religion, although only 38 percent are Catholic (89 percent of Hispanic students and 91 percent of White students report three or more years of religion). Among Black students, 52 percent report one year or more of vocal or performing arts, compared with 49 percent of Hispanic and 54 percent of White students.

The inconsistency between reported expectations and performance of the Black students is a cause for concern to Catholic educators. Black students report they have lower grades and do less homework than Whites or Hispanics. Blacks have lower achievement scores on entering and leaving Catholic high school than either of the other two groups examined. However, perceived educational expectations, especially for Black females, are higher than for Whites or Hispanics. This raises questions about the nature of the students' and their parents' expectations: are students "unrealistic" in their self-assessment or genuinely anxious to achieve? Is their achievement related to the high expectations they place on themselves and perceive from their parents? Are student perceptions of parental expectations accurate? The issues raised about student and parental expectations indicate there is a need for further study of Catholic high school students and their parents.

LIFE GOALS

In the study, students were asked to rank sixteen goals: four as "extremely important," four as "important," four as "somewhat important," and four as "not very important." This instrument rated student goals in two broad categories: those dealing with their own lives and those dealing with concern for others (see table 9.1).[13]

Table 9.1

Students' Ranking of 16 Life Goals
(listed in order of total group rank)

	Grade		Income[a]			Race[b]			Sex	
	9th	12th	VP	MP	NP	B	H	W	M	F
To have a happy family life	1	1	1	1	1	4	1	1	1	1
To get a good job when I am older	2	4	2	2	2	2	2	3	2	2
To be happy	5	2	4	3	3	7	6	2	3	2
To have God at the center of my life	3	6	3	5	5	1	3	6	4	6
To feel good about myself	7	3	5	4	4	6	7	4	5	4
To find meaning and purpose in life	6	5	7	6	6	5	5	5	7	5
To do my best in school	4	7	6	7	7	3	4	7	6	7
To make my own decisions	8	8	8	8	8	8	8	8	8	8
To have a lot of money someday	9	9	9	9	9	9	9	9	9	9
To help other people have a better life	10	10	10	10	10	10	10	11	12	10
To have lots of fun and good times	11	11	11	11	11	14	14	10	10	11
To be able to do whatever I want to do, when I want to do it	12	12	12	12	12	12	12	12	11	12
To do what I can to promote peace in the world	13	13	14	13	13	13	13	13	13	14
To do what I can to help people overcome hunger and poverty	14	14	13	14	14	11	11	14	14	13
To be active in church or parish	15	16	15	15	16	15	16	15	15	15
To help rid the world of social injustice	16	15	16	16	15	16	15	16	16	16

Source: Peter L. Benson et al., Catholic High Schools: Their Impact on Low Income Students (Washington, D. C.: National Catholic Association, 1986), p. 85

[a]VP= very poor (family income estimates less than $12,500 per year)
MP = moderately poor (family income estimates $12,500 – $22,000)
NP = non-poor (family income $22,001 or more)

[b]B = Black
 H = Hispanic
 W = White

Black students ranked as "extremely important": first, "to have God at the center of my life"; second, "to get a good job when I am older"; third, "to do my best in school"; fourth, "to have a happy family life." Whites and Hispanics rated "a happy family life" first. Overall, the goals ranked first through ninth deal with students' own lives; goals related to social concerns and the welfare of others rank tenth or lower. Whites place more emphasis on "having lots of fun" than Blacks and Hispanics, and less importance on "overcoming hunger and poverty." Otherwise, the lower ranking goals are quite stable across all groups.

ATTITUDES TOWARD NUCLEAR WEAPONS AND NUCLEAR WAR

Among Black students, 30 percent believe building nuclear weapons to defend one's country is "always or usually right"; 75 percent think the United States and the Soviet Union should immediately agree to stop making and testing nuclear weapons; 49 percent worry about the possibility of a nuclear war "a great deal or quite a bit"; 38 percent think it is "very or quite likely" that a major nuclear war will occur in their lifetime. On all four of these points Blacks differ only slightly from Hispanic and White students except for "worrying about the possibility of nuclear war." Comparable figures on this issue are 55 percent for Hispanics and 35 percent for Whites.

PERSONAL AND SOCIAL BELIEF

Among the three groups, Blacks score lowest on "being in control of their lives," highest on self-esteem. Blacks report the highest sense of purpose in life. Regarding others, Blacks endorse "women having all the same rights as men" more than Whites or Hispanics and are 10 percent less likely to believe that "minorities are getting too demanding in their push for equal rights" than Hispanics; Blacks are only 3 percent less interested than Hispanics in spending their own money to "make a better life for poor people in other countries," and 5 percent more inclined to help foreign poor than are Whites.

RELIGIOUS VALUES

As stated earlier, 36 percent of Black students in LIS Catholic schools are Baptist and 38 percent are Catholic. These students attend schools whose central purpose is to provide an environment in which Catholic moral values and religious teaching can be integrated with instruction in the basic academic disciplines in order to prepare the student for citizenship, career, and active Church participation. Eight measures of religious orientation were chosen for discussion in the study, based on measures initially suggested

by Gordon W. Allport and Peter L. Benson.[14]
The study report summarizes how LIS school students are
religiously oriented:

> ...girls, freshmen, Blacks and Hispanics tend to
> have an orientation toward religion that is more intrinsic
> (stresses prayer and the application of religion to all of
> life), and both more horizontal (concern for others) and
> vertical (emphasizing the importance of worshiping God)
> than their counterparts. They are more likely to view
> religion as an integral part of their lives. Blacks are
> more likely than Whites to see religion as both a system
> of rules and as a liberating force in their lives...[15]

STUDENTS LIFE SKILLS

In regard to life skills, students rated themselves in five categories:
interpersonal competence, competence in the world of business,
personal resources, global awareness, and political awareness.
Results show that student scores varied directly with the level of
family income. Very poor students scored lowest in these
competencies, non-poor highest. Racial and ethnic differences
were insignificant.

CONCLUSION AND IMPLICATIONS

The NCEA study is particularly useful in providing a rich data set
that includes nonacademic student outcomes in its focus on the
characteristics of the LIS Catholic high school. In serving low
income students, LIS Catholic high schools appear to offer these
students essentially the same opportunities they provide for the
non-poor, holding all students to the same standards. This
discussion of the NCEA study of LIS Catholic high schools should
reveal how it complements and adds to a significant body of
research on Catholic high school students' performance, most
notably the work of Coleman, et al., Greeley, and other
comparative studies based on the growing High School and
Beyond data set.

   While there is mounting evidence that Catholic high schools are
doing an exceptionally good job in serving poor students,
additional information is needed for Catholic educational efforts to
continue to serve the poor with increasing effectiveness, especially
about individual characteristics such as family background,
handicaps, motivation, aspirations, number of years in Catholic
school, self perceived school ability, and informal learning.

Parents of students in Catholic high schools are the focus of a proposed study initiated by the National Forum of Catholic Parent Organizations to build on the study under discussion. A major aim of the proposed study is to fill the gap in knowledge and understanding about what kinds of parent involvement make a difference in student outcomes identified as essential for the Catholic high school to fulfill its mission.[16]

Coleman and Hoffer report the importance of the adult community to high school students, both adults in the students' families and outside. Their study indicates that Catholic high schools provide students with additional access to "social capital" which, "with the human capital available in the family, is relevant to the child's development."[17]

The availability to students in Catholic high schools of additional social capital can perhaps be explained by the explicit purpose of the Catholic school, which includes building a "community of faith" which will spread beyond the school itself into the larger community and conversely, draws on the larger community to enrich itself. Among Catholic high school principals, 87 percent place "building community among faculty, students, and parents" as one of their top seven educational goals (out of a list of fourteen), ranking first or second for more principals than any other goal on the list.[18]

By choosing a Catholic high school, do parents implicitly endorse the school's mission to build a faith community? They need to be asked.

NOTES

1. R. J. Yeager et al., The Catholic High School: A National Portrait (Washington, D. C.: National Catholic Educational Association, 1985). P. L. Benson et al., Catholic High Schools: Their Impact on Low Income Students (Washington, D. C.: National Catholic Educational Association, 1986).

2. The National Catholic Educational Association is the nation's oldest and largest Catholic professional education association. Established in 1904, it serves over 90 percent of all Catholic educational institutions (schools, colleges, universities, seminaries), which are its members, with consultation services, workshops, seminars, meetings, publications, and sponsored research.

3. J. B. Benestad and F. J. Butler, eds., Quest for Justice: A Compendium of statements of the United States Catholic Bishops on the Political and Social Order 1966-1980. (Washington, D. C.: United States Catholic Conference, 1981), p. 361.

4. Chapter 8, in this volume; see also Harold A. Buetow, Of Singular Benefit: The Story of Catholic Education (New York: Macmillan, 1970), p. 179.

5. See Andrew Greeley, "The Ethnic Miracle," The Public Interest 45 (Fall 1976): 29.

6. Frank H. Bredeweg, C.S.B. United States Catholic Elementary and Secondary Schools (Washington, D. C.: National Catholic Educational Association, 1986-87), p. 16.

7. Yeager et al., The Catholic High School, p. 31 see also J. S. Coleman, T. Hoffer, and S. Kilgore. High School Achievement: Public, Catholic, and Private Schools Compared (New York: Basic Books, 1982). and Andrew Greeley, Minority Students in Catholic High Schools (New Brunswick, N.J.: Transaction Books, 1983).

8. Yeager et al., The Catholic High School, pp. 30-31 for tables of family income above and below $20,000.

9. See Benson et al., Catholic High Schools, p. 68 for an exhibit of students by grade, family income, race and sex.

10. See Yeager et al., The Catholic High School, p. 104 for an exhibit of median tuition costs and per-pupil expenditures in Catholic high schools by school type, gender composition of school, region, and enrollment size.

11. Ibid, pp. 103-111. A variety of strategies are employed by Catholic high school administrators, pastors, and parents to make up the difference between pupil costs and tuition income. Part 1 of the study reports particularly low development activity in schools with a high percentage of low-income students; it is unlikely that poor families can expect to get tuition assistance. It is more likely that LIS Catholic high schools struggle to cover the difference between per-pupil expenses and tuition with fundraising (9 percent), contributed services from men and women religious (10 percent), and other sources of income. In 1983-84 the average Catholic high school was dependent on some sort of subsidy (usually from a parish, a group of parishes, or a diocese) for 11 percent of its income.

Catholic dioceses and parishes invest in Catholic secondary education with contributions to cover expenses and keep tuition low. Traditionally, Catholic school costs have been subsidized by members of religious communities who staffed them, whose personal commitment to poverty kept salaries low. As their numbers have decreased, lay teachers and administrators have replaced them in two ways: with services rendered (as teachers and principals) and services contributed (low salaries).

12. Yeager et al., The Catholic High School, p. 116.

13. Benson et al., Exhibit 7.1, p. 85.

14. See G. W. Allport and J. M. Ross, "Religious Orientation and Prejudice." Journal of Personality and Social Psychology, 5 432-443; and Peter L. Benson and Dorothy L. Williams, Religion on Capital Hill: Myths and Realities (New York: Harper & Row).

15. Benson et al., Catholic High Schools, p. 98.

16. The National Forum of Catholic Parent Organizations is a department of the National Catholic Educational Association; the study proposal, Parent Choice, Parent Involvement and Student Outcomes, was completed in March, 1987, with a grant from the U. S. Secretary of Education's Discretionary Fund. James S. Coleman was an advisor to the project.

17. James S. Coleman and Thomas Hoffer. Public and Private High Schools: The Impact of Communities (New York: Basic Books, 1987); see chapter 8 for a discussion of social capital.

18. Yeager et al., The Catholic High School, p. 12.

10
Black Family Participation in Catholic Secondary Education
Patricia A. Bauch

Schools, whether public or private, serve as major agencies for socializing children into a specific ideology.[1] Compulsory attendance laws indicate the importance of the school in the socialization of children. The role of the educational system is to build upon the behavior and values that are established in the family and that represent the ideal values of society.

While public schools with their state-controlled curricula and teacher certification programs act primarily as agents of the state, private schools are viewed as agents of the family, or in the case of religious schools, as agents of the church of which the family is a part. The option of choosing a private school as an extension of family values need not always be in conflict with the desire of the state to bring the child into the larger society. Indeed, choosing a private school could strengthen family values, particularly for lower-income and minority groups.

The role of the school in strengthening family by building on its values and the ideal values of society implies the need for positive interconnections between parents and schools that vary across school settings as schools seek to provide programs and activities that fulfill community expectations.

When distrustful relationships arise between home and school, the school's potential for bringing the child into the larger society diminishes.[2] A growing body of literature supports the impor-

*The author appreciates the earlier collaboration in study design and data collection of Irene Blum, Nancy Taylor, Linda Valli, and Helen Wallace the statistical analyses of Thomas W. Small, and the editorial assistance of Sally M. Flanzer.

tance of parents' involvement in their own children's education and the academic and social benefits to the children of positive home-school interactions.[3]

The purpose of this chapter is to describe the participation of Black families, parents and their children, in Catholic education in the context of three different types of all-Black Catholic secondary schools: single-sex male, single-sex female, and coed. It is concerned with the kind of education Blacks are seeking in choosing Catholic schools, the contribution the school makes to Black family values, the extent and type of parent involvement in school-related activities, and whether specific types of Black families have advantages over others in generating social capital in Catholic schools through parent involvement. Special attention is given to a comparison between single-parent and two-parent Black homes, both Catholic and non-Catholic. Consideration is also given to the contribution that family choice arrangements and other school characteristics may make to the motivations and activities that characterize Black parents in Catholic secondary schools.

THE ARRIVAL OF BLACKS IN CATHOLIC SCHOOLS

Historically, Catholic schools largely served the children of European immigrant families, providing them with a familiar religious setting, a focused and stable environment, and membership in an ethnic and religious community that assisted their integration into the mainstream of American society.[4] Evidence that this has occurred for the majority of American Catholics, with the exception of Hispanics, can be seen in the considerable share of income and the high levels of education enjoyed by today's Catholics. Irish Catholics, for example, are exceeded in income and education levels only by Jews and Episcopalians. Blacks, including Black Catholics, along with other minority groups, remain at the bottom of the social strata.[5]

Once European immigrant Catholics became socialized and entered the mainstream of American society, their schools experienced a dramatic enrollment decline. Between 1965 and 1985, Catholic school enrollment decreased by nearly 50 percent from 5.6 million to 2.8 million students in 9,245 elementary and secondary schools. While enrollment is still falling in Catholic schools, one area in which it is continuing to rise is among Blacks in Catholic schools, especially in Catholic high schools. Although only about 17 percent of Catholic high schools serve 10 percent or more minority students, and approximately 80 percent of those enrolled in Catholic high schools are White students, the increase in minority students from 10.4 percent in 1969 to 21.3 percent in 1985 indicates a major shift in the populations these schools serve.

Given the success these schools enjoyed in the past in socializing minority groups, it would seem they have an opportunity again to repeat the "ethnic miracle" for a group of students who have recently arrived in their schools.[6]

The education of Blacks, most of whom are not Catholic, in Catholic secondary schools is a little studied phenomenon, although such studies have been done in elementary schools.[7]. In comparing high school students in public and private schools, Andrew M. Greeley and James S. Coleman et al. found that Blacks and other minority students achieve better in private, especially Catholic, schools than in public ones. They also found that parents of Blacks in Catholic schools are more interested in a rigorous education than parents of Blacks in public schools and tend to reinforce that view at home through greater television monitoring and other home factors.[8]   Catholic schools tend to provide a more rigorous and academically focused secondary school education and make greater demands on parents concerning involvement in their children's education than do public schools.[9] They may also provide additional "social capital," as argued by Coleman and Thomas Hoffer, that results from the social relations that occur among people as a result of their interactions. Social capital resides in a religious community with its power to shape and enforce norms for adolescents in the school.[10] Using as they do the large aggregated data base from High School and Beyond, neither the Greeley nor the Coleman et al. studies are able to investigate the specific school context in which Black families interact and how social capital is developed through home-school and within-school interactions at the level of Catholic secondary education, particularly in schools that serve non-Catholic students predominantly. Moreover, what parents want for their children in selecting a Catholic secondary school and how socialization occurs for Black adolescents and their families in these settings remains largely uninvestigated.

A STUDY OF CATHOLIC HIGH SCHOOLS

This study is part of a larger, ongoing field study of lower-income and minority families in Catholic inner-city high schools begun in conjunction with the National Catholic Educational Association's (NCEA) national study of Catholic high schools.[11]   For this study, data were gathered on parents' educational expectations of their children and the school, school goal accomplishments, parent involvement, curriculum, school climate, and the parent and school characteristics of five inner-city Catholic high schools, of which three served predominantly Black families, in an investigation of schools successfully serving the needs of lower-income families. Parent data reported here are drawn primarily from a survey distributed to all families in these schools resulting in a 64 percent return rate, or 1,070 families. Other data were obtained through formal and informal interviews with parents, students, teachers, and administrators and through participant observation. A team of six university researchers, including the author, spent the equivalent of ten days at each school in the spring of 1985, averaging two researchers per day. Detailed information concerning the research design can be obtained from the researchers.[12]

For purposes of this study, parent goal expectations are parents' responses to a series of survey questions concerning their children's expected future educational attainment and their most important reasons for choosing to send their child to a Catholic high school. Responses for future educational attainment level ranged from "not graduate from high school" to "obtain an advanced degree after college (PhD., M.D., or law degree)." For the reasons question, response categories were collapsed from twenty-five items to which parents responded representing four different types of reasons: (1) academic and curriculum; (2) discipline; (3) religion and values; and (4) noneducational reasons (e.g., safety, child's choice, location, affordable tuition).

For parent involvement, parents were asked to indicate their participation in a number of parent participation roles described by twelve items concerning: (1) helping at school, including serving as advisory, school board, or parent board members, and assisting teachers as classroom aides or substitute teachers; (2) monitoring homework, and (3) attending various types of school meetings. In addition, parents were asked to indicate the number of times in a school year that they talked with their children's teachers.

Among other demographic factors, parents were requested to provide information about whether or not they are Catholic, the number of parents living in the home, level of educational attainment, income level, employment, ethnic background, and their frequency of church participation.

The sample of schools was differentiated in the selection process to be representative nationally of "successful" inner-city Catholic secondary schools serving lower-income students. Thus, schools in this study were in five different metropolitan city districts in New York, California, Pennsylvania, Missouri, and Washington D. C. They were characterized by different organizational arrangements such as gender composition, governance structure, school size, and ethnic composition. Schools were judged to be successful as determined by criteria established by the NCEA researchers who had gathered survey data on the schools' teachers. These five schools scored in the top quartile of a scale constructed to measure teachers' beliefs concerning their own and the school's "effectiveness" in meeting the needs of lower-income and minority students from a field of

136 low-income serving schools.[13]   The focus of this chapter is on the three predominantly Black schools, their students, teachers, and parents.

THREE PREDOMINANTLY BLACK SCHOOLS: BRIEF CASE STUDY DESCRIPTIONS

The following ethnographic descriptions based on the field data provide insight into the academic and social life of each school, particularly as it relates to the school's goal focus and expectations for students, how teachers and students help shape the social and psychological context in which these goals and expectations are addressed, and what the results or school goal accomplishments are. These descriptions show how schools go about socializing students in the school community setting and serve as the context for examining parent values and participation. Several pertinent school characteristics for each of the three schools are summarized in table 10.1.

Table 10.1

Selected School Characteristics

	Characteristics				
Schools	Approximate Enrollment	% Blacks	% Catholics	Median Income	% Poverty[a]
Male	237	94	41	$22,737	16
Female	316	85	47	$18,617	29
Coed	288	99	43	$24,500	15

[a]Federal Poverty Level = approximately $10,000 for a family of four
(U. S. Census Bureau Report, 1985).

BOYS' SCHOOL FOR GENTLEMEN

The boys' school is located in a gentrified area of a large city where it occupies a romantically styled, turn-of-the-century building, originally a home for working girls. When the relocation of the school to its present site was announced in the 1970s, the White elite neighborhood brought a legal suit against the archdiocese over zoning which was settled eventually in favor of the school. The high chandeliers and gracefully winding, red-carpeted center staircase give the building's main interior a homelike feeling. A recently built gymnasium is diplomatically concealed behind the building. The school enjoys some athletic reknown. None of the students live in the immediate area. All commute from various parts of the city, with the broadest representation from its most depressed sectors.

At the time of its relocation, the archbishop invited the order of religious brothers who now staff the school to conduct it primarily for "lower-achieving students, specifically those who score too low on the archdiocesan cooperative examinations to be accepted at other area Catholic high schools." Here, a predominantly White male religious and lay faculty, several of whom have advanced degrees in reading and special education, help many students realize dramatic gains in math and reading during their first two years in the school, emphasizing the skills, habits, and attitudes that will lead students to "become more capable learners." A point is reached, however, when students are unwilling to be considered as general education or remedial students. By their junior year, everyone is assigned to a college-preparatory curriculum regardless of ability, although it is obvious that some students are still "barely literate," as reported by the academic dean. Not only are students not willing to be "tracked" after their sophomore year, neither are they willing to take advantage of a cooperative vocational education program that is offered at the local public high school, considering such programs "inappropriate to their life goals." Teachers report that "all students want to view themselves in adult life as going to work in a suit."

A sense of order, discipline, and a relaxed atmosphere pervade the school. Social pressures to keep up with the latest clothing fashions, to be "cool" by not appearing to have personal or home problems, which plague many students but are only addressed informally, and to set unrealistically high life goals, are tremendous. The school places a great deal of emphasis on the school's image as "a family" and students as "gentlemen," or the school's "macho image" as it was expressed by several students, expecting the type of behavior that those terms imply. Only modest pressure is applied for academic achievement because many faculty want to deemphasize failure. Most view failure as in conflict with the growth of self-esteem, acquiring positive attitudes toward life, and other developmental behaviors that the school stresses.

All students graduate with the same diploma. About 70 percent of the students are accepted at four-year colleges, many to a nearby city college, but most are not capable of sustaining a college program and drop out before they graduate. A few do graduate and some return to the school to speak in school assemblies and encourage students to attend to their academic studies.

GIRLS SCHOOL FOR LADIES

The girls' school is located in an industrialized area of a sprawling metropolis. The neighborhood consists mainly of commercial property, both developed and undeveloped, but is dotted occasionally with tiny, dilapidated houses. These are home to struggling minorities, mainly Blacks, Hispanics, and Asians. The community is characterized by social unrest due primarily to gang activities. About a third of the students come from the area, primarily Blacks, and some Hispanics. As with the boys' school, most of the students are low-achieving and are unable to gain admittance to other, more prestigious, Catholic high schools, which they say they would prefer to their present school.

The 1960s vintage school building is a split-level structure of modest size. Its two wings and a high chain-link fence empacted with a growth of thick shrubbery frame a blacktop parking area and inner yard, effectively enclosing the school. The connecting main entrance between the two wings is guarded by a high iron gate that is locked at the official beginning of the school day, reducing the tardy rate to zero. The school's hallways and classrooms are immaculately clean, polished, and bright. School offices are in a glass-enclosed area off the main entrance and resemble the lobby of the branch office of a local bank. Security concerns as well as the demand for "strict" observation of the school's many rules, including being on time for school, provoked a number of comments from students who characterized the school as "prison-like."

A Black teaching order of sisters who "preach" the ideals of a girls' finishing school direct the school. They are assisted by a mainly female Black and Hispanic faculty who care deeply about the students and give a tremendous amount of their personal time to them, particularly in the form of extracurricular activities. The school perceives itself as having an equally important goal as academics in preparing young ladies who will be "refined" in their attitudes, manners, and speech. "Ladylike behavior," "how to carry yourself," and classes in ethics that stress peer relationships and moral responsibility for one's sexual behavior permeate the school's curriculum. A goal frequently stated by faculty and students was the avoidance of teenage pregnancy. As reported by a faculty member, "parents send their girls here to keep them away from the boys. They expect us to do for them what they cannot always do."

Students were divided into three curricular tracks: college preparatory, business education, and general education, although all took the same academic core. The providing of a differentiated curriculum was disguised by use of the same textbook for the academic subjects taught at each level, but covering different amounts of material such that lower-track students might use a particular textbook over a two-year period. Students frequently complained about repetitious teaching, including those in the college-preparatory track. And seniors who had occupied the general education track as freshmen and sophomores complained of being "behind" as juniors and seniors.

An elite minority occupied the college-preparatory track. Girls in this track appeared to be more refined and gentle in their speech and behavior while those who occupied the general education track tended to be stereotypical: they were loud, disruptive, and had less refined manners and physical features. They perceived themselves as being more frequently corrected and "punished" than those in the college-preparatory and business tracks. A considerably larger proportion of first and second-year students occupied the lower tracks while few, if any, girls considered themselves general education students by senior year.

The social as well as academic demarcation had a noticeable negative effect on student relationships in terms of developing friendships with students in other tracks, liking one another, and teacher-student rapport. General-education Black students felt teachers favored college-preparatory students and liked Hispanic girls better "because they are more quiet." The faculty tended to relate to students on a one-to-one basis more than to groups. They prided themselves on the individual relationships they enjoyed with students and the successes they had experienced over the years in helping students from "troubled" homes, even taking them into their own homes when a domestic crisis occurred in a student's home.

About 20 percent of the students who graduate from the school receive a certificate rather than a diploma because they cannot read at the eighth-grade level, a state requirement for graduation. About a third pursue a four-year college degree, but most usually do not do so until several years after graduation, when they have become "more mature" and are "independent of their parents." Most enter the workforce directly and claim they more readily find jobs than if they had graduated from a public school. About two or three girls a year become pregnant. They are required to drop out of school.

COED SCHOOL FOR LEADERSHIP

The coed school formerly housed a girls' business education school constructed about fifty years ago. It was the newest school, founded six years before the study at the initiative of a well-organized community task force of Black parents and educators concerned about Black student achievement and preparation for college. Quite bland architecturally, though neat in appearance, the building has serious plumbing and other needed repair problems that daily affect life in the school. It lacks laboratories and athletic facilities. Students conduct the daily cleaning of the building and keep its interior attractive by creative use of bulletin boards, graphic wall designs, and other displays. Located in a neighborhood of modest homes, the area was described by one school official as a "low-income, high crime, Black ghetto" considered "dangerous" for students traveling into it. The school had slightly higher-achieving students than the other Black schools because it accepted and retained only students who intend to go to college and who maintain a "C" average.

The faculty are committed to preparing "Black leadership for service to the community." Students are required to enroll in leadership training classes that emphasize self-knowledge and practical interpersonal skills. The classes also focus on accomplishments of historical and contemporary Black leaders. These classes require a great deal of reading, writing, and public speaking. Student government, a grievance board on which students serve with parents and teachers, and the requirement of community service for graduation provide opportunities for application of leadership skills.

The faculty are more subject-oriented in their academic preparation and teaching than those at the other two schools. They provide for all students a sharply focused, four-year, college-oriented liberal arts curriculum that has been pared to its essentials and is taught rigorously and at a steady pace of increasing difficulty and complexity, culminating with a major research paper in the senior year. There is a great deal of interaction among the faculty concerning course content, teaching methods, and monitoring of individual student progress. In teaching, emphasis is placed on new material rather than review work and on becoming a scholar rather than on acquiring learning habits and attitudes, which are taken for granted.

Teachers press students to perform at the highest level of which they are capable, even beyond what some students think they can do. Students describe their teachers as "merciless," "demanding," and "unyielding" when it comes to completing their assignments, but they also express satisfaction with their accomplishments. Students who cannot keep up weed themselves out or are asked to leave the school at the end of their freshman or sophomore year. About half do so. Teachers are constantly concerned about the high levels of stress under which students are placed and their ability to cope with the rigorous curriculum the school offers. They provide a great deal of technical and personal support to students outside the classroom through before- and after-school tutoring sessions, Saturday trips to libraries, museums, and nearby colleges and universities, and by giving students their home telephone numbers for consultation about homework assignments. Students form their own study groups and tutor students who need it. A survival mentality generates cooperation among students and support for one another.

Most graduates are accepted at several colleges and close to 100 percent enter a four-year college, many on scholarships. The faculty guide and encourage students to choose Black colleges where, they report, students seem to do best. Many, however, also do well in traditionally White colleges and preliminary data indicate that the majority persevere through graduation.

The above descriptions indicate that each school strives to inculcate into students some basic set of societal values in which it specializes: cultivation of personal attitudes of confidence and success, development of moral behavior and social skills, and acquisition of academic knowledge and leadership skills. School climates vary from extremely demanding and rigorous psychological stress to a more relaxed, "laid back" school atmosphere and a social climate that is marked by its emphasis on rules and controls and contains some observable hostility. School organizational arrangements range from a highly-tracked curriculum to a single-track, college-preparatory curriculum and a more ambiguous arrangement where tracking is only partially used. Teaching methods range from repetition and drill in teaching skills and academic content to the presentation of challenging new material on a regular basis. Schools experience varying degrees of success in placing their graduates in college settings where student potentials differ in obtaining a four-year degree. Within this context, what are parents' expectations and participation at each school? Are they the same or different from school to school? Do parents get what they desire by choosing the school? Does the school's social structure and other characteristics influence parent participation?

PARENT GOAL EXPECTATIONS AND SCHOOL PARTICIPATION

School Comparisons

As indicated in table 10.2, parents have high educational expectations of their children. Even at the girls' school where the academic emphasis is noticeably less than at the other two schools, about 65 percent of parents expect their daughters to obtain a bachelor's degree or an advanced degree such as a PhD., M.D., or law degree. However, this percentage is considerably higher at the other two schools and is in direct proportion to the emphasis that each school places on academic pursuits.

Table 10.2

Frequency of Parental Goal Expectation and Involvement Variables by Single Sex and Coed Schools

Variables	Schools		
	Male (N = 174)	Female (N = 187)	Coed (N = 136)
Expectations for Child's Educational Attainment			
	127[a]	121	116
Bachelor's degree +	74.3[b]	65.4	87.9
Reasons for School Choice			
	83	57	89
Academic	47.7	47.1	78.1
	13	17	1
Discipline	7.5	14.0	.9
	23	19	11
Religion/Values	13.2	15.7	9.6
	55	28	13
Non-Educational	31.6	23.2	11.4
Participation			
	55	48	54
Help at school	32.2	29.6	45.8
	137	127	106
Monitor homework	78.6	78.9	86.2
	126	122	100
Attend school meetings	73.0	75.3	85.5
Talks with Teachers			
	13	32	8
None	7.6	17.5	6.1
	92	58	63
Three or more	53.4	31.7	47.7

Note:

[a] = number of subjects (parents);

[b] = percentages of the total number of parent subjects, by column throughout the table.

Correspondingly, parents chose the schools primarily for academic reasons, overwhelmingly so at the coed school, where 78 percent of parents reported that academic reasons, especially college preparation, were the most important ones in choosing to send their child to the school. Fewer than 50 percent of parents at the female and male school selected an academic reason as a priority in choosing the school, including choosing the male school for its remedial programs; rather, parents were more concerned about other values, particularly about their children's socialization. Discipline was a greater concern for parents at the girls' school than at the other two schools, with 14 percent of parents choosing it as the primary reason for enrolling their children. While religion and values were chosen at about the same rate by parents at the two single-sex schools, noneducational reasons overshadowed such reasons at both schools.   Parents at the boys' school, more frequently than any other school, indicated that their child "chose to attend" the school or attended because "their friends attend"; they also cited reasons such as "affordable tuition, "location," and for some, "athletics."   At the girls' school, parents indicated, more than at the other two schools, that "available public schools are unsafe".

Concerning participation, the academically focused coed school stands out from the single-sex schools in having the highest parent involvement in all categories: about 46 percent of parents report helping with class trips and other school-related activities such as sports, music, plays, and serving as board members and teacher aides; about 86 percent had attended school meetings, including meetings to discuss school problems and monthly meetings of parent organizations.   Communication patterns at the schools indicate that parents at the female school were least likely among the three schools to communicate with teachers. About 18 percent of parents reported that they had not talked with their children's teachers during the past year and only about a third reported three contracts or more, about 20 percent fewer than at the other schools.

School and Parent Effects

In separate analyses not presented here, parents' level of education, their reasons for choosing the school, and the individual school chosen were found to exert a statistically significant effect on parents' participation and communication.[14]   Parents who attended college were more likely to be highly active participators and communicators, reporting participation in three or more different roles represented by the items listed on the questionnaire or talking with teachers three or more times a year. Parents who chose the school primarily for academic reasons tended to communicate more frequently with teachers than those who chose the school for other reasons. The school itself, or the group of parents gathered at a particular school site, influenced all areas of participation and communication, suggesting that the school plays a strong role in parent involvement.

Results of other analyses indicated that there were no differences in the participation rates in school- and home-related activities of Blacks at either the predominantly Black schools or at the mixed-race schools where Blacks constituted about a 30 percent minority.   However, Blacks at mixed-raced schools and the all-Black schools had significantly higher rates of communication with teachers than did non-Blacks. Blacks appear to participate at least as well if not better than non-Blacks in these Catholic schools. Thus, predominantly Black schools had higher rates of participation overall than did mixed-race schools.

BLACK FAMILY CHARACTERISTICS AND PARTICIPATION IN CATHOLIC EDUCATION

Socioeconomic and Other Social Resources

Black families attending these three predominantly Black schools are not poor or less educated in comparison to Black families nationally. Black parents in these schools reported a median annual income of $20, 178 in 1985, approximately $4,000 higher than the U.S. Census Bureau estimates for a Black family of four, with about 55 percent reporting annual incomes over $20,000 and 30 percent over $30,000. About 23 percent received a 4-year college degree or higher degree and less than 4 percent reported that they did not graduate from high school.[15]   Compared to Whites and Hispanics in this study of Catholic schools serving lower-income families, Blacks were considerably more affluent than Whites and Hispanics attending similar schools as well as more affluent than Black families in general.

Although these families enjoy a relatively high socioeconomic status, the presumed social resources they bring to the Catholic school community that facilitate participation are low: 73 percent of these Black parents never attended a Catholic school, approximately 60 percent are not Catholic, 81 percent of mothers work, and only 49 percent of homes have both parents residing in them. These factors could be considered deficits to parent involvement in a Catholic school for this group. As newcomers to Catholic schools, Black parents may not initially feel as comfortable enrolling their children as would parents who themselves had attended a Catholic school, thus some social distance would have to be overcome. By not sharing in the main religious affiliation of the school, parents would not participate in church worship common to the school's sponsorship. Working mothers and the absence of a parent in the home are presumed deficits to participation since they greatly reduce the amount of time available to participate in activities outside work and the home.

Single-Parent and Two-Parent Home Effects on School and Church Participation

A series of analyses were used, including the 615 Black families from the five schools in the larger study, to determine whether specific types of families more frequently utilized opportunities to acquire social capital through interaction activities associated with Catholic education than did other families. For the analyses, Black families were separated into four types: single-parent Catholic, single-parent non-Catholic, two-parent Catholic, and two parent-non-Catholic.

Results indicated that there were no differences in participation and communication activities between or within the five schools by family type for these Black families. Parents from single- and two-parent family homes, whether Catholic or non-Catholic, were similar in the extent to which they participated in school-related activities and communicated with teachers. High communicators and participators were just as likely to be from single- as from two-parent homes, indicating that the absence of a parent in the home was not a deficit to school participation and communication. Differences, however, were found concerning church activity for family types (see table 10.3). Church activity, long an integral part of Catholic education, provides an additional opportunity for parents to interact and to obtain the social resources beneficial to their childrearing roles.

Table 10.3

Distribution of Church Activity for Black Family Types

| Church Activity | Family Types (N = 576) | | | |
	Single Parent Catholic %	Single Parent Non-Catholic %	Two Parent Catholic %	Two Parent Non-Catholic %
	66	104	72	122
Frequent	51.1	60.4	64.9	74.4
	63	68	39	42
Infrequent	48.9	39.5	35.1	25.6
	129	172	111	164
Total	100	99.9[a]	100	100

[a] Percentages do not always total 100 percent due to rounding.

Two-parent families were approximately 14 percent more likely to be involved frequently in church activities, whether Catholic or non-Catholic, than their counterparts in single-parent home situations, suggesting that the absence of a parent in the home lessons church attendance.   Over 74 percent of two-parent non-Catholic families reported that they participated in church activity "weekly" or "monthly," compared to about 60 percent of single-parent non-Catholic families; approximately 65 percent of two-parent Catholic families participated frequently compared to 51 percent of single-parent Catholic families.   Single-parent Catholics were the least likely to participate frequently in church activity whereas two-parent non-Catholic families were the most likely.

Although non-Catholics belong to a different church than the one affiliated with the school, they apparently seek this additional social support beyond the school by attending their own churches and attend at a higher rate than do Catholics, indicating that nonaffiliation with the school's religious denomination is not a barrier to acquiring the benefits of social capital associated with attending a Catholic school. In these schools, being a non-Catholic increases the likelihood of church attendance for both single- and two-parent families. For non-Catholics, the Catholic school may enhance Black family church participation by making parents more attentive to the need to nurture and retain in their children their own religious traditions not found in Catholic schools. Although they do not bring the resource of being Catholic, two-parent non-Catholic Black families participate as well, if not better, than Catholics in church activities.

In contrast, the single-parent Catholic is least likely to benefit from the social capital to be gained through church attendance, even though the parent is just as likely as any other family type to participate at school. Because many single-parent Catholics may be divorced or never married, they may perceive themselves as less accepted in the Catholic Church. This is strongly suggested by the fact that their non-Catholic counterparts are significantly more likely to be active in churches of other denominations. Other studies have shown that single-parent Catholics feel neglected by the Church.[16]

Thus, a group for whom Catholic schools might offer a greater benefit and who bring an additional resource to the school by being Catholic, appears to benefit less than its non-Catholic counterpart from the social capital that can be obtained through religious worship. The absence of a parent in the family is a greater deficit concerning church attendance for a Catholic than for a non-Catholic family.

DISCUSSION

The survey results indicate generally that these Black parents value education highly and are active participators in the school community in ways that are likely to enhance their child's academic and social development. They have high educational expectations of their children and choose Catholic schools primarily for academic reasons, especially for college preparation. While sharing similar values, including church attendance, parents are also involved in those school-related activities that are the most directly related to their child's educational progress, such as monitoring homework, participating in school meetings, and communicating with teachers. This type of involvement may help explain, in part, why Catholic schools are more successful than public schools in producing higher achievement scores among lower-income and minority students.

The survey and ethnographic findings together suggest a congruence or "fit" between what parents want and what the school provides by way of academic and social development. Not all schools were chosen equally by parents for their academic emphasis. Schools that were more oriented toward social and personal development (i.e., single-sex schools) emphasized academic pursuits less than the more academically focused coed school and reflected parents' reasons for choosing them. Each school had its own special character and contributed to Black family values in uniquely different ways, addressing parents' concerns by helping students gain greater self-confidence and an improved self-image at the male school, teaching students norms of social behavior at the female school, and preparing students for college success at the coed school.

Parent involvement patterns differed from school to school depending on the school's academic focus. At the academically focused coed school, parents were the most likely to participate at school and in school-related activities, including monitoring homework, and communicated frequently with teachers. At the more socially oriented schools where academic pursuits were stressed less, parent involvement was limited to communication. At the formally structured female school, with its norms and controls, parents were least likely to participate either at school or by communicating with teachers, leading to the speculation that parents may feel socially distant from a school that is more formally structured.

Blacks appear to be well-integrated into the Catholic schools they attend. They are involved at least as well if not better than non-Blacks, and non-Catholics are as involved as Catholics. Neither is their participation limited by so-called social deficits such as the absence of a parent from the home or presence of the mother in the workforce. In fact, these factors may motivate Black families to seek Catholic schools, where they can be affiliated with other families with whom they share similar goals and in a setting that is democratic in its equal treatment of those it serves. The association of non-Catholic Blacks with their own churches may enhance their commitment to Catholic education as a moral enterprise.

The varying patterns of reasons for school choice and their relationship to parent involvement suggests that parents may be involved in the school in ways that the school supports and encourages most and not involved in ways that might work against school socialization efforts, particularly efforts that are supportive of but not directly related to academic pursuits, such as were found in the two single-sex schools. Most likely, a compatibility between what parents want and what the school expects and provides determines the level of parent involvement.

CONCLUSION

This study suggests a framework through which student performance is shaped in Catholic schools, enabling them to contribute in a unique way to the education and socialization of Black students.

Parents have high expectations for their children's future educational attainment, motivating them to choose Catholic schools primarily for academic reasons but also for socialization reasons, that lead to success in life. The congruency or "fit" between what parents want and what the school accomplishes creates a level of confidence in the school and in the choice parents have made that facilitates parent involvement.

It should be recalled that teachers in these schools exhibited a high level of teacher efficacy, or belief that their efforts and those of the school were effective in meeting the needs of lower-income and minority students. Teachers who have a high sense of efficacy about their teaching capabilities can be confident not only in motivating students to enhance their cognitive and social development, but in communicating with students' parents. The confidence of parents in the school's efforts to address their concerns and in the choice they have made, coupled with the confidence of teachers in their teaching abilities, creates a compatibility between home and school that leads to mutual support concerning student progress. Thus, parents and teachers act together in ways that enhance student development.

Albert Bandura attributes increased psychological functioning to the confidence that comes from self-belief or efficacy. People will expend greater effort in the face of obstacles and be more persistent with less accompanying stress and frustration if they believe in the efficacy of their actions, that is, that their actions will result in favorable outcomes; they intensify their efforts when their performance falls short of their goals and actually produce the behavior that leads to results.[17] Thus, parent and teacher efforts to enhance student development produce greater effort and accomplishment on the part of students, creating a "community of belief" within the school setting that enables some schools to be more successful than others in accomplishing education and socialization goals. For these Black families, "deficits" such as the absence of a parent in the home and the presence of the mother in the workforce are not a limitation to their school involvement.

These Black families participate effectively in Catholic education because they have a set of characteristics that motivates them to value education highly and be involved in their children's learning. Black parents may be particularly disposed toward involvement because they, more urgently than non-Blacks, see the need for their children to do well in school in order to compete in the labor market. Although efforts were made to find the poorest Catholic high schools for this study, Blacks were more affluent than expected. This suggests the role played by education and income in parent involvement and student success.

Greeley hypothesizes that schools may be rather poor institutions for facilitating upward mobility of minority groups until minorities first acquire some kind of income parity.[18] In the process of socialization, those who are able to benefit the most from private schools are those with the highest levels of income and education. The American public and educators have generally perceived schools as producing equality of income. Just the opposite may be at work in the education of minority groups. As Blacks become more affluent, they become more at home in the Catholic school as evidenced by their involvement. Perhaps what matters most to these parents is a sense of acceptance and ownership in these schools. In the past, the Catholic Church generally did not provide Catholic schooling for Blacks, primarily because there were few Black Catholics; however, the Church's lack of presence among Blacks prior to their liberation from slavery has not gone unnoticed, as reflected in the comments of a Black administrator of one of the schools in the study:

> Historically the Catholic Church is a White church and has never really had an interest in evangelizing Blacks, although they are very spiritual people. They are mainly Baptists because, when we were still slaves, the Baptist Church was the one that welcomed us. And we bound together in that church and we're still there. The Catholic Church could have come, but it didn't. Maybe it's here for us now.

Perhaps the ethnic miracle can be repeated.[19]

NOTES

1. For various discussions of the role of the school as a social-
    izing agency, see Charles E. Bidwell, "The School as a
    Formal Organization," in James G. March, ed., Handbook of
    Organizations (Chicago: Rand McNally, 1965), pp. 972-1022;
    Robert Dreeben, On What Is Learned in School (Reading,
    Mass.: Addison-Wesley, 1968); and Talcott Parsons, "The
    School Class as a Social System: Some of Its Functions in
    American Society," Harvard Educational Review 29 (Fall
    1959): 297-318.

2.   See, for example, James P. Comer, School Power: Impli-
    cations of an Intervention Project (New York: Free   Press,
    1980), pp. 27-41; and Sara Lawrence Lightfoot, World's
    Apart: Relationships Between Families and School (New
    York: Basic Books, 1978), pp. 20-42.

3. For reviews of the literature, see Anne T. Henderson ed.,
    Parent Participation--Student Achievement: The Evidence
    Grows (Columbia, Md.: National Committee for Citizens in
    Education, 1981) and The Evidence Continues to Grow:
    Parent Involvement Improves Student Achievement (Columbia,
    Md.: National Committee for Citizens in Education, 1987);
    and Sharon L. Kagan, "Parent Involvement Research: A Field
    in Search of Itself" (Boston: Institute for Responsive
    Education, 1984, mimeographed).

4.   Extensive research on this topic has been done by Andrew M.
    Greeley and his colleagues. See, for example, Andrew M.
    Greeley and Peter H. Rossi, The Education of Catholic
    Americans (Chicago: Aldine, 1966); Andrew M. Greeley,
    William C. McCready, and Kathleen McCourt Catholic
    Schools in a Declining Church (Kansas City: Sheed & Ward,
    1976). See also James W. Sanders, The Education of an
    Urban Minority: Catholics in Chicago, 1833-1965 (New
    York: Oxford University Press, 1977).

5. The empirical evidence for this is based on an analysis of data
    from the General Social Surveys, 1982-1984, assembled at the
    National Opinion Research Center, Chicago, Illinois. The
    analysis was conducted at the Youth Research Center, The
    Catholic University of America, Washington, D. C., and is
    available from the author.

6. See Andrew M. Greeley, "The Ethnic Miracle," The Public
    Interest 45 (Fall 1976): 29.

7. See, for example, James G. Cibulka, Timothy J. O'Brien, and
    Donald Zewe S. J., Inner-City Private Elementary Schools: A
    Study (Milwaukee: Marquette University Press, 1982); and
    Diana T. Slaughter and Barbara L. Schneider, Newcomers:
    Black in Private Schools, ERIC, 1986 ED 274 768 and ED
    274 769).

8. See James S. Coleman, Thomas Hoffer, and Sally Kilgore,
    High School Achievement: Public, Catholic, and Private
    Schools Compared (New York: Basic Books, 1982; and
    Andrew M. Greeley, Catholic High Schools and Minority
    Students (New Brunswick: Transaction Books, 1982).

9. See Susan Abramowitz and E. Ann Stackhouse, The Private
    High School Today (Washington, D.C.: National Institute of
    Education, 1980), pp. 71-85; and Anthony S. Bryk et al.,
    Effective Catholic Schools: An Exploration (Washington,
    D.C.: National Catholic Educational Association, 1984).

10. For an extensive discussion of social capital, see James S.
    Coleman and Thomas Hoffer, Public and Private High
    Schools: The Impact of Communities (New York: Basic
    Books, 1987), pp. 221-231.

11. See National Catholic Educational Association, The Catholic
    High School: A National Portrait (Washington, D.C.:
    National Catholic Educational Association, 1985) and Catholic
    High Schools: Their Impact on Low-Income Students
    (Washington, D.C.: National Catholic Educational Assoc-
    iation, 1986). For a description of these studies, see chapter
    9, this volume.

12. The study design and data collection procedures can be found
    in Patricia A. Bauch et al., "Final Report to the National
    Catholic Educational Association on Field Study of Five
    Low-Income-Serving Schools" (Washington, D. C.: The
    Catholic University of America, Youth Research Center, 1985,
    mimeographed).

13. Teachers were asked to respond to seven survey questions
    concerning how "effective" they believed they were as teachers
    and how "effective" the school was in meeting the educational
    needs of lower-income and minority students in three goal

areas: promoting academic skills, values development, and faith development; and whether or not teachers and the school had a "special sensitivity toward lower-income families."

14. These analyses can be found in Patricia A. Bauch, "Family Choice and Parent Involvement in Inner-City Catholic High Schools: An Exploration of Psycho-Social and Organizational Factors" (Paper presented at the annual meeting of the American Educational Research Association, Washington, D.C., April 1987).

15. The U.S. Census Bureau reported that the median family income for a Black family of four in 1985 was $16,786 and that 14 percent of Blacks were college graduates. These are estimates based on yearly updated annual reports issued by the U S. Census Bureau. See U.S. Census Bureau Reports (Washington, D.C.: Government Printing Office, 1985).

16. In a recent survey of Catholics in the Archdiocese of Washington, D.C., 53 percent of those surveyed felt that single parents were not being adequately responded to by the Catholic Church. See Marjorie Hyer, "Sharp Decrease Found Among Catholics Here Going to Confession," Washington Post, July 4, 1987, p. D16.

17. See Albert Bandura, Social Foundations of Thought and Action: A   Social Cognitive Theory (Englewood Cliffs, N. J.: Prentice-Hall, 1986), pp. 393-395.

18. See Greeley, "The Ethnic Miracle," p. 29.

19. Ibid.

11

Catholic School Closings: Efficiency, Responsiveness, and Equality of Access for Blacks

James G. Cibulka

An important theme in the public versus private school debate is whether private schools are both more efficient and more responsive to consumers than are public schools. One stringent test for this argument is the way private school systems have used school closings as a response to enrollment decline and related problems. Catholic systems in urban areas, and to a lesser extent other religiously affiliated schools, operate numerous facilities. When falling enrollment and other problems beset a school, how have these difficulties been handled by Catholic authorities? Such problems eventually force school officials to choose between efficiency (closing or consolidating under-utilized schools to minimize costs) and responsiveness (keeping them open to meet an articulated "need"). It is by no means self-evident that private schools value efficiency over responsiveness when the two values are juxtaposed.

The purpose of this chapter is to describe the history and patterning of Catholic school closings. While the research literature on closings in the public sector is sizeable, very little attention has been given to private schools in this literature.

This issue impacts Blacks in that inner-city Catholic schools are among the most vulnerable to closing pressures and face a very uncertain future in many dioceses. Three factors heighten the vulnerability of these inner-city schools to closings. First, these are some of the oldest schools with the least adequate physical plants. The safety and/or effectiveness of maintaining such schools becomes problematic. Second, neighborhoods surrounding these schools frequently are in social and physical transition. Geographic areas where large numbers of immigrant Catholics once lived sometimes have undergone several demographic and commercial cycles, resulting in urban decay or redevelopment. These changes often result in fewer people living near the school. Sometimes its location comes to be viewed as undesirable. A third factor is the financially precarious plight of many inner-city schools. Newcomers to the school--Blacks and other minorities--may lack the ability to pay normal tuition. Parish or religious-order subsidies may have declined with the changing school population. Diocesan subsidies may be modest or offered on a conditional basis. Caught between declining enrollment and declining revenue with increased costs for personnel and other items, the schools face a precarious future.

When the racial dimension is considered, the issue of school closings raises two questions for Catholic school officials. Will efficiency or local responsiveness be valued more highly? Second, how responsive will Church policy be to Black Americans in particular? This second issue raises broader questions about equality of access to private schools, which shall be addressed in the concluding section of the chapter.

LITERATURE OVERVIEW: FINDINGS FROM PUBLIC SCHOOLS

Space does not permit, nor do my purposes here require, a full review of the literature on school closings and cutback management in public education. Nonetheless, reviewing some of the key themes and conclusions in that research will help to anchor the present study's findings.

The response of public school officials to enrollment declines was inordinately slow. Their failure to scale back operations promptly can be traced to a variety of factors. Competing public demands for service increases, budgetary increases even in a period of enrollment loss, and bureaucratic inertia are some of the major ones.[1]

When public officials attempted school closings, frequently they encountered community opposition. This political problem became more complex in urban environments with mobilized constituencies capable of building coalitions to fight officials' plans. Inevitably, these constituencies challenged the efficiency assumptions guiding the logic of bureaucrats and often caused elected board members, fearing voter reprisals, to retract their support for school closings.

On their part, professional administrators often misguaged the political dimensions of closing a school, tending to define the issue as a technical organizational problem. They remained committed to a highly centralized planning approach, conceding to community involvement only for purposes of coopting opponents or legitimating their own plans.

This attempt to assure bureaucratic hegemony throughout the closing process created problematic outcomes. Large numbers of schools serving inner-city minority populations were closed because their schools were by objective criteria "deficient," frequently in terms of facilities. Equity criteria were more often than not ignored, unless imposed by court orders constraining this technical orientation. A second outcome was heightened community mobilization to fight school officials, lessening the success rate for closing schools. In short, the literature on public school closings documents the difficulties of this policy, owing both to the actions of public school officials and the environmental constraints which surround public schools as governmental institutions.

METHODS

The focus of this study is the nation's Catholic schools. This is the only sector of private schools to experience enrollment decline. In fiscal 1981, Catholic schools represented 63 percent of the private school enrollment, whereas they had constituted 87 percent in 1965-66. In secular and all other church-related and sectors, enrollment grew during the period.

Two data collection methods were employed. Existing databases were examined from the National Catholic Educational Association (NCEA), the National Center for Education Statistics, and the U. S. Bureau of the Census. In addition, phone interviews were conducted in thirty-two dioceses. These included the twenty-five largest Catholic school systems as well as seven smaller systems which were added on the basis of information provided by one or more phone respondents. The largest dioceses were selected to represent the major portion of the sample because in 1983-84 they represented 57 percent of the Catholic enrollment and 48 percent of the schools.

Many of the school systems selected have substantial Black and other non-White enrollment. Minority enrollment in the ten largest dioceses (which comprise about a third of the national enrollment) are listed in table 11.1. Some other dioceses in the sample also have substantial non-White enrollment, e.g., Black concentrations in New Orleans (23 percent) and Washington, D. C. (32 percent), Hispanics in Miami (39 percent) and San Antonio (60 percent), Asians in San Francisco (21 percent), and Asians and Blacks in Oakland (20 and 10 percent respectively). Most school systems in the sample, regardless of overall minority percentages, have had one or more predominantly Black or other minority school in the diocese.

Table 11.1

Catholic School Minority Enrollments in the Ten Largest Dioceses 1983-1984

Minority Enrollment in Percentiles

Urban Dioceses System	Total Enrollment (Rounded)	Black	Hispanic	Asian	Indian	Total Minority
Chicago	178,700	16.6	11.0	3.0	0.1	30.7
Philadelphia	159,800	10.2	2.4	1.2	0.2	14.0
New York	125,800	15.2	23.0	4.2	0.1	42.5
Los Angeles	109,800	9.6	41.4	6.7	0.4	58.1
Brooklyn	107,400	17.6	18.0	4.4	0.2	40.2
Detroit	79,900	16.1	2.5	0.7	0.5	19.8
Cleveland	78,900	8.1	2.1	1.2	0.2	11.6
Newark	74,100	12.7	15.6	3.0	0.1	31.4
Boston	71,500	3.6	2.6	0.7	0.3	7.2
St. Louis	65,500	8.5	0.8	0.8	0.2	10.3
Total	1,051,600	131,300	134,900	29,500	2,200	297,900
Percentage Distribution	100.0	12.5	12.8	2.8	0.2	28.3

Source: United States Catholic Elementary and Secondary Schools 1984-1985 Washington, D. C.: National Catholic Educational Association, 1985), p. 18.

In some school systems, phone interviews were supplemented by mail surveys when phone contact was not possible or additional factual material was needed.

The structure of the interviews followed the tradition of elite interviewing.   The format was semi-focused.   Areas covered included the number of closings in recent years, the reasons for the closings, who initiated the closings, who approved them, what other processes are employed, what controversy surrounds the closings, what clientele are most affected by closings, the effect of the diocesan subsidies, if any, on closings, the role of the pastor and principal, and related matters.

DISCUSSION OF FINDINGS

The above findings pertaining to public schools are in some ways very unlike the school closing process in Catholic schools. During the early years of enrollment decline--the late 1960s and early 1970s--Catholic dioceses closed large numbers of schools. Efficiency concerns dominated the thinking of these officials as they considered two interrelated problems--a projected shortage in "religious" staff to teach in their schools and the prospect of declining enrollment in future years.[2] The rising costs of shifting to lay teaching staff combined with likely reductions in revenue accompanying fewer students led many local parishes, religious orders, and in some cases dioceses to conclude that they should close the doors of their schools. Closing schools created further reductions in pupil enrollment, although presumably these decisions led to a more efficient match between available space and student demand.

So far these facts seem consistent with the conception of Catholic schools as market institutions responsive in their supply decisions to the ebb and flow of consumer demand. They behave far less ponderously than their public counterparts.

Yet a more complex picture emerges when the behavior of Catholic officials is mapped over a longer period. When the number of school closings across the nation is compared with the magnitude of enrollment loss for each year between 1967 and 1983, one finds that the school closings never kept pace with student decline. In fact, the gap grew wider as time passed. Since the late 1970s the number of closings has fallen off appreciably despite steady enrollment decline.

Three reasons account for this apparently inefficient response to the problem. First, Catholic officials sometimes decided that the Church had an obligation to serve certain populations and geographic areas even where numbers and costs otherwise dictated closing the schools. Among these "special" populations were impoverished Blacks in inner-cities, many of whom were non-Catholic. This dimension will be discussed later. Second, officials in some dioceses decided to postpone closings by requiring local planning. This was to assure that all local factors were involved in the decision to remain open or close, to improve the likelihood of a school surviving by fostering local self-help efforts, and, if this failed, to plan an orderly closing. Third, some dioceses primarily wished to reduce community opposition to closings, public criticism, and negative media treatment.

Depending on their motives, dioceses evolved different strategies of response. Before examining these responses, it is important to review how the authority structure of Catholic school systems differs from public schools.

Catholic schools within a diocese form a unitary administrative and governance system only in the loosest sense of the word. Elementary and secondary schools are technically owned by one or more local parishes, the diocese, or by private religious communities. At the elementary level, approximately 85 percent are single-parish schools, while high schools are sponsored primarily by religious communities (38.5 percent), followed closely by dioceses (35.5 percent). Superintendents, school boards, and the bishops have no direct authority over the educational activities of religious communities, which are free to open or close a school without consulting or even informing the diocese. Parish-run schools ultimately are controlled by the local pastor. Their legal and political autonomy is less complete than that of privately run religious schools. Parish priests are selected by the bishop and are in certain respects politically and/or financially dependent on the diocese.

Given these complexities, Catholic school systems are better understood as a federation. This is, of course, a simplification because some units within the federation are truly independent while others enjoy autonomy in many realms of decisionmaking.

The fact that Catholic schools are highly decentralized has had two important effects on the way school closings have been managed. First, the initiative for closings usually has come not from central officials but from the local schools, where management authority and often ownership rests. Typically, local officials determine that their particular school must close. In the late 1960s and early 1970s, the main reason was the decline of "religious" to staff the schools. Since then it has been declining enrollment, loss of paying clients, and decline of the parish subsidy system in inner-cities.

The decentralization to which I have referred has made the role of the diocesan officials in the school closing process a problematic one. In the 1960s and 1970s, they found themselves reacting to local decisions. There were many parental protests and much bitterness directed toward diocesan officials because of the perception, sometimes reinforced by the media, that ultimate authority to reverse the local pastor and parish council, or religious community, rested in the bishop's hands. The perception existed, in other words, that the system was ultimately a hierarchy of authority, however decentralized in name. Such confusion pervades federal governmental systems, so it is not surprising to find it in this context as well.

With respect to closings, diocesan officials faced two authority problems. For one, as was suggested, their legitimacy was challenged when they were targets of repeated community protests. Moreover, they were in no position to bring a positive outcome to most protests because conflict had polarized.

Under those circumstances, most dioceses during the 1970s consolidated greater authority over school closings in the hands of central officials. They made it explicit that no closing would occur without final approval by the bishop. Also, they set timetables forbidding last minute closings. And since these steps alone would hardly resolve the problem of reacting to change, most dioceses developed procedures to govern the closing process. In general, these procedures touched on the length of time needed to process a closing, who had to be involved in making a decision, what criteria had to be considered, and what alternatives had to be explored first. All of these were intended to give central officials some capacity to gain greater influence over the actions of local officials.

The difference between this federated system and the public school situation could not be drawn more clearly. For Catholics, initiating authority rests with local, not central, officials. In addition, both parties have shared authority, and the problem has been one of articulating that shared authority more clearly. In the public sector, local schools have no legal autonomy and there is a strong tradition of centralized decisionmaking. The weak authority structure of Catholic school systems led most dioceses to respond to the challenge by improvising new structures rather than using existing bureaucratic authority and structure to impose a solution on local schools.

These differences between public and private sectors did not guarantee that closings would be handled well, as the early years of closings remind us. But they provided a foundation for collaboration in which each party is recognized as having a legitimate stake in the outcome as well as distinct responsibility for shaping a satisfactory outcome.

Response Patterns

Officials in the various dioceses have evolved different balance points between local and central authority. Five patterns of decisionmaking emerged, distinguished by the degree of authority assumed by diocesan officials. These are centralized initiative; centralized initiative with local participation; local initiative with mutual decisionmaking; local initiative with central ratification; and local initiative. Each is discussed below.

Centralized initiative. This decisionmaking style prevails in a small number of dioceses and resembles the pattern in many public school systems with respect to school closings. The superintendent of schools in the diocese, or his/her representative, identifies schools which should be closed, based on enrollment, cost, or other factors (access to alternative schools, age of facility, etc.). Frequently this approach is employed with respect to diocesan high schools. The diocesan leadership identifies a rational plan for closings. In one case, this entailed closing a school whose enrollment was not the lowest but which was located in a depopulated area and whose faculty was deemed inadequate. According to this logic, it is better to plan than to rely on market forces to shape events.

This was one of two patterns (the other being local initiative) which lead to a high degree of conflict. It tends to be viewed by the affected schools as authoritarian. Typically, it leads to ad hoc protest groups which label themselves the "Save Our School Committee." It may involve covert negotiations to keep the school open, but more often than not, one of the disgruntled parties leaks the information to the press, unleashing a storm of protest which places the diocese in a defensive posture. Thus, even if this approach involves some covert discussions, it is soon labeled as unilateral or conspiratorial.

Central initiative, local participation. In this case, diocesan officials also target certain schools, but typically they do so to serve early warning that the school is in trouble and is headed for closing unless some action is taken. In certain dioceses these schools are flagged or even given probationary status. The schools may be run by parishes or the diocese.

Typically, the diocese will require that all parties at the local school (parish council, pastor, school board, principal, teachers, etc.) come together to develop a plan for the long-term viability of the school.[3]   This will involve an assessment of baptisms and other indicators of the potential market, a study of possible sources of revenue such as a development program or, tuition increases, and an expenditure plan. The diocese, based on its overall plan, which may include an assessment of diocesan enrollment, personnel, demography, and academic programs, may establish specific regulations for the schools, including a reporting timetable.

There was a degree of controversy associated with this approach. Sometimes the local resistance came directly from the local school board, pastor, and other authorities. In other cases, parents protested the school's acquiescence to the diocese. In most cases, however, there was local acceptance of responsibility to try saving a school from closing. In such instances, diocesan officials feel they have succeeded in rescuing a school from disaster by forcing local actors to confront reality and plan accordingly. This requirement is no guarantee that all the parties will buy into a new plan, and when closings occur, it is often because of such resistance by the teachers, pastor, or some other key local actor. Yet this strategy of central initiative and local involvement gives a diocese some opportunity to alter the course of events rather than react to a foregone conclusion that the school will close.

Local initiative, mutual decisionmaking. This style differs from the preceding one cited above in one important respect. Diocesan officials are less interventionist in identifying problem schools. Typically they will mandate that all schools engage in a planning process and will then provide consultation services to each school. If a school initiates a decision to close, the bishop, who retains final decisionmaking authority, will refer them back to diocesan school officials for a thorough review of the plan to make certain that all avenues have been exhausted. In this approach, then, the diocese has not identified problem schools as part of an overall plan, but does require that democratic planning occur. This is meant to counter two situations: local inaction until a crisis occurs, and unilateral decisions by the local pastor without adequate consultation with the parish council. The premise here is that: (1) local schools will plan more effectively if all schools are required to participate and the diocese avoids imposing a stigma on certain problem schools; (2) the diocese maintains informal influence over the planning by providing technical assistance; and (3) the decision to close rests with local schools, based on collaboration with the diocese.

Accordingly, this approach tends to be associated with less controversy. At the same time, the price paid by the diocese is perhaps less efficient decisionmaking than that provided by the styles enumerated previously.

Local initiative, central ratification. This approach moves further in the direction of the diocese merely ratifying local decisionmaking. The diocese does not require all schools to plan, but it does not automatically ratify a school closing. When a parish pastor comes forward to request the bishop's approval to close a school, the diocese will then intervene to check the validity of this choice. This may involve the diocese conducting a study, alone or in consultation with the local school. The bishop may then ask whether the superintendent and/or school board concur in the request. Sometimes the local request is reversed. While this is less likely to result in a protest, since the school is kept open, there may be considerable local resentment.

Local initiative. This approach prevails in two situations. First, a religious order may peremptorily decide to close its doors. This is an
unavoidable scenario in many dioceses, unless diocesan officials can gain a voluntary commitment from religious communities that they will consult with the diocese when they might be contemplating a closing.

Second, this highly decentralized approach exists with respect to parish school closings in some dioceses. There is no requirement that planning occur, so the diocese merely waits for local initiative.

Like the highly centralized approach, this decisionmaking style leads to great controversy. This can occur because the bishop on occasion will not approve a request for a closing, or because there is no guarantee that the local decision has involved all affected parties, in which case some are inclined to protest. Very few dioceses any longer utilize this approach, since it created so many difficulties in the late 1960s and early 1970s.

In this extremely decentralized approach, the system is perhaps the most responsive to local requests for school closings. By contrast, other decision patterns which rely on local initiative attempt to incorporate some of the efficiency assumptions of rational, democratic planning, at some sacrifice to being totally responsive to local demands. There is a clear trade-off between efficiency and responsiveness, and most dioceses have found a pattern which, while not as decentralized as it was a decade ago, still aims toward responsiveness more than efficiency. The contrast to the public schools could not be more clear.

At the same time, this institutional response has created or reinforced inadequacies which the Catholic schools must resolve. Two important ones will receive attention here.

RESPONSIVENESS AND EQUITY

It is important to ask how these closing decisions have affected Blacks, who heavily utilize inner-city Catholic schools. It is true that Catholic officials have been less enamored than their public school counterparts with seeing the closing process as technically neutral--a policy which resulted in large numbers of public school closings in inner-cities. Yet it does not follow that a policy sensitive to local concerns has uniformly favored the maintenance of predominantly Black inner-city Catholic schools. Large numbers of such elementary and high schools have closed since the 1960s.[4]

Three forces are at work, with quite different results in various cities or even in the same city at different periods. Two of these forces are negative. First, many of these schools no longer enjoy a firm base of local support, whether normative or financial. Parishes operating an inner-city school may no longer have school-age children and have lost any interest in the sacrifices required to keep the school open. The parish membership may be too small or impoverished. The pastor may have other priorities for ministry to the poor than the high costs associated with maintaining a school. Similar dynamics may impel the decisions of religious orders operating a school.

Second, Black schools have the added jeopardy that most Blacks attending them are non-Catholic. Within the Church it is debated what obligations extend to ministry toward those of another faith, who may wish to attend the school for largely secular reasons. This doctrinal issue confounds any clear treatment of racial equity, for one's view on one matter is not predictive of one's perspective on the other.

Weighing in favor of keeping Black schools open is the policy of many bishops, unwritten or official, to subsidize the continued existence of such schools with diocesan funds. Bishops sometimes have treated Black schools quite differently than their overall policy on school closings would dictate. The rationale for such a policy is a matter of racial equity combined with the conception of the Church as ministering to the poor, as it has historically for other groups in America. Yet there is no national policy on this matter adopted by bishops, and it remains a controversial one in some dioceses. For example, some dioceses require or encourage subsidies from more prosperous parishes. Another strategy has been to underwrite such schools for a period of time until they can develop a sounder financial and enrollment base.

The degree of central initiative taken by a bishop has been an important weathervane of the survival of these predominantly Black (sometimes Hispanic) schools. Where bishops have left the matter to local parish leadership, the chances of mortality for Black inner-city schools have been higher. This is not necessarily because local actors lack sensitivity to Black needs, but because the elements of the school's infrastructure (funding, staffing, leadership, sponsorship, patron support) are all too fragile to survive without moral and logistical support from the spiritual leader of the diocese. Thus, as one surveys the national landscape on this important matter, diocesan leadership appears to be a key element determining whether such schools will remain open.

Alternatives to Closing a School

If a decision is made to keep a school open, regardless of who makes it, the school may still close eventually. Only a limited number of options are available for rescuing an ailing school. None of these are easily accomplished, especially by inner-city Black schools.

One approach is to try to find additional students by changing the school's target population or better publicizing the school. For schools with neighborhood or regional identities, it is difficult to find a large new population. Drawing on a larger service area or creating a special emphasis usually requires greatly improving the image of a school; if they are to travel any distance to a new school, students and parents must be convinced that there is something special about it.

Another approach is to improve the funding base of the school through new nontuition revenues or cost savings. For example, a sophisticated development program can help, but officials must be able to sell donors on the worth of the school.

Alternatively, two or more schools may consolidate. This approach was originally intended by diocesan officials to reduce the cost of closing schools. Two parishes join forces to operate a school, so in theory the parish whose school is closed loses little. In some places, consolidations have worked well, but in roughly half the situations I studied (and in over half the dioceses) consolidations led to new conflicts. These revolved around ownership. Conflicts sometimes occur between pastors over who is responsible for hiring, budgeting, and other policy setting and administrative matters. The parish which no longer has the facility located in its environs may lose a sense of commitment. Arguments arise over the portion of revenues to be borne by each parish, particularly as enrollments shift. In certain cases, this has led to discontinuation of the consolidation.

Some dioceses have found ways of mitigating this difficulty. Formal agreements are codified in writing so that they serve as a record of initial understandings. When new priests are selected for a parish by the diocese, they are asked about their commitment to the consolidation arrangement. Other dioceses have placed greater emphasis on voluntary consolidations, arguing that arrangements posed by the diocese fell apart. As an alternative, some dioceses have begun to look at regional arrangements, with schools limited to particular grades and serving specific geographic boundaries.

In short, none of the alternatives to closing a school are easy paths. The decision to try to keep a school open will not always result in its long-term survival. Inner-city schools are especially vulnerable because they have limited capacity to utilize these options. If the school has opened its doors to large numbers of poor Blacks, it is a reality that drawing back a middle-class clientele--Black or White--is difficult. Both class and racial attitudes interfere. Cutback management seldom yields many dividends because such schools usually are run on a shoestring already. Financial development is difficult because potential donors view the risks of helping such schools as very high.

CONCLUSION

These findings suggest that Catholic school officials, in confronting the problem of declining schools, have been sensitive to local community needs. In recent years at least, they have valued responsiveness over efficiency as a legitimating principle in addressing this problem. At the same time, this responsiveness has not prevented sizeable numbers of inner-city schools serving Blacks and other minorities from closing their doors. Only special treatment by bishops has kept many of these schools open, and without a national policy by the Catholic Church, the schools face an uncertain future.

Why is access to Catholic schooling important for Blacks and other minorities? First, the principle that parents shall not be compelled to have their children attend a public school has been well established since the landmark Supreme Court decisions in Pierce vs. Society of Sisters (1925) and State of Wisconsin vs. Yoder (1972). There is not, of course, any comparable requirement that freedom from compulsion to attend public schools will guarantee equal access to private schools for various racial groups or socioeconomic classes. Indeed, the strong historical barriers to public support for private schools virtually guarantee that equality of access shall not be equally distributed among economic groups in America. Because Black Americans as a group are disproportionately poor, particularly those residing in inner-cities, they have unequal access to private schools. Tuition costs act as an important barrier for low-income parents.[5]

Equality of access is limited in other ways besides the funding structure. It is here that the issue of school closings becomes a critical component. Obviously, seats must be available; where demand exceeds supply it is likely that poor Blacks will be underrepresented. Admissions and expulsion policies tend to become more selective under such conditions.

Equally important, closing inner-city schools creates inequality in the geographic distribution of available seats. Low-income parents in the inner-city are less likely than middle-class parents to have transportation to reach distant Catholic schools, except in the unusual cases where it is provided by the Catholic school or publicly subsidized.[6]

Of course, equal access to private schools for Blacks and other minorities could be improved through public policy initiatives. If constructed with the goal of equalizing access, public subsidies in the form of tax credits or vouchers could make it easier for low-income parents to send their children to private schools. The merits of these proposals have been hotly debated, yet their political liabilities appear so formidable as to render them moot in the foreseeable future.

Without a public policy which seeks to improve equality of educational opportunity by improving access to private schools, the issue of equal access becomes an organizational and managerial problem for private school officials. Whether to permit further closings of inner-city schools is a central part of the challenge for Catholic school officials. The debate over closings of public schools has all but disappeared because of rising birth rates. The Catholic school sector, too, can be expected to gain enrollment for this reason. Yet the special financial and doctrinal issues pertaining to predominantly Black inner-city schools serving large numbers of non-Catholics will not be resolved so easily or quickly. To be sure, Catholic school officials have avoided large-scale school closings; they have not operated according to strict proprietary, market principles. In the marketplace we expect equity issues to be sacrificed to efficiency demands. Nor have Catholic officials succumbed to the bureaucratic rigidities and efficiency assumptions frequently characterizing public-sector approaches to school closings. Between these two extremes, of market and bureaucratic responses, however, there remain many unanswered questions about the policy responses which Catholic officials will evolve.

Will they handle the challenge of survival and well-being for inner-city Catholic schools as well as they have addressed the school closing problem overall?

NOTES

1. An excellent sourcebook for this literature, up to the point of its publication, is Ross Zerchykov, Managing Decline in School Systems: A Handbook (Boston: Institute for Responsive Education, 1983); see also two special journal issues pertaining to cutback management in public education. One issue, edited by Joenathan Dean, is in Education and Urban Society 15, no. 2 (February 1983): 147-264; the other edited by Michael Berger, is in Peabody Journal of Education 60, no. 2 (Winter 1983): 1-119.

2. A related doctrinal issue also arose: could schools staffed primarily by laypersons carry out their Catholic mission? This issue was less one of resources than perceived quality.

3. This process of "development" is discussed in R. J. Burke, Understanding and Implementing Development (Washington, D. C.: National Catholic Educational Association, 1984).

4. No exact figures are available because racial enrollment data are not uniformly available for the entire period since 1967. Also, dioceses do not define inner-city schools in any uniform manner.

5. These costs can, however, be partially offset by an institutional policy of offering scholarships to needy individuals. The offset is only partial because some low-income patrons will still be discouraged from applying because of a school's reputation for exclusiveness, whether accurate or not, or due to an unwillingness to face the possible stigma of receiving special aid. Of course, middle-class parents hardly are free of pricing barriers in realizing their private schooling preferences for their children. However, the tuition pricing system tends to be more sensitive to them than to low-income parents' preference schedules. This is because tuition will not rise above what most targeted consumers can pay, because officials fear losing clients. By the same token, tuition will not fall to the point which most low-income consumers can afford because this equilibrium point would be below the cost of supplying the service.

6. Wisconsin and some other states provide such transportation under certain conditions.

Summary and Discussion
Thomas B. Hoffer

The chapters included in this section touch on a number of important issues both for Catholic school governance and for public policy toward Catholic schools. Rather than summarize and critique the findings of the separate chapters point by point, I believe it is more useful to set forth some unifying themes that cut across the chapters and to indicate where our knowledge stands and how it might be improved.

From a public policy standpoint, Blacks in Catholic schools represent a phenomenon worthy of detailed scrutiny for at least two reasons. On the one hand, there is the long-contested issue of public aid to private schools, the outcome of which hinges in part on comparisons of educational opportunities and outcomes in public and private schools. On the other hand, related to the issue of public support, is the problem of how to improve the education of Black Americans in general, whether in public or private schools.

How do Blacks fare in Catholic schools? Previous research, particularly that using the ongoing High School and Beyond survey, has found that Blacks realize substantial advantages in their rates of high school graduation, academic achievement growth, and subsequent college attendance from attending Catholic as compared to public high schools. These findings are based on extensive statistical controls for family background differences and earlier (sophomore year) levels of achievement.[1] Within the Catholic sector, the recent research effort by the National Catholic Education Association has shown that Blacks are generally well-integrated into the Catholic schools they attend. As Mary Barnds has shown in chapter 9, racial differences in homework, coursework, and program enrollment are quite small in the Catholic schools. Blacks do show lower levels of high school completion and academic achievement than Whites in Catholic schools, but the racial gaps are smaller than in the public schools.

Finding positive effects for a type of school attended, while important, is from a practical point of view only a point of departure. What is needed is an understanding of how the school effects are generated, and whether and how the key mechanisms can be applied to settings where they currently do not exist. The research record on this score, unfortunately, is quite deficient. One line that has been pursued with some success is to try to identify differences in the academic and disciplinary demands of public and Catholic schools, differences which could account for the higher achievement of Blacks in the Catholic schools. Research along this line has found that Blacks in Catholic schools do indeed complete more homework, are more likely to be in an academic program of studies, and are less prone to absenteeism and class-cutting than their public school counterparts with comparable family backgrounds. These differences, particularly in the area of academic demands, account for much of the Catholic schools' greater effectiveness in promoting academic achievement among Blacks.[2]

While suggestive, these findings are less than satisfying in two key respects. On the one hand, the explanatory variables lack the degree of specificity needed to guide instructional and administrative practice. Not all kinds of homework and coursework within nominally "academic" programs are equally beneficial. Curriculum specialists are well aware of the range of variability in the ways in which the content of nominally identical courses are conducted, but this body of knowledge has not yet worked its way into sociological discourse on schools.

But even with greater specificity of these explanatory variables, this line of explanation would still be deficient in another important respect. The problem is that the question of why public and Catholic schools differ in their academic demands and disciplinary standards remains largely unaddressed. One approach to this question that has gained attention recently is to examine the relationships between schools and their constituencies. The problem of how to characterize these relationships is an issue addressed by three of the four chapters in this section, and one that James Coleman and I have devoted attention to as well.[3] One idea is that Catholic schools are able to make greater academic and disciplinary demands because they are more responsive to the families they serve than are the public schools. Coleman and I built this hypothesis on the observation that Catholic (and other religious schools) largely serve families that not only share a common set of beliefs about the kind of education their children should receive, but also maintain ongoing relations with one another through their church membership. These ongoing relations provide parents with both more information about their children's school experiences and a channel to transmit their preferences to school officials.

This formulation is questionable as an explanation for the success of Blacks in Catholic schools, however, since most Blacks in Catholic schools are not members of the Catholic Church. As Patricia Bauch finds in her case studies of predominantly Black high schools, Catholic religious affiliation does not seem to be a factor in the involvement of Blacks parents in the life of these schools. By actively promoting parental involvement, Catholic schools may be able to compensate for the absence of ongoing relationships among Black parents. But it must be kept in mind that most Blacks in Catholic schools are enrolled in schools where a majority of the students are members of the Catholic Church. It may very well be, then, that Blacks are able to benefit from the structure of relationships that the dominant functional community defines, even though many of the Black families are not a part of that community. If this is the case, then we should find that Catholic schools are less effective when the proportion of Catholics in the school is lower.

What we do know is that Catholic school attendance is beneficial for Black students generally. Franklin and McDonald, Bauch, and Cibulka indicate American Catholic schools have made a sincere effort to reach the Black community and facilitate its integration into the larger society. In reaching out to the Black community, the Catholic schools have not compromised their tradition of academic rigor and high expectations for student performance. By all indications, the schools have succeeded in gaining the active support of their Black students' parents and have encouraged, if not required, the parents to maintain high standards for their children. For the foreseeable future, though, the great majority of Black students will receive what education they can from the nation's public schools. Thus while the success of the Catholic schools should be given the public praise and support it has long deserved, the overriding goal of public policy toward schools must be to find ways to establish the responsiveness characterizing the Catholic schools in the public sector.

As a way of orienting research on this issue, it is useful to place the debates over public and Catholic school comparisons in a broader institutional context. Behind the issue of relative effectiveness is an ongoing concern over how to improve the effectiveness of American education as a whole. Indeed, the debate over public aid to private schools occasionally assumes the form of a debate over the pros and cons of a "market solution" to this larger problem. While the introduction of greater choice into American education has much to recommend it, particularly for minority groups which have historically been denied choice, the problem of who will take responsibility for effectively delivering education services remains. In the public schools, the dominant response to pressures to improve outcomes has been to implement greater bureaucratic control over schools and teachers. In recent years we have witnessed a tremendous growth in system-wide standardized testing and assessment along with centrally determined performance standards for students and teachers. This movement may well be strongest in the nation's urban school districts, where most Blacks are enrolled. Despite their intention of providing greater accountability to the public, these procedures have a decided tendency to move decisionmaking over classroom conduct away from teachers, and serve to undermine teacher-student and parent-school relationships by introducing standardized evaluation and intervention techniques. Whether by virtue of financial constraint or educational philosophy, Catholic schools incorporate far less bureaucratic administration and show a correspondingly higher degree of local autonomy and teacher control over their classrooms. But if the opportunity is greater in the Catholic schools for teachers to work as subject-matter specialists with professional authority, these advantages are offset by certain disadvantages. Catholic schools face pressures for public accountability no less than public schools. But while accountability has led to standardization and bureaucratization in the public sector, it is more likely to lead to "public relations"--accentuating the positive and ignoring the negative--in the private sector. Neither response, it seems, makes much of a contribution to the education of children. Future research comparing public and Catholic schools would be well-directed to examine ways of combining the virtues of each system into new models of school organization that move control to the local school and teachers within the school, while at the same time providing for real accountability to the families of students.

NOTES

1. James S. Coleman and Thomas Hoffer, <u>Public and Private High Schools</u> (New York: Basic Books, 1987); Thomas Hoffer, Andrew M. Greeley, and James S. Coleman, "Achievement Growth in Public and Catholic Schools," <u>Sociology of Education</u> (April 1985): 74-97.

2. Thomas B. Hoffer, "Educational Outcomes in Public and Private High Schools." (Ph.D. dissertation, University of Chicago, 1986).

3. Coleman and Hoffer, <u>Public and Private High Schools.</u>

Part 3
Independent Schools for
Black Children

From the perspective of Black parents, independent Black schools offer many of the same advantages to Black families and children as do mixed-race private schools. Whether segregated school settings are an advantage or disadvantage depends upon the goals of individual parents, the needs of the children, and the type of school. In these alternative independent neighborhood schools, children are exposed to quality educational environments, often enriched environments, small class sizes, and access to many resources, including extracurricular activities. The authors of chapters in this section argue that Black independent educational institutions offer the added advantage of a cultural context which is particularly helpful and nurturing to developing Black children. They also argue that there is much diversity in the nature of cultural contexts among schools, and that the importance of these contexts to the motivations and achievements of Black children appears undeniable. Finally, the schools provide a model for reform of public education.

In chapter 12, Lomotey and Brookins discuss the Black educational model provided over the past fifteen years by the Council of Independent Black Institutions (CIBI). According to Lomotey, CIBI schools have students who consistently score one to three years ahead of their peers in public schools on standardized achievement tests. The authors argue that CIBI students have stronger self-concepts and a greater sense of responsibility to their family, community, and race. They also argue that even if the majority of Black children attend public schools, this model is important because it points to Black self-determination with respect to education and can serve as a source of inspiration to public schools. Brookin's findings as a result of an exploratory study of ten independent Black urban schools, all of which were members of CIBI, are presented. Two-day site visits were conducted at each school in an effort to determine each school's philosophical, ideological, organizational, and curricular characteristics. The data were content-analyzed; implications for the education of the attending Black children are considered.

In chapter 13, Ratteray and Shujaa offer an important perspective on parental choice through a detailed discussion of the concerns and academic expectations of some Black families who have a tradition of sending their children to independent neighborhood schools. We are therefore reminded that not all families whose children attend these independent neighborhood schools are first-generation members of such school communities. The respective roles of religion and culture in the schools are primarily viewed as strategies Black parents ultimately pursue to fulfill their educational goals for their children. The religious and cultural contexts of these schools contribute critically to the nurturing environments in which the Black children learn.

12
Independent Black Institutions:
A Cultural Perspective
Kofi Lomotey and Craig C. Brookins

The American public school is in a rapidly increasing state of deterioration.[1] Many studies have been done recently and many reports have come out speaking about the condition of the public school in terms of the academic achievement of all students.[2] Also, fewer people are now going into the teaching profession and, partly as a result of this, the quality of teaching is deteriorating across the country in all communities. In addition, several reports have shown that the education of students in America compares unfavorably with that received by students in some other developed countries.[3] To say that the situation in terms of public education is critical should not be surprising to anyone.

This situation does not have a tremendous impact on the quality of education afforded African American children. Historically, the education of African Americans has always been poor. This is not only true in academics, but in terms of cultural and social development. African American students have, on the whole, historically performed significantly below the norm within the public school system.[4]

The high school dropout rate for African Americans is abominable. In New York City it exceeds 70 percent for males and some believe that it approaches that same figure for African American males nationally.[5] In California, for males and females, it exceeds 40 percent.[6] In East Palo Alto, California, it was reported in 1983 that nine out of ten African American students dropped out of high school before graduation.[7]

We can look at the achievement gap that exists between African American and Caucasian students nationally. At the sixth grade level, this gap was between two and three years in reading, writing, and arithmetic in 1986. Moreover, these statistics appear to represent a trend that continues.

The point is that poor-quality education, in terms of basic skills acquisition, is not a new situation for African Americans. The deterioration of the entire system is new, but inadequate education for children of African ancestry is something that has been going on since it became legal to educate African American children. Despite virtuous aims and copious oratory with regard to educational equality and equal opportunity, African American children have failed, for the most part, in the public school system.

It is important to point out that it is possible to educate African American children effectively. Since the early 1970s there has been a significant body of research--the effective schools research--that looks at public schools where African American children have been educated effectively.[8] One of the leading researchers in this area was Ron Edmonds, who, before his untimely death, had done a significant amount of research primarily in the Midwest and on the East Coast looking at schools that had been providing effective education for African American children.[9] That research is continuing. Models of effective education for African American children are being looked at across the country. The reality is that these models are a very small exception and not the rule. Another model exists also--the independent Black educational institution (IBI), which is the model discussed in this chapter.

In an effort to define and better understand some of the IBIs in existence, one of the authors conducted an exploratory study of ten IBIs in the midwestern and eastern portions of the United States.[10] This study focused on the philosophy and ideology, pedagogy, and academic rigor of these schools and provided a description of how these areas are operationalized in the schools. The findings of the study are cited throughout the subsequent discussion.

THE PURPOSE OF EDUCATION

Others have adequately discussed elsewhere universal goals for an individual's education. Such goals include the development of creativity, an inquiring mind, and the ability to learn from experience.[11] We will focus here on the functions that education serves for society--as the understanding of these functions contributed to the birth and nurturance of IBIs. Schools in any society serve three major functions. The first is that they provide information for the students. When comparing the curriculum in a predominantly African American community versus that offered in a predominantly Caucasian community, the quantity and quality of that information varies depending upon the clientele. That is, the academic goals of students in urban school districts (where the large majority of African American students are found) are significantly lower than those found in suburban school districts (that are more often than not populated by Caucasian students).

The second function of education is to control people. If we look in the African American community, we see that most students are being prepared to fit into blue-collar second-class employment positions where there are specific rules. They are told that if they break rules they are going to be penalized severely, i.e., be fired. That is the kind of education that most African American children receive for the most part in their communities, an education which pigeonholes individuals into certain often predetermined options in the larger society.[12]

The third function of any educational system is to instill values or a cultural frame of reference. Particularly in America, this function is second nature to us. People do not think twice about the fact that within the American educational system we are being immersed within the White Anglo-Saxon Protestant Male (WASPM) value system. The reason people do not think about it is because institutions throughout the entire society behave similarly. The mass media, churches, and social institutions throughout American society foster this WASPM value system. Not surprisingly, it is the predominant value system in society, and in every society the predominant value system is the one that is emphasized in the various institutions. Rarely does the emphasis on a WASPM value system arise in talks about educational institutions in this society.

In summary, these are the three primary societal functions of educational institutions--sharing information, controlling people, and imparting values or a cultural frame of reference.

HISTORICAL OVERVIEW OF THE IBI

African American people have had their own independent Black institutions for at least two centuries. Quality education has always been, contrary to popular belief, a primary concern and interest of African American people.[13] As early as the eighteenth century, African Americans began developing their own schools. One of the earliest schools was the African Free School that operated in New York City in the late eighteenth century.[14]

More recently there have been a number of schools, some that the reader may be familiar with--Afrikan People's Action School in Trenton, New Jersey, New Concept Development Center in Chicago Illinois, Omowale Ujamaa in Pasadena, California, and Shule Ya Taifa in East Palo Alto, California. All of these schools, for the most part, are small--with enrollments between fifty and 200 students. These schools have been developed by African American people, usually with funding from within the African American community, to provide not only an academic education for African American children but to provide a cultural frame of reference that has particular relevance to the students in the schools.

We differentiate between the traditional African American private school and the IBI by focusing on the emphasis in the IBI on dealing with African American culture as the basis of the curriculum.

The current proliferation of IBIs began about twenty years ago, in part as a consequence of community control concerns primarily on the East Coast, where parents were attempting to have some say within the public school system and were not being successful.[15] Parents made the decision that they had to go out and begin their own schools in their own communities. That is how Uhuru Sasa Shule in New York developed--in part, as a result of the Oceanhill-Brownsville community control movement.[16]

In addition to being relatively small, most of the schools are preschool and early elementary, although there are some IBIs that are middle schools and high schools. In fact, there were two institutions of higher education; there was Malcolm X College in Greensboro, North Carolina, and Nairobi College in East Palo Alto, California. Both of these institutions closed after being in existence for less than ten years.

THE ACADEMIC PROGRAM OF THE IBI

With regard to the academic experience in the IBI, Brookins found that the emphasis is on providing the child with a superior education in terms of emphasizing high achievement and basing the curriculum on academic content beyond the "basics" (standardized objectives) of the public school systems.

Many of these schools administer standardized achievement tests. This is done for several reasons. One reason is that they want parents to be aware of how their children compare on a national level with children who are in public schools or other private schools. Another reason is because they want to know how the children are progressing academically over the course of the year (in most IBIs, exams are administered twice a year). A third reason is that they want to be equipped with data to demonstrate that African American people can educate their own children effectively.

When IBIs administer standardized achievement tests, for the most part their students perform anywhere from one to three years ahead of their peers in public schools.[17] Contrary to the belief that has been predominant in the African American community--that African American people cannot provide services for themselves as well as other people can--IBIs provide quality education.

One of the authors has worked in East Palo Alto in Shule Ya Taifa, an IBI that has been operating since 1980, serving children between the ages of three and ten. Each year they administer the CAT test and, invariably, children who have been in the school for one or more years score at least one year above grade level in reading, spelling, and mathematics.[18] The same is true with IBIs in other parts of the country. Whenever these children go into public or other private institutions, usually at either the fourth, sixth, or ninth grades, invariably these children are placed ahead of their peers by age or are placed in accelerated classrooms because of their superior academic work within the IBI.

Brookins's findings are consistent with this observation in that his research indicates that students from IBIs enter more traditional school systems better prepared than the average student because of their high academic competence and exposure to a wider variety of educational content.

An understanding of the political component in the IBI curriculum is crucial in order to fully appreciate the nature of the academic program. Brookins notes that through the political experience, the IBI provides the child with a realistic and analytical understanding of world events. Political education is interwoven within all the lesson plans and subject areas that are taught, including math and science. Again, the emphasis is on the African experience and how world events affect African people. In general, it is the schools' belief that no events occur outside of a political context and that this realization will assist the child in making appropriate life decisions in the future.

Teachers

Teachers are considered the most important component within each of the schools' educational philosophies. All of the academic, social, and cultural knowledge and information is filtered through the teachers. In Brookins's study, several teachers expressed the belief that any person is capable of teaching African American children if they are enthusiastic and willing to learn and share the school's philosophy. However, the philosophies of the schools dictated that an African American teacher is most capable of transmitting culture and properly socializing the child.

A difference was observed in the self-motivational characteristics of the teachers within the different schools studied by Brookins. Most of the teachers tended to be naturally motivated in the sense that their lifestyles very closely corresponded with the ideals of the program. Although the academic training of the child was important, their pedagogical emphasis was more culturally oriented.

Other teachers tended to be more academically oriented and the cultural motivation came as a result of the training and education received through the school.

Pedagogy

The various teaching approaches found by Brookins included (1) multilevel groupings of students that gave the younger students the opportunity to interact and be assisted by the older students, (2) early academic exposure for preschool and early primary-grade children, (3) small teacher/student ratios, and (4) a formalized teacher training program that emphasized the cultural and political aspects of the teaching process.

In an attempt to develop and implement new and innovative means of educating African American children, a few of the schools have very extensively developed frameworks for the teaching/and learning process, such as a variation on open-space environments and an approach based on a traditional East African method of socializing children.[19]

Several other aspects of the teaching process seen as necessary in effectively teaching African American children, regardless of the theoretical approaches used, are:

o   Content and information must be interesting and challenging to the child

o   Content must be related to the child's environment

o   Affection and love must be generously given

o   Pedagogy should consist of common sense approaches that are a combination of knowledge and experience

o   Learning must be viewed as both a positive and negative experience

o   Expression must be encouraged. This was observed in varying degrees in each school, but was generally geared toward the belief that expression leads to confidence in ability, self-control and understanding of appropriate and inappropriate behavior, and active and natural learning

Perhaps the most significant and frequently mentioned aspect of the teaching process concerned the need for the expression of love and caring. This was seen as an essential part of any effort to relate to African American children. This involved frequent touching and holding, concern for the child as a human being, and a sincere concern for the child's life experiences, including their family and home life, their community, and their future.

The schools looked at by Brookins departed significantly from the typical orderly, quiet, and instructional school programs. Although the environment was instructionally oriented, a very informal analysis showed that the "time on task" spent by the students was low in many cases. Interestingly, the schools made a conscious effort to encourage student expression. This was consistent with research that suggests that African American children need an environment that takes advantage of their natural high energy level and vibrancy.[20] Also, the necessity for quiet and order may not have been applicable to such small school environments in which a low student/teacher ratio generally led to a more manageable classroom situation, reflected by less confusion and more order.

SOCIAL AND CULTURAL ASPECTS OF THE IBI

While academic excellence is stressed in the IBI, social and cultural development are given comparable emphasis. Moreover, it is the focus in the IBI on the development of a positive self-concept for African American children that, perhaps more than any other characteristic, has for many years distinguished the IBI from the public school in America.

The social and cultural development of children in IBIs has also been a success. Brookins found that, through the provision of a cultural experience, the IBI attempts to expose children to the values, history, and cultural aspects of their heritage through purposeful and explicit methods. The goal of the schools is to help the children understand their heritage in an intrinsic and nonsuperficial manner. Many of the schools are structured to reflect the society and the individuals within that society that they are trying to create; that is, they focus on the development of the "new" African man and woman. This "newness" or "uniqueness" is of crucial importance in understanding the IBI. The schools represent an attempt to present a solution for the disillusionment presently found in many African American communities.[21]

For the most part, students within the IBI are very disciplined. There is a focus on self-discipline within these schools. Since self-discipline does not always work with young children, sometimes discipline has to be externally imposed. However, these children are, for the most part, very well disciplined and respectful of themselves, their peers, their parents, and of other adults within the community.

In Brookins' study, the type of discipline problems most frequently reported had to do with issues related to the students' respect for themselves and others, including: talking back to teachers, gestures toward the teacher and peers, playing in the classroom, and running through the school. Cursing and fighting were occasionally reported, but not by most schools.

In general, discipline problems were reported to be minor. According to the teachers and administrators, the most effective method of maintaining an orderly and disciplined atmosphere is to create a positive and well-structured classroom environment. This involves classroom management techniques in which the teacher plans activities that correspond to the attention span, interests, needs, and abilities of the students. Rules must be explicit and rewards consistent.   Teachers must effectively maintain communication with the student, constantly discuss and identify problems, and emphasize problem solving techniques. Constant communication with other teachers and consistency among teachers was also mentioned as important.   Other factors are also responsible for effective discipline. Small class size, concerned and active parents, and the fact that most of the schools are able to put a limit upon the number of children they enroll most likely contribute to this lack of serious discipline problems.

Students in the IBI are also very determined. They are conscious of their ability to do well academically, socially, and culturally. They are not turned off to the sciences at a very young age. In fact, within the Council of Independent Black Institutions (CIBI) there is a focus on the science achievement of African American students. There is an Annual Science Exposition that takes place in April in a different part of the country each year. The children of IBIs come together to demonstrate their science achievements in a noncompetitive environment--the projects that they have been working on in the areas of science over the course of the year. As the reader might suspect, the children get very excited about this.

Children in IBIs are not turned off by education. They are not turned off by science or mathematics. They do not feel that these are areas that they cannot delve into. They feel very good about their ability to excel in those areas. In addition, these students have developed a very positive sense of themselves as African American children. They have also developed self-confidence in terms of their ability to do whatever they want to do once they grow up.

All of the schools studied by Brookins were highly intensive in their pursuit of academic goals. However, this intensity did not always extend to the social and cultural realms. The IBIs that were studied by Brookins can be categorized as being of low, moderate, or high intensity in their pursuit of social and cultural effectiveness.

The schools that were of low intensity were characterized by two or more of the following characteristics:

o   They were in a transition stage from one type of educational program to a nationalist/pan-Africanist orientation

o   They began as an alternative to public school as opposed to a consciously distinct educational model oriented specifically toward African American children

o   They provided a cultural education primarily through a historical teaching perspective

Schools that were of moderate intensity were those that:

o   Exposed children to a political and cultural education that is characteristic of a survival orientation, emphasizing development of the skills and knowledge needed by African American people to survive in the present society

o   Enrolled a substantial number of children with professional and high-income parents

The schools that were highly intense were those that:

o   Adhered strongly to a nationalist/pan-Africanist orientation

o   Strongly pursued a cultural education experience in an explicit effort to create the new African society.

This was essentially accomplished through a curriculum that strongly emphasized the behaviors, attitudes, knowledge, and values characteristic of an African personality.

THE PHILOSOPHY OF THE IBI

Revolutionary Pan-African Nationalism

In terms of the philosophy of the IBIs, the focus is on three basic components--revolutionary pan-African nationalism, the Nguzo Saba, and familyhood. Many who are involved with IBIs would not subscribe to the use of these terms to describe their organizational philosophy, but most would subscribe to the spirit of the basic definitions offered.
    Revolution has two aspects--tearing down something (psychologically or otherwise) that is not working in your interest and building up something in its place. In the case of the IBI,

African Americans have observed a system that is not operating in their interest (i.e., the public schools) and have not only condemned that system, but are building up something in its place. This is what is meant by revolutionary.[22]

Pan-Africanism is the notion that African Americans are a part of a worldwide community of African people and that we acknowledge that relationship to other African people around the world.[23]

For African Americans associated with IBIs, nationalism means the communities that they live in make up a nation and they have to strive to develop institutions within that nation--educational, political, cultural, religious, and whatever other kinds of institutions one would normally think of within a society. The schools operate on the notion that African Americans are a nation within a nation.

In the IBI philosophy, African Americans are a people who reject a system that is not working for them, develop a new one to replace it, identify with other African people around the world, and view themselves as a nation. This is the first part of the philosophy within these institutions--revolutionary pan-African nationalism.

The Nguzo Saba

One of the most important aspects of the pedagogy of the IBI is its value orientation. The value orientation focuses on the cultivation of positive and humanistic values and those directed in the best interests of African American people. This value system serves as the foundation on which the cultural system is developed. Utilizing the principles of the Nguzo Saba (Seven Principles), the schools incorporate this value education into every aspect of the school day, including recess, mealtime, and class time.

In the mid-1960s Dr. Maulana Karenga developed a doctrine called Kawaida that he felt was useful for African people in America. His view is that African Americans have been operating for too long from someone else's frame of reference and that they need to draw from their own past and current situation to develop a value system that will be of benefit to them. One component of the doctrine that Dr. Karenga developed is the Nguzo Saba, or the Seven Principles of Blackness. Within the IBI there is an attempt to instill these values within the children.

o   Umoja (unity)--There is a striving within the institutions and within the communities for unity in the family, the community, nation, and race

o   Kujichagulia (self-determination)-- The children are encouraged to speak for themselves, and name themselves, not allowing other people to do so o   Ujima (collective work and responsibility) - One of the most devastating things that has affected African Americans in this country with regard to education has been the tracking system that has been in place ever since it became legal to educate African American children. Within IBIs, children are encouraged to work together to enable each of them to develop their skills so that tracking does not become significant. All of the children are working toward a collective good. Children are encouraged to work together in terms of their other responsibilities around the school, such as cleaning up

o   Ujamaa (cooperative economics)--Children are encouraged to do what they can to help each other economically in terms of the development of businesses and whatever other kinds of economic ventures they may be involved in

o   Nia (Purpose)--People within these institutions do everything that they do with a reason behind it, rather than not thinking about why they are doing it

o   Kuumba (creativity)--They strive to do all that they can in the most creative way that they can within the institutions and communities

o   Imani (faith)--Children are encouraged to have faith in what they are doing, in their people, in their teachers, and in their own communities

Brookins found that in the schools he studied, formal and informal methods are used to transmit these cultural values to students. The formal methods were those that were directly structured into the school program. These methods are usually written into the school policy or curriculum guidelines. They included the celebration of special African and African American holidays, field trips and community events, certain rituals and protocols (school songs and pledges), dress codes requiring African attire, and African cultural and historical materials incorporated into the curriculum.

The informal methods are those that teachers use to supplement the formal methods. These include the use of African proverbs and stories, writing African American and African stories and book reports, and structuring classroom activities to encourage cooperation, sharing, and writing. The schools also rely upon the teachers to act as role models for the students by personally practicing the values being taught. These seven values provide the second part of the cultural basis that is fostered within these institutions.

Familyhood

The notion of family institutions is equally important. The family orientation and the open expression of love and caring contribute to the schools' ability to maintain their effectiveness. Such an environment allows students to feel comfortable, secure, and, most importantly, seems to create a sense of continuity between the child's home and the school.

Historically, African American parents in this country have been told that they do not have a say in what goes on in schools. They have been told that the administrators and teachers are the primary decisionmakers in the school. As a result, many African American parents are reluctant to raise questions about their children's education. That reluctance develops as a result of administrators' attitudes, but it is also based upon the fact that many African American parents had negative experiences in the schools when they themselves were students. As a result, they do not really have a desire to be involved in what is going on in the schools. They expect that once they send their children there, they will be taken care of by the administrators and teachers.

In IBIs, parents are encouraged to be involved on all levels with whatever is going on. Parents are told initially when they first express an interest in the schools that they have not only a right but a responsibility to be involved in their children's education. Parents are, in fact, the primary educators of their children. They merely delegate that responsibility to schools on a temporary basis. They still have the major responsibility for what is going on with their children. Parents are encouraged to understand this perspective at all times. In IBIs, parents are involved as teachers, teacher aides, and helpers administratively, on field trips, and in curriculum development. Certainly the situation is not an ideal one, but if parents enter into a situation with a different attitude about what parents' roles are, the situation is going to be different than it would be in a traditional public school setting. So parents are involved within these schools on a regular basis.[24]

The philosophy and ideology of the IBIs studied by Brookins were not absolutely identical, yet several commonalities were identified. These are:

o   An emphasis on high or superior academic achievement

o   An emphasis on the transmission of culture (and in some cases cultural development)

o   Developing a sense of commitment to African and African American people o   Teaching self-determination, including the necessity for the schools themselves to be independent

o   Basing an educational process on distinct and explicit values

o   Developing a strong African American identity and self-concept

o   The belief that African American people are an African people with a common ancestry, a common condition or experience, and a common destiny

o   Providing political education through an understanding of current and historical events and how they relate to African and African American people

o   Development of a lifestyle based on humanistic values

The desired outcomes as expressed by the staff of the schools were:

o   A strong sense of oneself as an African American child--including a positive self-concept, identity, and attitudes, a strong cultural identity, and an appreciation of one's heritage

o   Confidence in one's ability, comfortable in any environment, and not easily influenced

o   Academic competence--students are expected to achieve at grade level or above and possess good study habits; reading ability is particularly emphasized

o   The ability to think analytically, critically, and independently; students should learn problem-solving skills

o   An understanding of the Nguzo Saba and the ability to make value decisions based on its principles

o   A commitment to African and African American people throughout the world

o   Disciplined and self-determined attitudes and behavior

o   An awareness of political issues and current events, particularly as they relate to African Americans

o   Strong historical knowledge

o   Social and emotional competence regarding the importance of people and the ability to effectively communicate and relate to all people

o   Understanding of the needs and purposes of education

o   Recognition of the importance of family and familial relationships

o   Possession of the urge to create and institute change in society

Although the intensity level varied, the philosophical and ideological orientation suggested above was present, to some degree, in each school.

ADMINISTRATION OF THE IBI

Governance

There are basically three levels of governance at IBIs. Most IBIs have a board of directors composed generally of individuals who support the goals and objectives of the schools and who have services or goods that they can provide to help develop the school. Additionally, parents have a say in how the schools are run. Most schools have a functioning parent organization that is involved in all aspects of operating the school. Most also have a director who reports directly to the board and deals with the responsibilities of the day-to-day operation of the school.

Parent Involvement

Parental involvement with IBIs as a result of their children being in our schools or as a result of parents themselves being educated and wanting to be involved in what we are doing, has also been a tremendous success. Parents, once involved in the school, generally maintain that involvement over a long period of time, in large part because of the fact that the children do well academically. Some parents are also impressed with the fact that there is a different cultural reference being emphasized--an African American frame of reference--one that is relevant to their children and to their families.

CONCLUSION

The Importance of the IBI

The IBI is an important model within the African American community for several reasons. First, it is a demonstration that African American people can effectively educate their own children. That is important because African Americans have looked to others to provide education within their community and need to know that that is not necessary. Most African Americans do not believe that they can effectively educate their own children.[25]

Second, IBIs provide inspiration for committed parents and teachers who are involved in the public school. Within the IBI movement it is understood that the IBI is not the answer. In fact, we realize that education is not the entire answer. It is only a part of the answer. The IBI is not going to be the answer even in the area of education, because it is understood that for a long time to come the large majority of African American children will be in the public schools. Over 90 percent of African American children are going to be in the public schools for a long time.[26]

Praise goes to those African American teachers and other committed teachers who are in the public schools trying to do something effectively for African American children. The IBI model is an inspiration for them in terms of what can be done in a positive environment with African American children--academically, socially, and culturally.

Third, it is felt that the IBI is a valuable model in terms of institutional development within the African American community. We focus on that because in any society, community, or nation, there is a need to develop institutions--all kinds of institutions--in order to foster the culture of the people.[27] Educational and other institutions foster the culture of the people in control.

There is a need for African Americans to foster the development of their own institutions in order to perpetuate their own culture and fulfill other responsibilities that institutions undertake. It is especially important because it is very clear (particularly looking at education) that one cannot expect one's oppressor to facilitate the liberating process.[28] America is not about to develop educational institutions or any other institutions that will bring about freedom, justice, and equality for people of African ancestry. If African Americans are concerned about that happening, they have to provide the models themselves, both within the IBI movement and the public schools. The reality is that the status quo is not working, and has never worked in the interest of African American people. There needs to be radical alteration and, in some cases, replacement of the institutions in American society.

The IBI is important also because it is a demonstration that African American people can finance their own institutions. The large majority of these schools survive primarily as a result of tuition payments, which provide 80-90 percent of the budgets of these schools. The reason for this is clear. IBIs could, of course, receive federal, state, or local government funding, or they could receive funding from corporations and foundation; but the view is that since they have rejected the system in this country, it would be contradictory to seek funding from people who are supporting and perpetuating that same system. Generally, when you receive funding from someone, they attempt to control (at least in part) what you are trying to do. This has been observed in other schools, and the view is that in order for IBIs to maintain the values that have been established initially in setting up the schools, there is a need to get the "front money" for the schools from within African American communities. That has, of course, created problems for these schools, but they have been, for the most part, very firm with this aspect of the philosophy regarding outside funding.

These schools are also seen as training grounds for tomorrow's leaders in the African American community. The students are being trained to bring their skills back into the African American community. That is not to say that they cannot go to work for the large national or multinational corporation--it just means that some part of their time and/or money needs to be devoted to the development of the African American community. If you study other racial/cultural groups in this society, you see that this is not an unusual notion. Other people train their children to be committed to developing their own community. The current education of African American children is not achieving this aim for the African American community.[29] Instilling African American culture and values is also a key factor in terms of the development of IBIs.

Summary

There is a need to believe that all African American children can learn, because they can. For so long, African Americans have been instilled with the notion that they do not have the cranial capacity that Caucasian people have--that they do not have the ability to learn as much as White people can.[30] Surprisingly, views such as these are still being fostered within schools of education. African American and Caucasian educators are being told, day in and day out, in subtle and sometimes not so subtle ways, that African Americans are not able to do all that other people can do academically. One sees African American children being labeled at a very young age as slow learners. One sees African American children in African American communities being retained in kindergarten en masse.

We are familiar with a school in an African American community where an entire class--32 students--was retained in kindergarten. While many educators say that some students are not socially prepared to deal with kindergarten and need to repeat it, our view on that is very clear. Anytime a child cannot reach the minimal goals that are required of them in kindergarten, it is a reflection on the school, not the child.

Invariably, when African American children are labeled slow learners and educably mentally retarded, those labels are indicative of the situation in the school. It is a result of the lack of cultural relevance of the curriculum, the lack of motivation on the part of the student as a result of that lack of cultural relevance, and the view of educators that these children cannot learn. Invariably, if a teacher does not believe that a child can learn, the child is not going to learn because that belief is going to have an impact on the way that the teacher teaches.[31] Educators, African American and Caucasian, need to believe that African American children can learn, because all of them can.

Moreover, those who are involved in teaching should teach African American children from an African American perspective. For example, when teaching the concept of one plus one, one should focus on physical things that come from the African American community. Teaching one plus one and using the example of two cars in the driveway is not something to which most African American children can relate. The referents need to be relevant to their lives. There have been many studies done that have shown that children do better if their culture is the focus that the currriculum emanates from.[32] It is important to understand that African American children will only do well in general (certainly some of them will always do well) if the curriculum that they are exposed to emanates from their culture.

The number of IBIs is increasing. Inquiries are received at CIBI on a regular basis from people who are either interested in starting IBIs or who have started IBIs and need to get information about curriculum development, teacher training, or other topics.

Since CIBI began in 1972, it has been offering an annual Teacher Training Institute (TTI) that takes place at Kent State University in Kent, Ohio. Not only are teachers from IBIs involved in these TTIs, but public school teachers also. Theoretically, the goals of both groups are the same in terms of providing quality education for African American children. People in CIBI do not see themselves as being separate from African American teachers within the public school system. They come together often, locally and nationally, to talk about ways to improve the quality of the education that African American children receive, wherever they may be.

Finally, at some point the scope of the IBI must move beyond the education of the young. It must extend its efforts to the parents and surrounding community with the objective of affecting the values, standards, and goals of all who come in contact with it. A key objective is to create a physical and intellectual arena that allows for the full development of the abilities of its clients while it diminishes the impact of institutionalized White racism.

The ultimate objective is the creation of permanent African American institutions, families, and individuals whose priorities and energies ensure the achievement of the goals of independence, self-determination, and dignity for African Americans and Africans the world over.

NOTES

1. See National Commission on Excellence in Education, <u>A Nation at Risk: The Imperative for Educational Reform. A Report to the Nation and the Secretary of Education</u> (Washington, D.C.: Government Printing Office, 1983).

2. National Science Foundation, "Educating Americans for the 21st Century: A Plan of Action for Improving Mathematics, Science and Technology Education for all American Elementary and Secondary Students so that Their Achievement is the Best in the World by 1995." A Report to the American People and the National Science Board (Washington, D. C.: National Science Foundation, 1983).

3. National Academy of Sciences, "The Underachieving Curriculum: Assessing U.S. School Mathematics from an International Perspective" (Washington, D. C.: Government Printing Office, 1987).

4. See, for example, James Coleman et al., <u>Equality of Educational Opportunity</u> (Washington, D. C.: Government Printing Office, 1966); Lawrence Marcus and Benjamin Stickney, <u>Race and Education: The Unending Controversy</u> (Springfield, Ill.: Charles C. Thomas, 1981); Sol Adler, ed., <u>Cultural Language Differences</u> (Springfield, Ill.: Charles C. Thomas, 1984).

5. "Future of Young Black Men Looks Bleak, Panelists Say," <u>New York Times,</u> May 19, 1985, sec. 1, p. 34; "Challenge To Teachers: Reduce Dropout Rate," <u>National Black Teachers Network</u> 1, no. 3 (undated): 1.

6. Reginald Wilson and Sarah E. Melendez, eds., 1985. Fourth
    Annual Status Report on Minorities in Higher Education, 1985,
    Office of Minority Concerns (Washington, D. C.: American
    Council on Education, 1985).

7. Peninsula Times Tribune, April 18, 1983.

8. See, for example, George Weber, Inner City Children Can Be
    Taught to Read: Four Successful Schools (Washington,
    D. C.:   Council for Basic Education, 1971);   Richard
    Veneskzy and Linda Winfield, "Schools that Succeed beyond
    Expectations in Teaching Reading" (Newark, Del. University
    of Delaware Studies on Education, Technical Report #1, 1980);
    Kofi Lomotey, "Black Principals for Black Students," Urban
    Education, 22 (July 1987): 173-181.

9. Ron Edmonds, "Effective Schools for the Urban Poor,"
    Educational Leadership 37 (October 1979):   15-24. It is
    important to emphasize that here we are referring specifically to
    academic excellence, since this is the effectiveness criteria
    relied upon consistently in the literature. As we move into the
    discussion of the independent school, an increased emphasis
    is placed on social development, including self-concept
    and cultural development.

10. Craig C. Brookins,"A Descriptive Analysis of Ten Independent
    Black Educational Models" (M. A. thesis, Michigan State
    University, Department of Psychology, 1984).

11. Julius Nyerere, Education for Self-Reliance (New York:
    Uhuru Sasa School, Inc., 1973).

12. Samuel Bowles and Herbert Gintis, Schooling in Capitalist
    America: Educational Reform and the Contradictions of
    Economic Life (New York: Basic Books, 1976); Bob
    Suzuki,"Education and the Socialization of Asian Americans:
    A Revisionist Analysis of the 'Model Minority' Thesis,"
    Amerasia 42 (1977): 23-51.

13. Carter G. Woodson, The Miseducation of the Negro
    (Washington, D.C.: Associated Press. 1969).

14. Mwalimu Hannibal Tirus Afrik, Education for Self Reliance,
    Idealism to Reality: An Analysis of the Independent Black
    School Movement, (Stanford: Council of Independent Black
    Institutions, 1981).

15. Ibid; Kasisi Jitu Weusi, A Message from a Black Teacher (New York: East Publications, 1973.)

16. Ibid.

17. While there is no documentation available on a national level for this assertion, one of the authors, Lomotey, who has been involved with these schools since 1970, is personally familiar with most of these schools and has seen the test scores. Moreover, the Institute for Independent Education is in the preliminary stages of developing a report that will document this assertion. For more information on this forthcoming report, the reader should contact the Institute at P.O. Box 42571, Washington, D. C., 20015.

18. These scores are available by contacting the Shule Ya Taifa at P.O. Box 51661, East Palo Alto, Calif. 94303. Persons interested in obtaining information regarding the test scores of individual schools may contact the schools directly.

19. J. P. Ocitti, African Indigenous Education: As Practiced by the Acholi of Uganda (Nairobi: East African Literature Bureau, 1973).

20. Beverly M. Gordon, "Towards a Theory of Knowledge Acquisition for Black Children," Journal of Education 164 (1982): 90-108.

21. Amos N. Wilson, The Developmental Psychology of the Black Child (New York: Africana Research Publications, 1978).

22. Kwame Nkrumah, Consciencism (New York: Monthly Review Press, 1970).

23. Maulana Karenga, Kawaida Theory: An Introductory Outline, (Inglewood, Calif.: Kawaida Publications, 1980); Haki Madhubuti, Enemies: The Clash of Races (Chicago: Third World Press, 1978).

24. Joan Davis Ratteray and Mwalimu Shujaa, Dare To Choose: Parental Choice at Independent Neighborhood Schools (Washington, D. C.: Institute for Independent Education, 1987).

25. Madhubuti, Enemies: The Clash of Races.

26. Frank Satterwhite, ed., <u>Planning an Independent Black Educational Institution</u> (New York: Moja Publishing House, Ltd., 1971).

27. Haki Madhubuti, <u>From Plan to Planet-Life Studies: The Need for Afrikan Minds and Institutions</u> (Detroit: Broadside Press, 1974); Kofi Lomotey, <u>Nationbuilding in the Afrikan Community: It's Time to Build Solutions to the Education Problem</u> (Stanford Council of Independent Black Institutions, 1981).

28. See Nyerere, <u>Education for Self-Reliance</u>.

29. A. Babs Fafunwa, <u>New Perspectives in African Education</u> (Nigeria: Macmillan, 1967); Madhubuti, <u>From Plan to Planet-Life Studies</u>; and Lomotey, <u>Nationbuilding in the Afrikan Community</u>.

30. This view has been purported most notably by Arthur Jensen, Milton Schwebel, and William Shockley. See, for example, Milton Schwebel, <u>Who Can Be Educated</u> (New York: Group Press, 1968); Arthur Jensen, "How Much Can We Boost IQ and Scholastic Achievement?" <u>Harvard Educational Review</u> 39 (Winter 1969).

31. William Ryan, <u>Blaming the Victim</u> (New York: Pantheon Books, 1971).

32. See, for example, Janice Hale-Benson, <u>Black Children: Their Roots,Culture, and Learning Styles</u> (Baltimore: Johns Hopkins University Press, 1986) for a discussion of this topic as it relates to African American children.

13

Defining a Tradition: Parental Choice in Independent Neighborhood Schools

Joan Davis Ratteray and Mwalimu Shujaa

For over 200 years, African Americans have fought for equal access to educational institutions and opportunities. An apparent victory was achieved with the 1954 ruling of the U.S. Supreme Court in <u>Brown vs. Board of Education</u>, which declared segregation unconstitutional. The spoils, however, are proving bittersweet. The urban public schools to which many African Americans are fiercely loyal continue to be of poor quality, have inordinately high dropout rates, and consistently produce dismal academic results.

A recent study by Ratteray and Shujaa reveals that a number of African American families are withdrawing their children from public institutions. They are not sending them to "ivy league" preparatory academies, which are usually owned and operated by and for affluent European Americans. Neither do they favor the so-called "alternative schools," which are less rigorous and less competitive than traditional programs. These families have dared to choose from a growing number of independent neighborhood schools.[1]

This chapter outlines the long tradition of which contemporary independent neighborhood schools are a part, describes why parents say they choose these schools, and draws some implications for the future education of African American children.

TWO CENTURIES OF TRADITION

Some of the earliest independent schools were formed by African Americans themselves because there were few opportunities for them to receive an education. Between 1796 and 1798, members of the African Church, later known as St. Thomas African Episcopal Church, began a day school in Philadelphia.[2] Prince Hall, a Black man, Revolutionary War veteran, and the father of freemasonry among Blacks in America, started a school in Boston in 1798.[3] Other private day schools were formed in the early 1800s by Bethel A.M.E. Church, founded by Richard Allen; by John Gloucester of the First African Presbyterian Church; and by other Black individuals. The Oblate Sisters of Providence, an order of Black nuns in Baltimore, started a school in 1829 that is still operating today. The curricula at all these schools included reading, writing, computation, science, and foreign languages.

There is a strong legacy of schools in the South, too. Near the turn of the century, Tuskegee Institute was founded by Booker T. Washington. Piney Woods Country Life School in Mississippi has been nurturing Black youth since 1909, while Laurinburg Institute in North Carolina, formed in 1904, peaked at 1,500 students in the 1940s. Numerous other schools, such as the Ivy Leaf School in Philadelphia, began all across the country in the 1960s and 1970s.

Many schools closed in the mid-twentieth century, because African Americans relentlessly continued to surrender their independent options as they gained greater access to mainstream educational institutions.[4]

The history of American education unfortunately became a long chronicle of disparate treatment for Blacks. State and local funds were systematically allocated to provide unequal financial and other resources to schools serving African American youngsters.[5] Furthermore, after the U.S. Supreme Court mandated equal access, state and local governments engaged in many tactics to avoid the desegregation mandate.[6]

From the beginning, African Americans have responded differently to evidence of unequal treatment based on race. Some have measured their relationship to mainstream education in quantitative terms, while others have done so qualitatively.

The question of equal access in education is a quantitative issue. It is measured, for example, by the numbers of Black and White children that attend schools in particular jurisdictions or who can get into magnet schools.

This does not mean that the struggle to gain full and equal access to education has not included improving the quality of schooling for African Americans, but there has always been an implicit assumption that quality would improve automatically once access was achieved. However, African Americans are finding that even with the right of access protected, the dream of quality education remains largely unfulfilled. Families in major inner-city areas still find themselves in segregated schools, with no access to the academic quality often maintained in suburban schools.[7]

On the other hand, the Ratteray and Shujaa study reveals that some African Americans are turning their attention to the environment in which learning takes place, questions of curriculum content and demonstrated academic achievement, and the importance of the religious or cultural (i.e.., African American) perspectives from which content is taught. This is a focus on qualitative measures, which are central to parental disillusionment with public education and the growing interest in independent neighborhood schools. These environmental, academic, religious, and cultural elements are what parents believe constitute a "good education" for their children.

The idea that African American families need to reevaluate their loyalty to traditional public education was raised fifty-four years ago by Carter G. Woodson in The Miseducation of the Negro:

> "Highly educated" Negroes denounce persons who advocate for the Negro a sort of education different in some respects from that now given the White man. Negroes who have been so long inconvenienced and denied opportunities for development are naturally afraid of anything that sounds like discrimination. They are anxious to have everything the White man has even if it is harmful. The possibility of originality in the Negro, therefore, is discounted one hundred percent to maintain a nominal equality...
>
> ...the educational system as it has developed both in Europe and America [is] an antiquated process which does not hit the mark even in the case of the needs of the White man himself. If the White man wants to hold on to it, let him do so; but the Negro, so far as he is able should develop and carry out a program of his own.[8]

Independent neighborhood schools represent efforts by African Americans to do exactly what Woodson suggested--carry out their own program.

WHY PARENTS CHOOSE

A written survey of 399 parents at forty schools included two open-ended questions eliciting multiple responses, which the researchers then classified under relevant headings.

In one question, each family was asked what they expected their children to achieve once they were enrolled in these schools. Of the total responses, 65 percent said they expected academic achievement, 24 percent wanted children to have their culture affirmed, and 11 percent expected instruction in religious values.

When asked why they chose an independent school, 48 percent described the learning environment, 29 percent gave academic reasons, 12 percent focused on religious education, 7 percent anticipated the schools would be culture-affirming, and 4 percent were concerned about cost.[9]

Thirty-five of these families at ten schools were interviewed in depth. Transcripts of the interviews provided the following representative examples of reasons for each of the survey categories.

The Learning Environment

Most of the reasons given for rejecting public schools and enrolling children in independent neighborhood schools relate to the learning environment. They include the need for individualized attention, high teacher expectations, effective administration, and the personal safety of the students.

Individual Attention. Overcrowding and the inability of teachers to provide sufficient individual attention to the needs of various children are examples of problems associated with the learning environment, as seen in the following example:[10]

[The] classrooms [were] very large...I tried him...for kindergarten for one year and...I thought it was waste of time. He actually did not learn anything. He was way above the rest of the students. Therefore, he just sat with the students, and because the teacher wasn't able to find out what he knew, at the end of the year she couldn't tell me he could count to a hundred. When he left Montessori at three years old, he was counting to a hundred by fives, tens, and hundred, and she didn't even realize....I tried to tell her, but she didn't believe me. So that's why I made sure he didn't go to public school. (58.31)

Teacher Expectations. The learning environment is also shaped by the expectations teachers have for the children:

[The teachers at an independent school] want coming to school to be a positive experience...[My daughter] gets up and she wants to come to school. She wants to learn. [The teachers] promote asking questions. That's a positive thing to me. She comes home with that same type of attitude...

There aren't two recesses in the morning or this long expanded recess. They go out, they play, they're back in. The day is strictly constructed toward learning...The expectations the teachers have of the children and the standards are high. (77.81)

Sometimes parents recall their own experiences with large classes and their feelings of being neglected, and this prevents them from sending their children to public schools; others focus on their children's needs:

I didn't feel that he was getting the personal attention that he needed. I felt...that he needed a closer atmosphere and he needed constant hands-on care...The private school would be better for him because of the sizes of the classes, and this school offered a limited amount of children per class and...I felt like the teachers would get to know him better and he would do better. (76.33)

A parent and former public school teacher expressed additional fears:

I think that basically in public school the teacher teaches towards the average child, and if you can do more than the average child then a lot of teachers are not perceptive enough to give your child...you know, to just kind of sit there and wait until someone catches up. Or if you're a little slow, that teacher doesn't often always have the time to foster that learning that perhaps you have missed. (76.52)

Effective Administration.   One parent said administrative difficulties prevent public school teachers from being effective:

Years ago we found teachers really seemed to take a special interest in the children, and I'm not saying that to say that there are teachers who still don't, but I'm saying that the teachers have such a load on them now in the public schools, they have overcrowded classes and some schools don't have adequate materials. So therefore...they can't really do the job they would like to do. I have a lot of friends who are teachers, and they complain a lot that they can't do the job because there's so much paperwork to be done...So it's the system working against them more than anything else. But my children have never really wanted to go to public school, because they also recognize there are problems there. (58.57)

The first meeting with the director of an independent neighborhood school provides families with their first impression of what the learning environment might be like at that school. Administrators were frequently described as sincere, caring, professional, and religious. Some families recall their first meetings this way:

They came very well recommended by the [state] accrediting board and that was why I chose it. And then when we came and talked with [the director] and [two assistants] and they seemed to be very nice people, church-going people and that was a plus in my corner. (19.2)

I...had a long conversation with [the director] and when I saw how sincere she was about...not only Black kids, but I'm saying educating children...I just took it from there. (19.58)

In contrast, one father is very disheartened over a seemingly uncaring attitude by a public school principal who did not acknowledge a noteworthy achievement by this man's son in a national event:

In the public school [my son] was in the second grade when he participated in the "Olympics of the Mind" competition and...his teacher decided he was going to be it. And he took them, he was a star performer, he took them to the second place award championship in Akron, Ohio...He came back and they did not even congratulate this kid...The school in large did not congratulate this kid. I mean they had all these preliminary competitions and what have you, and support just was not there. (23.119)

Before enrolling their children, some families assess a school by the manner in which the administrator conducts business:

One of the things I'm most impressed with is, the school is run like a business. They're very serious. They're very professional. The appearance of the school, the decorum, the reception, the sense of order, all of those things. And if children are...educated in an environment like this, it will order their lives. If they're educated in a chaotic environment, it will disorder their lives, and I think too much of that is happening. (52.4)

Personal Safety.   Fear for personal safety was another factor families cited for leaving public schools. This is an example of a mother's concern for a sixth grade boy who became the victim of gang terrorism:
I thought he was on drugs... when he come home he won't do anything, just lay across the bed and say, "Please, I don't want to go to school today." I said,

"What's wrong, you don't want to go to school? You're just lazy."

Finally he got to the point he couldn't even get back home. Somebody stole his watch, his bookcase, his tennis shoes, bus pass, everything...When he got off the bus they would come there three of them and just rip his pockets and take everything out...

He...got in a fight with three boys, and he kicked one on the leg. They expelled him two weeks for fighting back...I took him out of that school and he didn't go to school the rest of the year. (18.17)

Academic Expectations

The second set of reasons for choosing independent schools concerns academic issues, especially the school's concentration on fundamentals, its ability to challenge the student academically during a child's early years, and the school's reputation. In other words, parents want a well-rounded academic curriculum to be the foundation of a school:

> I wanted him to be able to get a very solid background in the fundamentals that...would give him a good basis to be able to go to a good high school and...get scholarships to a university...I wanted him to be able to communicate well...I found that many, many Black people aren't able to write or to express themselves in college. I mean, most of the time we take the remedial courses...The public school system was not doing an adequate job, to me. (40.67)

> [The school] put a lot of emphasis on reading and writing and English. I know that the math is coming up. But, the beginning basics that I noticed, there was a lot of emphasis on reading and English, and they have science fairs for the kids...They work with them to give them self-confidence...If they need criticizing, they will do that in a constructive manner. (40.70)

On the other hand, the absence of training in fundamentals has been an important reason why some parents have turned away from public schools. One parent, whose child had been tested in public school and placed, without her knowledge, in a learning disability class, had her child retested at an independent neighborhood school:

[When the administrator] tested her, he found out that there was no problem. The main thing was that she had not been taught the basics.

[The reason] I didn't start the children off in the beginning at [an independent neighborhood school] was, I felt that I wasn't financially able to handle it. So I had just kept her in public school...I said I can make the sacrifice because there's only one thing I can give my children in life and that's an education. All these other material things will fade away and will profit nothing. (52.26-27)

Parents want their children to be challenged because they feel that this is the best way to prepare them to be "self-sufficient and self-supporting" in adult life. One parent describes what she looked for:

The science, the social studies and phys. ed, they'll fall in place, but that foundation of math and English, math and reading, they must have. So, I guess when I'm picking a school, I'm looking for a curriculum that has a strong academic--and that's English, math, science...social studies... (58.37)

There is a general feeling that public schools are not as challenging academically as they should be, and one parent looked at the curriculum for the public school her son was to have attended:

Before I had made my decision, I did go to a teacher that taught at...the school my son would attend if he went to public school...I told him what he could do, and should I just go ahead and send him to private school where he'll get that kind of special attention, or should I send him to public school...He went over the curriculum with me, and I just felt that he would be more challenged going to a private school setting. (76.48)

Preschool programs at independent neighborhood schools are also regarded as more challenging. Public-sector preschool programs, which are based on accepted models of early childhood education, are seen as places where children play all day, and are cared for, but are not given "real" work:

A nursery setting is a little like play, you know. They get the basic stuff, like they learn their alphabet and how to count...But, insofar as writing and learning all these other different things, math and science and Spanish...they were not getting that in nursery school because nurseries cannot afford to provide that. (19.7)

Most of the families that were interviewed had a definite awareness of the possible negative effects of pushing children toward academics at too early an age. However, there was also the belief that "pushing kids to do whatever they can do at their age" is what schools are supposed to do. Families did not want their children pushed beyond their abilities, but most of them believed that children needed to be pushed to reach their potential.

Administrators and principals who go the extra mile to support their academic programs are also highly valued. A mother, speaking about her daughter, said she is pleased that an independent school "recognized" her child's need and did something about it in a timely manner:

She's a little behind in her reading. She was having problems, and she was getting kind of frustrated because she couldn't read at the level she thought she would...so [the administrator] secured...a volunteer to come in and tutor the children in reading after school. And in one week, I could just see the progress. I was just surprised. (58.7)

Many parents depend on the reputation of the school, experienced either firsthand or on the advice of a friend:

We both decided that this was the school that she would come to...because by working here, I know some of the ins and outs and I knew that she would get a good...education. (48.25)

In another family, keeping their daughter in an independent neighborhood school created severe transportation problems. They considered withdrawing her, but friends helped to convince the family that the daughter would benefit more academically by being in an independent neighborhood school than in a public school:

One of my girlfriends...was saying, "You don't want to let her go to public school. Let her stay where she's at. She's getting this [reference to academic offerings]"...And then another one of my friends said the same thing: "If you can't afford it, I'll help you." (23.3)

In another instance, a parent notes the progress being made by her nephew at an independent neighborhood school:

My sister-in-law has her son here. He started in kindergarten, and I was so very pleased with what I saw from him...He was reading, really reading. He could stop on the street and see a sign or something and sound it out with the phonics teaching that they had given him here. (52.47)

Parents demonstrate, therefore, that they expect independent neighborhood schools to be stronger in basic academics than public schools, because this is what they define as "a good education."

Religious and Cultural Contexts

Religion and culture are important factors for African Americans who seek a context for the acquisition of knowledge and to reinforce the development of the individual as a member of society after he or she leaves school.

Role of Religion.   Religion is seen by some families as a means of providing their young with moral guidance. For one parent, religion is an aid to raising a child in a difficult environment:

> [My daughter is] younger than her academic grade level and she's higher than [her] age level. So I wanted to put her in an environment which I thought would keep her from becoming too involved with children older than herself. And I wanted her to have a Christian education and make a different commitment to ensure there were some safeguards with her having to go into college at a very young age. (52.10)

Another parent blends spirituality with the academic curriculum:
> There is one scripture that I think just about every teacher here in this school uses as far as motivating and prompting the children, as far as gaining more self-confidence..."I can do all things through Christ who strengthens me." And this is the same thing we reinforce in our home. (52.57)

The lack of "Christian discipline" in the public schools is something to which a number of families object:
> So many things are happening in the public school until I wanted to give [my daughter] a Christian atmosphere to be able to be disciplined properly. (52.24)

Two other parents, who relate prayer to discipline, explain their views in this way:
> I think schools throughout the country, the United States as a whole, have suffered greatly since they took prayer out of the school system....And prayer in schools, I think,

makes it better, and I think it hasn't helped the public
school system. So that's why I chose to leave--or have my
son brought up in Christian academy. (52.73)

I also believe in the religious program they took out of the
public schools some time ago, and I really feel it's lacking.
I can recall we...had respect and manners. But after
teaching...I feel we need prayer back in the schools.
(58.38)

One mother describes her son's public school classmates,
whom she also claims exert negative peer pressure on him:
I would say 97 percent of them didn't go to church...There
was one little boy in his class that even asked him what do
the praying hands mean when he saw it on the bulletin
board, and did it have anything to do with God... (58.12)

On the other hand, some families wanted to focus their highest
priority on academic pursuits, in spite of their religious orientation:

I might have a stronger belief in religion, but I know if you
have religion and don't know math and reading, you're not
going to get that job. So I want him prepared. (58.39)

Role of Culture.   A cultural context is one in which a child finds
that the curriculum content and learning process affirm his or her
cultural/racial/ethnic identity. While many parents did not consider
cultural issues important when they first chose an independent
school, they did consider it an important reason for keeping their
children there.

As Woodson forewarned, the tradition of struggle against racial
segregation creates a degree of apprehension at the prospect of
voluntarily enrolling one's child in an all-Black school.   The
parents in this survey reacted in two different ways: some were
ambivalent about the role of culture, while others were more
positive.

Some parents were defensive about being perceived as anti-
White, and some even wished that there were "token" Whites at
their children's school to provide opportunities for cultural
exchange. Many are sometimes apologetic about having enrolled
their children in an all-Black school:

We are not just going to deal with us. We're going to be
dealing with Hispanics. We're going to be dealing with
Caucasians. I would really love to see my child in school
where there were all cultures, a melting pot, because that's
the kind of society he's going to face when he walks out of
these doors. (76.13)

On the other hand, without clearly defining a racially homogenous environment as important, some families caution against an integrated setting:

I notice at the schools where the staff is predominantly White they just don't seem to know how to love our children for themselves. They tend to want to group children into some category, like this is a bright kid, this is a kid who causes some problems because he is a little disruptive or he daydreams...and they base everything that child does oftentimes on...their prejudicial kind of feeling... (58.77)

Some parents go to great lengths to avoid acknowledging the importance of cultural awareness. This is true of the mother in the following example, although later in the interview, it is easier for the father to accept the role of culture:

MOTHER: When we made the choice, we really were not looking for a Black program. We chose this because it had a good program, and it happened to be Black. But had we found a good program in a White setting...I would not have a problem putting her there.

FATHER: If kids go into a predominantly White environment, those school systems will change them. You know you see a Black kid that's maybe not groomed properly. Whereas here, in a Black environment, he's going to get that tender loving care that he needs. In a White school, that kid could very well be labeled as a kid with a problem, with learning disabilities because nobody wants to take the time to get close to him. (19.139)

Often, parents have not developed criteria for assessing how their child's school handles the issue of culture. They are motivated by their own feelings of "miseducation" to seek a culture-affirming environment:

I didn't learn anything about Black history until I was in college. Dr. Martin Luther King? I didn't know who he was until after he died. (58.42)

For some, cultural-affirmation is indeed no more than knowing the names of famous Black people:

One thing I wanted [our son] to have was...to know these different Black people...because he probably knows quite a few...that I don't know... (23.161)

Another parent reports that his level of cultural awareness increased his disillusionment with public schools:

> These Black kids, teach them their heritage. [Public
> schools] weren't about that. Black History Month...it
> dwindled to a week and that type of thing...it was
> absolutely pathetic. (23.119)

Even some independent schools do not stress their African
American cultural foundations. Cultural affirmation occurs
implicitly, through the racial composition of the staff, which helps
make it a "Black environment." As a parent notes:

> It's not drilled into the children's head, "Black is
> positive"...but from the actions and example of the staff,
> the overall attitude is conducive to say this is a positive
> experience. We are a Black school... (77.82)

In spite of an apparent lack of cultural focus in this school, that
same parent is very clear about her own objectives in educating her
child:
> I don't want my child to be in a school and to get the
> subliminal message that White means you're superior or
> you have to strive to be like a person of the Caucasian race
> to succeed. I want my child to understand that there is a
> basic level of intelligence that man needs to achieve...and
> that learning...will enrich your life regardless of your race.
> (77.82-83)

Likewise, some families are very comfortable with the
quality of instruction and the perspective from which the
curriculum is delivered. They believe that a Black school
can prepare a child to function in different environments:
> My idea of a Black school would be that my son could go
> through here, and then he could go to Harvard Business
> School....It's not that he would necessarily become a civil
> rights activist. If he wanted to, he could. But he wouldn't
> be one or the other. That he would be very, very
> sophisticated, you know what I'm saying. That he would
> be able to go into any White arena and be very, very
> comfortable going into any Black arena. That's my ideal
> concept of what his education should be like. (23. 152)

The role of cultural affirmation in decisionmaking about
schools, therefore, is a sensitive area. In fact, only a few schools in
the survey were found to have evolved an intellectually based
definition of what it means to be African American and to have
infused that into the curriculum.
During the interviews, a few families were self-confident and
forthcoming in their explanations. Many families initially glossed

over the role of culture, and not until they were pressed for the meaning of their responses did they admit that culture was very important. For some, it appeared to be a source of deep, unresolved conflict and fear of alienating their children from the larger society. For others, it was sufficient if the school merely had external symbols, such as pictures of the late Dr. Martin Luther King, Jr. Finally, some had intuitively gravitated toward institutions where the teachers and staff were Black, but those parents had made no conscious examination of the perspective from which the curriculum was being taught.

IMPLICATIONS

Parents choose independent neighborhood schools because they find that mere access to educational institutions is not enough. They are looking for what they perceive to be nurturing environments, where children can take advantage of learning opportunities and are fortified by an understanding of the religious or cultural contexts of knowledge. Ironically, each of these criteria for a good education is precisely what African Americans are able to do best for each other, and it has been true throughout our long tradition of independent education.

Culture, therefore, is the foundation for all learning, though this is seldom admitted on first encounter. It must be recognized by independent schools as an integral part of their marketing plans, for it is what sets them apart from their competition and will enable them to retain their enrollment.

Parents have shown that they can move beyond access and want to focus on issues of content and context. They are ready to be encouraged to express and act on their convictions about the role of culture in the learning process. Parents are leading the way, and education policymakers should follow, for only then can African American children understand what they have to offer America and the world.

NOTES

1. Joan Davis Ratteray and Mwalimu Shujaa, <u>Dare to Choose: Parental Choice at Independent Neighborhood Schools.</u> (Washington, D.C.: Institute for Independent Education, 1987). This study identified several hundred self-help educational institutions, most of which serve African Americans. The schools are usually operated by parents and teachers of various ethnic and cultural groups. Half of them are secular, although the curricula at the remaining religiously affiliated schools are usually independent of church control.

The parents, who usually come from families of four or five, have a wide range of incomes. Some earn less than $15,000 annually, others more than $50,000, but most are between $15,000 and $30,000; 44 percent of them have two or four-year degrees, and 19 percent have completed postgraduate study. Half of the families live less than three miles from their school, making these true neighborhood institutions.

2. Horace Mann Bond, Education for Freedom (Lincoln, Pa: Lincoln University Press 1976), p. 76; see also Vincent P. Franklin, The Education of Black Philadelphia (Philadelphia: University of Pennsylvania Press, 1979); and R.R. Wright,The Negro in Pennsylvania: A Study in Economic History (Philadelphia: A.M.E. Book Concerns, 1911), p. 124.

3. Charles H. Wesley, Prince Hall: Life and Legacy, 2d ed. (Chicago: Drew Sales Lodge Regalia, 1983).

4. Joan Davis Ratteray, "Independent Schools: Challenge Reborn," American Visions (March/April 1986): 55-56.

5. Lyman Beecher Brooks, Upward: A History of Norfolk State University, 1914-1975 (Washington, D.C.: Howard University Press, 1983), p. 15; see also Richard W. Cooper and Herman Cooper, Negro School Attendance in Delaware: A Report to the State Board of Education in Delaware (Newark: University of Delaware Press, 1923), p. 17.

6. John Ogbu, Minority Education and Caste (New York: Academic Press, 1978), p. 105.

7. Gary Orfield, et al., "School Segregation in the 1980s: Trends in the States and Metropolitan Areas," report by the National School Desegregation Project to the Joint Center for Political Studies (Chicago: Office of Public Affairs, University of Chicago, 1987).

8. Carter G. Woodson, The Miseducation of the Negro (Washington, D.C.: Associated Press, 1933), p. xi.

9. Unlike the other categories, cost was not discussed elsewhere by parents and, therefore, is not discussed in this chapter.

10. The numbers in parentheses following quotes are used to protect the confidentiality of the informants while permitting distinctions to be made between their responses.

Summary and Discussion
Barbara A. Sizemore

The African American struggle for education in the United States has progressed through four phases since the seventeenth century: entry, or the right to attend public schools; egress, or the right to work in the public schools as administrators, teachers, clerks, janitors, etc.; equity, or the right to the same resources and service; and excellence, or the right to the best education the state has to offer.[1] Lomotey and Brookins and Ratteray and Shujaa argue that African American parents chose the Independent Black Institution (IBI) or independent Black neighborhood school because the public schools had deteriorated so that their children could not get equity and excellence there. Therefore, as Diana T. Slaughter[2] has pointed out, the entry of African Americans into private schools is a continuation of this 300-year-old struggle.

Ratteray and Shujaa administered a written survey to 399 parents at forty such schools and found that 65 percent expected their children to have high academic achievement, 24 percent expected cultural affirmation, and 11 percent expected religious instruction; 48 percent chose the independent school because of the learning environment, 29 percent for the academic curriculum, 12 percent for the religious emphasis, 7 percent for the cultural value, and 4 percent for cost.

Thirty-five of these parents at ten schools were interviewed more extensively. Most of the reasons given for rejecting public schools and enrolling children in independent neighborhood schools related to the learning environment. Parents perceived that their children would benefit from more individual attention, higher teacher expectations, more effective administration, and better guarantees of personal safety in these schools, satisfying their need for equity or an equal share of the resources. They also felt that independent schools concentrated more on the fundamentals and provided a more academically challenging curriculum.

Some wanted more religious and cultural contexts emphasizing moral guidance and cultural/racial/ethnic identity. Ratteray and Shujaa see culture as the foundation and basis for all learning and urge the schools to stress this reality as a vital part of their marketing plans. But, they found that cultural affirmation was a sensitive area around which some families exhibited ambivalence, others a deep, unresolved conflict, and still others a quiet denial. Yet, parents seeking the IBI or neighborhood school did want more than mere access. They were concerned about context and content and sought a nurturing environment or excellence.

Lomotey and Brookins reported a descriptive study (conducted by Brookins) of the philosophy, ideology, pedagogy, and academic rigor of ten IBIs in the Midwest and East to define and better understand the IBIs. Details of the design and implementation of the study were not given, but findings of positive student outcomes in academic achievement were reported.

The schools manifested most of the characteristics found in the Effective Schools' literature[3] except for the finding that the schools were not typically orderly or quiet and not much time was spent on task. In addition, what Brookins calls the informal curriculum in the IBI is the formal aspect in the Effective Schools and vice versa. Still, the IBIs produced students who were better prepared as determined by standardized test scores.

Lomotey and Brookins report the following as desired positive student outcomes at IBIs: strong self-concept; self-confidence; academic competence; ability to think critically, analytically, and independently; ability to understand the Nguzo Saba (Kawaida cultural values system), commitment to African and African American people; political awareness; self-discipline and self-determination, strong knowledge of African and African American life, culture, and history; social and emotional competence; an understanding of the needs and purposes of education; recognition of family; and willingness to struggle for change.[4]

The authors saw the IBI as a model of African American competence; an inspiration for parents, teachers, and students in public schools, a model of institutional development and finance, and a training ground for future African American leaders. For them, as for Ratteray and Shujaa, culture was the central concept. IBIs stress revolutionary pan-African nationalism, the Nguzo Saba, and familyhood. Political education is part and parcel of every subject and skill taught in the curriculum and the emphasis is on how world events affect African people. IBI teachers are culturally and politically oriented and committed to African and African American people; their ultimate objective is the creation of permanent African American institutions. To understand Ratteray and Shujaa and Lomotey and Brookins, the reader must come to them with definitions for their undefined terms: culture, nationalism, values and education. The African American struggle has certainly been cultural. Culture is the sum total of artifacts generated by a group in its struggle for survival if defined Afrocentrically.[5] Survival is the ability of the group to preserve the health and strength of its individual members so that they can reproduce themselves and care for their progeny. Nationalism is the condition which exists when a group has developed solidarity and cohesion through a pseudospecies declaration (e.g., we are the chosen people made in the image of God), an identity specification (the name the people call themselves), and a territorial imperative (a homeland). Values are the overriding guidelines of the culture-the imperatives which designate what is of worth, good and bad, right and wrong, etc.[6]

Education is the acquisition of knowledge, information, skills, and experience which train, socialize, and enlighten the individual members of the group.[7] Education therefore, is the means for the transmission of the culture, its values, and the spirit of nationalism to members of the group. If education does not do this, the ability of the group to survive becomes more difficult.

Carter G. Woodson discussed this problem in his now famous book, The Miseducation of the Negro, in which he said that the education of Negroes seldom does any good because they do not learn about their own group and its culture. They do not know their group's history, literature, art, or music. Nor do they know what the best interests of their group are. Woodson knew the importance of a group's culture to survival and advancement:

> The so-called modern education, with all its defects, however, does others so much more good than it does the Negro, because it has been worked out in conformity to the needs of those who have enslaved and oppressed weaker peoples...
>
> No systematic effort toward change has been possible, for, taught the same economics, history, philosophy, literature and religion which have established the present code of morals, the Negro's mind has been brought under the control of his oppressor. The problem of holding the Negro down therefore is easily solved. When you control a man's thinking you do not have to worry about his actions. You do not have to tell him not to stand here or go yonder. He will find his "proper place" and will stay in it. You do not need to send him to the back door. He will go without being told. In fact, if there is no back door, he will cut one of his special benefit. His education makes it necessary.[8]

Moreover, cultural knowledge could enhance one's self-concept and motivate one to use one's potential for the greatest good.

The philosophy which Lomotey and Brookins found in their schools reflects Woodson's point of view. The three views were: revolutionary pan-African nationalism, a value system (Nguzo Saba), and familyhood (a cultural orientation). Woodson saw cultural foundation as a necessity for political action. So did Harold Cruse some thirty years later in The Crisis of the Negro Intellectual, in which Cruse argued that the Negro will never advance to first-class citizenship without a cultural foundation for the economic and political progress.[9]

A look at past excluded groups reveals a power inclusion model which gives importance to Lomotey and Brookins's overview of IBIs. Most excluded groups started with a separatist movement by which group solidarity and cohesion were generated, leading to a strong group feeling of nationalism which resulted further in religions where God looked like the people, traditions of self-help and self-reliance, and great respect for the elders or holders of the culture. Because this group solidarity was vested in religion, separate schools were often found attached to the "church." These separate schools taught the values of the culture as well as the religion. Nationalism and religion, then, became the most important dynamics in motivating people to struggle for their cultural self-preservation.[10]

The family was the first educational bulwark. Here religion, culture, and the tradition of self-reliance were reinforced. In such cases, three institutions worked to define, defend, and develop the interests of the group.[11] Business and job opportunities were generated by such solidarity and cohesion and a capitalist niche was created for the group. Self-help organizations were formed to accumulate and distribute capital and the group then began to operate in the pluralist political arena, jockeying for power.

Today the African American family is in trouble because of its inability to care for its progeny and bring them to a higher standard of living than the generation before. Single-parent families will soon be the norm if no changes occur in the near future. When headed by females, such families are poorer because of the instrumental value of male superiority in American society. The assault against African American males in the market place has resulted in an unemployment rate which militates against a two-parent family. Job and career opportunities exist for them in athletics, entertainment, the military, and crime. Since only a few will enter into the millionaire spaces available in athletics and entertainment, too many African American males wind up in the army or prison.[12]

The ambiguity or conflict found among some African American families around cultural affirmation in schools by Ratteray and Shujaa may be a manifestation of the double-consciousness defined by W. E. B. DuBois in book <u>The Souls of Black Folk</u>:

> ...It is a peculiar sensation, this double-consciousness, this sense of always look at one's self through the eyes of others, of   measuring one's soul by the tape of a world that looks on in amused contempt and pity. One ever feels his twoness...an American, a Negro; two souls, two thoughts, two unreconciled strivings; two warring ideals in one dark body, whose dogged strength alone keeps it from being torn asunder.[13]

Each African American must wrestle with this desire to be African and American at the same time. Institutional racism, or the preservation of White superiority by laws, rules, regulations, traditions, and custom, is still alive and well in the United States. Its eradication is dependent on the continuation of struggle. Struggle comes from education. If the education does not generate struggle, survival becomes more difficult.

The fear of many today is that the integrated education which we fought so hard to get fails to prepare African Americans for struggle against institutional racism. One reason may be our failure to integrate the curriculum, or what we teach, how we teach it, and how it is administered. African American history, life, and culture should be intergrated into American history and culture. We should no longer need to have African American History Week or Month. We should no longer need supplementary texts which deal with African America's literature, poetry, and drama. African American cultural artifacts are American. The fact that our curricula in private, parochial, and public schools are Eurocentric and monocultural reflects the instrumental value system at work in our larger society: the superiority of White affluent males of European descent. This value system creates an ascriptive continuum which classifies people according to race, sex, class, and point of national origin.

While we do know, according to Ron Edmonds, all that we need to know to educate all of the children, the continuing question is whether or not we will do it. While there are now Effective Schools where African American children are scoring at or above the national norms on standardized tests in reading and mathematics in large numbers, only in the IBIs is the African American's history, life and culture integrated into the entire curriculum.[14] These Effective Schools can train and socialize African Americans, but whether or not they can enlighten them remains a question.[15] Enlightenment is the prerequisite for defining the group's interests and waging the struggle to defend and develop them.

Lomotey and Brookins and Ratteray and Shujaa emphasize the cultural model as the most important for excluded and oppressed groups. They agreed with Woodson's statement:

> The program for the uplift of the Negro in this country must be based upon a scientific study of the Negro from within to develop in him the power to do for himself what his oppressors will never do to elevate him to the level of others.[16]

Although Effective Schools can and do train and socialize African American students to perform well academically, they do not prepare them for struggle. Only a curriculum based on the culture of a people can do that.

> Chinua Achebe said in Things Fall Apart: Does the white man understand our custom about land? How can he when he does not even speak our tongue? But he says that our customs are bad; and our own brothers who have taken up his religion also say that our customs are bad. How do you think we can fight when our own brothers have turned against us? The white man is very clever. He came quietly and peaceably with his religion. We were amused at his foolishness and allowed him to stay. Now he has won our brothers, and our clan can no longer act like one. He has put a knife on the things that held us together and we have fallen apart.[17]

African American people get inaccurate conceptual maps of reality from a Eurocentric curriculum. The knowledge which is disseminated preserves certain symbolic universes which make certain groups powerful and others powerless.[18]

NOTES

1.   Barbara A. Sizemore, "The Limits of the Black Superintendency: A Review of the Literature," Journal of Education Equity and Leadership 6 (1986): 180-208.

2.   See chapter 2, written by Slaughter, of the report: Diana T. Slaughter and Barbara L. Schneider, Newcomers: Blacks in Private Schools, ERIC, 1986 (ED 274 768 and ED 274 769).

3.   Barbara A. Sizemore, "Pitfalls and Promises of Effective Schools' Research," Journal of Negro Education 54 (1985): 269-288; see also: Barbara A. Sizemore, Carlos A. Brossard, and Birney Harrigan, An Abashing Anomaly: Three High Achieving Predominantly Black Elementary Schools. (Washington, D.C.: National Institute of Education, January 1983).

4. See Maulana Karenga, <u>Introduction to Black Studies</u> (Inglewood: Kawaida Publications, 1982) regarding Nguzo Saba. The Nguzo Saba consists of seven principles: unity, self-determination collective work and responsibility cooperative economics purposecreativity, and faith.

5. Sizemore, "Limits of the Black Superintendency;" see also: Sekou Toure, "A Dialectical Approach to Culture," <u>Black Scholar</u> (November 1969): 13.

6. Barbara A. Sizemore, "Making the Schools a Vehicle for Cultural Pluralism," in Madelon D. Stent, William R. Hazard, and Harry N. Rivlin, eds., <u>Cultural Pluralism in Education</u> (New York: Appleton Century Crofts, 1973), pp. 43-54.

7. Sizemore, "Pitfalls and Promises," p. 273.

8. Carter G. Woodson, <u>The Miseducation of the Negro</u> (1933; reprint, New York: AMS Press, 1977), p. xii.

9. Harold Cruse, <u>The Crisis of the Negro Intellectual</u> (New York: William Morrow, 1967), p. 456.

10. Sizemore, "Making the Schools a Vehicle," p. 45.

11. For example, see Karenga, <u>Introduction to Black Studies</u>, pp. 42-147.

12. Lawrence Gary, <u>Black Men</u> (Beverly Hills, Calif.: Sage Publications, 1981).

13. W. E. B. DuBois, <u>The Souls of Black Folk</u> (1903; reprint, Greenwich, Conn: Fawcet, 1961), pp. 16-17.

14. Sizemore, "Pitfalls and Promises," p. 274-275.

15. Jules Henry. "Is Education Possible? Are We Qualified to Enlighten Dissenters?" in Donald A. Erickson ed., <u>Public Controls for Non-Public Schools</u> (Chicago: University of Chicago Press, 1969), pp. 83-102.

16. Woodson, <u>The Miseducation of the Negro</u>, p. 144.

17. Chinua Achebe, <u>Things Falls Apart</u> (Reprint, Greenwich, Conn.: Fawcet , Paperback, 1959), p. 162.

18. Sizemore, "Making the Schools a Vehicle," p. 48.

Part 4
Parental Perceptions and Goals: Independent and Parochial Schools

Parental perceptions of desirable schools, parents' socialization goals, and their individual orientations toward childrearing enter into the process of choosing the appropriate private school for their child. These perceptions, goals, and orientations are empirically described by the authors in this section, particularly as they relate to the various types of private schools in which Black children are enrolled. Parental expectations of private schooling, the role of parents' educational expectations in the children's school experiences, and the nature of the family/school partnership are central points of investigation in the following chapters.

In chapter 14, Arnez and Jones-Wilson present data indicating that disenchantment and dissatisfaction with public education are important reasons for the increasing enrollment of Blacks in private schools. Survey questionnaire data from 2,668 Black parents of children in private schools in the greater Washington, D. C., area (grades K-12) serve as a database. The authors find that lower-income parents perceive their children's upward mobility to be blocked in local public schools; higher-income parents refer to poor academic quality.

In chapter 15, Slaughter, Johnson, and Schneider report the results of a content analysis of interview data focused on the educational goals of Black parents. The authors assumed that Black parents had intuitive educational philosophies which served as stimulants relative to educational prescriptions for their children. This led to the development of a coding system by Slaughter and Schneider designed to classify the preferred educational goals of Black parents. Considerable diversity of parental educational goals could be tolerated within one school community. Among the six inductively identified family goal types, three that are particularly stressed by Black parents, in contrast to non-Black parents, focus on the family's educational role, the importance of good teaching to quality education, and the role of education in the child's subsequent social mobility. A second study also contrasts the seventy-four Black respondents in the Slaughter and Schneider study with forty-one Black respondents obtained from three predominantly Black urban private schools by Johnson. In both studies, schools were members of Catholic, independent elite, and independent alternative networks.

In chapter 16, Johnson reports on the racial socialization strategies of Black parents whose children attend three types of predominantly Black private schools (elite, alternative, and parochial). Johnson focuses on how coping strategies differ from one school to another. Findings are discussed in terms of their consistency with parental socialization goals and the conduciveness of various school settings to the development of coping options for children.

14

A Descriptive Survey of Black Parents in the Greater Washington, D.C., Area Who Chose to Send Their Children to Nonpublic Schools

Nancy L. Arnez and Faustine C. Jones-Wilson

Historically, Black parents and guardians have exhibited a firm commitment to public schooling for their young. The continuous efforts of such adults to increase their children's access to public schooling and improve its quality are well known.[1] Along with this traditional behavior, however, within the last two decades it has been increasingly apparent that larger numbers of Black adults are selecting nonpublic schools for their young. Little research has been conducted to ascertain the reasons for these parental choices of private schools over public schools, and definitive information is still being sought. Of the existing literature, little has been contributed by Black researchers. Their perspectives could be very different from those of their non-Black counterparts because Blacks live a different experience daily.

This study provides empirical information about an emerging phenomenon in the field of education, Blacks in private schools. Since public schools have long been regarded as a unifying factor in society and a primary agent for socializing the young into common societal values and expectations, as well as a place where microcultures meet to develop and appreciate multiculturalism as an appropriate societal concept, what happens to these notions as increasing proportions of the nation's largest minority group pull their young out of public schools? If private schools are going to play a larger part in the education of Black youth, we need to know more about those schools and what they do well. The findings from this study may assist private and public schools in their planning and assessment for the coming decade.

*With the assistance of Deborah Carter, then graduate assistant, Dept. of Educational Leadership, School of Education, Howard University; now M.A.

For the sake of clarity, we establish the following definitions for key terms: nonpublic and private are used interchangeably to refer to elementary and secondary schools that are established and maintained by churches and/or independent persons and groups. Public schools refer to elementary and secondary schools established by states through their counties or cities, and by the District of Columbia, to educate "all the children of all the people." The greater Washington, D.C., metropolitan area includes Washington, D.C., northern Virginia, adjacent Maryland suburban areas, and one Pennsylvania jurisdiction.

OVERVIEW OF RELATED LITERATURE

The literature on the subject of Black parental choices of nonpublic schools over public schools is not very extensive. Much of it consists of essays or newspaper reports. In reviewing this scant literature, we will discuss nonempirical and empirical reports and studies.

The articles and reports that appeared in the popular press and other such sources seemed to begin to document the recent phenomenon of many Black parents choosing nonpublic schools. This choice is of interest primarily because historically, most Blacks have looked to public schools as a means for educational achievement and occupational upward mobility. During the years of segregation, public schools in Black communities were sources of culture, personal pride, and educational fulfillment. Teachers and principals were highly respected and admired community leaders.

Even as school desegregation increased, Blacks were still strong supporters of their local community schools. Their strong support reflected their enduring commitment to education. It is our belief that the commitment to education existed in all socioeconomic groups and geographic areas, although the commitment might have been strongest in the South and in border states where discrimination was harshest and life chances poorest for most Blacks.

Several authors have suggested that Black parents may have rejected public schools and established their own or enrolled their children in other private schools because these schools may have emphasized African values and lifestyles.[2]   However, we have suggested that one of the primary reasons given by Black parents from all socioeconomic levels for enrolling their children in nonpublic schools was to provide for them a sense of family, a sense of caring, and a quality education.

Some authors have suggested that, for the most part, children in private schools are from middle-income homes. Dennis P. Doyle and Patrice Gaines-Carter have argued, for example, that children enrolled in nonpublic schools were usually from middle-class families.[3]

Joan Davis Ratteray has suggested that many parents of minority and poor children were disillusioned with traditional public school systems. Her site visits to forty nonpublic neighborhood schools between July and September, 1983, revealed that the parents perceived their children to be trapped in a public school system that promised them low achievement. To solve the problem these poor and minority parents founded or created nonpublic schools that met their needs. Further, Ratteray's survey noted that although these nonpublic schools suffer from financial constraints, they have excellent teachers and course work guided by a cultural or religious doctrine, but containing high-level mathematics, several foreign languages, and computer literacy, as well as an emphasis on reading and writing skills tested by standardized measures. Ratteray's findings suggest that not only middle-class parents enroll their children in nonpublic schools, and that perhaps Black parents chose nonpublic schools as a rejection of public schools.[4]

In 1981, Sarah Edwards and William Richardson surveyed a sample (313 of 1,927) of parents who withdrew their children from the Montgomery County, Maryland, public schools (MCPS) to enroll them in private schools. Minority groups constituted 15 percent of the student withdrawals, compared with 20 percent of the total MCPS enrollment. Results suggested that the most important reasons for withdrawal from public schools were their lack of discipline (53 percent), desire to have children taught values/religion (44 percent), and smaller class sizes and more individualized instruction in nonpublic schools.[5]

In a 1982 followup study to the Edwards and Richardson project, Joy Frechtling and Steven Frankel surveyed 277 parents of students leaving MCPS for private schools, and 281 parents who enrolled their children into MCPS from private schools. Results of the telephone interview survey revealed that most parents who put their children in private schools wanted smaller classes, more individualized instruction, and higher academic standards. Parents who transferred their children into the public schools from private schools gave convenience and cost as major reasons for the transfer.[6]

Diana T. Slaughter and Barbara L. Schneider have found that Black families' choice of private schooling appears to be "less of a rejection of public schooling, and more of an evolution of a new strategy for insuring future levels of sustained and/or upward mobility for the family."[7] They also found that many Black parents preferred educational programs that were very teacher-centered ("deliberate"), whereas others stressed the importance of parental involvement in schools ("authoritative"). White parents preferred schools that were more child-centered ("humanistic"). White parents were also more likely to endorse private schools as the best form of education ("traditional"). Further, more Black than White parents link desegregation and quality of education. Deborah J. Johnson found that Black parents who choose Black independent schools may be seeking or reaffirming racial identity, and/or a strengthening of the Black community.[8]

Other studies have suggested that parents choose private religious schools because these schools offer a higher quality of education, because of the lack of discipline in the local public schools, because of religion (95 percent of the non-Catholic parents, representing over 40 percent of the total, cited religion as a factor in their choice of the school), and because the schools taught social, moral, and cultural values. In addition, some of these authors (e.g., George Ballweg) found that social class did not affect the reasons for parents' choice of nonpublic schools.[9]

Studies have also pointed out that many non-Catholic Black families choose Catholic schools because of their perception that the quality of teaching and discipline are better in those schools than in public schools. Also, Catholic schools are accessible and less costly than many other private schools. Further, values are important even though the families may not completely endorse Catholic values. Finally, some parents believe that Catholic school authorities are more responsive to them than are public school authorities.[10]

In 1984, John Holmes and David Hiatt surveyed forty-four evangelical Christian schools in south Los Angeles County, California, in order to ascertain parental expectations of private Christian schools and to determine if there were differences between parental expectations of Black, Hispanic, and White ethnic groups attending these schools. The results indicated that 71 percent of all parents, and 67 percent of the Black parents, chose a Christian school because of its religious focus in the educational program. Among Blacks, 16 percent chose the Christian school because of its academic program, and 15 percent had other expectations, including a caring staff, as primary reasons for enrollment of their children.[11]

In summary, Black parents who choose nonpublic schools may do so because they believe their children will receive a higher quality of education there, they want some emphasis on the development of values/morals/character, or they perceive a breakdown in discipline in public schools and want their children to avoid being involved in this disintegration. Some Black parents want desegregated schooling for their children, others want more caring teachers and more individualized instruction than they think public schools provide, and still others view private schools as the new avenue for upward mobility for their children.

The major purpose of the study was to ascertain from Black parents/guardians their reasons for choosing nonpublic schools for their young, and to assess the relationship between parental choice of nonpublic schools and their attitudes toward public schools.

METHODS AND PROCEDURES

Instrument

Preliminary planning for this study began in the spring of 1985. A fifty-item questionnaire was constructed by the authors, adapting items from the questionnaires of the Montgomery County School System, with permission.[12] Other items were adaptations from the annual Gallup poll, which inquires about public attitudes toward education, and from the U.S. Department of Education, A Study of Alternatives in American Education: Family Choice in Schooling, by R. Gary Bridge and Julie Blackman.

The survey questionnaire had five major components, four of which will be addressed in this chapter. The first was descriptive, asking respondents to supply demographic information. The second component questioned respondents about possible considerations that may have influenced their decision to send their child(ren) to nonpublic schools. The third component, not addressed in this chapter because of space limitations, asked parents for possible reasons for not enrolling their child(ren) in public schools, and asked parents to grade the public schools in their communities. Component four solicited parental opinions about school choice in general (the concept of choice in schooling). Component five asked parents to grade the independent school that they chose.

Sample Selection

Using directories of nonpublic schools obtained from the Association of Independent Schools in Greater Washington and from the D.C. Public School System, sixty-four principals of nonpublic schools were contacted in September 1985, and asked for cooperation by providing us with the names and addresses of Black parents to be included in the study.

By January 1986, thirty-six nonpublic schools, more than half of those contacted, had agreed to participate in this survey. Twenty-two of the schools are in the District of Columbia, eleven in Maryland, two in Virginia, and one in Pennsylvania.

Twenty-four of these schools are private but not parochial; ten are Catholic, and two are church-related but not Catholic. Principals agreed to cooperate with this study with the option of having the principal distribute and collect the questionnaires, thereby assuring anonymity of their parents.

Although 2,668 questionnaires were distributed, there is no way to know how many of these instruments actually reached Black parents, or were returned to the schools by student carriers. Nonetheless, 409 usable questionnaires were returned to the researchers. Generalizations should not be made from this random sample to the larger Black population without further study.

Of the 409 parental responses, 111 came from the twenty-four private, non-parochial schools. The largest number, 259, came from the ten Catholic schools, 24 from parochial, non-Catholic schools, and 15 parental responses could not be linked to specific school code numbers. Usable responses were determined to be those where respondents replied to 90 percent or more of the questions asked, using the response format indicated.

The respondents are a random sampling of the universe of Black parents in this geographic area who chose private schools for their children. We have no reason to believe that they differ from nonrespondents in any way except that they were willing to take the time to respond to the questionnaire and see that it was returned to the school or to the researchers directly.

RESULTS

Demographic Data

Respondents' ages ranged from twenty-two to sixty-two years, with an average of thirty-nine, while the age range for the respondents' spouses was from twenty-two to fifty-eight, with an average age of forty-one years. Of the 394 respondents who answered the question on marital status, 57 percent were married, 14 percent single, 9 percent separated, 17 percent divorced, and 3 percent widowed. It should be noted that the majority of the respondents were married, which suggests that the study reflects the attitudes and behaviors of intact Black families.

Family income covered a wide span, with the poorest respondents earning less than $10,000 annually (4 percent), and the most affluent earning $50,000 or more (29 percent). Between these extremes were 9 percent earning $10,000-$14,999; 12 percent $15,000-$19,999; 10 percent between $20,000-$24,999; 16 percent $25,000-$34,999; and 20 percent earning $35,000-$49,999 annually. The number of persons depending on these incomes ranged from one to twelve, with the most frequently cited number of children being three or four. Thus, approximately

75 percent of the families in the study reported incomes at or above $20,000 per year. These figures should be interpreted in light of the fact that 57 percent of the participants may have both parents working outside the home, plus the median income in the Washington D.C., metropolitan area--including Blacks--is higher than the national median income.

In terms of occupation, most respondents and their spouses were professionals (68 percent of respondents; 66 percent of their spouses). Educational attainment was high; 46 percent of the respondents and 43 percent of their spouses were college graduates or above.

The following information regarding occupation and residency, which shows that a high proportion of the respondents were professionals, tended to be married to professionals, and lived in Washington, D.C., may support the notion that the higher income, occupational, and educational attainment of this group may be a function of the opportunities for Blacks in the federal and District of Columbia governments, and the numerous public and private colleges and universities in the area.

The majority of the respondents (61 percent) lived in the District of Columbia, while 39 percent resided in the suburbs; 71 percent had resided in this area for fifteen years or longer. Homeownership was high; 69 percent of the respondents owned their own homes.

Protestants represented 37 percent of the respondents, while 34 percent were Catholic and 29 percent "other." "Other" included Muslims, Jews, atheists, and "none." Differences in response patterns by religiosity will not be included in this report.

It is important to note that 79 percent of the respondents had not attended private schools. Of those who had attended a private school, the average length of attendance was 8.3 years. This suggests that for most respondents, the option to attend private schools is new and may be related to their upwardly mobile strivings; or perhaps the nonpublic school choice is a reflection of Blacks' historical struggle for a better life in the United States.

Parental Choice of Nonpublic Schools

The section of the questionnaire which pertained to parents' decision to select nonpublic schools consisted of fifteen items, fourteen of which loaded sufficiently to be included in the following analysis. The fifteen items were factor-analyzed to determine the relative importance to parents of each item on the list.[13] Three factors emerged. Six items loaded together on the first factor, which might be labeled "perceptions about the school's program." The second factor consists of five items and might be labeled "development of academic and social characteristics in children." The third factor contains three items and might be labeled "quality of school and program." The items for these three factors are listed in table 14.1. Only one item, "discipline," did not load into any of the three factors.

Factor 1 can be defined as representing an attitudinal dimension about the school's program, formed, apparently, as a result of discussions, feelings, and beliefs--coupled with a minimum of evidence (e.g., high test scores of students) that is immediately verifiable. Parents believe these schools will benefit their children now and in the future.

Table 14.1

Factors: Loadings After Varimax Rotation for Parental Choice of Nonpublic School Items

---

Factor 1: Perceptions about the School's Program

e.	Kinds of children in the program	.43
f.	High test scores of students	.41
g.	What other parents say about the program	.67
h.	What teachers say about the program	.56
i.	How well children like it	.38
n.	Beneficial contacts for the future	.55

Factor 2: Development of Academic and Social Characteristics in Children

j.	Values taught children	.43
l.	Developing a strong positive self-concept within children	.64
m.	Cultivates the intelligence of the child	.64
k.	Your own child's test score	.42
o.	School has high expectations for students	.37

Factor 3: Quality of School and Program

a.	Reputation of the school and program	.43
b.	Quality of teachers in the program	.67
c.	Quality of curriculum	.63

Note: Factor items are designated by letters in Tables 14.1 - 14.2 for convenience in cases of repetition; items were enumerated by alphabet on the original parent questionnaire

Factor 2 presented a set of items that focused on academic and social characteristics of children, for example, their values and self-esteem, along with cultivating intelligence and making high test scores possible. Note that parents want the whole child--not just cognitive possibilities--to be affected positively by the schooling process.

Factor 3 contained three pertinent items, with the emphasis on quality of teachers and quality of curriculum.

Within and among the three factors, the highest loadings on items that seem to influence parental choice of nonpublic schools are on quality of teachers, what other parents say about the program, developing a strong positive self-concept within children, cultivating the intelligence of the child, and quality of curriculum.

In the item-by-item analysis, parents were asked to indicate whether an item was extremely important, important, somewhat important, or not at all important. What should be noted is that parents are uniformly stating that the itemized characteristics are important or extremely important to them. In every case the means are at the 1 or 2 level, "extremely important" or "important." In no case do they fall to the 3 or 4 level, which would indicate only "somewhat important," or "not important at all."

In general, regarding the perception theme (factor 1) what other parents say about the program was rated important by 60 percent of respondents. What teachers say about the program was rated important by 83 percent of respondents. How well children liked the program was thought to be important by 83 percent of the respondents. Concern about the characteristics of children in the program was expressed by 64 percent of respondents. High test scores were important to 73 percent of respondents and 71 percent felt beneficial contacts for the future were important.

The second factor pertained to the development of academic and social characteristics in children. Again, in the item-by-item analysis, 97 percent of parents felt values taught children were important. Similarly, 98 percent of parents felt that developing a strong self-concept was important. Cultivating the child's intelligence was rated as important by 90 percent of the respondents, while 94 percent saw the child's test scores as important. Similarly, 95 percent of parents wanted the school to have high expectations of children.

Within the third factor, quality of the school and program, 94 percent of parents thought the reputation of the school was important while 99 percent thought the quality of the teachers was important. Further, with respect to the quality of the curriculum, 99 percent thought it important.

The one item which did not appear in the factors, but was asked about, had to do with discipline. However, 93 percent of respondents felt discipline was important and only one respondent expressed the belief that discipline was not at all important.

Which factors were most important to these Black parents? Which items within a factor seemed most important to them in choosing nonpublic schools? The factor with the lowest mean (highest importance) was the third, quality of school and program. It appears that Black parents may have selected nonpublic schools because they were perceived to have good reputations, quality teachers, and quality curricula. It is apparent from these findings that the quality of the school's program is an extremely important consideration for Black parents. This finding coincides with what other researchers have discovered with respect to the choice of private schooling by Black parents.

The second factor, development of academic and social characteristics in children, seems to be next in importance. Inspection of the means for items within this factor suggests that developing a strong positive self-concept, cultivating intelligence in the child, and the values taught may be the more salient items. This finding coincides with the results of other researchers, who discovered that values, the expectations of the school for the children, and enhancing the child's self-concept are important to Black parents.

Within the least salient factor, perceptions about the school's program, the most important considerations seem to be how well children like it and what other parents say.

Opinions about Choice

A series of questions designed to assess parents' opinions and beliefs regarding differences, advantages, and disadvantages of both nonpublic and public schools was included in the study. A comparison of some of the parental responses is provided in table 14.2.

The respondents seemed to believe that public schools had poor physical plants, did not offer challenging curricula or good extracurricular activities, had mediocre books and instructional materials, had average teachers, and did not offer their children a good education that would prepare them for the work force or to enter college. In addition, these Black parents seemed to believe that public schools lacked discipline, had poor academic standards, usually had large schools and overcrowded classes, and that public school teachers were not much interested in their pupils. It should be noted regarding discipline that these Black parents believed it was not only lacking in the public schools, but also in the homes of many public school children.

One possible explanation for the poor perception of public schools by these Black parents is that they may feel cut off from the public school system. It may be that public schools are perceived as the self-proclaimed domain of educational authorities (e.g., teachers, principals, etc.) who do not represent the interests of Black parents. Even when those authorities may also be Black, as is the case for most schools in Washington, D.C., it may be that the public school (or the public school system) is no longer responsive to parents, but to teachers, boards of education, and other political groups. Another possible explanation is that offered by Schneider in chapter 19--that Black parents may believe public schools have become obstacles to their children's upward social mobility. An examination of Black parents' choice of nonpublic schools bears this belief out to some extent.

Table 14.2

Factors: Loadings After Varimax Rotation for Ratings of Public and Nonpublic School Items

	Public Schools – Not Chosen	Nonpublic Schools – Chosen
Factor 1: Quality of Educational Institution and Programs		
a. Physical plants and facilities	.56	.49
b. Curriculum (subjects offered)	.69	.67
c. Handling of extracurricular activities (sports, theater, etc.)	.64	.64
d. Books and instructional materials	.64	.66
e. Quality of teaching	.53	.70
f. Education student receives	.50	.73
h. Preparing students for college	—	.50
Factor 2: Effectiveness of Program Administration		
g. Way schools are administered	.64	.46
h. Preparing students for college	.63	—
i. Way discipline is handled	.76	.85
j. Preparing for jobs – those students not planning to go to college	.63	.27
k. Behavior of students	.70	.74
l. Desegregation	.35	—

Note: Two sets of factor analyses were performed on questionnaire — one pertaining to public schools and one to nonpublic schools.

We found that quality of school and program were primary motivating forces behind Black parents' choice of nonpublic schools. In particular, these parents were concerned with the reputation of the school and the quality of the curricula and teachers. Secondly, these respondents wanted their children to be taught values, acquire positive self-concepts, and have their intelligence cultivated. Black parents wanted their children to perform well on tests, and they wanted schools to have high expectations of their children.

It also seemed important to Black parents what type of children attended the schools, whether their children liked the schools, and what teachers and other parents said about the school. These considerations seemed to reflect the Black parents' sense of community, which is often exhibited by Black people's oral tradition and group orientation--values which have been found to characterize Black American culture.[14] Further, these parents' behaviors may be corroborating the belief of Slaughter and

Schneider that Black parents have distinctive educational ideologies, and often choose schools that tend toward teacher-centered educational programs.

This study has found that parents who choose nonpublic schools are not necessarily middle and upper-income people. Carol Ascher has observed that nonpublic schools, especially in urban areas, do not seem to be attended primarily by middle and upper income Black students.[15] In fact, James G. Cibulka, Timothy O'Brien and Donald Zewe, in their study of Catholic schools in urban areas, found that half of the students enrolled were Black and that approximately 33 percent of them came from families with incomes below $10,000 annually.[16] The present study also found evidence which suggests that Black parents of all social backgrounds choose nonpublic schools.

CONCLUSIONS AND RECOMMENDATIONS

We believe that the historical struggle of Black Americans to obtain quality education for their children, in spite of a continuing system of institutionalized racism and second-class citizenship, causes them now to continually choose between public and nonpublic schools. Further, these parents make selections within each type of schooling (public or nonpublic) based on their financial means and the perceived intellectual abilities of their offspring. Overall, the choice of nonpublic schools seems to be a critique of otherwise preferred public schools.

We also believe, as do other writers (e.g., Ascher, Slaughter and Schneider, and Cibulka et al.) that Black parents' choice of nonpublic schools reflects their desire to provide the best possible quality of education for their young. Nonpublic schools have been perceived to provide basic skills instruction, cultivate higher-order thinking skills, have higher academic standards, and be more successful in preparing their students for college or the workplace. Taken together, these qualities may provide the necessary ingredients for Black youth to become socially skilled and academically prepared so that they can be more successful in a predominantly White society.

Black parents' choice of nonpublic schools underscores their determination to use education as a vehicle for upward mobility, regardless of their socioeconomic status.[17] Black parents may also be expressing their frustration with being powerless in the American public educational system. It may also be that Black parents want to be able to choose schools that may be more congruent with their own personal and cultural beliefs and values.[18]

Nonetheless, the message in the emerging Black flight from public schools may prove instructive to public school administrators. They may want to work toward increasing Black parental involvement in planning, curriculum, selecting teachers, and establishing academic standards. Perhaps public school administrators and teachers could enlist parents in developing programs to instill respect for authority and others in schools. It seems clear that parents need to be enlisted to help solve what are perceived as serious discipline problems in public schools. Such measures could be offered by a public school system, assuming these schools want to stem the loss of students.

If public schools expect to retain the Black constituency that they have enjoyed historically, they will need to examine perceptions and beliefs of Black parents who no longer elect to use public schools for their children's education--even though choices are made available to them within the public school system, for example, magnet schools. Research is needed on Black parental choices of and among public schools, rather than assuming that such selection is automatic.

Private school officials and teachers should be encouraged to retain and maintain their high standards of academic performance. They should perhaps consider including more of the culture and values of Blacks in their staffs, courses, and activities. As costs of these schools escalate, it is entirely possible that Black youth may need more financial assistance in order to continue to benefit from nonpublic schooling.

Black individuals and communities must consider the costs and benefits of education in nonpublic schools versus education in public schools--not only for themselves, but for the nation at large.

In general, perhaps more effort needs to be made to involve parents in their children's education. The education of our children is not the exclusive domain of teachers, principals, and/or educational organizations. Black parents seem to be saying that they want a voice in their children's education. Maybe it is time that school officials begin to listen.

NOTES

1. See, for example, Meyer Weinberg, A Chance to Learn: A History of Race and Education in the United States (New York: Cambridge University Press, 1977); and Minority Students; A Research Appraisal (Washington, D.C.: Government Printing Office, 1977);and The Search for Quality Integrated Education: Policy and Research on Minority Students in School and College (Westport, Conn.: Greenwood, 1983).

2. Shirley Moskow, "New Alternatives in Education: Three Case
    Studies," Tuesday Magazine monthly supplement to the News
    American (Baltimore) May 1973; Deborah Daniels, ed.,
    Education By, For and About African Americans A Profile of
    Several Black Community Schools (Lincoln, Neb.:
    University of Nebraska, Student Committee, Study
    Commission Undergraduate Education and the Education of
    Teachers, n.d.); Joan D. Ratteray, Alternative Educational
    Options for Minorities and the Poor, An Interim Project
    Report (Washington, D.C.: National Center for Neighborhood
    Enterprise, September, 1983) ERIC, 1984 (ED 242 828);
    Joan D. Ratteray, "Pulling Together for Education, " Black
    Family 4, no.4 (1984): 42-43, 63; Rukiyah Foster, "Ujamaa
    Teaching Instills African Values," Hilltop December 5, 1980:
    1; Hakim Eitiope, "Basing an Education on African Values,"
    Times Tribune, February 20, 1985:1.

3. Dennis P. Doyle, "A Din of Inequity: Private Schools
    Reconsidered," Teachers College Record 82, no. 4 (1981):
    661-673; Patrice Gaines-Carter, "Choices Difficult for Many
    Parents," Washington Post, District Weekly, February 14,
    1985: D.C. 1.

4. Ratteray, Alternative Educational Options for Minorities and the
    Poor; and "Pulling Together for Education."

5. Sarah Edwards and William Richardson, A Survey of MCPS
    Withdrawals to Attend Private Schools. ERIC, 1981 (ED 226
    096).

6. Joy Frechtling and Steven Frankel, A Survey of Montgomery
    County Parents Who Transferred Their Children Between
    Public and Private Schools in 1980-81. ERIC, 1982 (ED 234
    483).

7. Diana T. Slaughter and Barbara L. Schneider, Newcomers:
    Blacks in Private Schools. ERIC, 1986 (ED 274 768 and ED
    274 769).   See also   Diana T. Slaughter and Barbara L.
    Schneider, "Parental Goals and Black Student Achievement in
    Urban Private Elementary Schools: A Synopsis of Preliminary
    Research Findings," Journal of Intergroup Relations 13, no. 1
    (1985): 24-33.

8. Deborah J. Johnson, "Identity Formation and Racial Coping
    Strategies of Black Children and Their Parents: A Stress and
    Coping Paradigm"   (Ph.D. dissertation,   Northwestern
    University, 1987).

9. Virgil Blum, Quality Education for Inner-City Minorities Through Education Vouchers. ERIC, 1978 (ED 171 844); William Turner, "Reasons for Enrollment in Religious Schools: A Case Study of Three Recently Established Fundamentalist Schools in Kentucky and Wisconsin" (Ph.D. dissertation, University of Wisconsin, 1979); George Ballweg, "The Growth in the Number and Population of Christian Schools since 1966: A Profile of Parental Views Concerning Factors Which Led Them to Enroll Their Children in a Christian School" (Ph.D. dissertation, Boston University, 1980); Janet Huck, "The Bells of St. Michaels," Newsweek, April 20, 1981, p. 67.

10. James G. Cibulka, Timothy J. O'Brien, and Donald Zewe, S.J., Inner-City Private Elementary Schools: A Study (Milwaukee: Marquette University Press, 1982).

11. John Holmes and David Hiatt, Parental Expectations of the Christian School. ERIC, 1984 (ED 244 363).

12. Appreciation is expressed to Dr. William M. Richardson and Dr. Joy A. Frechtling of the Montgomery County, Maryland, School System for sharing their questionnaires with us and permitting adaptation of some of their items.

13. The traditional social science approach to factor analysis was used in making these computations. The Statistical Package for the Social Sciences was used. The number of factors extracted is determined by the number of factors with an eigenvalue greater than or equal to 1.0; the diagonals of the correlation matrix are initially replaced by squared multiple correlations; the iteration is stopped if the convergence reaches the .001 criterion; the maximum number of iterations is 25. The method of rotation used was an orthogonal varimax technique which simplifies the columns of the factor matrix.

14. Robert Carter and Janet E. Helms, "The Relationship of Value-Orientation to Racial Identity Attitudes," Measurement and Evaluation in Counseling and Development 19, no. 4 (1987): 185-195.

15. Carol Ascher, "Black Students and Private Schooling," Urban Review 18, no. 2 (1986): 137-145.

16. Cibulka, O'Brien, and Zewe, Inner-City Private Elementary Schools: A Study.

17. Slaughter and Schneider, Newcomers, p. 572.

18. Deborah J. Carter, "Parental Schooling Choice: African American Parents' Choice of Black Independent Schools" (M.A. thesis, Howard University, 1986).

15
The Educational Goals of Black Private School Parents

Diana T. Slaughter, Deborah J. Johnson, and Barbara L. Schneider

This chapter primarily reports data from a study which used an ethnographic approach to investigate the family-school relations of Black children and their parents. Impetus for the study came from observations of two related educational trends. First, increasing numbers of Black families are enrolling their children in urban nonpublic schools.[1] The percentages of Black children enrolled in all types of private schools, sectarian and nonsectarian, have nearly doubled in ten years. Second, though under no legal mandate to desegregate, many urban private schools have begun to systematically recruit Black pupils. The trends provide an excellent opportunity for carefully study of family-school relations because both families and schools could reasonably be expected to be very self-conscious of their educational goals. Importantly, the choices of the Black parents, particularly those choosing a desegregated, nonsectarian school, represent a historically unparalleled trend within Black American communities.

The study addressed two research questions: first, why do Black parents send their children to urban private elementary schools, and second, what are the experiences of the children in these schools? This chapter focuses primarily on the first question, using parent interview data obtained from Black and non-Black parents of children attending desegregated private schools.

*An earlier version of this chapter was presented at the first annual Conference on Ethnic and Minority Research, the International Association of Cross-Cultural Psychology, June 24-28, 1985, at the School of Education, Lund University, Malmo, Sweden. Another earlier version was presented at the annual meeting of the American Educational Research Association, March, 1985, in Chicago.

The aim was to achieve a holistic understanding of the socialization contexts in which the children were studying and learning, and therefore, the specific contribution of family-school relations to the children's schooling experiences. The ethnographic approach to study of families and schools combined hypothesis-testing with deliberate exploration.[2]

Several assumptions were made. First, it was assumed that families would differ in their reported educational goals, despite their common willingness and ability to make educational expenditures for their children. Second, it was assumed that as school philosophies differed, so too would the educational experiences of the children. Third, it was assumed that the Black parents could have different educational goals, even from a subset of non-Black parents whose children had already been friendly to some of their Black school peers. Finally, it was assumed that if a holistic ethnographic approach were used to study these families and schools, the results could contribute significantly to the field of education in two specific ways: first, by helping to establish criteria for excellence in Black education, and second, by improving substantially upon present understanding of how the in-school lives of middle-school children are impacted by behavioral patterns reflecting considerable consensus between families and schools.

In a separate study conducted by Johnson described in chapter 16, similar data were collected on Black parent educational goals, using the parent interview questions from the initial study.[3] However, the Johnson study was conducted in three predominantly Black private schools. Black parents have used such schools to educate their children for a number of years.[4] The availability of the Johnson data permitted contrasts in this chapter between the parental educational goals of Black parents sending their children to desegregated schools and the goals of those Black parents sending their children to predominantly Black private schools. Schools were deliberately chosen to have highly diverse educational programs, and to have a reputation for academic excellence.

Other researchers have offered reasons for why families enroll their children in private schools. They speculate that families are seeking: (1) a higher level of academic achievement for their child, (2) greater control and authority of the family in the child's education, and (3) greater value congruence between themselves and the school.[5] Additional reasons could include: (4) disaffection with public schools in urban neighborhoods where the families reside; (5) new availability of the necessary economic resources; (6) the schools' response to the potentially available student population, given changes in the racial and ethnic composition of cities; and (7) the "zeitgeist" of America since the 1954 Supreme Court decision.[6]

Unlike prior studies, a major assumption of the initial ethnographic study conducted by Slaughter and Schneider was that parents, including Black parents, have intuitive educational philosophies which contribute to school choice for their children. When parents have options, these "philosophies" will guide their selection of, and continued support for, particular types of educational programs. Specific reasons for school choice, therefore, would be embedded in an overall philosophy about the role of education and formal schooling in both their own and their children's lives. In the ethnographic study, the researchers inductively generated and characterized these philosophies, portraying them primarily as differing educational goals. In the second study, the initially identified goal types were cross-validated, and no new ones identified. After describing the identified goal types, including rationale, the results of a comparison of goals between the two groups of Black parents, as well as the non-Black parents, will be presented.

BACKGROUND

The dictionary defines goal as an end that one strives to attain; aim."[7] It is reasonable to assume that parents differ in their educational aims. American society has achieved consensus on the value of education, but there is consistent evidence of diversity of opinion as to the aims or purposes of education. The evidence is found in historical and philosophical analyses of education in America. It is found in the diversity of schooling arrangements and school types that exist. It is also found in the results of educational studies.

Over time, consensus has formed around differing educational aims. Early aims to provide for a literate citizenry were supplemented, some would say subrogated, by the aim of providing for social equity via equal educational opportunity. An emphasis on multiculturalism in the 1970s was overshadowed by emphasis upon a return to the basics.[8] John Dewey emphasized the child's preparation for life in the real world.[9] Today, many are concerned that education prepare children to cope as adults within an increasingly technological, service-oriented society.[10] Given the coexistence and prevalence of such differing views in society, it is reasonable to assume that parents differ in their perceptions of the desirable outcomes of their children's education and the desirable qualities of any school.

Coherent, but quite different, educational philosophies also coexist in American society. For example, some philosophies are far more child-centered than others.[11] The structure, sequencing, and pacing of curricula are less important than that an optimal match be achieved between what the child knows and what it can know and be taught. In the child-centered approach, it is thought that children are naturally motivated to explore and master novelty. Provided that they feel secure, such new learning is extraordinarily pleasurable, and therefore, self-reinforcing. More traditional approaches often assume children have to be motivated to learn, and stress the importance of the structure and organization of curricula, as well as adult sanctions, to the learning process.[12] In this study, parents were expected to differ in their perspections of how children learn and develop, and the respective roles of parents and teachers in children's learning.

Historically, schools have been organized and managed differently within American society. Some are largely parent-supervised and operated; others are managed by elected and/or appointed community boards of trustees. Both types are likely to be small and relatively self-contained with respect to having ultimate responsibility for the child's education. Other schools (e.g., parochial schools, public schools) are members of larger bureaucratic structures in which educational authority is ultimately held by persons equivalent to district superintendents or superintendents who report to boards of education. Apart from school organization and management, many other factors such as geographical location, extent of urbanization of the school's community, racial/ethnic mix of the school population, and school size, combine to determine the unique type of schooling experienced by a child's parents. It seems reasonable to assume that parents' educational goals for children would be partly influenced by appraisals of the contexts surrounding their own earlier educational experiences.

Both families and schools are institutions within a larger culture, in this instance, American culture. Both share, though unequally, in the child's socialization into that greater culture. Socialization research literature documents that as families differ in structural ties to the broader culture, their perceptions of the means and ends of childhood socialization differ.[13] Further, as society changes and introduces different demands upon its existing institutions, the socialization contexts experienced by children also change.[14] Families could be expected to differ in characterization of the role of their child's school in current family life according to their structural placement in society and the extent to which they have been impacted by societal changes. Such differences also partly influence perceptions of the aims of education because American families, as primary socialization institutions, perceive schools to be major secondary socialization settings for their children.

In summary, many factors converge to determine parental educational goals. The open-ended questions in the Family Educational Goals section of the Slaughter and Schneider parent interview addressed six topics thought important to an analysis of parental goals:

o   Prior educational experiences of the one or two responsible parents

o   Parental perceptions of how children learn and develop

o   Parental perceptions of the respective roles of teachers and parents in the child's learning

o   How parents characterize the role of their child's school in current family life

o   What parents envision as the desirable qualities of any school

o   Parental perceptions of the desirable outcomes of their child's education and schooling experiences

When the preceding six criteria were systematically applied to an examination of obtained parent interview data from the ethnographic study, it was possible to distinguish six different response patterns. The patterns were labeled: (1) Authoritative, (2) Deliberate, (3) Humanistic, (4) Moral, (5) Practical, and (6) Traditional.[15] The patterns were thought to relate to one another as follows:

First, families differ as to whether they see the primary authority for the child's education and schooling to reside within the family or within the school. Patterns classified as Authoritative or Humanistic emphasize the importance of the school in realizing the family's own educational goals for its children. Conversely, patterns classified as Deliberate, Moral, Practical, or Traditional emphasize school-centered authority for the child's education. Educational goals are to be defined by educators; the family supports the school's efforts.

Second, families differ in their perceptions of the centrality of the child's feelings in the educational process. Concern for the emotional climate of the school, the child's personal and social development, and the roles of teachers, parents in motivating children typify either Humanistic or Practical response patterns. These themes are not recurrent in other patterns.

Third, emphasis on the social or reputational standing of schools occur more frequently in the Authoritative and Traditional response patterns. The standards of the school and its educational curriculum, insofar as these are public, are particularly stressed in these response patterns.

Fourth, emphasis on definite linkages between curriculum and other educational experiences and child learning and development outcomes is most characteristic of the Deliberate and Moral response patterns. The outcomes may stress either personal capability for improved social standing in the future (Deliberate) or improved personal character (Moral). Other patterns tend to stress the quality of the child's immediate in-school experiences. All of the other patterns either more often stress specific child achievement or occupational outcomes and/or emphasize that if provided with a responsive learning environment, children will develop optimally, capable of selectively determining their own future.

HYPOTHESES

The following hypotheses were implicit in the research question, "Why are Black parents sending their children to desegregated private elementary schools?"

o   There is no difference in the educational goals of Black and non-Black parents who send their children to desegregated private elementary schools

o   There is no difference in the educational goals of Black parents who send their children to desegregated, in comparison to predominantly Black, private elementary schools

o   The educational goals of Black parents will not be related to the type of private elementary school (i.e., independent elite, independent alternative, catholic) attended by the children

Hypotheses one and two, as null hypotheses, argue against the assumption that there is anything special about parents who are Black and who send their children to desegregated private elementary schools. Hypothesis three argues against the assumption that type of school choice and family educational goals are related. Given the limitations of available resources, no comparison was made between Black private and public school parents, though the comparison was also implicit in the research question. During data analysis, the relationship of reported family income to parental educational goals was also determined.

METHOD

This chapter presents data on parent educational goals from seven private elementary schools, six of which are in Chicago.[16] Three schools are independent elite, two are independent alternative, and two are Catholic. Two elite schools, one alternative, and one Catholic school, all racially mixed, were the site for initial data collection from parents about their educational goals for their children (Study 1). The remaining three schools were the sites in which preliminary confirmation of the goal types identified in Study 1 was made, this time with Black parents whose children attended predominantly Black schools (Study 2).[17] Presentation of the rationale for school and parent selection in both studies will be followed by a brief discussion of the process used to identify the six types of parent educational goals and a description of the goal classifications.

School Selection

Study 1. Schools were deliberately selected from three different private school networks: independent elite, independent alternative, and sectarian (Catholic). All four schools had solid academic reputations and had existed for over ten years, and three of the four were both racially mixed <u>and</u> desegregated: Monroe (alternative, N = 126, 50-percent Black); Oak Lawn (elite, N = 331, 28-percent Black); Roman (elite, N = 564, 6-percent Black); and St. August (Catholic, N= 126, 35-percent Black).

Schools were contrasted with 1980 national averages for their networking affiliation on pupil enrollment, number of teachers, and pupil/teacher ratios. One significant difference was obtained. Roman's pupil enrollment was significantly greater than the national average for the Independent Schools Network ($\underline{Z}$ score = 3.54, $\underline{p}$ =.05). Similar results were obtained when the four schools were contrasted, using state data tapes, with their Chicago counterparts.

Unlike most private schools in Chicago, the schools were located in racially diverse neighborhoods. Two of the four schools, Oak Lawn and St. August, had shown increments greater than 10 percent in Black enrollment over the eleven years (1970-1981) prior to the study, but two, Monroe and Roman, had not. Local population characteristics indicated that the schools were located in economically and educationally advantaged census tracts, but the tracts also reflected the socioeconomic diversity characteristic of metropolitan Chicago.

Study 2. Five criteria were relevant to the selection of schools for the study. The schools should: (1) reflect diverse private school networks (alternative, elite, sectarian); (2) have fifty or more pupils; (3) have 90-100 percent Black enrollment; (4) have been established for ten or more years; and (5) be located in metropolitan Chicago. All three schools met at least four of these criteria; one school was located in Washington, D.C. The schools were located in predominantly Black communities, typically lower middle-income. Among the institutions selected were a parochial school (St. Benedito), a traditional school (Chaucer), and an alternative school (Watoto). Located in Washington, D.C., Watoto had a pan-African sociocultural orientation. Each school had 60-100 pupils.

Parent Selection

For Study 1, parent interviewers were identified from school-supplied lists of households of children attending grades K-7 in each school in the spring of 1983. The lists included all of the Black households and a subset of non-Black households (White, Asian, Hispanic) whose children were observed by teachers to be friendly to one or more Black children in the school. Non-Black households were selected to maximize the likelihood of similarities with Black households; therefore, obtained differences between the two parent groups would be especially significant. Black parents were interviewed by Black interviewers, non-Black parents by White or Asian interviewers.

For Study 2, parent interviewees were identified from either school-supplied lists (St. Benedito and Watoto) or director/teacher nominations (Chaucer). As in Study 1, the Black parents were interviewed by Black interviewers. The interviews obtained are depicted in table 15.1 by school type and parent race.[18]   In Study 1, data were obtained from 131 households, 73 Black and 58 non-Black parents. Typically, the 2 1/2 hour interview was conducted with mothers, in the home of the family. However, interviews were conducted with five fathers (all single parents), and in 21 interviews, both parents were present. The study assumed that the primary caregiver and respondent (s) presented the dominant views as to the family's educational goals for the child.

Table 15.1

Households Interviewed by School and Race of Parents

Parents Interviewed	Study 1				Study 2			Total
	Monroe (Alternative)	Oak Lawn (Elite 2)	Roman (Elite 1)	St. August (Catholic)	Watoto (Alternative)	Chaucer (Elite)	St. Benedito (Catholic)	
Black	22	16	15	20	10	17	14	114
Non-Black	15	13	15	15	—	—	—	58
Total	37	29	30	35	10	17	14	172

A total of 114 Black parents from a sample pool of about 294 Black families across the seven schools were interviewed, or approximately 38.8 percent of the available sample pool. Across the four Study 1 schools, a total of 71 eligible Black and 139 eligible non-Black parents were not interviewed. In Study 2, across two of the three schools, 65 eligible Black parents were not interviewed. At the third school, 17 of the 20 nominated families did not participate, but no complete list of interviewees was made available. About 50 percent of the eligible parents who did not participate were never contacted for scheduling, and the other 50 percent refused to participate when contacted. In Study 1, refusals focused on scheduling problems and the anticipated time required to administer the interview. In Study 2, given the aims of that study, refusals were typically related to racial issues rather than issues concerning identification of the family's educational goals for the children.[19]

STUDY 1: IDENTIFICATION OF PARENTAL
RESPONSE PATTERNS

Coding began in January, 1984, with inductive derivation of the patterns of response to nineteen interview questions, ranging from "Thinking back to your own school days, what would you most want to change if you could relive them?" to "Between the two of you, who feels most strongly in favor of private schooling... and why?" and "At this time, what is your idea of the essential elements of a quality education for your child?"

Each of the six response patterns emerged within the context of the preliminary detailed research team discussions of thirteen parent interviews (four Deliberate, two Authoritative, two Humanistic, two Moral, two Traditional, and one Practical). Black and non-Black parents were represented in four of the six patterns; Practical and Authoritative occurred only among Black parents in the initial thirteen cases.

After preliminary consensus was established about the salient features of each of the six inductively derived response patterns, and tentative descriptions were written, seventy-three interviews were coded by two members of the research team. The four schools had been deliberately chosen to maximize the probability of differing educational philosophies. However, student readers knew little of these philosophies, and readers did not judge interviews they had conducted. The relative naivete of the student members of the team was very important because Slaughter and Schneider had jointly interviewed top administrators at each school. However, during the team meetings, the schools attended by the parents' children were not discussed; the focus was on classifying the response pattern of the individual interviewee.

The purpose of having two judges was to achieve consensus on the classification of a particular response pattern. Whenever Slaughter or Schneider were not among the judges, the judges were to be mixed-race pairs. Black interviews were rated first, and a Guttman scale was used to assign interviews in sequence to each pair of judges. Major identified discrepancies in classification were discussed and resolved with the group. Later, three additional female raters (two Black, one White) were added to the team. They assisted in coding the remaining interviews and resolving earlier discrepancies. The two new Black judges had conducted parent interviews, but not at the schools of the parents they rated. Finally, Slaughter and Schneider reviewed all 131 classifications, even in instances where there had been no discrepancies (63 of 131 cases, or 48 percent). Therefore, every case had a minimum of three readings, and some had more. Judges had the verbatim tapes of this section of the interview to refer to whenever the interview protocol left them in doubt of the most viable classification. Raters routinely identified, on a coding form, the key responses and phrases that determined their classification. Though raters were instructed to identify any newly emergent response patterns that could not be readily classified into one of the existing six categories, none were identified. In a subsequent study of interrater reliability (percent agreement of classification category) using thirteen cases, the interrater reliability was found to be .77.[20]

THE SIX PARENTAL EDUCATIONAL GOALS: KEY ELEMENTS AND APPLICATION TO PRIVATE SCHOOL CHOICE

In the final classification, the 131 response patterns were distributed as follows: Authoritative (n = 19); Deliberate (n = 33); Humanistic (n = 34); Moral (n = 10); Practical (n = 13); Traditional (n = 22).

The key elements of each response pattern will be listed prior to a more descriptive, holistic definition. These elements essentially distinguish each response pattern from the other five because they are not found, in combination, in any of the other patterns. The definition is a thumbnail sketch of the pattern, with a primary focus on how the elements converged to cause the parents to choose private schooling for the child.

The distinction made throughout between the key elements of the response pattern on the one hand, and the choice of a private school on the other, is important. The response patterns may be generalizable to public school parents, insofar as the patterns reflect differing educational ideologies. However, in this sample, these ideologies are used to rationalize the specific choices of private schooling. The key descriptive elements implicate private schools per se only in the Traditional response pattern, and this pattern contains the most mixed group of responses.

Authoritative Response Pattern

Key Elements. There are six key elements of this response pattern; in order of greatest to least priority, they are:

o   These parents decided where to send their child to its school after a very systematic investigation of alternative options, primarily because they see themselves as being very responsible for the quality of education their child receives inside and outside of school

o   These parents are very vocal and articulate about the educational philosophy of their child's school. They easily evaluate the strengths and weakness of the school, in so far as they affect their child o   The parents believe they are responsible for ensuring teacher accountability. Mechanisms for clearcut teacher accountability and high academic standards are perceived to be lacking in many American schools

o   These parents believe that the essential elements of a quality education for their child include exposure of their child to children of socially and culturally different backgrounds

o   The parents believe that the ideal school should have, in addition to a strong, broad academic program that is intellectually challenging, a focus on the social fabric of society, including social problems

o   The parents believe that the optimal educational environment plays an important role in the formation of children's social identity and the maintenance of their self-esteem

Summary Definition.   Parents who stress the importance of their own responsibility for their child's education are parents who choose a school primarily because they perceive that it offers them the best opportunity to protect their children from adverse in-school social experiences.   These parents often vividly describe the negative educational experiences that children can have, and are determined that these experiences not become part of their own children's lives.   They are very aware that education occurs in a larger American social and cultural context, and seek ways to both minimize the impact of perceived negative features of our society and maximize perceived positive ones.   The specifics of these "features" may vary between families, but interests are very similar: these parents want to retain influence vis-a-vis teachers and school administrators in their child's education.   They believe that a deficient education is the probable outcome of relinquished parental responsibility.   They choose a school whose faculty and staff can be trusted to adhere very closely to the family's educational standards.   They are sensitive to any aspects of the school environment which could attenuate their family's control and influence over the child.

The desire to maintain control of educational standards often led the family to select private schooling.   However, such parents are not overly child-centered.   When they discuss the child's learning and development, they generally emphasize the quality of instruction that the child receives, rather than the child's feelings about it.

These parents believe that the child's teacher must expect that he or she can learn, and deliver the curriculum accordingly.   They want teachers to be on task as much as possible.   Their specific ongoing parental role is to support the school in its maintenance of high academic standards.   However, these parents also firmly believe that they are competent judges of whether children are being adequately instructed. They prefer that, in relation to their child, the authority of teachers and administrators be subject only to the authority of themselves.

Deliberate Response Pattern

Key Elements. There are five key elements of this response pattern

o   These parents believe that good teachers are absolutely essential for children to learn. Because the parents firmly believe that children cannot learn without good teachers, the hallmark of an excellent school is excellent teaching. In short, parents are not educators, teachers are

o   These parents believe that good schooling provides training in communication, organization, and other social skills. Success in school and life, requires exposure to such training in part because it enhances self-confidence

o   These parents openly express dissatisfaction with the poor quality of education they experienced as children. They are very determined that their children receive something better; they want a good educational foundation, order and structure in the classroom, and an enriched curriculum that provides for the special needs and talents of their child

o   These parents have very high educational and occupational standards. They typically project professional status for their child; they are definitely not content to let the child decide for itself

o   These parents particularly like small classes because they believe they provide more opportunities for personalized individual attention and instruction. They frequently emphasize that the special attention received and needed by their child could not be provided in schools with larger classes

Summary definition. Parents in this category choose private schooling primarily to introduce academic as well as social skills they perceive they are unable to give their child elsewhere (e.g., at home or in public schools). The school is perceived as playing a vital, independent role in the total development of the child. It is the school's responsibility to nurture the individual talents of the child in order to maximize her or his opportunities for social mobility. Parents expect the school to provide an educational experience for their child that includes quality instruction in basic skill areas and exposure to desirable social skills.

School is a place to "learn all about the world and how to get along in it." Communication and organizational skills are as important as learning to read and write. Teachers, rather than parents, can accomplish these tasks because of their pedagogical expertise; therefore, dedicated teachers are highly respected.

These parents believe the private school experience will extend the child's college and career choices. Such choices may not have been available to the parents when they themselves completed high school. A private education will ensure that the child has the necessary qualifications to enter a "good college," which will eventually guarantee the child high occupational status attainment.

Humanistic Response Pattern

Key Elements. There are six key elements in this response pattern:

o   These parents want their children to learn in an environment that is pleasant, joyful, and relatively non-competitive. They judge the goodness of a school according to whether children are both academically productive and happy within it, and they feel very competent in making such a judgment

o   The parents stress the importance of teachers who create an atmosphere that fosters curiosity, creativity, and problem-solving as necessary components of the learning process

o   These parents believe that parents and teachers generally should have an open, close relationship; communication about the child's welfare and development should be frequent and both formal and informal channels should be used

o   Parents believe that small classes and individualized instruction are important elements to a child's productive and happy life in school

o   Parents expect the school to play an important, significant role in the child's general personal and social development

o   Parents believe that excessive bureaucratic rigidity and constraints in many schools thwart these essentials of quality education

Summary Definition. Parents who choose private schooling primarily for humanistic reasons emphasize the kind of person they want their child to become, and the kind of personal and social relationships they want their child to have while in the process of "becoming." They are keenly aware of their child's unique talents, strengths, and weaknesses, and they expect the child's schooling experiences to capitalize on the child's unique individual expressions.

They may stress that they want their child to be challenged academically, but they are just as likely to stress that they want their child to mature socially as a consequence of close, personal contacts with adults and children who may hold different, but complementary, values and perspectives.

These parents expect close ties between their family and the school. They view the child's learning and development as essentially a result of a partnership between themselves and their child's teachers. The school's role is one of extension of the family's role as educator. Feelings generated as a result of the child's interaction are important dimensions of the teaching-learning process. Teachers are expected to thoughtfully attend to children's feelings, and to respond to them. In short, the school is perceived as an extension of the family; parents are looking for an educational environment that is child-centered and affect-based; the focus is on what the child needs to develop.

Flexibility and responsibility are highly desirable qualities of a school as far as these parents are concerned. Children should be able to learn how to learn independently; this means that all school activities are considered from the vantage point of their contribution to a quality education for the child. Further, teachers and administrations are expected to accommodate to any immediate familial exigencies which could affect the child's learning and participation in school. They understand that the willingness of school faculty and staff to accommodate is frequently contingent upon the expected close ties established as a result of continuing, reciprocal exchanges of both material and nonmaterial resources between themselves and the school.

Moral Response Pattern

Key Elements. There are two key elements of this response pattern:

o   These parents firmly believe that a quality education addresses the spiritual side of a child's development, equally as well as the basics and/or an enriched curriculum. Therefore, a key focus of the child's education is the development of moral and social character

o   The parents prefer a disciplined, ordered learning environment in which children learn to behave in accordance with respected adults' standards and expectations

Summary definition. Parents who choose private schooling primarily for moral reasons consider ethics and morality to be essential elements of a good school's curriculum. Learning obedience, respectfulness, and the difference between right and wrong are as highly valued outcomes for children by these families as is learning the basics of reading, writing, and mathematics. Other studies and school activities are considered secondary and/or more appropriate for discussion at home.

Teachers are revered as the ultimate authority in academic as well as social issues. Learning is best accomplished in an ordered and disciplined environment. Parents expect that the child's education will equip him or her with the academic requisites to pursue a higher education. When describing what their career goals are for their child, the parents tend to be very specific about acceptable occupations, such as doctor or lawyer.

One or more of the parents is likely to have attended a parochial school. The school's role is to carry on the cultural and moralistic tradition that the parents may have received as children. The school is viewed as the key factor in transmitting the cultural and moral history of the family across generations.

Practical Response Pattern

Key Elements. There are five key elements of this response pattern.

o   These parents expect teachers to be nuturing, and thus demonstrate concern for the academic and social-emotional needs of the child

o   These parents are especially sensitive to any signs of rejection or indifference on the part of school faculty or staff toward themselves or their children; such behavior is intolerable

o   The parents look to the school for support of their own learning and parenting; they highly respect the expertise and advice of school personnel

o   The parents believe that the "good parent" provides the best education affordable for the child

o   The parents believe that the goal of education is to prepare oneself for a respectable job in society; schools have the ultimate authority in this preparatory process

Summary definition. Of utmost importance to those parents who exemplify the practical choice model is that the teacher must demonstrate care and concern for the academic and emotional needs of the child. Often based on their own reported past and/or present experiences and observations, unfairness, insolence, and rudeness by the school to themselves or their children is intolerable. In a world that these parents frequently perceive as dangerous and unstable, the school serves as a sanctuary where the child can be safe and thus learn in a protected environment. Therefore, school climate is very important to these parents, and they respond loyally and warmly to a climate which they feel is caring, supportive, and respectful of their child and themselves.

These parents look to the school for support of their own learning and parenting. They respect the advice and expertise of the school personnel on all educational matters as they may not necessarily be knowledgeable as to how children learn and develop.

In the view of these parents, good parents are those individuals who try to provide the best education they can possibly afford for their child. Consequently, it is not unusual to find that many of these parents are making considerable personal sacrifices to send their children to private school.

Finally, these parents, while maintaining that education is very important, firmly believe that the primary aim of education is to prepare oneself for a respectable job.

Traditional Response Pattern

Key Elements. There are five key elements of this response pattern.

o   These parents believe firmly in the importance of a high-quality college preparatory learning environment, beginning as early as elementary school, if not before

o   The parents believe that the best education is in private schooling because such schools provide the necessary exposure to an enriched curriculum. One or both family members often have a prior history of private school attendance, and the options considered for the child were usually limited to the pool of available private schools

o   The parents emphasize the importance of competence, knowledgeable teachers to the educational process, however

o   These parents also have a strong belief in their child's intellectual potential; they place considerable emphasis on training the child to be an effective competitor

o   These parents emphasize that the social reputation of the child's peers is very important; peers' families should share similar educational and social values

Summary definition. Parents who exemplify the traditional choice model are committed to a belief that the best training for the high achievement goals they have for their children is found in private schools. They want their children to be inspired to work hard, compete successfully, and excel. They look to an enriched college preparatory curriculum and the reputation of a rigorous learning environment to develop these attributes. The school should provide the child with a strong foundation in the basic skills, but should also prepare the child, through an enriched curriculum, to assume a leadership position in society.

In contrast to other parents, teachers per se are not perceived by these parents as having special status; they are expected to be competent and knowledgeable in their subject fields so that they can contribute significantly to the development of the child's inherent intellectual potential. Almost as important as teachers is the school social environment. After-school peer group contacts are encouraged among schoolmates, and many parents may go to elaborate lengths to ensure that their children interact with socially acceptable peers. Parents are especially sensitive to what others (perceived) like-minded parents do with, or provide for, their children. Comments such as "Everybody sends their child to private school in this area..." are not uncommon. It is likely that one or both parents attended a private elite school, and therefore, private education per se is a social symbol, a symbol of familial prestige. These parents believe that the good school provides the socially appropriate "lens" through which children, by observation and actual experimentation, learn about the good life and the best that this civilization offers. Therefore, the good school conserves the essential values of family and home, as these parents understand them.

RESULTS

Results will be presented in order of hypotheses 1-3. First, the background characteristics of the parents in Studies 1 and 2 are summarized (these characteristics have been detailed elsewhere).[21] Key similarities and differences between the Black and non-Black groups in study 1, and between Blacks in Studies 1 and 2 are summarized preparatory to discussion of the parents' educational goals.

Parental Background

Black and non-Black parents (mothers, and fathers) in Study 1 did not differ significantly in age or years of educational attainment; college completion was the norm. However, Black families were significantly more likely to report less annual family income. In 1982, the mean for Black families was $35,000-$44,999, with a mode (20 percent) of $15,000 -$24,999, but the mean for non-Black families was between $45,000-$54,999, with a mode (24.5 percent) of $100,000 or above. The majority of parents in both groups (78.9-percent Black, 80.7-percent non-Black) reported that their children did not receive scholarship aid.

The 1980 U.S. Census code was used to classify occupations, as well as the related industry in which the occupation was pursued. The majority of working mothers and fathers engaged in either professional or executive/managerial/administrative occupations. Black parents tended to work in industries related to educational services, non-Black parents in industries related to health services.

The majority of Black (68 percent) and non-Black (81 percent) mothers had not attended a racially desegregated elementary school; Black mothers were nearly twice as likely to have attended a desegregated school as non-Black mothers (32 percent versus 19 percent). Black mothers were about equally likely to have had White teachers (47.2 percent) as Black teachers (45.7 percent). However, the overwhelming majority of non-Black mothers (83 percent) reported having only White teachers. Significantly more non-Black mothers reported that they and the fathers of their children had attended private elementary schools. However, the majority of parents in both racial groups, at all schools, had not attended private elementary schools. No significant race differences were found in the educational aspirations or expectations. Parents at all schools reported that they hoped that their child would obtain a college degree, and they expected the child to attain one.

In summary, Black parents had lower family incomes and were more likely to have attended a racially desegregated school and experienced other-race teachers, than non-Black parents. However, Black parents were less likely to have attended a private elementary school. Otherwise, the two groups of parents were similar in age, years of education, occupational rank, and educational aspirations and expectations for their children.

The Black parents in Study 2 were not significantly different from those in Study 1 on either the average years of maternal education or average annual family income. The mean family income category for Black parents in the predominantly Black schools was also $35,000-$44,999, and the mode (21.1 percent) $15,000-$24,000.

Parental Educational Goals

Hypothesis one predicted no difference in the educational goals of Black and non-Black parents who send their children to desegreated private elementary schools. In this study, this hypothesis was not supported by obtained data (see table 15.2). Chi-square analyses indicated a significant effect for race, X^2 (5, $\underline{N}$ = 131) = 11.43, $\underline{p}$ = .04. Compared to non-Blacks, Blacks were twice as likely to have response patterns classified as Authoritative or Practical, and almost twice as likely to have them classified as Deliberate. Non-Blacks were twice as likely to have response patterns classified as Humanistic.

Table 15.2

Frequency Distributions by School Racial Composition, Parental Race, and Educational Goals

	Auth.	Del.	Hum.	Moral	Prac.	Trad.	Total
			Parental Educational Goal				
Racially Mixed Schools (n = 4)							
Black Parents	14	22	13	6	9	9	73
(%)	(19.2)	(30.1)	(17.8)	(8.2)	(12.3)	(12.3)	(100)
Non-Black	5	10	21	6	4	12	58
(%)	(8.6)	(17.2)	(36.2)	(10.3)	(6.9)	(20.7)	(100)
Predominantly Black Schools (n = 3)							
Black Parents	12	4	4	4	9	8	41
(%)	(29.2)	(9.8)	(9.8)	(9.8)	(21.9)	(19.5)	(100)
Total Black Parents							
	26	26	17	10	18	17	114
(%)	(22.8)	(22.8)	(14.9)	(8.8)	(15.8)	(14.9)	(100)

Hypothesis two predicted no difference in the educational goals of Blacks who send their children to desegregated private elementary schools, in comparison to Blacks who send their children to predominantly Black schools. This hypothesis was supported by obtained data. Chi-square analyses indicated a nonsignificant effect for school racial composition, X^2 (5, N = 114) = 9.651, p = .09. The trend in these data toward significance (i.e., $p < .10$) was probably caused by the finding that at least one response pattern, Deliberate, occurred three times more frequently among Black parents who sent their children to desegregated schools.

Hypothesis three predicted that the educational goals of both Black and non-Black parents would not be significantly related to the type of private school attended by their children. Conclusive testing of this hypothesis must await the results of other studies because the conventional assumptions of the chi-square analysis were not met in the present one. Specifically, a number of cells had Expected Frequencies (EF) less than 5, accumulating to more than 20 percent in both Black and non-Black matrices, whenever school was treated as an independent variable. Even given that there is some flexibility and diversity of opinion about interpreting data under such conditions, we prefer to interpret this new data conservatively.[22] With this proviso, therefore, we note that when the total group of Black parents (i.e., N = 114) is considered according to school type (i.e., private elite, private alternative, Catholic), with five of 18 cells (27.8 percent) being less than the minimum EF of 2.8, chi-square analyses are highly significant, X^2 (10, $\underline{N}$ = 114) = 76.6, $\underline{p}$ = .00.

Specifically, the Moral and Practical response patterns are more likely to be given by parents whose children attend the two parochial schools, which account for 100 percent ($\underline{N}$ = 10) and 72 percent (N = 18), respectively, of all responses in these two classifications. The Deliberate and Traditional response patterns are more likely to be given by parents whose children attend the three elite schools, which account for 65 percent ($\underline{N}$ = 26) and 76 percent ($\underline{N}$ = 13) of all responses in these two classifications. Finally, the Authoritative and Humanistic response patterns are more likely to be given by parents whose children attend the two alternative schools, which account for 58 percent ($\underline{N}$ = 26) and 59 percent ($\underline{N}$ = 17) of all responses in these two classifications.

On an exploratory basis, families with annual incomes below $35,999, in comparison with families at or above this level of income, were more likely to be impacted by school racial composition. At the lower income levels, the two groups of Black families tended to differ in their educational goals. In particular, Deliberate and Humanistic response patterns were more prevalent in the desegregated school situation.

DISCUSSION

Many factors determine a family's choice of a school for their children, and therefore, it was decided that no one response to a particular interview question would be sufficiently informative for purposes of this ethnographic research. Rather, it was decided to develop criteria to guide the research team in making a holistic judgment about the nature of the rationale offered by the parent(s) in response to selected parent interview questions.

This chapter provides evidence that individual Black parents differ in their educational goals when, as a group, they are financially secure enough to afford private schooling for their children. It also provides evidence that Black parents differ from a similar socioeconomic group of non-Black parents in the types, though not the nature, of goals more often emphasized, but that school racial composition (racially mixed versus predominantly Black) does not significantly relate to how educational goals are conceived by these parents for their children. Finally, evidence from the study suggests that parental educational goals, within the same racial group, may also be associated with the type of school attended by the children.

Although Black parents do have preferred educational goals (i.e. Deliberate, Authoritative), they respond flexibly to the school environments in which their children participate. The Deliberate response pattern encapsulates the vision of education as a vehicle of social mobility and opportunity; the school is a crucible in which the necessary socialization skills are acquired for this purpose. Schools are expected to transform their clientele into persons able to realize that which is best about the American dream. Here are some themes from the protocol of one such Black parent, including *what they believe are essential elements of a quality education:*

[My school was characterized by] brutality--kids were paddled in the hand. Writing on the board 100 times...The subject requirements and different subjects added. History was limited and biased. The teachers needed to be changed because of inadequate materials and preparation...I wanted something different for my children and I've had an opportunity to realize just what is important for a person's future. The academic requirements are more advanced. More individualized instruction, more parent participation. More parent input and concern about the curriculum. Just the reverse of what was in my school. Pupil composition. The pupil composition is mostly White in my daughter's school while it was only Black in my elementary school...My child needed more of a challenge...I found my daughter was two and a half to three levels above her peers...I was looking for the best. Convenience also a factor..[Essential elements of a quality education include] A school that is aware of change for the purpose of preparing children to meet those changes. Since this school meets my standards, I would rely on the school to select the proper instructors...[I want my child to be prepared for college years--to meet challenge of any college, not a specific career....[for] a society where middle and upper income people function...(for) cultural exposure...[learn to be a] self-motivated, self-starter.]

The Authoritative response pattern projects a vision of education in which the family assumes an assertive, protective stance in relation to the totality of the child's socialization experiences, both at home and in school. The quality of the child's social relationships must be monitored if the child is to be productive in a complex, too-frequently hostile, world. The family is ultimately very responsible for the child's emergence as an "educated" person. Here are some themes from the protocol of one such Black parent, *including what they believe are essential elements of a quality education:*

Lot of politics [in reference to own schooling experiences]. Teachers got jobs that way; a lot of them were not qualified...If I had been properly motivated [I] could have achieved more--you couldn't aspire to be certain things when I was young--only certain things. No one ever used their imagination to think of how times would change for us and direct us toward the future. Hopefully, our [Black] kids won't have to face this. I wanted my kids to have the best they could get...We aren't that sold on private schools. We're sold on a good education...We're striving. [We want] <u>foreign languages, math proficiency, good reading and writing knowledge of English</u>...Children learn from parents. Teachers are to supplement that learning with more particular goals in a more structure sense. The federal government says you have to have schooling; it's not left up to a particular municipality to decide that...but I don't feel that teachers are responsible for education...They're the catalyst--the parents are responsible to see to it that their kids are educated... A good education--the only thing I feel I'm responsible for--the one legacy I have to give...

Detailed contrasts are beyond the scope of this chapter. However, it is instructive to quote four parents, two of whose response patterns were classified as Traditional, as to what they, too, believe are essential elements of a quality education for their children.

Humanistic (first parent): High motivation; an environment where he feels happy; challenging work, the ability to compete with himself, and an excitement for learning...that's my main criteria. I am not as concerned about competition. The excitement for learning should carry over after school hours. Humanistic (second parent): Creates desire or curiosity, joy in learning process, as [the] child gets older, more importance of curriculum...teacher [must] enjoy what [he or she is] doing, well-versed in subject area.

Traditional (first parent): Material must include the basics, reading, writing, and arithmetic and approached...thoroughly, especially reading comprehension has to be stressed. Writing, expressing himself, and science. In the younger grades, I prefer females [teachers]. Children who come from homes where the parents are concerned about their education are the kind of children I want him to attend school with. Traditional (second parent): Challenging peers--[other intellectual kids]. Competition...teachers would have to set high goals for kids...Teach them how to critically think...

Other researchers have found that parents whose children attend parochial schools are not necessarily adherents of the school's religious faith.[23] In this study, the parents of these children particularly appreciated the warmth, caring, and respect that they perceived their families received from school personnel. The goals of education were to include basic respect and valuation of individual students and their families, in a community setting in which perhaps all too often, such esteem and deference may be missing.

Generally, there are three alternative interpretations of these findings. First, the parents may have chosen the schools in accordance with their educational goals. Second, the schools may have chosen pupils whose parents have educational goals that initially coincide with their own. A corollary is that the children of such parents are more likely to be retained in the schools. Third, parents and each school, from the moment of initial inquires about admissions, engage in a reciprocal, interactive socialization process in which the school's philosophy is gradually internalized by the sending parents, partly because of perceptions of benefits to the child. Given study findings, this third position is the one most favored.

Few parents reported being as systematic and rational as might be expected, given the personal costs to them, in their educational planning for their children. In fact, response patterns differed in this very respect, with Authoritative and Humanistic response patterns being far more definite about the family's authority for the child's education. Frequently, parents (non-Black) offering Traditional and Moral response patterns simply continued to support a habitual preference for private schooling that had continued in their families for one or more generations. These parents firmly placed the majority responsibility for education with the schools.

All of the schools tolerated a wide range of educational aims within their communities. No fewer than three of the six response patterns (goal classifications) were found in each of the seven schools, whether among Black or non-Black parents. In fact, there were more identified parental educational goals than schools. Although all schools had a central tendency, each individual school community also embraced a wide range of values among its families. The schools accepted and retained children whose parents disagreed in part with the school's perception of its educational mission.

Only the third interpretation seems especially useful: schools and families engage in mutual transactions over time in which the overall school community's sense of educational purpose, mission, or identity is continually defined and reaffirmed. These "rituals of reaffirmation" constitute a socialization process that is educationally beneficial to entire families.

Not all parents sought greater control and authority over their children's education; not all showed evidence of high value congruence between themselves and the schools. Other data indicated that not all parents were especially supportive of desegregation. In any event, the distinguishing features between Black and non-Black parents did not pivot around finances, disaffection with neighborhood public schools, or racially separate schools. Goals also did not differ in the degree to which Black children's education for positive racial identity development was affirmed, whether or not the parent sent the child to a predominantly Black school. Therefore, the educational goals of middle-income, professional Black parents for their children may currently be being achieved at the expense of the children's longer-term commitment to the Black community.

Schools were selected from different private school networks; it is not surprising to have found that sending parents have differing educational philosophies. The contribution of this study has been to articulate those philosophies from the parents' perspectives. It is concluded that Black parents are sending their children to private schools because the schools have an educational purpose or mission with which they can eventually identify. It is precisely the diversity in available schools that is attractive to the Black community. Each family may find a school whose educational goals, even if not entirely isomorphic to its own, are found to be sufficiently engaging and satisfactory when expressed in the many rituals of reaffirmation.

NOTES

1. Diana T. Slaughter and Barbara L. Schneider, Newcomers: Blacks in Private Schools. ERIC, 1986 (ED 274 768 and ED 274 769); ED 274 769 is the document which contains the Coding Manual for use in classifying parental educational goals. See also Barbara L. Schneider and Diana T. Slaughter, "Educational Choice for Blacks in Urban Private Elementary Schools," in Thomas James and Henry Levin, eds., Comparing Public and Private Schools (London: Falmer Press, 1988), vol. 1, pp. 294-310.

2. Data collection techniques included the use of open-ended and informal interviews, narrative observations of student life in participating schools, and tests and inventories administered by teachers to children. Data were obtained from school records and publications.

3. Deborah J. Johnson, "Identity Formation and Racial Coping Strategies of Black Children and Their Parents: A Stress and Coping Paradigm" (Ph.D. dissertation, Northwestern University, 1987).

4. See, for example, chapters 8 and 13, in this volume.

5. S. Abramowitz and A. Stackhouse, The Private High School Today (Washington, D. C.: National Institute of Education, 1981); Rev. Virgil Blum, "Private Elementary Education in the

Inner City," Phi Delta Kappan, 66 (1985): 643-646; James Coleman, Thomas Hoffer, and Sally Kilgore, High School Achievement: Public, Catholic, and Private Schools Compared (New York: Basic Books, 1982).

6. Institute for Research on Educational Finance and Goverance. Policy Notes: Public and Private Schools (Stanford: Stanford University, School of Education, CERAS Building, 1985), Winter/Spring issue.

7. David Guralnik ed., Webster's New World Dictionary (New York: Macmillan, 1962), p. 321.

8. Gwen Baker, "Policy Issues in Multicultural Education in the United States," Journal of Negro Education 48 (1979): 253-266; James Banks, "Black Youth in Predominantly White Suburbs: An Exploratory Study of Their Attitudes and Self-Concepts," Journal of Negro Education 53 (1984): 3-17; Carl Bereiter, "Schools without Education," Harvard Educational Review 42 (1972): 390-413; C. Cheng, E. Brizendine, and J. Oakes, "What Is 'An Equal Chance' for Minority Children?" Journal of Negro Education 48 (1979): 267-287.

9. See, for example, John Dewey, The Child and the Curriculum and the School and Society (1902; reprint, Chicago: University of Chicago Press, 1968), and Experience and Education (1938; reprint, New York: Collier Books, 1972).

10. See, for example: Paideia Proposal, The Paideia Proposal: An Educational Manifesto. (New York: Macmillan, 1982).

11. See, for example, Dewey, Child and the Curriculum and Experience and Education; Lawrence Kohlberg and Roberta Mayer, "Development As the Aim of Education," Harvard Educational Review 42 (1972): 449-496; and Bereiter, "Schools Without Education."

12. See Patricia Minuchin et al., Psychological Impact of the Schooling Experience (New York: Basic Books, 1969) for an excellent study of the potential impact of this diversity upon children's learning and development.

13. Jacob Getzels, "A Social Psychology of Education," in Gardner Lindzey and Elliot Aronson, eds., Handbook of Social Psychology, rev. eds. (Reading, Mass.: Addison-Wesley, 1969), vol. 5, pp. 459-537.

14. Robert Hess and Susan Holloway, "Family and School as Educational Institutions," in Ross Parke, ed., <u>Review of Child Development Research</u> (Chicago: University of Chicago Press, 1985), vol. 7, pp. 179-222.

15. Slaughter and Schneider, <u>Newcomers</u>.

16. The seventh school was located in Washington, D.C. As part of the larger aims of her study (see chapter 16, this volume), Johnson needed a private alternative school, predominantly Black, whose grade levels ranged from kindergarten through grade 8. No such school then existed in the Chicago area.

17. Slaughter and Schneider, <u>Newcomers.</u>

18. In Study 1, field interviewers in the spring of 1983 were instructed to obtain twenty Black and fifteen non-Black interviews of parents with children primarily in grades 4-7. The same children would be in grades 5-8 in the fall of 1983, the time of the planned school observations. Interviewers were instructed to select parents of children in grades K-3 only if time permitted and/or to meet quota demands. Similar instructions were given in Study 2, where the forty-one interviewed parents had children in grades 1-8.

19. Johnson, "Identity Formation ."

20. Additionally, one of the original research team members in the Slaughter and Schneider study (not Deborah Johnson) coded the Parental Educational Goals interview section of the forty-one cases in the Johnson study.

21. Slaughter and Schneider, <u>Newcomers.</u>

22. For a good discussion of this issue, see Bryan S. Everitt, <u>The Analysis of Contingency Tables</u> (London: Chapman and Hall, 1977), pp. 40-41.

23. James G. Cibulka, Timothy J. O'Brien, and Donald Zewe, S. J. <u>Inner-City Private Elementary Schools: A Study</u> (Milwaukee: Marquette University Press, 1982); see also chapters 8-11, in this volume.

16
Racial Socialization Strategies of Parents in Three Black Private Schools

Deborah J. Johnson

The interdependent roles of parents and schools are crucial to the issue of social mobility and the future of Black children. The way in which these roles influence each other are important to the development of the child's self-perception and the ultimate shaping of a viable coping style. Many researchers view Black parents as effective socializers of their children, particularly in their ability to successfully prepare the children to cope with the exigencies of our society while maintaining a positive sense of self.[1]

Achieving the delicate balance between creating an awareness of racial discrimination and prejudice, which are stressful, and encouraging racial coping strategies which protect the child's positive sense of self, is the challenge of Black parenthood.[2] The literature on children's group identity and personal self-esteem shows that many Black parents have been successful in achieving this goal.[3] Many Black children have a positive sense of self-worth and highly value the Black community to which they belong.[4] How is this achieved? One way is through the positive racial coping and socialization strategies of parents. This chapter describes the racial socialization strategies of parents whose children attend three different Black private schools.

BACKGROUND

Black families are particularly vulnerable to the ecological stress factor of race.[5] Within the ecology of the Black existence, all Black families develop strategies to cope with the exigencies of racism and discrimination.[6] Moreover, Black parents face the daily dilemma of simultaneously protecting their children's sense of self and preparing them to cope successfully with issues of race which they anticipate will occur in the child's future experiences.

Diana T. Slaughter and Barbara L. Schneider conducted a study which investigated Black parental educational goals, school type, and the experiences of Black children in four desegregated private school settings (see chapter 15).[7]   The authors concluded that the schools and Black families work together to affirm the overall private school community's sense of educational purpose, mission, and identity.   The ensuing socialization context was educationally beneficial to Black children.[8] However, the authors also found that many Black parents were concerned about the positive racial identity development of their children.

Since the most recent body of research suggests that self-esteem and group identity operate independently, parental emphasis on the one may result in no effect or a deleterious effect on the other.[9]   A study by Margaret Beale Spencer demonstrated this point.[10]   Spencer reported that preference patterns of children aged 3-9 years old were related to the cultural childrearing strategies of their parents.   Specifically, the Eurocentric racial attitudes of Black children were negatively related to parent's teachings about civil rights, the child's knowledge of Black history, and discussions about racial discrimination. Spencer concluded that the "lack of direct teaching of specific cultural values resulted in the learning of Eurocentric racial attitudes/preferences".[11]

Harriette Pipes McAdoo studied stress and coping in middle-class Black families.[12]   Like poor Black families, they suffer the effects and stresses of racism, discrimination, and economic isolation. Black families attain and maintain middle-class incomes through dual careers.   Her findings indicate that middle-class Black families also utilize extended kin networks to abate the impact of ecological stress factors.

In an environmental ecology presupposing Black stress, the task of childrearing is a particular dilemma. Black parents are especially concerned with developing racial coping strategies (RCSs) in their children that will allow them to surmount blocked opportunity while simultaneously protecting their self-esteem. McAdoo explains that Black parents are acutely aware of the contradictions, particularly in the context of education, but push beyond them toward the ultimate goal of upward social mobility for their children.[13]

Positive affect to one's reference group has been shown to be related to effective racial coping and school success. Two studies of Black college students examined achievement and coping behavior.[14]   These studies focused on the individual personality characteristics of high and low achievers. Specific coping strategies were conceptualized not in relation to race and culture, but in relation to whether, within a dominant cultural control ideology, or a personal control ideology, a student operated from an internal or external control system.

Phillip J. Bowman and Cleopatra Howard extended the work of Patricia Gurin and Edgar Epps in a study of intergenerational race-related socialization.[15]   Bowman and Howard found that intergenerational transmission of self-development orientations was related to adolescents' greater sense of personal efficacy, while emphasis on racial barrier awareness was associated with higher school grades.   They concluded that the coping orientation transmitted by Black parents to their children is an important component of their motivation, achievement, and career aspirations.

Depending upon the school, parents can primarily either achieve insulation of the child's racial self, create coping opportunities (proactive, reactive), or work toward a balance between the two. From the point of view of Black parents, because education is so highly valued in the Black community and is the primary mechanism of social mobility, these racial coping strategies become intervening routes to upward social mobility.

Thus, by identifying which route a parent has chosen to protect the child's sense of self and understanding the parent's coping orientation, we may determine how the school environment complements or confounds parental racial socialization processes. The interaction of the parent with the school is a process which triangulates on the child. The child is at the apex of the triangle, with the school at one base angle and the parent(s)/home at the opposite base angle. The triangle itself is set within a circle of racial stress.

The research presented below is part of a larger study involving parents and children. However, in this chapter only parent data are reported. The strategies of Black parents who send their children to private schools were of particular interest because of the greater effort expended toward quality education for their children.

HYPOTHESES

These hypotheses follow from the question, "What are the coping orientations of Black parents and how are different school settings reflected in their coping orientations?"

1. Parents whose proactive orientations require them to assert positives and/or minimize their child's contact with negative racial experiences, will most often have children who attend an alternative school.

In one school there exists a strong Black ideology which emphasizes Black pride, political awareness, unity (communalism), and accountability to the larger Black community. Parents are encouraged to participate in the school and be a part of the school family and the school identity. The school is child-centered in its educational approach. It is especially concerned about who the child is as a person and how the school might enhance the child's racial identity development. Stresses which enter from the outside are discussed and interpreted within the context of a Black ideology.

2. Parents who have reactive coping orientations will primarily be found in traditional and parochial school settings.

It is assumed that these types of schools emphasize the basics of education. Such a school is focused on the child's acquisition of the basics and on eliminating those elements which might interfere with that acquisition. Parents emphasize the child's positive personal differences apart from the group.

METHOD

The design of this study uses qualitative and quantitative methods to explore these issues and identify their important elements. Given the socializing influence of the school and the objective of obtaining information on a wide range of possible RCSs, rather than have many schools participate, only three schools (representing particular types) were selected for participation in this study.

Subjects

At least one parent from each of forty-one families having a child aged 5-14 years old participated in the study. Parents had their children enrolled in one of three all-Black private schools. Two of the schools were located in Chicago and the third was in Washington, D.C. The schools were selected to be representative of small, stable, Black independent institutions for children. Among the institutions selected were a parochial school (14 families), a traditional school (17 families), and an alternative school (10 families). The alternative school in this study had a pan-African sociocultural orientation.

Within the three schools there was some variation in educational attainment and family income. Cross-tabulations of school with educational level resulted in significant differences in mother's education (X^2 (39) = 0.82, p = .00), but not in father's education (X^2 (32) = 0.38, p = .67). The annual family income in each school varied. Within the traditional school, Chaucer, at the alternative school, Watoto,19 percent of parents reported incomes below \$34,999, while 82 percent reported incomes above \$35,000 and at the parochial school, St. Benedito, about 70 percent of parents reported an annual family income below 34,999 and 30 percent reported incomes above that figure.

School Selection

Five criteria were considered in the selection of schools for the study: diverse private school networks; 90-100 percent Black enrollment; fifty students or more; established for ten years or more; and location in metropolitan Chicago. All schools in the study met at least three of these criteria.

Racial Coping Interview-Parents

The interview schedule was adapted from the Slaughter and Schneider (1986) study of Blacks in private schools. The adult interview in their study was comprised of six sections (A thru F). Section F of their interview, questioned parents about their expectations of problems of child racial coping as Black Americans and was used as the Racial Coping Interview in this study to identify parental RCSs. Racial coping strategies were coded from four questions in the parent interview:

1. What do you anticipate and how are you planning to protect your child (regarding the child's experiences as a Black American)?

2. How does your family go about ensuring that your child will have a positive Black identity ?

3. What other day-to-day experiences in reference to being Black have you and your child talked about?

4. Describe any special features of your family's overall educational program for your child because (s)he is a Black American child.

Eighteen racial coping strategies (RCSs) were identified in an adult pilot study using the Slaughter and Schneider parent interview data.[16] Eleven new RCSs were identified in this study and eleven were either maintained or amplified from the pilot study.

Reliability

Reliability was calculated from the percent agreement between RCSs coded by two independent raters. If one rater coded strategies not coded by the second rater, those RCSs figured negatively into the percent agreement calculated. Both raters coded each of the forty-one cases. Using this conservative method, interrater reliability was established at .75 on this instrument.

PROCEDURES

Data Collection

The goals and procedures of the study were discussed with administrators, parents, students, and teachers in each school. Parents were generally interviewed in their homes.

Ten interviewers were trained in the following manner. Initially, they were given a tape of an adult interview, a packet of interview and test materials, and a manual of instruction. Two of the ten trainees were further required to observe an interview or were observed conducting an interview. The remaining eight interviewers were trained exclusively by taped interview) seven of these eight interviewers had prior interview experience through either clinical or research training).

Refusals

The rate of refusal at Watoto was about 33 percent and at St. Benedito about 50 percent. At Chaucer, of twenty contacts, only three parents refused. However, a complete parent list was not obtained from this school. The rate of refusals for parents in these schools brings into question the representativeness of this sample not only for Black families in general, but for the families in the particular schools studied. Caution is especially important in the context of the St. Benedito and Chaucer schools.

Decision Rules

The twenty-two RCSs listed in table 16.1 (column 2) were the basis for coding adult strategies from the parent Racial Coping Interview.[17]

Table 16.1

Comparison of Adult Pilot Study RCSs (1984/85) with Adult RCSs (1985/86)

1984/85 (N = 74)	1985/86 (N = 41)
1. No elaboration	1. Defer to authority *
2. Ignore	2. Engage authority *
3. Project to others	3. Physical confrontation *
4. Project superiority	4. Verbal confrontation *
5. Meet problem on own terms	5. Authoritative directive *
6. Can't protect	6. Moral reasoning (nonracial) *
7. Internalization of stereotypes	7. Moral reasoning (race-related) [3, 16]
8. Select educational environment	8. Legal reasoning *
9. Build self-esteem/confidence	9. Strategic planning [5]
10. Positive Black role models	10. Explore the problem [12, 14]
11. Extended family interaction	11. Develop support systems [11, 13, 17]
12. Exploration of child events	12. Project racial pride [10, 12, 15]
13. Family activities	13. Project superiority [4]
14. Exploration of contemporary politics/events	14. Project inferiority [7]
15. Exploration of family history and struggles	15. Assert personal selfhood [9]
16. Racial awareness	16. Persist *
17. Involvement in helping others	17. Conform *
18. General discussion	18. Change or choice of environment [8]
	19. Ignore/do nothing [2, 6]
	20. Avoid or withdraw *
	21. Negate racial group *
	22. No racial coping [1]

[ ] = RCS (= Racial Coping Strategy) identified/amplified from 1984/85 pilot study data

* = New RCS identified from 1985/86 data

In the earlier pilot study of parental racial coping strategies,   RCSs were categorized as proactive, reactive, or neutral prior to the data analysis.[18]. Applying these categories to this study, examples of neutral RCSs (defined as a racial coping strategy having both negative and positive connotations or having neither connotation) are "persist and change or choice of environment". Examples of reactive RCSs (consistently used negatively) are "negate racial group" and "avoid or withdraw". Proactive RCSs (consistently used positively) "assert personal selfhood" and "strategic planning".

Many of the twenty-two RCSs identified in the study were not used frequently enough to warrant consideration in determining reactive, proactive, or neutral racial coping orientation(s). Therefore, in order to test the hypotheses decision rules were instituted to eliminate those RCSs not used consistently across RCS instruments. Below is a brief description of those rules.

A dominant strategy list was developed from the preferred and overlapping RCSs of participants responding to the racial coping instruments. Five such strategies qualified; three were proactive ("defer to authority," "moral reasoning (nonracial)," "assert personal selfhood") and two were reactive ("ignore /do nothing," "superiority"). When one of the dominant RCSs was used in conjunction with a minor RCS, the pair was assessed with respect to the connotation of the dominant RCS. These pairings are referred to as combinations. Coping orientations were designated according to the predominant use of strategy combinations identified as proactive or reactive.

In order to enhance the reader's understanding of the findings in this section, examples of parents' proactive and reactive statements are presented below. Responses are to one of the four questions used, question #170, which asked, "How does your family go about ensuring that your child will have a positive Black identity?" Following each statement, the RCSs number(s) from table 16.1 (column 2) indicating the RCSs coded for each statement are listed in parentheses.

Proactive:

He has different role models. All the fellow police
officers. The family is close. [We] meet and share every
holiday, talk... (10, 11)

[We expose him to] artifacts and evidence of his cultural
tradition.
If he understands where his roots are and they are in
Africa, then he will have a positive Black identity (12)

Reactive:

We don't. We don't do nothing to ensure that he has a
positive Black identity. (19)
Can't think of anything right now. (22)

RESULTS

Hypothesis Testing

Hypothesis 1 predicted that alternative school parents would have a predominantly proactive orientation. This hypothesis was upheld by data from the parent interview. Watoto parents were largely proactive (67 percent) in their RCSs. Hypothesis 2, however, was not upheld. Although Chaucer parents were mostly reactive (67 percent), parents at St. Benedito departed significantly from the hypothesis in that they were overwhelmingly proactive (83.3 percent).

Table 16.2

Frequency of Articulated Parent Racial Coping Strategies (RCS)

Chaucer (n = 112)		Watoto (n = 63)		Benedito (n = 84)		Total (N = 259)	
RCS	%	RCS	%	RCS	%	RCS	%
Explore	26.8	Pride	34.9	Nocope	19.0	Pride	21.6
Pride	19.6	Explore	17.5	Pride	14.3	Explore	19.7
		Assert	12.7	Explore	11.9	Nocope	11.6
				Assert	10.7	Assert	10.0
				MoralR	10.7		
Superior	8.9	Environ	9.5	Infer	6.0	Environ	6.6
Assert	8.0	Support	7.9	Persist	6.0	Superior	5.4
Nocope	8.0	Nocope	7.9			Persist	4.6
Environ	7.1	Super	4.8			Support	4.6
Persist	6.3					MoralR	4.2
Support	3.6	MoralN	1.6	Support	3.6	MoralN	2.9
Ignore	3.6	Plan	1.6	Environ	3.6	Inferior	2.9
MoralN	2.7	Ignore	1.6	MoralN	2.4	Ignore	2.9
MoralR	1.8			Plan	2.4	Plan	1.5
Legal	0.9			Conform	2.4	Avoid	1.2
Plan	0.9			Avoid	2.4		
Infer	0.9			Negate	2.4		
Avoid	0.9			Super	1.2		
				Ignore	1.2		
Defer	0	Defer	0	Defer	0	Conform	0.8
Engage	0	Engage	0	Engage	0	Negate	0.8
Physical	0	Physical	0	Physical	0	Legal	0.2
Verb	0	Verb	0	Verb	0	Defer	0
Direct	0	Direct	0	Direct	0	Engage	0
Conform	0	MoralR	0	Legal	0	Physical	0
Negate	0	Legal	0			Verb	0
		Persist	0			Direct	0
		Conform	0				
		Avoid	0				
		Negate	0				

Note: The total number of parents represented by this table is 41; there were 17 at Chaucer; 10 at Watoto; and 14 at St. Benedito.

As indicated in table 16.2 the most highly preferred parental strategies were consistent across schools. The strategies "explore the problem" and "project racial pride" represented 26-47 percent of all parent RCSs.   "Assert personal selfhood" was usually articulated as the third or fourth most frequently used RCS.

Chaucer's pattern emphasized "explore the problem" (26.8 percent), "project racial pride"   (19.6 percent), and " project superiority" (8.9 percent). Watoto's emphasis on "project racial pride" (34.9 percent) far exceeded the articulation of the other RCSs, "explore the problem" (17.5 percent), "assert   personal selfhood" (12.7 percent), and "change or choice of environment" (9.5 percent).   Although St. Benedito parents also frequently identified racial pride, "explore the problem," and " assert personal selfhood" as RCSs, they were distinguished by their relatively high inarticulation of RCSs. As a result their configuration assumed the following pattern; "no racial coping indicated" (19.0 percent), "project racial pride" (14.3 percent), "explore the problem" (11.9 percent), "assert personal selfhood" (10.7 percent), and "moral reasoning (race-related)" (10.7 percent).

Overall, there were few differences in RCS usage between parents of boys and girls on the parent interview; parents were largely egalitarian in usage of preferred RCSs. However, sex of the child was important in the use of certain RCSs. For instance, "negate racial group" and "conform" were used exclusively by parents of boys.   Conversely, "avoid or withdraw" was used exclusively by parents of girls. Parents of boys were twice as likely as parents of girls to articulate "persist", "project inferiority" (internalization), and "develop support systems" as prescribed ways of coping.   Finally, parents of girls were twice as likely to articulate "moral reasoning" (race-related and nonracial).

Factor Analysis: Typologies

The basis for interpretation of factors (designated coping orientations) began far in advance of the statistical analysis. Prior to conducting the factor analysis, a detailed review of each child and adult case on each RCS measure was undertaken.   Each protocol was categorized according to the RCS emphasized in the response.   Each cluster of RCSs was labeled according to their apparent function. This made categorization more consistent. For each RCS measure, between five and eight patterns were distinguished. While not statistically sound, this procedure allowed the author to develop an intimate knowledge of how RCSs operated conceptually and functionally. Since RCSs were rarely used in isolation, it was important to understand how they might combine. The process described, then, was a critical step in interpreting the factors, presumed to represent parental coping orientations.

In preparation for the factor analysis, the data from the racial coping measures were subjected to a natural log transformation in order to normalize the data. Within each RCS measure, a strategy was excluded from the variable list if its absolute frequency was less than or equal to one. Those RCSs remaining in the variable list were factor analyzed separately for each measure.[19] Within each measure, three factors met the criterion set (eigenvalue greater than 1.84). Individual RCSs having factor loadings greater than or equal to .46 were identified as significant contributors to a factor. After the factors had been identified, factor scores were generated and assigned using statistical software (SPSS, version 8).

Parent Interview. Adult prescriptions for and orientations toward child coping were reflected in responses to the parent interview. In this section, both quantitative and contextual information on parents' responses will be presented by school type. Quotes from individual parent interviews correspond by number to each of the four questions mentioned earlier:

1. What do you anticipate and how are you planning to protect your child (regarding the child's experiences as a Black American)?

2. How does your family go about ensuring that your child will have a positive Black identity?

3. What other day-to-day experiences in reference to being Black have you and your child talked about?

4. Describe any special features of your family's overall educational program for your child because (s)he is a Black American child.

Three factors accounted for nearly 50 percent of the variance.[20] Factor 1, described as insulatory (self-denying), explains 28.3 percent of the total variance and was a strongly reactive orientation composed of self-effacing and passive RCSs. The mean factor score was highest ($F(2,38) = 3.69$, $p = .03$) for parents at Benedito ($M = .55$), followed by Chaucer ($M = -.27$) and then Watoto ($M = -.32$).

The components of this coping orientation, consistent with several edicts of Christian ideology and ethics, include "ignore/do nothing," "avoid or withdraw," "moral reasoning race-related" (humanistic), and "moral reasoning-nonracial" (ethical). In combination with these RCSs, "persist" becomes both a reactive and a nonverbal strategy. This insulatory (self-denying) orientation deemphasizes and even rejects the racial self, both individually and as part of a devalued group, in favor of a global self which transcends race through humility and moralistic behavior and pursuits.

The following response of one parent to three of the four questions on the parent interview typifies the factor 1 coping orientation:

Question 1: No problems. I've always sacrificed and put him in private school--higher standards in private [school], I wouldn't pay for harassment. And most of the kids at school are Black.

Question 2: I just trained her to have self-respect and respect to others--not to regard people of their color or status. Not to feel low esteem because racist thing no bearing on ability to. We study Blacks who have made outstanding contributions--historians.

Question 3: Instilling in her that all she has to do is have faith in God. Never let anybody discourage her cause she's Black or brainwash her.

St. Benedito was significantly low, even of negative valence ($M = -.67$) on factor 2, described as competitive (assertive) orientation, in contrast to Chaucer's ($M = .53$) and Watoto's ($M = .03$) relatively high mean factor scores ($F(2,38) = 7.30$, $p = .002$). The higher mean factor scores of Chaucer and Watoto parents on this proactive coping orientation indicated their attempts to foster competence in their children by emphasizing the superiority of Blacks either through historical or familial links. The children are encouraged to explore and understand the many facets of Black life. Often the children are guided through an interpretation and resolution of both child and adult events experienced as discriminatory or oppressive. This coping orientation is typified in the responses of the following parent:

Question 1: The degree of education that he will receive if he is in a totally Black environment in High school-inferior education in the school system. By sending him to a school that will give him the tools I feel he needs as a Black person.

Question 2: By discussing Blacks and their goals, what successful Blacks are doing, exposure to Black literature, not let Blackness become a product to make you feel inferior.

Contemporary-cultural versus global-historical characterizes the bipolar dimension of factor 3. Chaucer ($M = .14$) and, secondly, St. Benedito ($M = .10$) parents focused on the strength and solace of the contemporary Black community and family members (contemporary-cultural focus). Conversely, the projection of racial pride which links the broad historical context of African accomplishments to the present-day African-American potential and accomplishments (global-historical focus) was offered most often by Watoto parents (M = -.67). This coping orientation is illustrated by the following statements of one parent:

> Question 1:   I expect that because she will express herself as being African--she will have strong discussion and may be intimidated ...depending on strength or weakness of character, I don't know how she will deal with Euro-Americans.... [I will] continue to emphasize the importance of who she is and what her role is in the community on this continent and on Africa. Identify with the role of the ancestors in history.

> Question 2:   By reinforcing what the school has. Maintaining African frame of references in house and lifestyle. When she identifies with Africa as part of her past--then she will see it as part of her present and future.

Intercorrelations: Racial Coping Orientations and the Schools.   Factor scores were generated which allowed adult coping orientations to be correlated among themselves and the schools. The schools were arrayed from high to low according to the degree of emphasis upon race in the school philosophy: Watoto, Chaucer, St. Benedito. School correlated significantly only with the second factor, competitive (assertive)   (r = -.27, p <.05). Specifically, parents from St. Benedito, in contrast to Chaucer and Watoto parents, were least likely to be represented by the competitive (assertive) coping orientation.

SUMMARY AND CONCLUSIONS

Parents in the three independent, predominantly Black private schools reported that they used as many as seventeen of twenty-two possible different racial coping strategies, some proactive, some reactive, in socializing their children. In particular, "explore the problem," "project racial pride," and "assert personal selfhood" were popular strategies among parents at all schools. Overall, St. Benedito parents, followed by Watoto and Chaucer parents, respectively, were most likely to use a greater number of individual proactive racial coping strategies. When strategies were clustered using factor analysis techniques, three factors (designated coping orientations) accounted for nearly 50 percent of the variance: factor 1--insulatory (self-denying), factor 2--competitive (assertive), and factor 3--contemporary-cultural versus global-historical. On factor 1, St. Benedito parents, followed by Chaucer, and then Watoto parents, scored highest. On factor 2, Chaucer and Watoto parents scored considerably higher then Benedito parents. On factor 3, Chaucer and St. Benedito parents tended to cluster toward the contemporary-cultural pole, while Watoto parents clustered toward global-historical.

The evidence presented demonstrates the varying approaches middle-income Black parents in three types of independent schools report teaching and modeling in preparing their children for school and beyond. The findings also indicate that the parents choose schools for their children which are certainly compatible, if not complementary, with the parent's racial socialization goals and strategies. However, some school environments were associated with a wider variety of coping options. Parents of boys were somewhat more likely than parents of girls to report encouraging primarily reactive racial coping strategies. Findings from the factor analyses and related analyses demonstrate the importance of both parents and schools as major socializing forces in children's lives.

This study underscores the partnership between parents and schools. Schools could potentially be involved and helpful in expanding parents' and children's options for coping. Future study in this area should focus on bringing mental health issues back into the classroom. In Black or predominantly Black schools, notwithstanding socioeconomic factors, identity diffusion is a primary concern.[21] The problem is balancing the goal of social mobility with the reality of blocked opportunity. Within a dominant American culture boasting of unlimited options, too often Black children, upon discovering their "Blackness," learn only about what they (and Black people generally) cannot do or become. Despite this dilemma, if Black children are to even survive into the next century, healthy identity-formation must be fostered. This responsibility should be jointly shared by parents and schools.

As one example of an effort to extend this research, this study has been expanded to include younger children who attend public elementary schools and their parents.[22] Hopefully, these data will aid in helping to determine those coping orientations which are effective and promote resilience in children. Another purpose of the new study is to identify and perhaps model those empowered parents whose children attend public schools.

The exigencies of racism cannot be ignored or pushed aside and Black families must be offered the resources to shape their approach to racial socialization with effective, proactive racial coping strategies and to eliminate or modify ineffective ones. More empirical work on racial socialization can be the foundation underlying and guiding this process.

NOTES

1. Virginia Young,"Family and childhood in a Negro Community," American Anthropologist 72 (April 1970): 269; John Ogbu, "Social Stratification and the Socialization of Competence," Anthropology and Education Quarterly 10 (1979): 3; Marie F. Peters and Grace C. Massey, "Mundane Extreme Environmental Stress in the Family: The Case of the Black Family in White America," in Hamilton L. McCubbin, Marvin B. Sussman, and Joan M. Patterson, eds., Stress and the Family:Advances and Developments in Family Stress Theory and Research (New York: Hayworth, 1983), p. 193; and Diane S. Pollard, "Perspectives of Black Parents Regarding the Socialization of Their Children." (Manuscript).

2. Peters and Massey, "Mundane Extreme Environmental Stress"; Marie F. Peters, "Parenting in Black Families with Young Children: A historical perspective," in Harriette P. McAdoo, ed., (Beverly Hills: Sage, 1981), p. 211.

3. William E. Cross, "Black Identity: Rediscovering the distinction between Personal Identity and Reference Group Orientation," in Margaret B. Spencer, Geraldine K. Brookins, and Walter R. Allen, eds., Beginnings: The Social and Affective Development of Black Children (Hillsdale New Jersey : Erlbaum, 1985), p.155; Margaret Beale Spencer, "Personal and Group Identity of Black Children: An Alternative Synthesis," Genetic Psychology, 106, (1982): 59; Margaret Beale Spencer, "Cultural Cognition and Social Cognition as Identity Correlates of Black Children's Personal Social Development," in Spencer et al., Beginnings, p. 215.

4. Robert Taylor,"Black Youth and Psychological Development," Journal of Black Studies 6 (1976): 353.

5. Chester Pierce,"The Mundane Extreme Environment and Its Effect on Learning," in S. G. Brainard, ed., Learning Disabilities: Issues and Recommendations for Research, (Washington D. C.: National Institute of Education, 1975). Jean Carew,"Effective Caregiving: The Child from Birth to Three," in M.D. Fantini and R. Cardenas, eds., Parenting in a Multicultural Society, (New York: Longman, 1980). p. 170.

6. Diana T. Slaughter and Gerald A. McWorter, "Social Origins and Early Features of the Scientific Study of Black American Families and Children," in Spencer et al., Beginnings, p. 5;

Peters and Massey, "Mundane Extreme Environmental Stress"; and Peters, "Parenting in Black Families."

7. Diana T. Slaughter and Barbara L. Schneider, <u>Newcomers: Blacks in Private Schools</u> ERIC, 1986 (ED 274 768 and ED 274 769).

8. See chapter 15, this volume, for a discussion of some of this work.

9. Leachim Semaj, "Reconceptualizing the Development of Racial Preference in Children: A Socio-Cognitive Approach," <u>Journal of Black Psychology</u> 6 (1980): 59; Cross, "Black Identity"; Spencer, "Personal and Group Identity"; and Deborah J. Johnson, "Racial Preference and Biculturality in Interracial Preschoolers" (M.A. thesis, Cornell University, 1983).

10. Margaret Beale Spencer, "Children's Cultural Values and Parental Childrearing Strategies," <u>Developmental Review</u> 3 (1983): 351.

11. Ibid, p. 359.

12. Harriette Pipes McAdoo, "Stress Absorbing Systems in Black Families," <u>Family Relations</u> 31, (1982):479.

13. Ibid.

14. Yvonne Abatso, "The Coping Personality: A Study of Black Community Students," in Spencer et al., <u>Beginnings</u>, p. 131; and Patricia Gurin and Edgar Epps, <u>Black Consciousness, Identity, and Achievement</u> (New York: John Wiley and Sons, 1975).

15. Phillip J. Bowman and Cleopatra Howard, "Race-Related Socialization, Motivation, and Academic Achievement: A Study of Black Youths in Three Generation Families," <u>Journal of the American Academy of Child Psychiatry</u> 24 (1985): 131.

16. Deborah J. Johnson, Diana T. Slaughter, and Barbara L. Schneider, "Parental Coping and Identity Formation in Black Children: Coding Manual IV," <u>Newcomers</u>. Contact the senior author for the most updated version of this manual.

17. Deborah J. Johnson, "Identity Formation and Racial Coping Strategies of Black Children and Their Parents: A Stress and Coping Paradigm," (Ph.D. dissertation, Northwestern University, 1987).

18. Johnson, Slaughter, and Schneider, "Coding Manual IV."

19. Norman H. Nie et al., Statistical Package for the Social Sciences, 2d ed.," (New York: McGraw-Hill, 1975); and John Scanzoni,"Sex Roles, Economic Factors, and Marital Solidarity in Black and White Marriages," Journal of Marriage and the Family 37, (1975): 130.

20. Factor 1 contained the following RCSs in highest to lowest order: avoid or withdraw (.82); legal reasoning (.80); negate racial group (.74); project inferiority (.71); moral reasoning (nonracial) (.61); ignore/do nothing (.53); strategic planning (.53); moral reasoning (race-related) (.52); persist (.51). Factor 2 contained the following RCSs in highest to lowest order: explore the problem(.75); project superiority (.61); no racial coping (-.75). Factor 3 contained the following RCSs in highest to lowest order: develop support systems (.59); strategic planning (.46); project racial pride (-.69).

21. Erik H. Erikson, Identity: Youth and Crisis (New York: W. W. Norton and Company, 1968).

22. Postdoctoral research was conducted under the auspices of the University of California at Berkeley, Department of Afro-American Studies.

Part 5
Educational Policy Issues:
Blacks and Private Schools

Increasing the access of Black families, particularly poor Black families, to quality education has been a consistent concern within the Black community and a growing concern among the nation's policymakers. Tax credit incentives and educational voucher systems have been seen as potential routes toward this end. Debates on this issue stress on the one hand, expanding the access of economically disadvantaged groups to nonpublic schools and stablizing enrollment among those students from disadvantaged backgrounds already attending these schools, and on the other hand, pushing the goal of attaining quality education and upward mobility that much further from the grasp of these children and their families. These debates are most informative when they are cast in the larger context of educational policymaking generally as it applies to Black people. The chapters in this section, representing quite different perspectives, both attempt to address this larger context.

In chapter 17, Schneider focuses on the state of the public educational system and the attitudes toward the system which spawned initiatives to ameliorate some of the problems. Diverse Black perspectives on these policy initiatives, such as tax credits and vouchers, are discussed, as is the possible impact on private schooling and the education of poor and minority children, especially Black children.

In chapter 18, Yeakey examines the phenomenon of increasing numbers of Blacks in private schools from the perspective of an educator committed to public schools. She acknowledges that the trend in the past generation is an implicit critique of public schooling. Her analysis of the social and historical influences upon the education of Black children leads her to conclude that community-based control of schools is the only viable educational reform capable of forestalling further abandonment of hope for these schools.

17
Private Schools and Black Families: An Overview of Family Choice Initiatives

Barbara L. Schneider

Over the past twenty years, problems with American public education, particularly within large urban school systems, have increased in scope and intensity. The failings of public education and the need for major reforms have become the repeated themes of recent numerous reports, the most notable being <u>A Nation at Risk.</u>[1] The seriousness of the educational situation for Blacks and other minorities can perhaps best be exemplified by examining the academic performance and dropout rates of Chicago public school students.

The Chicago public school system serves about 430,000 students, 87 percent of whom are Black, Hispanic, Native American, and Asian. Nearly half of the students come from families with reported incomes at poverty level. Students in elementary schools where the population is entirely minority tend to score on basic skills achievement tests significantly below the national average at most grade levels. This trend is even more dismaying in predominantly Black high schools, where the average eleventh grader's reading achievement is lower than that of 85 percent of his or her peers around the country. Of students enrolled in ninth grade, 50 percent fail to graduate from high school.[2]

On October 5, 1987, Chicago teachers returned to their classrooms, ending the longest public school strike in Chicago's history. The strike had lasted for nineteen days. Many of the students, especially those who did not attend summer school, were out of school for nearly four consecutive months. This loss of school time is particularly serious in light of research showing the negative effects of insufficient exposure to schooling on the academic performance of minority and economically disadvantaged students.[3] These are the very students who constitute the majority in the Chicago public school system.

During the Chicago teacher's strike, local newspapers frequently published feature stories on families who because of the strike were placing their children in private schools. Yet the decision of Black parents to leave the public system for religious or independent private schools cannot simply be explained as a preference for a more stable educational system. Private school choice must be understood in light of individual family characteristics such as parent schooling history, financial resources, and childrearing practices as well as changes in society such as desegregation policies which make it possible for families to exercise the option to choose.[4]

The problems with education are not endemic to Chicago, but can be found in other inner-city public education system,[5] What the Black community in Chicago shares with other Black groups nationwide, is a commitment to quality education for Black children. Where the differences in opinion occur is how this can be achieved and sustained in American society. Support in the Black community for family choice initiatives reflects in part the ways different groups believe excellence in education for Black children can be achieved.

BLACK SUPPORT FOR PUBLIC EDUCATION

Black support for public education has often been misinterpreted by many scholars. Throughout America's history, Blacks have expressed dissatisfaction with public education.[6] Although Blacks have been dissatisfied with public education as it has been practiced in relation to them, public education was generally viewed as the only option for Blacks to gain equal education and financial opportunities in American society. As public education continues to fall short of Black expectations for social mobility, one can reasonably assume that support for public education will decline.

Wavering support for public education among Blacks and other minorities is clearly evident in results of the annual Gallup Poll of "Public Attitudes toward the Public Schools" over the past ten years.[7] Since 1975, a random nationwide sample of adults has been asked to grade the public schools on a scale of A, B, C, D, Fail, and Don't Know. With the exception of one year (1981), non-Whites have consistently given public education lower marks than White respondents. The difference between White and non-White combined A and B grades for the public schools from 1975 through 1987 (excluding 1977 and 78) is shown in figure 17.1.

Figure 17.1

White and non-White Grades of the Public Schools from 1975 through 1987

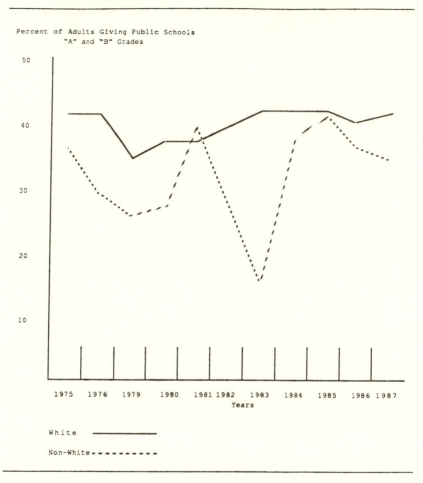

Percent of Adults Giving Public Schools
"A" and "B" Grades

White ——————

Non-White ----------

Source: "Annual Gallup Poll of the Public Attitudes toward the Public Schools" for years cited.

The graph clearly shows that non-Whites are less likely to give
public education high marks than Whites. Whereas White scores
show one steep period of decline, gradual improvement, and then
relative stability, non-White scores tend to be more volatile. The
trend lines between Whites and non-Whites are decidedly different.
For example, in 1983, when White scores returned to their
previous 1975 high of forty-three, non-White scores reached their
all-time low of twenty.

This pointedly demonstrates that support for public education is not commonly perceived across the ethnic and racial lines. Alex Gallup and David Clark have recognized this schism and believe that as the population of inner-cities grows, dissatisfaction with the public schools will increase.[8] In the instance of Blacks, it is often assumed that, because Blacks ardently support desegregation policies, that they also support public education.[9] It is not widely understood that there are many Black families who are dissatisfied with the type of public education Black children receive. The dissatisfaction of these Blacks can be seen in their movement to private education and their positions on family choice initiatives.[10]

FAMILY CHOICE INITIATIVES

One solution advocated by various policymakers and scholars to ameliorate the problems of public education is to allow families to choose the type of school they want their children to attend.[11] Varying considerably in their financial and regulatory policies, the general theme of such family choice initiatives is to provide families with vouchers or tuition subsidies to use in public or private schools of their choice.[12] Two family choice initiatives, education vouchers and tuition tax credit plans for private schools, are briefly described in the following section. The major emphasis is on Black perceptions of these initiatives in relations to their interests in quality education.

Educational Vouchers

Touted for two centuries by a small number of economists and clergymen, the voucher concept finally received considerable attention by educators and policymakers when Milton Friedman, the renowned economist, advocated that the government issue education grants to parents.[13] Under Friedman's plan, parents would receive a voucher for each child they had in elementary and secondary school. The value of the voucher would equal the cost of an average public school per-pupil expenditure, which was redeemable in state-approved schools. Treating elementary and secondary education as a free-market commodity, the quality of schools would undoubtedly increase. Because this system assumes the parents can be informed and effective shoppers of educational alternatives high-quality schools would be in demand while poorer schools would close.

According to the Gallup Polls, seven out of ten Americans believe that families should have the right to choose their child's school. Yet, when asked if they would favor a voucher system which would enables parents to choose among public, parochial, or private schools, the voucher idea is supported by only a small margin (44 percent "yes" to 41 percent "no"). Researchers contend that the "lukewarm" support for vouchers in comparison to the strong support for choice is based on the belief that vouchers would ultimately hurt the public schools by drawing away the best students.[14] There is, however, little empirical evidence to confirm or refute this explanation.

Since the 1960s, advocates of voucher plans have worked on altering Friedman's "unregulated model" so that it is more responsive to issues of family financial need. Most of these proposals have not been implemented. Only one voucher experiment has been seriously studied by social scientists. Even this experiment could not be considered as a "true" voucher plan because private schools were not included.

In the early 1970s, the U.S. Office of Economic Opportunity funded a voucher experiment based on a proposal by Christopher Jencks for the Alum Rock School district in San Jose, California.[15] The school district served a predominantly poor and minority population (From 1970-71 through 1976-77, the percentage of students with Spanish surnames grew from 47.2 to 57.2; the percentage of Black students increased from 10.1 to 11.5; and the percentage of Whites decreased from 42.7 to 31.3). During the years of the project, parents of elementary students (K-8) could choose among school programs for their children, in any of the fourteen voucher schools. Free transportation was provided for students who attended non-neighborhood schools.

Evaluation of results of the Alum Rock experiment indicated that initially, families with high income and educational levels had a greater awareness and concrete knowledge of school program alternatives. However, over time, information differences between family groups were reduced. As for the type of programs the families selected, the economically and socially disadvantaged families more often chose programs that were highly structured. Regardless of their social and economic backgrounds, most of the parents did not choose programs on the basis of their instructional merits but rather because of the proximity and social composition of the school offering the program.[16]

Although results of the Alum Rock experiment were limited by design, the study did produce important information on several key issues. With respect to equity considerations concerning choice and family resources, this study suggests that less economically advantaged families will choose different programs if given the opportunity. Choice patterns seem to be constrained by the limits of information families have concerning alternatives and their assumptions given the location of the school and composition of the student body.

The Alum Rock study reveals very little about the choice patterns and educational values of Black families. When taking into account family income and educational attainment, there is no evidence that Blacks behave differently than other racial groups in choosing school programs for their children. Results specifically pertaining to Blacks indicate that the Black families were the least satisfied group with the educational system at the beginning and end of the experiment. Given that Blacks were the least satisfied with the public system, it is unclear whether they would be more or less likely to choose private education were that alternative option available. Without including private schools as an option, this study does little to clarify the assumed positive or negative social consequences of a voucher system for minority and poor families.

Tuition Tax Credits

In the last fifteen years, tuition tax credit proposals have frequently been introduced at both state and federal levels. These bills typically allow families to take a federal or state tax deduction based on a percentage of the tuition they pay at a private school. Tuition tax credit proposals vary considerably in regard to equity issues. Specifically, bills tend to favor the wealthy or poor by including regulations which limit the amount of credit and portion of tuition covered by the credit. In some instances, the bills also may contain refundability provisions for families whose incomes are so low that they would not benefit from a credit. Another provision often included in these proposals is a requirement that the tax credit apply only to eligible schools. While designed to ensure civil-rights guarantees, these school eligibility requirements vary considerably in their enforcement provisions.[17]

Congress has yet to pass a tuition tax credit plan, although several have been introduced in the senate and by the administration. The Packwood-Moynihan-Roth plan introduced in the early 1980s was the only bill to receive serious consideration. The plan allowed for a deduction of up to 50 percent of tuition expenses, up to a maximum amount not to exceed $1,000. Hotly debated, this plan failed to receive congressional approval.

Minnesota has been the only state to pass a tax credit plan which was challenged locally but upheld by the Supreme Court. The Minnesota legislation allows families with children in public or private elementary or secondary school to deduct educational expenses from their income when calculating their state income tax liability. Expenditures on tuition, instructional materials, and transportation qualify as deductions.

As in the case of educational vouchers, there have been few studies which have attempted to examine the effects of tuition tax credits on family school choice. One exception is an investigation conducted by the Rand Corportation (summer, 1984), which examined the effects of the Minnesota tax deduction legislation.[18] In this study a sample of 476 families with children in public and private schools were contacted by telephone. Parents were asked about family choice, knowledge and use of the income tax deduction, and propensity to switch to private schools as a consequence of changes in deduction policies. Results of this study contradicted other research on family choice. Neither income nor race were found to be related to public or private choice. Factors considered important to selecting private education included school quality, moral and religious instruction, and school discipline.

Black Opposition to Tuition Tax Credits and/or Vouchers.

Among Black community organizations, the strongest opposition to tuition tax credit legislation has come from the National Urban League and several of its regional affiliates.[19] The NAACP has also issued a statement about the detrimental effects tax credits would have on public education.[20] In a period of limited funds for education, these groups believe tax credit legislation would further divert scarce resources from public schools.

In the view of these groups, the financial benefits of recent tuition tax credit bills would favor Whites and middle and upper-class families. Poor families having no tax liabilities would not be eligible for a tax credit. Thus, those most likely to take advantage of the situation and leave the public schools would be middle-income families. One possible outcome of this situation is that private schools would raise their tuitions, given the increasing demand. This would make private school completely out of reach for most poor families. Another consequence might be that, as more students enroll in private schools, the base of support for private education would increase, making additional federal support more likely. Public schools would become the "institution" for the poor and minority.

Black Support for Tuition Tax Credits and/or Vouchers.

Many persons maintain that quality education for Black children can best be achieved through privately controlled schools.   These individuals advocate Black private separatist schools administered by individuals who share their ideology and values.   Blacks supporting tuition tax credits or vouchers share the belief that public education has not met Black children's needs.[21]   Rather than allocating additional resources to public schools, parents of this persuasion are seeking ways to strengthen their abilities to generate educational alternatives for their children. For example, Black parents who sent their children to independent neighborhood schools are particularly partial to voucher initiatives rather than tax credits, because they potentially offer immediate financial assistance.[22] Continuation of present policies, they believe, can only limit their educational choices.

Many parents who send their children to parochial schools have also supported tax credits. These parents believe their children can get a better education in Catholic schools than in public ones, primarily because of the emphasis on traditional religious values and academic standards.[23] These families are willing to make considerable financial sacrifices so their children can attend Catholic schools. In a recent study of inner-city Catholic schools, 81 percent of the sampled families reported earned incomes between $5,000 and $10,000 a year.[24] Yet these families paid $300 or more in annual tuition to send their children to Catholic schools.

Generally, families sending their children to Catholic schools have been strong supporters of tuition tax credits and vouchers.[25] Without some financial relief, supporters fear many Catholic schools will have to close. Scarce resources make it extremely difficult to keep high-quality teachers and adequate facilities. Increasing tuition payments is problematic, since many families are barely able to pay existing fees. Moreover, scholarship aid is limited. For these families, tax credits would be of tremendous help.[26]

Black families on the average pay higher tuition and fees in private schools than families of White students.[27] This is probably the result of the large number of Blacks in Catholic schools, who, because they are non-Catholic, pay higher tuition rates. Studies of Catholic schools have found that half the Blacks in Catholic schools are not Catholic.[28] Andrew Greeley reported that many of these families are not necessarily supporting private schools because of religious values and convictions, but because they believe that the Catholic schools provide a better education for their children. He states, "Perhaps the principal reason for choosing a Catholic education for one's child if one is a minority family is that the child's chances of graduating from college are perceived as being enhanced by such an educational experience."[29] James Coleman and Thomas Hoffer take a different but complementary position as to why non-Catholic Blacks matriculate to Catholic schools. They believe that the lack of a stable community network that provides the child with moral values has led many inner-city Black parents to Catholic schools and for other Blacks to establish small independent schools.[30]

SUMMARY AND CONCLUSIONS

Equity issues regarding both education vouchers and tuition tax credits are concerned with who will benefit monetarily and educationally under either system.[31] Proponents for family choice initiatives contend that wealthy families have greater opportunities to exercise a variety of educational alternatives for their children in the public or private sector, while poor families have only one option, the public schools.[32] Supporters of educational vouchers maintain that a system which includes a tuition add-on-supplement for poor families would increase the educational options of poor families and make them more equal to those of wealthier families.[33] Tuition tax credit advocates argue that current taxation policies encourage economic and racial segregation by providing tax incentives for middle-income and wealthy families to choose segregated, exclusive private schools while providing no such incentives for lower-income families to choose private schools.[34] As for the educational benefits, supporters maintain that private schools tend to enhance academic achievement more than public schools.[35] If more poor children were given access to private schools their educational achievements would presumably improve.[36]

Critics of both plans assert that both proposals would ultimately benefit only the wealthy.[37] The amount of aid being proposed would do little to encourage poor families to choose private schools. Rather than providing opportunities for low-income families to attend private schools, tuition tax credits would most likely encourage middle-income families to select private education. Breneman states: "Tuition tax credits will increasingly split the public and private schools along socioeconomic lines, with the public schools in many areas becoming educational wastelands, ignored but tolerated by a society that has taken care of the more demanding parents through private alternatives."[38] With respect to educational benefits, critics maintain that the academic achievement differences between public and private school students are very slight.[39] Moreover, private schools do not seem to be especially effective at promoting the academic achievement of disadvantaged and minority students.[40]

Controversies over the establishment of a voucher or tuition tax credit system are likely to continue. One of the sources of contention between the supporters and opponents of either plan is directly tied to the administration and distribution of benefits. Whether the poor and minorities stand to gain or lose educationally and monetarily if vouchers or tax credits become a reality is of major importance to the Black community. Differences in opinion among Black community members regarding the use of public funds for educational vouchers or tuition tax credits center on whether the education that the majority of Black children receive today would be likely to improve if aid to private schooling were to be increased.

The bases of these diverse opinions on the merits of vouchers and tuition tax credits are partially reflective of the dearth of studies that have been conducted in these areas. There are relatively few empirical studies on family choice and private schools. For this reason, this overview included information obtained from interviews, organizational position papers, and policy documents, to trace and differentiate between various Black positions on family choice initiatives.

More studies on the conditions and constraints of a voucher or tuition tax credit plan for the communities and the families who participate are needed both to protect the poor from unanticipated adverse consequences of these educational policies, and to obtain data from more nationally representative sample populations. Ethical and legal issues associated with the potential fusion of church and state interests should be considered in all proposed educational policies reflective of family choice initiatives.

NOTES

1. National Commission on Excellence in Education, A Nation At Risk: The Imperative for Educational Reform (Washington, D. C.: Government Printing Office, 1983).

2. Education Policy Task Force, Report of the Education Policy Task Force of the Washington Transition Committee (Chicago: Internal Document, Mayor's Transition Committee, 1983).

3. Barbara Heyns, Summer Learning and the Effects of Schooling (New York: Academic Press, 1978).

4. Diana T. Slaughter and Barbara L. Schneider, Newcomers: Blacks in Private Schools. ERIC, 1986 (ED 274 768 and ED 274 769).

5. Barbara L. Schneider, "Schooling for Poor and Minority Children: An Equity Perspective," in William Boyd and James Cibulka, eds., Private School and Public Policy: International Perspectives (Philadelphia: Falmer Press, in press).

6. For discussion of this point, see Slaughter and Schneider, Newcomers; Roger Pulliam, "Historical Review of Black Education: Chicago," Negro Educational Review 29, no. 1 (1978): 22-32; Diane Ravitch, The Troubled Crusade: American Education, 1945-1980 (New York: Basic Books, 1983).

7. Reported in Phi Delta Kappan 57 (December 1975), 58 (October 1976), and 61-69 (September 1979-1987).

8. Alec Gallup and David Clark, "The 19th Annual Gallup Poll of the Public's Attitudes toward the Public Schools," Phi Delta Kappan, 69 (September 1987): 17-30.

9. Slaughter and Schneider, Newcomers.

10. Barbara L. Schneider and Diana T. Slaughter. "Educational Choice for Blacks in Urban Private Elementary Schools," in Thomas James and Henry Levin, eds., Comparing Public and Private Schools: Institutions and Organizations, Volume 1 (Philadelphia: Falmer Press, 1988).

11. Henry Levin, "Educational Vouchers and Social Policy," in James W. Guthrie, ed., School Finance Policies and Practices, (Cambridge, Mass.: Ballinger, 1980). pp. 235-263.

12. Ibid; see also, E. West, "The Prospects for Educational Vouchers: An Economic Analysis," in R. E. Everhart, ed., The Public School Monopoly (Cambridge, Mass. Ballinger, 1982), pp. 369-391.

13. Milton Friedman, Capitalism and Freedom (Chicago: University   of Chicago Press, 1962).

14. Gallup and Clark, "The 19th Annual Gallup Poll."

15. Christopher Jencks, "Is the Public School Obsolete?" Public Interest 2, no. 2 (1966): 18-27;"Private Schools for Black Children," New York Times Magazine, Sec. 6 (November 3, 1968): 30; "Giving Parents Money for Schooling: Education Vouchers," Phi Delta Kappan 51, no. 1 (1970): 49-52; and Education Vouchers: A Report on Financing Elementary Education By Grants and Parents (Cambridge, Mass.: Center for the Study of Public Policy, 1970).

16. R. Gary Bridge and Julie Blackman, A Study of Alternatives in American Education, vol. 4, Family Choice in Schooling (Washington, D. C.: National Institute of Education, 1978).

17. Joel Sherman et al., Congressionally Mandated Study of School Finance. A Final Report to Congress from the Secretary of Education, vol. 2) (Washington, D. C.:   Government Printing Office, 1983).

18. Linda Darling-Hammond and Sheila Kirby, Public Policy and Private Choice: The Case of Minnesota. Conference, Comparing Public and Private Schools. (Stanford: Institute for Research on Educational Finance and Governance, October, 1984).

19. Personal communication, Dr. Gwendolyn LaRoche, Education Director, Chicago Urban League, July, 1985.

20. Beverly Cole, Tuition Tax Credits (New York: National Association for the Advancement of Colored People, 1982).

21. For further discussion of this point, see Roger Freeman, "Educational Tax Credits," in Everhart, The Public School Monopoly, pp. 471-500; Joan Ratteray, "One System is Not Enough: A Free Market Alternative for the Education of Minorities," Lincoln Review, 4, no. 4 (1984): 25-31; and Rev. Virgil Blum. "Private Elementary Education in the Inner City," Phi Delta Kappan 66 (May 1985): 643-646.

22. Ratteray, "One System"; Robert Woodson, Testimony for the Select Committee on Children, Youth and Family, 96th Congress, U.S. House of Representatives (June, 1984).

23. Donald Erickson and George Madaus,   Issue of Aid to Nonpublic Schools. Report to the President's Commission on School Finance (Chestnut Hill, Mass.: Boston College, 1971); Andrew Greeley and William McCready, Catholic Schools in a Declining Church (Kansas City: Sheed & Ward, 1976); Philip Cusick, "A Study of Inner City Parochial Secondary Schools" (Paper presented at the annual meeting of the American Educational Research Association, New Orleans, 1984); Patricia Bauch, "Five Low Income Schools: A Sketch," unpublished paper (Washington, D. C.: Catholic University, 1986); and John Maddaus, "Families, Neighborhoods and Schools: Parental Perceptions and Actions Regarding Choice in Elementary School Enrollment" (Paper presented at the annual meeting of the New England Educational Research Organization, Maine, April 1985).

24. James Cibulka, Timothy O'Brien, and Donald Zewe, Inner-city Private Elementary Schools: A Study (Milwaukee: Marquette University Press, 1982).

25. Blum, "Private Elementary Education."

26. Ibid.

27. Mary F. Williams, <u>Private School Enrollment and Tuition Trends</u> (Washington, D. C.: Center for Education Statistics, 1986).

28. Cibulka, O'Brien, and Zewe, <u>Inner City Schools</u>; and Catherine Hickey and Bruce Cooper, "The Challenge of Non-Catholic Children in Catholic Schools" (Paper presented at the annual meeting of the American Educational Association. Quebec, Canada, April 1984).

29. Greeley and McCready, <u>Catholic Schools.</u>

30. James Coleman and Thomas Hoffer, <u>Public and Private High Schools</u> (New York: Basic Books, 1987).

31. Stephen Arons, "Educational Choice. Unanswered Questions in the American Experience," in M. Manley Casmer ed., <u>Family Choice in Schooling: Issues and Dilemmas</u>.
(Lexington, Mass.: D. C. Heath & Co., 1982), pp. 123-31; James Guthrie and A. Zusman,"Unasked Questions," <u>Harvard Educational Review</u> 51, no. 4 (1981): 515-518; Barbara Heyns, "Policy Implications of the Public and Private School Debates," <u>Harvard Educational Review</u>, 51, no. 4 (1981): 519-525; and Richard Murname, "Evidence, Analysis, Unanswered Questions," <u>Harvard Educational Review</u> 51, no. 4 (1981): 481-489.

32. B. Cohen, "Equality, Freedom and Independent Schools," <u>Journal of Philosophy of Education</u> 12 (1978): 121-128.

33. Jack Coons and Stephen Sugarman, <u>Education by Choice: The Case for Family Control</u> (Berkeley: University of California Press, 1978).

34. Nathan Glazer, <u>The Future under Tuition Tax Credits</u> (Stanford: Institute for Research on Educational Finance and Governance, March, 1982); and Thomas Vitullo-Martin, "The Impact of Taxation Policy on Public and Private Schools," in R. E. Everhart ed., <u>The Public School Monopoly</u>. (Cambridge, Mass.: Ballinger Publishing Company, 1982), pp. 423-469.

35. James Coleman, Thomas Hoffer, and Sally Kilgore, Public and Private Schools (Chicago: National Opinion Research Center, 1981); and "Achievement and Segregation in Secondary Schools: A Further Look at Public and Private School Differences," Sociology of Education 55, no. 2/3 (April/July 1982: 219-34; Andrew Greeley, Catholic High Schools and Minority Students. New Brunswick, N. J.: Transaction, 1982; and Thomas Hoffer, Andrew Greeley, and James Coleman, "Achievement Growth in Public and Catholic Schools," Sociology of Education, 58, no. 2 (1985): 74-97.

36. Chester Finn, "Why Public and Private Schools Matter," Harvard Educational Review 51, no. 4 (1981): 510-514.

37. Henry Levin and James Catterall, "Public and Private Schools: Evidence on Tuition Tax Credits," Sociology of Education 55, no. 2/3 (April/July 1982): 63-182; David Frey, "The Tuition Tax Credit: Uncertain Directions in Public Policy," in M. Manley-Casmer, ed., Family Choice in Schooling: Issues and Dilemmas. (Lexington, Mass.: D. C. Heath & Co., 1982), pp. 135-148; and Arthur Wise and Linda Darling-Hammond, "Educational Vouchers: Regulating Their Efficiency and Effectiveness," Educational Researcher 12, no. 9 (November, 1983): 9-18.

38. David Breneman, Should We Agree to Go? The Case against Tuition Tax Credits (Stanford: Institute for Research on Educational Finance and Governance, 1982).

39. See J. Douglas Williams, Patterns of Academic Achievement in Public and Private Schools; Implications for Public Policy and Future Research. Conference, Comparing Public and Private Schools. (Stanford: Institute for Research on Educational Finance and Governance, October, 1984); and "Catholic School Effects on Academic Achievement: New Evidence from the High School and Beyond Follow-Up Study," Sociology of Education 58, no. 2 (1985): 98-114.

40. Karl Alexander and Alexander Pallas, School Sector and Cognitive Performance. Conference, Comparing Public and Private Schools. (Stanford: Institute For Research on Educational Finance and Governance, October, 1984).

18
The Public School Monopoly: Confronting Major National Policy Issues
Carol Camp Yeakey

Color is not a human or a personal reality (in America); it is a political reality.

James Baldwin[1]

Amidst the euphoria over a discernible Black presence in private schooling in tandem with notable achievement gains, one must be mindful of the larger social reality that such a presence serves to conceal. The more generous numerical approximations of the Black presence in private schooling suggest that Blacks comprise roughly 10 percent of the overall student population. Unfortunately lost in some of the more provocative arguments in favor of Black visibility in private schooling is the fact that, despite identifiable progress made by a few Blacks, public schooling for the masses of Black Americans is actually deteriorating. The fact is that there will be no significant reform in public schooling for Blacks without manifest changes in political and economic empowerment in local Black communities and society at large.

Schooling in America, whether public or private, has always been more of an economic and, correlatively, a political issue than a pedagogical one, concerned methodologically with tools and techniques.[2] A number of interdisciplinary scholars have attempted to analyze schooling within broader confines, within its proper historical, social, political, economic, and ideological context.[3] An exacting analysis of the various theoretical perspectives is beyond the scope of this paper; yet the signal contribution of these theorists is that they advance our knowledge relative to the nature and function of schooling in industrial terms, by informing their deliberations with the language of power, hegemony, and social control. In so doing, they strip schools of their purported innocence and expose inequities in the distribution of economic goods and services and certain forms of cultural capital as well. It is within this political and economic context that one can examine the relationship between schooling and social control. Schools find themselves in a deceptive paradox. Charged with the responsibility of educating those who will, in turn, educate future generations, they play a pivotal role in the legitimation and reproduction of a society characterized by a marked degree of social and economic inequality. It is, at best, anachronistic to ignore the allocative functions of schooling in this regard.[4]

Departing from the major focus of this volume, this chapter discusses what portends for the masses of Black youngsters in the public schools of America today. An examination of the current political and educational reform agenda reemerging in Black America is preceded by a brief analysis of the educational and economic marginality of Black Americans. The chapter concludes with an analysis of some of the major national policy issues as well as a summary discussion of the social, political, and economic quagmires America must indubitably face. Although this chapter centers largely on Blacks and public schooling, it has relevant implications for the schooling of lower-status Whites and other racial and ethnic groups of color.

Finally, mention must be made of the fact that a chapter devoted to a discussion of public schooling, in a book concerned largely with private schooling, is no mere oversight or inadvertence on the part of the editors of this volume. We would do well to remember that it is the public schools, in particular, that have virtually monopolistic control over the schooling, and, as some suggest, the future status attainment of the masses of Black Americans today. More importantly, however, the existence of the phenomenon of Blacks in private schools is an implied critique of the public schools themselves. An examination of that implied critique is, in part, the substance of this paper.

EDUCATIONAL MARGINALITY PARALLELS ECONOMIC MARGINALITY

Educational marginality parallels the economic marginality of any racial and ethnic group in America. To understand the current educational and economic marginality of Blacks today, it is necessary to examine the historical conditions which gave rise to the present status of millions of Black Americans. Blacks and their lack of social mobility in American society are persistently compared to White immigrants who have experienced a marked degree of social status attainment. Yet the experiences of Blacks and White immigrants are hardly analogous, for the experiences of Blacks cannot be understood under the framework of immigration and assimilation that applied to European ethnic groups. The fundamental issue is both political and economic and draws a basic distinction between the voluntary immigration of White immigrant groups and the forced enslavement of Blacks.

There are three major factors which differentiate the reality of the non-White group experience from that of European immigrants.[5] The first is forced entry into a society. Second is the subjugation to various forms of unfree labor that restrict the physical and social mobility of the group and its participation in the political arena. The third is a cultural policy that not only constrains, but transforms and destroys the values, traditions, and ways of life of an enslaved populace.

The most sophisticated version of the argument explaining how European immigrants improved themselves economically over time is capsulized in what might be called the waves theory.[6] This theory claims that groups of European immigrants came to America at different times, met discrimination, and after numerous trials of varying length, overcame adversity and ascended the social-class ladder of American prosperity. This process was repeated time and again by each new wave of immigrants. According to this theory, Blacks are viewed as one of the more recent groups of "immigrants" to go through this process; for it was not until the twentieth century that large numbers of Blacks moved to the cities and to the North and thereby began to encounter modern social problems of adjustment. The proponents of this view argue further that, in time, these newcomers, just as their European counterparts, will eventually become a part of the mainstream and share in America's riches.

This view overlooks several fundamental aspects of the American experience, which, if accurately portrayed, do permanent damage to such faulty analysis. A cursory examination of the Black experience in America provides some interesting insights. For example, along with the first English immigrants, those who arrived before the Mayflower, Blacks were living in America. Blacks are by no stretch of the imagination newcomers to America. In terms of language, tradition, mores, and culture--the most important avenues for acculturation into a society--the Black American, even with his distinct cultural identity and diversity, was as qualified for American citizenship as the first or even second-generation European immigrant. Certainly this was true as early as 1880, when the major waves of Europeans began to arrive, over 250 years after the first African slaves were brought to America. Moreover, this sociological claim to share in America's bounty is made without considering the enormous contribution Blacks made in winning independence for this nation or their subsequent military participation in preserving it afterwards. It is made, also, without mentioning the decisive role Blacks have played in the economic development of the nation.

In reality, when the first nineteenth and twentieth-century European immigrants initially arrived, at worst, they dislodged Blacks from their meager hold on the bottom rung of the economic ladder, pushing Blacks off or beneath them. At best, the Europeans began at a level slightly above. Some immigrants suffered and fought against discrimination; they moved up the ladder and witnessed other White ethnic groups, arriving after them, go through the same process. But the masses of Blacks have been kept at virtually the same socioeconomic position--at the bottom of the economic ladder--as their predecessors. The irony is that Blacks often taught European immigrants the skills which would, at times, enable White ethnics to replace and even move up and beyond them on the economic ladder. Also, tragically, along with other qualifications for citizenship, far too often the immigrants manifested racism towards non-Whites as a necessary characteristic of their newly adopted Americanism.[7]

Blacks in America are not just another urban migrant group with a marked potential for assimilation into the mainstream of American society. Rather, as a group they have failed, for generations, to gain the rewards and status attained by others. It is somewhat illusory, therefore, to characterize contemporary urban problems in employment and schooling as transitory and capable of resolution over time. Many of these problems have grown worse over the years and have been strongly resistant to solution. While the ghettos of White ethnics dissolved as social and economic opportunities increased, today's non-White ghettos have become more isolated and crowded as urban renewal in the city centers, the suburban drift of Whites, and the geographical relocation of jobs have depressed opportunities in employment, housing, and schooling. Moreover, most of the earlier immigrants arrived knowing that generations of their predecessors had worked their way out of poverty by diligence and perserverance, and believed that they could do likewise. Today's Black groups share no such conviction. For too long, they have experienced little in the way of reward for hard work, regularity, and frugality; and they have little optimism for that which the future portends.

CLARIFYING MISCONCEPTIONS

It is most useful here to dispel some glaring misconceptions in the social science research literature relative to schooling and its relationship to status attainment. The old adage that knowledge is power has been extended to imply that schooling is the key to elevated social and economic status attainment. The belief that schools should act as social levers is attributable, in large measure, to progressive educational ideology. Underlying this almost impervious faith in the value of schooling is the notion that public schooling provided the means by which European immigrants moved into the social, cultural, and political mainstream, while Blacks, Hispanics, and American Indians have evinced far less prosperity. Yet, research sustains the fact that only with certain notable exceptions, city schools were not the ladders of social-class mobility for European immigrants, for in many fundamental respects, city schools related to European working-class immigrants in much the same way as they now relate to non-White groups and lower-status Whites.[8] Census data in 1920 and in succeeding decades up to and including 1960 make it clear that even when European immigrants became Americans, neither schools nor society offered quite the social-class mobility imagined.[9]

Relative to the school's response to European immigrants, the arrival of massive numbers of immigrant pupils coincided with the emergence of achievement and IQ testing, vocational guidance, and the movement to diversify instruction and curriculum in city schools. Such practices were employed, if not conceived, as a way of limiting the amount and type of schooling presumed suitable for children of the lower social strata.

It should be noted here that heightened debates centered on the comparative intelligence of immigrants that parallels, quite precisely, the debate over the intelligence of Black Americans. Central to these debates were the questions of whether measured differences were environmental or genetic and whether the tests utilized were culturally and linguistically biased.

Research debunks the legend that the schools were an effective antipoverty agency that taught poor immigrant children so well that they eventually became affluent Americans.[10] The reality was quite different, for the actual function of the public school was the reverse of its legendary function: to certify lower-status youngsters as socially inferior at an early age and initiate the process that kept many of them economically and socially inferior in adulthood. The school was coined an agency of negative credentialism. Because the legend is so pervasive, social programs and policies founded on the legend persist. And so unswerving is America's faith in the school as the vehicle for social mobility that the search for more effective vehicles to obviate poverty is neglected.

The unassailed assumption, as evidenced by the school's institutional policies and processes, is that all persons start from roughly the same vantage point. The fact is that the legend has permitted our nation to maintain a high degree of inequality while concurrently thwarting any challenges to the underlying assumptions that are perceptibly false. On a societal scale, a notion of equality has been propagated while the victims, the non-White groups in America, are blamed for their failure to use the school as it is envisaged, however erroneously, that European immigrant groups have done.

So the legend supports a social policy which is secure in its faith that the agency for the amelioration of most social problems already exists--and that those problems whose solution eludes us now either will be resolved, or are beyond solution, through no fault of that great nation, but because of deficiencies in particular people who cannot seem to solve their problems as countless other Americans have before them. [11]

The legend has persisted because the schools have been viewed altruistically, as apolitical institutions above the self-interests so pervasive in our economy and detached from the very structural alignments that perpetuate inequality. [12] It was only in the late 1950s and 1960s that radical critiques of the school's role and relationship to lower-status individuals, as well as attempts to inter the legend, gained currency. The legend endures in part because in the early twentieth century in America, unskilled jobs were plentiful, and immigrant youngsters who failed in schools entered the economy and progressed economically. In the main, this romanticized view of historic slums and social-class mobility is mindless of the fact not that European immigrants "made it," but "how" they made it.

Despite the plethora of Great Society programs and compensatory aids that have been dismantled by the Reagan administration, the belief persists that there are no sound solutions to alleviate the dire straits of today's non-White groups confined to lower social-class status. The public school is deemed powerless. Yet this same logic has been utilized to argue quite the reverse for White immigrant groups. Thus European groups "made it" because of the school, while non-White groups have been excluded from America's prosperity through no fault of the school. [13]

The public schools are not failures. They are highly successful enterprises, holding firm to the constancy of their task to select individuals for opportunities according to a hierarchy closely paralleling existing social class patterns. That certain racial and ethnic groups remain the underachievers and the bulk of society's burden evinces the class-based nature of racial and ethnic group derivations in American society.

Both intelligence and academic achievement follow too closely a cultural-economic line to be held to be the product of genes, unless, of course, one is prepared to identify specific gene pools in identified ethnic groups, taking full account of intermarriage, when and how often for various subgroups, as if the aforementioned is possible without the convenience of skin color. [14] The unalterable fact in our society is that educational marginality parallels the economic marginality of any racial and ethnic group. And, school has a less pervasive influence on students than home background. [15] Perhaps the most profound and unheeded implication of the foregoing pages is that, historically, poor people did not succeed economically through the school, but that when they succeeded economically, they exerted political pressure to ensure that their children would succeed through the schools. The import of this statement suggests that educational success follows upon the heels of economic success, not the converse.[16]

We shall see how this pattern replicated itself in the Black community to stimulate, in part, the growth of the Black middle class in the industralized North from the 1940s to the 1960s. Yet the present deindustrialization of the North has precipitated the growing educational and economic underclass of Black Americans today.

STATUS REPORT ON BLACK AMERICA

While there have been notable gains made by Blacks over the past two decades as a result of the civil rights movement, a second nation has grown up within Black America-- the Black underclass. The term itself is rather controversial and connotes a special subculture beyond hope and suffering who live in the inner-city, trapped in an unending cycle of joblessness, broken homes, welfare, drugs, and violence. The picture, at best, is disheartening.

The evidence overwhelmingly points to the fact that lingering racism, the lack of economic opportunities, and radical changes in the job market are the direct causes of the swollen ranks of the Black underclass.[17]   Unlike ethnic groups in the first half of the twentieth century, unskilled Blacks have been unable to shed poverty by taking manufacturing jobs that offer decent wages. By 1970, the door to these jobs was virtually shut. In the last fifteen years, only 1 percent of the 23 million jobs created in the private sector were in manufacturing, while more than 90 percent were in the service sector.[18]   Many new jobs required relatively high education levels and were in the suburbs. As a result, members of other ethnic groups or White women took a significant proportion of these jobs. Young Black men took only one out of every 1,000 new jobs created between 1970 and 1983.[19]

University of Chicago sociologist William J. Wilson suggests that what feeds the cycle of the underclass is not welfare, but the loss of jobs from the inner-city and chronic unemployment.[20] Wilson says you have to look at where the jobs are, not just how many were created.   Blacks have borne the brunt of deindustrialization with their heavy concentration in the steel, automobile, rubber, and textile industries. He contends that the data on Blacks moving out of poverty into the middle class from the 1940s through the 1960s shows that much of that movement was due to securing higher-paying jobs in the industrial sector. Subsequent, notable advances in academic achievement have been largely attributable to this group. That has all been reversed. The four large cities of New York, Chicago, Philadelphia, and Detroit account for more than one quarter of the nation's central-city poor. They lost more than a million manufacturing, wholesale, and retail jobs between 1967 and 1976, at the same time that their populations were becoming minority-dominant. For most inner-city Blacks, new service jobs--janitor, messenger, busboy--have not compensated for the loss of manufacturing jobs. Whereas cyclical unemployment was the problem for Black men in the past, permanent unemployment is at the core of the Black underclass today. Wilson disassociates himself from the self-help crowd who feel that Blacks should just deal with the conditions in the underclass themselves. "These problems are so massive and overwhelming that it's unrealistic to think that the Black community can solve them on its own."[21]

In the inner-city today, the only institutions with a record of consistently getting people out of the underclass are the parochial schools. In the Catholic schools, teacher salaries are much less than what public school teachers are paid, and they screen their applicants. Further, principals can hire and fire teachers as well as impose many rules on both students and their parents. Chicago's Father George Clements, the pastor of the Holy Angels Catholic Church, describes the regimen at its elementary school this way:

We have achieved honors as an academic institution above the national norm in all disciplines. We bear down hard on basics. Hard work, sacrifice, dedication. A twelve-month school year. An eight-hour day. You can't leave the campus. Total silence in the lunchroom and throughout the building. Expulsion for graffiti. Very hard emphasis on moral pride. The parents must come every month and pick up the report card and talk to the teacher or we kick out the kid. They must come to the PTA every month. They must sign every night's homework in every subject. They must come to Mass on Sundays. They must take a required course on the Catholic faith. The kids wear uniforms, which are required to be clean, pressed, no holes. We have a waiting list of over a thousand, and the more we bear down, the longer the list gets.[22]

Poverty is one of the firmest predictors of subsequent academic performance, not because low income in and of itself makes a child a dunce, but because the circumstances of poverty often erode supportive and attendant expectations that would likely enhance learning. How do Blacks fare once they reach public school? Not surprisingly, given the difficulties many encounter along the way, they do less well than White children. Although the gap between Blacks and Whites in reading achievement, as measured by the National Assessment of Educational Progress (NAEP), is substantial, it has been narrowing, especially for elementary

students and for children who live in the Southeast, where the gap
has been greatest. It is important that the narrowing of the gap
coincided with and may have been caused by some of the Great
Society programs, such as Head Start and Title I, programs which
have suffered cutbacks under the Reagan administration.[23]
Under the guise of the "New Federalism," the Reagan
administration has elevated private interest over the public good.[24]
Since the 1980s the right to a public education has been undermined
at the federal level by antibusing legislation, severe budget cuts in
education and student assistance, proposals for tuition tax-credits,
the granting of tax-exempt status to schools that blatantly
discriminate, the exemption of certain schools from civil rights
regulations, the negation of affirmative action requirements, and the
abdication of the federal role in monitoring and enforcing equal
access to quality education.[25] Moreover, a climate of indifference
and insensitivity from the federal government to the local school
official has had the net effect of once again "blaming the victim."
Thus progress made by a few Blacks has proved inadequate to
significantly close the gap between Black and White educational
attainments. Such attainments are miniscule given the number of
Blacks in poverty and the overwhelming educational needs of
Blacks.
Conversely, there is the Black middle class, that is, those
Blacks who are perceived to have "made it."   To be sure, a Black
middle class certainly exists, but the 1980 census figures indicate it
lags far behind its White counterpart.[26] For example, out of
1,222,452 Black individuals in the New York metropolitan area
who received income in 1980, only 2,733 made over
$50,000--0.24 percent. More than 2.5 percent of White adults in
the New York vicinity with reportable incomes fell into this
category. And of the area's 464,082 Black families, less than 2
percent had incomes over $50,000. About 10 percent of the White
families exceeded that amount. The 1985 national update indicated
that the disparity is continuing. Almost 20 percent of all White
families in the U.S. had incomes over $50,000; only 7 percent of
Black families did.
It is important to note here that the Black middle-class
professional has served to refute degrading, humiliating, and
offensive stereotypes and has given incentive to Black youth. On
the other hand, such an image has caused frustration and
aggression as well. According to many Black professionals, true
integration on a personal and professional level remains an
unrealized dream. It appears that despite the most lofty academic
achievements,"... that there's a ceiling for Black people in the
White world...People look at me, and all they see is Black."[27]
Seemingly, the drive toward achievement and accomplishment that
the image inspires is overwhelmed and distorted by the social
reality it conceals.[28]

As most Blacks still attempt to use the public schools to overcome their educational and economic marginality, it is appropriate to discuss some of the current reforms being proposed to offset Black underachievement.

REFORM EFFORTS

In this part of the chapter, we look at some of the major reform proposals, albeit briefly, in the Black community. As the succeeding pages will show, community control is the reform strategy which provides the greatest opportunity for alleviating Black underachievement in the public schools.

Historical Perspectives: Ocean Hill Brownsville and Black Parent-Teacher Estrangement

Viewed historically, the demand for local control may be seen as a natural--indeed, inevitable--extension of the doctrine of maximum participation of the poor established by the Office of Economic Opportunity in the various Community Action Programs that it had begun to fund. The Anti-Poverty Program, Model Cities, and Title III of the Elementary and Secondary education Act, among others, were set up to encourage local participation in policymaking as a concommitant or even a prerequisite to achieving substantive goals. Federal money was used to finance local elections and to establish special governments for these programs in inner-city neighborhoods. Federal programs, then, not only increased the expectations of participation for many community residents, but they also created new sets of local leaders with neighborhood rather than citywide support and perspectives. Schools quickly became the institutional battlegrounds for the testing of these new forces.

At one point in the early 1960s, teachers were allied with Black urban community groups and each supported the other, viewing themselves as oppressed by and powerless relative to the centralized boards of education. But events during the Ocean Hill-Brownsville controversy in New York in the late 1960s did much to cement the estrangement which presently exists among minority parents and teachers.

However, before the Ocean Hill-Brownsville incident shattered the alliance, there were signs of community discontent with teachers'-union bargaining demands. During the 1967 negotiations between the United Federation of Teachers (UFT) and the New York City Board of Education, minority parents were outraged at the union's demand for a contract provision granting teachers the right to exclude from class pupils labeled disruptive.[29] The disruptive pupil provision, still unresolved when the UFT went out on strike, led large segments of the Black community to openly oppose the teachers' efforts.

The teacher-community alliance completely disintegrated during the Ocean Hill-Brownsville, New York City teachers' strike of 1968.[30] The strike was ignited when the community-controlled local school board transferred nineteen teachers. The teacher's union contended that the teachers were transferred without benefit of due process, while the predominantly Black board maintained that it had the authority to transfer and/or dismiss personnel. The central issue was one of control and accountability.

Shock waves from Ocean Hill-Brownsville spread across the country.[31] Unions in other cities became wary of pending decentralization plans which involved community participation in decisionmaking. For instance, the influence of the Detroit Federation of Teachers in the Michigan legislature made the passage of the Detroit decentralization plan contingent upon the union's maintaining its right to bargain an overall agreement covering the decentralized districts.[32] At the American Federation of Teachers (AFT) convention held in New Orleans in 1969, delegates led by Albert Shanker and the UFT defeated a strong resolution supporting the concept of community control in urban districts.[33] Similarly, pressure was brought to bear against community control advocates in union locals throughout the United States.

By 1972, a committee report of the New York Bar Association made clear the limitations of the transfer of power to local school boards under New York's decentralization act of 1969. "The legislature did not vest in the community boards the most significant aspect of labor relations; the negotiation of a contract."[34] During the 1975 negotiations between the UFT and the New York City Board of Education, the exclusion of the community boards from the bargaining process surfaced as a major point of contention. It is the contention of the community boards that they were excluded from having any impact on the negotiation's outcome.

The major reason teachers' unions were and are opposed to community control is the increased accountability resulting from a transfer of public educational power from one large bureaucracy to several smaller school districts. To accept community control, the union must accept a sharing of its power through a new responsibility and accountability to the client community it serves. Thus, any attempt to dilute the union's authority, as community control does, is viewed as an unconscionable threat to the very existence of the union itself. The real issue for the community is what a teacher's union ought to be and more importantly, what ought to be its responsibility to its client communities.

Research has substantiated the failure of teachers' unions to even identify with the masses of poor Blacks.[35] Ideally, the union movement in general was conceived of as a struggling, fighting, and marching force side by side with the least privileged. If the union and the Black parents had been in alliance, they could have had tremendous impact on the social and political powers in the country. But the tragic fact is that the union wanted no part of such a coalition; on the contrary, the union placed itself in the position of being an adversary of Blacks and other minorities. Not only have the teachers' unions opted not to support the legitimate desires of the poor for a fair share in society, they, as well as virtually all of the trade union movement, have sought gains at the expense of Blacks.[36]

The failure of teachers' unions to influence or even attempt to influence public policy or action for poor Blacks is most dramatically illustrated by the teachers' irrelevance to the course of racial desegregation in public education. For many years, equality of educational opportunity has been a major rallying cry among teachers' organizations, especially in their efforts to secure federal aid to education. The inequalities due to racial discrimination have been more flagrant and almost as pervasive, yet it cannot be said that teacher organizations have been an important factor in the fight to eliminate racially segregated schools.[37] It was the NAACP, not the professional organizations of teachers, which successfully attacked differential salary schedules for White and Black teachers, the practice of forcing Blacks to go out of the state for certain kinds of professional training, and the obviously unequal facilities for Black students in the South. Since the Supreme Court decision in 1954 declared racial segregation in public education unconstitutional, the teacher's unions have failed to provide leadership for gaining acceptance of the decision and for implementing the necessary reorganization of teacher-pupil assignments.

The Commission Reports

In April 1982, A Nation at Risk, the report of the National Commission on Excellence in Education, marked the beginning of a tidal wave of reports that sought to reform and raise the academic standards of America's schools.[38] Overnight, the "buzz" words were accountability, back to basics, competency, and basic literacy. The motivation for the rash of reports was the fear that America would lose its world market dominance and the belief that raising academic standards would enhance American industrial productivity. While significant research questions such an assumed cause-and-effect relationship, for our purposes we will examine the reforms, in summary fashion, to ascertain whether there is potential for significant Black achievement gains from the larger reform efforts.

The substance of the commission reform reports calls for a national curriculum, the lengthening of the school day, more standardized testing, proposed curricular changes (more rigorous mathematics, science, social studies, and English requirements), computer literacy, and the abandonment of bilingual education programs for Hispanic youth and new-wave immigrants. Few believe the proposed changes will evidence greater achievement among White students, not to mention Black youngsters.[39] In fact, Black students and other lower-status youth may suffer disproportionately because a longer, low-quality school day will do more harm than good and even increase the dropout rate. What is being prescribed is a "high-tech," inherently elitist form of schooling with no accommodation for students of differing skill, interest, or aptitude levels from those prescribed by the commission reports.

In effect, Blacks and others are asked to subscribe to the discredited notion that all students, irrespective of their social status, sex, and racial, ethnic, or religious background, will be treated equally by being held to the same academic standards. "They are left with the absurdity that treating people the same, is the same as treating them equally."[40] The crux of the problem with the contemporary commission reform reports is that they lock-in the preexisting inequities of the present public school system and make no attempts to address or ameliorate them. Others have drawn similar conclusions:

> Despite the attention generated by the 1983 reports, what marks them most, I believe, is their overwhelming ordinariness and conventionality. They actually provide no new departures from the fundamental character of the existing school system. What we see in the reports is little more than a set of proposals for schooling as usual: for technical training to meet industrial needs, for scientific preparation to combat the communist threat, for socialization to ensure discipline in the office or on the shop floor. What they advocate, more than anything, is more of what already exists rather than something profoundly different.[41]

If the commissions have their way, such a reformed school would be more highly stratified along more rigid class distinctions. We would come perilously close to emulating the educational systems of those with whom we are locked in competition. Why? Because there is a price to pay for the reforms and it will be borne by those who can afford it the least. If one understands the heightened synergistic relationship between achievement and family income, the argument becomes not only irrefutable, but moot.

Community Control

Black communities today are well-versed in the grim realities with which the larger White American society must now grapple. Black communities in the large urban centers in the 1950s and 1960s foretold much of the educational malaise in which America now finds herself. In the 1960s, Black urban parents did not ask for school integration, but for accountability through community control of their schools. Instead they were given decentralization. How fortuitous that almost twenty-five years ago, urban parents were among the first to question the competence of school professionals.[42]

For Black parents, the issue twenty-five years ago and the issue today is a political question involving accountability and a sharing of power and decisionmaking. From the perspective of this author, community control through political empowerment is the most viable alternative for redressing the political, economic, and educational ills afflicting Black America. One has only to witness the community mobilization of Black parents in the major cities, e.g., Chicago, New York, Philadelphia, and St. Louis, who are beginning, through pressure politics, to alter the course of schooling for their youngsters. Consider that White suburban and rural public schools have always been community controlled. On the urban scene, while many of the particulars have yet to be finalized, it is important at this stage to understand the ideological underpinnings upon which the concept of community control is founded.

Decentralization and community control are two terms which are often used interchangeably, albeit erroneously.[43] Decentralization is defined as the shift in decisionmaking within an organization in such a way as to bring the process as administratively close as possible to the individuals who will implement the decisions being made. Usually this means moving the responsibility for decisions downward--that is, rather than keeping all decisions in the hands of some centralized authority, the process is delegated by stages to the various levels within the organization. Decentralization is a strategy for modifying the internal hierarchy of authority and control in a school system, and often occurs without any involvement of a school's client community.

Community control is defined as a political strategy for reconstituting the interfacing relationship between a school and its client community. Typically including decentralization of authority and control, community control also implies other kinds of organizational changes as well. Such responsibilities as the hiring and firing of personnel, the design of curricula, allocation of resources, and pupil policy would be the responsibility of the community. Inherent in community control is the premise that the schools, teachers, and administrators would be accountable to the residents of the community they serve. Community control implies a redistribution of power within the educational system. Implicit here is a redefinition of community participation from involvement or expressed interest, to direct engagement in the policymaking process and in the exercise of power. For many years, particularly during the 1960s, urban parents and urban communities were demanding a shift in decisionmaking from the centralized authorities to the grass-roots level through decentralization and community control, without realizing that the former could occur without the latter.

The failure of school integration provided the Black community with insights into their exclusion from the school decisionmaking processes.[44]   Community participation in urban school decisionmaking emerged out of the failure of the existing system to fulfill its promises to large numbers of Black and Puerto Rican parents, who, at some time in the early 1960s, became convinced that integration, as a means of improving the education of their children, was not going to work. The issues debated in the struggle for integration, in quite unanticipated ways, gave rise to the current movement towards community control of school decisionmaking. It is crucial to remember that integration was not abandoned by Black parents, but by boards of education who consistenly failed to deliver on the promise of integrated schools.[45] The demand for community control was a direct response by Blacks to the lack of access to decisionmaking processes that vitally affected the lives of their children.

Prolonged dissatisfaction with the academic performance of Black and minority youngsters has led to questions regarding the legitimacy of the urban school.[46] This is particularly true when a specific clientele is the school's victim and ameliorative efforts have made no discernible difference. The massive dissatisfaction of Black parents regarding the academic performance of their children was and is, in effect, a rejection of the experts' professed claim of expertise.[47] This occurs at a time when education is widely seen as the vehicle for social and economic mobility, the place to break the cycle of poverty.

An increasing number of urban schools have gradually lost the kind of authority that clients typically accord an institution on the basis of its competence. When institutions thus lose the support of client groups, they lose, as well, much of the base for their real authority and control. The mounting crisis of confidence in relations between city schools and their constituents is unlikely to subside until the schools either meet the demands of their critics or alter their traditional prerogatives.

The failure of urban schools to raise the achievement levels of Blacks is not, however, the sole justification for community control. What makes community control a special kind of demand, essentially different from other proposed educational reforms, is that it relates to a variety of social and political issues that go beyond the question of educational attainment.[48]

Community control of schools is the beginning of a significant drive toward not just equal educational opportunity, but full equality. This belief is based on the view that as long as Black Americans lack political and economic power, they will not be able to improve the conditions under which they live. Community control of schools is presented as the leading edge of a political wedge that will begin to redistribute decisionmaking power to those affected by the decisions. Control of the schools is viewed as the first step in effecting a more just distribution of political power and a greater degree of self-determination for Black citizens.

Community control further implies a redistribution of decisionmaking power within the educational subsystem that it attempts to answer the political failure in education systems; as regards the educational failure, community control is intended to create an environment in which more meaningful educational policies can be developed and a wide variety of alternative solutions and techniques can be tested. Community control is an instrument of social change. The redistribution of power is in itself an aspect of that change.[49]

The advocates of community control are correct in assuming that the pedagogical problems which afflict the schools are political problems and that their children will not learn to read until a substantial shift of power takes place within the city. In essence, the fight over community control must be seen as part of a broader struggle for the redistribution of political power.

Support for community participation is voiced by the educational establishment and teacher organizations, but their concept of community participation is more loosely related to the traditional parent-teacher-association (PTA) concept, and has nothing to do with community control of decisionmaking. Community control of the schools involves local control over such key policy decisions as the hiring and firing of personnel, design of curricula, allocation of resources, and pupil policy.

Inherent in community control is the premise that the schools, teachers, and administrators are accountable to the residents of the community they serve. Distinguishing features of the present traditional school system and a system that has undergone fundamental reform through parent-community participation are presented in table 18.1. Governing bodies would be locally selected and mechanisms for encouraging broader community involvement would be developed.

A major source of power for minority communities is ethnic solidarity, for which voting provides one outlet. Within the Black community, there is increasing interest and hope in getting "a piece of the action," and this means a redistribution of power in the city

Table 18.1

Characteristics of Traditional and Reformed School Systems

Distinguishing Feature	Traditional System	Reformed System
Center of control	Professional monopoly	The local community
Role of parents	To interpret the school to the community, for public relations	To participate as active agents in matters substantive to the educational process
Bureaucracy	Centralized authority, limiting flexibility and initiative to the professional at the individual school level	Decentralized decisionmaking allowing for maximum local lay and professional initiative and flexibility, with central authority concentrating on technical assistance, long-range planning, and system-wide coordination
Educational objectives	Emphasis on grade-level performance, basic skills, cognitive achievement	Emphasis on both cognitive and affective development; humanistically-oriented objectives; for example, identity connectedness, powerlessness
Test of efficiency and promotion	Emphasis on credentials and systematized advancement through the system	Emphasis on performance with students and with parent-community participants
Institutional philosophy	Negative self-fulfilling prophecy, student failure blamed on learner and his background	Positive self-fulfilling prophecy–no student failures, only program failures; accountable to learner and community
Basic learning unit	Classroom, credentialized teacher, school building	The community, various agents as teachers, including other students and para-professionals

to allow the Black community a greater role in the policy process. Community control advocates are fully aware of the difference between the right to participate in the policy process and the power to achieve their objectives. Implicit here is a redefinition of community participation from involvement or expressed interest, as reflected in attendance at meetings or voting, to direct engagement in the policymaking process and in the exercise of power. Reform agendas in major cities across the country speak poignantly to the notion of shared decisionmaking in the execution of power.

CONCLUSION

For decades, the American dream of upward mobility has nourished the aspirations of millions of Americans. Schools are envisioned as the ru du passage, the ladder upon which ambition climbs to privilege.[50] America's Blacks are attempting to use the schools as a social lever, as they perceive previous waves of European immigrants have done and as present waves of Asian immigrants are now doing. It should come as no surprise, therefore, that the public schools have become the battleground around which Black communities have mobilized to influence the educational decisions affecting the lives of their children. The quest for control of the schools is mobilizing the Black community. Yet the issue is beyond schooling per se. Schools as institutions are merely the conduits through which the redress of larger social, political, and economic injustices will be made.

To understand the current educational crisis facing America generally, and Black America, in particular, is to understand the larger social, political, and economic policy crises which penetrate the lives of America's citizens. The present educational crisis is firmly rooted in the racism, dominance, and inequality emblematic of the larger society, in the widening class divisions between the "haves" and "have nots," and in the conspicuous consumption of material goods and services that aggrandizes individualism yet leaves one bereft of spiritual fulfillment or social consciousness. Moreover, as America experiences a no growth economy, there is a very real possibility that many, even most of the children of the poor will become fathers and mothers of the poor. As this replicative phenomenon takes place, America witnesses the perpetual regeneration of a hereditary underclass.

As shown in previous pages, educational marginality parallels economic marginality. Inadequate resource allocation to city schools, residential segregation and housing quality, the location, structure, and placement of public transportation systems, discriminatory hiring and promotion practices, academic underachievement of Black youth, unavailability of decent health care, prejudicial behavior of policeofficers and judges, stereotypical images of Blacks in the media and school curricula, price gouging in ghetto stores, morbidity, mortality, and longevity rates, lack of political clout and effective legislative representation--these and myriad other forms of social, political, and economic discrimination concurrently interlock to determine the status, income, and welfare of Black people.[51] Such factors cannot be considered inconsequential to one's social mobility or the lack thereof in the economic arena, for such processes are not simply additive, but are mutually sustaining and reinforcing. Noneconomic factors neatly interlace with economic factors becoming, on a systems level, operationally inseparable.

The root exploitation of Black Americans lies in a system of economic power and privilege in which ascriptive variables such as race (skin color), sex, age, and family background have a stratifying and mutually reinforcing effect. The lower school performance of Blacks is not the central problem, but an expression of a more fundamental one, namely racial barriers and the ideologies that support and legitimize inequality. DuBois said it best: "the problem of the twentieth century is (still) the problem of the color line..."[52]

Given the foregoing, we must applaud, embrace, and participate in the mobilization of the Black community, through community control, as it attempts to offset ,through the schools, the many injustices that have been heaped upon it. In so doing, our task is not simply to enable Black youngsters to maintain the social system that perpetrates inequality, but to change that system as well, through a renewed sense of social and political commitment, of social consciousness.

NOTES

1. J. Baldwin, The Fire Next Time (New York: Dell Publishing Company, 1963), p. 139.

2. C. C. Yeakey, "Schooling: A Political Analysis of the Distribution of Power and Privilege," Oxford Review of Education 7, no. 2 (1981): 173-191.

3. See S. Bowles and H. Gintis, Schooling In Capitalist America: Education Reform and Contradictions of Economic Life (New York: Basic Books, 1976); B. Bernstein, Class Codes and Control, volume 3, Towards A Theory of Educational Transmission (London: Routledge and Kegan Pual, 1977); M. F. D. Young, ed., Knowledge and Control (London: Collier-Macmillan, 1971); M. MacDonald, The Curriculum and Cultural Reproduction (Milton Keynes, England: Open University Press, 1977); C. Loparte, "Approaches to Schools: The Perfect Fit," Liberation (September-October 1974): 26-32; S. Gorelick, "Schooling Problems in Capitalist America," Monthly Review 29 no. 3 (January 1977): 20-36; H. A. Giroux, "Teacher Education and the Ideology of Social Control," Journal of Teacher Education 162 (Winter 1980); H. Mehan, Learning Lessons: Social Organization in the Class-room, (Cambridge, Mass.: Harvard University Press, 1979); R. Sharp and A. Green, Education and Social Control (London: Routledge and Kegan Paul, 1975); and C.C. Yeakey and E.W. Gordon, "The Policy Implications of Status Variables and Schooling," in A. Lieberman and M. W. McLaughlin, eds., Policy Making in Education (Chicago: University of Chicago Press, 1982), pp. 104-132.

4. Yeakey, "Schooling: A Political Analysis."

5. R. Blauner, Racial Oppression in America (New York: Harper, 1972), pp. 52-53; see also L. Litwack, North of Slavery (Chicago: University of Chicago Press, 1961).

6. Yeakey and Gordon, "Policy Implications of Status Variables" p. 118.

7. F. R. Westie, "The American Dilemma: An Empirical Test," American Sociological Review 30 (August 1965): 527-38.

8. See C. Greer, The Great School Legend (New York: Basic Books, 1972); D. K. Cohen, "Immigrants and the Schools," Review of Educational Research 40 (February 1970); 13-27; J. Addams, Democracy and Social Ethics (Cambridge, Mass. Harvard University Press, 1902); and Twenty Years at Hull House (New York: Macmillan, 1914); and The Second Twenty Years at Hull House (New York: Macmillan, 1930).

9. N. Glazer and D. P. Moynihan, Beyond the Melting Pot: The Negroes, Puerto Ricans, Jews, Italians, and Irish of New York City (Cambridge, Mass.: MIT Press, 1963); Niles Carpenter, Immigrants and Their Children, 1920,"Census Monograph no. 7 (Washington, D.C.: Government Printing Office, 1927), vol. I., p. 32, table 16; Walter Laidlaw, Statistical Sources for Demographic Studies, Greater New York, 1910 and 1920 (New York: New York Census Committee, 1932), pp. 52-76; C. Jencks and D. Riesman, "On Class in America, "Public Interest, no. 10 (Winter 1968): 79; Bureau of the Census, Current Population Reports, series P-20, (Washington, D.C.: Bureau of the Census, 1970), pp. 7-8; R. Coles, Still Hungry in America (New York: New American Library, 1969); and C. McCarthy, "40 Million Americans and a Broken Odyssey," Washington Post, 13 July 1970, p. 29.

10. Greer, The Great School Legend, p. 3.

11. Ibid, p. xi.

12. Ibid.

13. Ibid, 103.

14. M. J. Mayo, "The Mental Capacity of the American Negro," Archives of Psychology, no. 28 (New York: Science Press, 1913): 10-21.

15. J. S. Coleman et al., Equality of Educational Opportunity (Washington, D.C.: Government Printing Office, 1966).

16. Greer, The Great School Legend, p. xiii.

17. See, for example, W. J. Wilson and K. M. Neckerman, Poverty and Family Structure: The Widening Gap between Evidence and Public Policy Issues, IRP Conference Paper, (Madison, Wis. Institute for Research on Poverty and the U.S. Department of Health and Human Services, 1984); and A. Cohen, Economics, Marital Instability and Race, (Ph.D. dissertation, University of Wisconsin at Madison, 1979).

18. "A Nation Apart," p. 20.

19. Ibid.

20. "Debating Plight of the Urban Poor," U.S. News and World Report, March 3, 1986, p. 21.

21. Ibid, p. 22.

22. N. Lemann, "The Origins of the Underclass" Atlantic Monthly, July 1986, p. 67.

23. P. Graham, "Black Teachers: A Drastically Scare Resource," Phi Delta Kappan 68 (April 1987):   601; see also Education Week, May 14, 1986, p. 27.

24. See C. C. Yeakey, "School Reform in Perspective: Emerging Educational and Social Policy Dilemmas," in C. C. Yeakey and G. S. Johnston, eds., Schools as Conduits: Educational Policymaking During the Reagan Years (Westport, Conn.: Greenwood/ Praeger, in press).

25. B. P. Cole, "The State of Education for Black Americans," Education Digest, 49 (December 1983):   28.

26. E. Hopkins, "Blacks at the Top: Torn between Two Worlds," New York, January 19, 1987, p. 22; see also G. Davis and G. Watson, Black Life in Corporate America Swimming in the Mainstream (New York: Anchor Press/Doubleday, 1982).

27. Hopkins, "Blacks at the Top," p. 22.

28. C. C. Yeakey and G. S. Johnston, "A Review Essay," American Journal of Orthopsychiatry (April 1979):   353-359 (especially p. 357).

29. C. Cheng, "Community Representation in Teacher Collective Bargaining: Problems and Prospects," Harvard Educational Review 46 (May 1976) 157.

30. Ibid.

31. For an interesting analysis of the community control movement in Chicago, headed by Dr. Barbara Sizemore, and the Chicago Teachers' Union response to it, see John Hall Fish, Black Power White Control (Princeton, N.J.: Princeton University Press, 1973). Similarities between this movement and the Ocean Hill-Brownsville incident are strikingly similar.

32. Joseph M. Cronin, The Control of Urban Schools; Perspective on the Power of Educational Reforms (New York: Free Press, 1972), p. 198.

33. Cheng, "Community Represention," p. 160.

34. Association of the Bar of the City of New York, The New York City School Decentralization Law and its Effect on Collective Bargaining (New York: Association of the Bar of the City of New York, 1972), p. 1.

35. J. O'Neill, "The Rise and Fall of the UFT," in A. Rubinstein, ed., Schools against Children The Case for Community Control (New York: Monthly Review Press, 1970), p. 176.

36. T. E. Linton and J. L. Nelson, Patterns of Power, Social Foundations of Education (New York: Pitman, 1968), p. 580.

37. Ibid.

38. For the major national reform reports, see College Entrance Examination Board, Academic Preparation for College: What Students Need to Know and Be Able To Do (New York: College Board Educational Equality Project, 1983); National Coalition of Advocates for Students, Our Children at Risk: An Inquiry Into the Reality of American Public Education (mimeographed); National Commission on Excellence in Education, A Nation at Risk: The Imperative for Educational Reform (Washington, D.C.: Government Printing Office, 1983); National Science Board Commission on Precollege Education in Mathematics, Educating Americans for the 21st Century (Washington, D.C.: National Science Foundation, 1983); Task Force on Education for Economic Growth, Action for Excellence: Comprehensive Plan to Improve Our Nation's Schools (Denver: Education Commission of the States, 1983); Twentieth Century Fund, Making the Grade: Report of the Twentieth Century Fund Task Force on Federal Elementary and Secondary Education Policy (New York: Twentieth Century Fund, 1983); U. S. Department of Education, The

Nation Responds: Recent Efforts to Improve Education (Washington, D.C.: Government Printing Office, 1984); Business Advisory Commission, Reconnecting Youth, the Next State of Reform (Denver: Education Commission of the States, 1985); Holmes Group, Tomorrow's Teachers: A Report of the Holmes Group (East Lansing, Mich. Holmes Group, Inc., 1986); Task Force on Teaching as a Profession, A Nation Prepared: Teachers for the 21st Century (New York: Carnegie Forum on Education and the Economy, 1986); National Task Force on Educational Technology, Transforming American Education: Reducing The Risk to the Nation (Washington, D.C.: Government Printing Office, 1986. For related studies, see M. J. Adler, The Paideia Proposal (New York: Macmillan, 1982): E. Boyer, High School: A Report on Secondary Education in America (Princeton, N.J.: Carnegie Foundation for the Advancement of Teaching, 1983); L. Darling - Hammond, Beyond the Commission Reports: The Coming Crisis in Teaching (Santa Monica, Calif.: Rand Corporation, R-3177-RC, 1984); and T. R. Sizer, Horace's Compromise: The Dilemma of the American High School (Boston: Houghton Mifflin, 1984), among others.

39. C. C. Yeakey, "American Schooling and the Retreat from Democracy: The Limits of Contemporary Educational Reform Policy," in J. Stanfield, ed., Research in Social Policy: Historical and Contemporary Perspectives (Greenwich, Conn.: JAI Press, in press), p. 7.

40. Ibid, p. 32.

41. S. Shapiro, "Choosing One Educational Legacy: Disempowerment or Emanicpation?" Issues in Education 2 (Summer 1984,): 12-13.

42. C. C. Yeakey and G. S. Johnston, "Collective Bargaining and Community Participation in Educational Decision Making: A View toward Trilateral Bargaining and School Reform," Journal of Collective Negotiations in the Public Sector, 8, no. 4 (1979): 347-366.

43. See N. Levine, Ocean Hill-Brownsville: A Case History of Schools in Crisis (New York: Popular Library, 1969), p. 11; and L. J. Fein, The Ecology of the Public Schools: An Inquiry into Community Control (New York: Pegasus, 1971), p. 5.

44. See Levine, Ocean Hill-Brownsville, p. 11 and Fein, Ecology of the Public Schools, p. 5.

45. New York Civil Liberties Union, "The Burden of Blame: A Report on the Ocean Hill-Brownsville School Controversy," in M. Gittell and A. G. Hevesi, eds., The Politics of Urban Education (New York: Praeger, 1969), p. 340.

46. Fein, Ecology of the Public Schools, p. 71.

47. Ibid, p. 72.

48. Ibid, pp. 58-62; see also H. W. Pfautz, "The Socialization Process," in H. M. Levin, ed., Community Control of Schools (New York: Simon and Schuster, 1970), p. 14.

49. See M. Gittell, "A Typology of Power for Measuring Social Change," American Behavioral Scientist 9 (April 1966): 23-28.

50. Yeakey, "Schooling: A Political Analysis," p. 182.

51. Yeakey and Johnston, "A Review Essay," p. 356.

52. W. E. B. DuBois, "Worlds of Color," Foreign Affairs, 3, (April 1925): 423.

Summary and Discussion
Edmund Gordon

Doxey Wilkerson, my first professor of education and--for the last twenty-five years--my dear friend, once observed that Black parents are not lacking in their aspirations for the education and career development of their children. Rather, he argued, they often lack the knowledge and skills required to translate those aspirations into high academic and career achievement. Professor Wilkerson's insightful observation is important to appreciating and understanding many of the issues raised in this volume. The growing Black presence in private and parochial schools in the United States is in part a reflection of the high aspirations some Black Americans hold for their children. Unfortunately, this presence, the manner in which choices are made, and the goals or purposes behind the choices reflect limited know-how concerning the facilitation of academic achievement and intellectual development.

In chapter 14, Arnez and Jones-Wilson report that parents' perception of the type of school program, the academic and social characteristics of the students in the school, and the quality of the academic program are major factors influencing the choice of schools among parents who choose nonpublic schools. These perceptions appear to be based on the reputations of the schools. It is not clear how much detailed information is available to these parents concerning each of these dimensions of each school. Rather it appears that judgments are based on colloquial notions of the characteristics of the schools. In the Slaughter, Johnson, and Schneider study (chapter 15), decision models are described as authoritative, deliberate, humanistic, moral, practical, and traditional. These models do not appear to be mutually exclusive with respect to the decision process or its component elements. We do see, however, more of the specific considerations which go into the choices made. Their study suggests that parents have some knowledge of what they want in a school or what they want the school to achieve. However, these goals appear to be broadly described, with little apparent sensitivity to just what a "good teacher," "structured program," or "broad curriculum" should be. In chapter 16, Johnson identifies racial socialization strategies which reveal a concern for socialization to Black identity. These parents do not appear to depend on the independent school primarily for this aspect of their children's education, but may in fact use the strategies because the private school experience tends to isolate the children from the Black community. Factor analysis of the strategies reveals three factors or coping designations: (1) insulatory, (2) competitive, and (3) contemporary-cultural versus global-historical. What apppears to be important to the parents who use these strategies is that the school experience complement the value implicit in the strategy. What seems to be common in all three studies is evidence in aspirations and goals for their children. They expect these aspirations to be served by their choice of private rather than public schools. However, much of their behavior in support of these aspirations reflects poorly informed faith rather than specific and detailed information concerning how the schools they choose and they themselves should go about achieving the goals implicit to their aspirations.

In chapters 17 and 18, public policy issues are examined relating to the financing of alternatives to public school and the quality of public education. Schneider reviews some of the recent debate concerning vouchers and tuition tax credits, both of which come up wanting as solutions to the problems of parental choice and effective schooling. Wilkerson's distinction between aspirations and know-how is also relevant here. It is the better-educated and more affluent parents who seem best able to benefit and make sophisticated choices when schooling is being purchased. But the Yeakey critique of the quality of public education for low-status people in the United States highlights the paradoxical situation facing this segment of the population. Yeakey argues that the public schools have a monopoly on schooling for the masses and that it is a monopoly which has never served low-status people well, but is able to maintain its hegemony because the public schools serve the sorting and status-maintenance purposes of the dominant forces in the social order. If we are to accept this argument, and it is persuasively presented, it is not simply a problem of parental aspirations which are not supported by parental know-how, but parental aspirations and goals for their children which are impossible to achieve through public schools which are by definition under the control of the dominant forces in society. Thus, the retreat to independent and parochial schools.

But have the Blacks who are now visible in independent and parochial schools found a solution to the problems of effective education? The answer is obviously yes and no. Chapters 2 through 13 describe a wide variety of schools outside of the public sphere. Some of these schools are excellent institutions. Some are good for some purposes and not so good for others. Still others are probably better than the mode for public schools but are not so good by an reasonable standard of what schools should be. Here we face a problem. How are laypersons--parents--to choose between these options, when it appears that the choices are made on the basis of limited knowledge and, as I will argue momentarily, incomplete understanding of the nature, purpose, and processes of adequate education.

Most observers seem to agree that private schools do a better job of educating low-status children than public schools. Some skeptics argue that the apparent success is due to selection factors which give these schools the privilege of excluding the hard-to-teach. It is argued that if the private sector has to serve the same population which is served by public schools, they would do no better. But there are more subtle and complex problems. It can be argued that the availability of a private or parochial school provides a choice for more effective training, but not for more effective education. Most of the outcomes measures by which private schools have been judged emphasize content and skill mastery, socialization, and postsecondary opportunities. These are important outcomes, but some of us feel that these are the products of training. The products of education include intellect development, critical thinking, independence of thought, and creative analytic and synergistic conceptual competence. Since private as well as public schools are the institutions of the established social order, the development of intellect has not been their primary goal. Socialization and skill mastery are the more typical goals and purposes of schooling in conservative and reactionary societies. Intellect development is a more revolutionary function and has the potential for formenting radical change even when that is not its purpose. According to this argument, private schools may be no better for low-status and oppressed persons than public schools, since the need is that they be educated to change the social order and not to simply fit it.

It may well be that the problem of parental choice in the selection of schools and the improvement of education for low-status children cannot be resolved in the private versus public school arena of choice. In the first place, most low-status children will continue to be educated in the public schools for the indefinite future. The urgent task is to improve those schools and change what these families and communities do in support of education. In the second place, Wilkerson's concern with know-how relative to academic development would focus our attention not so much on the public versus private school setting, but on the nature of the educational experiences which are made available to children at home, in the community, and at school (be it public or private). What seems inadequately understood is that the development of intellect and academic competence requires more than a "good school" experience. Rather, there must be congruence between the specific needs of the child and the resources of the school. It is not just good teaching that is needed, but teaching which is targeted on the individual learning needs of the learner.

We are beginning to understand that intellect development requires that learners actively engage the material to be learned. Passive learning appears to be counterproductive to the development of higher-order intellectual competence, yet it is often discipline, structure, and receptive learning that are colloquially associated with many of the parochial and other private schools to which our parents turn. There is growing evidence that excessive dependence on the "school" and failure to recognize that home and community must support academic development are also culpable factors in the undereducation of minority group children. The expectations, models, and resources which are made available may be more important in the development of dispositional characteristics needed for academic development than the specific school in which learning occurs. The opportunity to use the knowledge and conceptual and problem-solving skills is increasingly recognized as important to academic development. In the choice of the more elite schools, insufficient attention may be given to the fact that these schools have built their reputations through their success in educating children who have done their preacademic learning in settings which prepare them for the exercise of choice in selecting learning experiences, which have embedded knowledge structures (information, "cultural literacy," cognitive skills) upon which additional learning is scaffolded, and which are congruent with the demands of academic learning situations.

We do not have information on the availability of this kind of understanding in the population of Black parents who are making choices concerning the education of their children. Their choice of private schools reflects their high aspirations for their children. The variations in the schools, the complexity of the issues, and the continued existence of an achievement gap between Black and White children in these schools all support the Wilkerson assertion that the high aspirations are not matched by a high degree of sophistication concerning how these aspirations are best achieved.

19
Epilogue
Diana T. Slaughter and Deborah J. Johnson

MODELS FOR STUDYING FAMILY-SCHOOL RELATIONS

Existing models differ with respect to how relationships between students, families, and schools are defined. The criteria include: (1) the degree of emphasis upon the community or neighborhood for understanding life in school, (2) the amount of specific attention to the family as part of a community or neighborhood and its effect on school relations, (3) the degree of focus upon the child's familial home environment, as contrasted with (4) primary attention to pupil characteristics obviously derived from family background for explaining student performance in schools. Throughout the history of educational research in this area, studies have varied along these dimensions. Educational studies of Black children largely began with a focus on pupil characteristics.

Focus on Pupil Characteristics

Researchers initially focused on the contribution of pupil characteristics associated with family background to student learning and achievement. Allison Davis and his colleagues, for example, stressed the contribution of social-class background.[1] Researchers such as Eleanor Leacock, Ray Rist, and Janet Schofield have stressed the contribution of race and status distinctions within race to students' learning experiences in schools.[2] Some researchers who take more macrosocietal perspectives argue that family background has its greatest effect upon minority education in the kinds of persons the children become. Coleman, for example, has argued that the Black student's sense of personal efficacy determines relatives educational success.[3] What these otherwise highly diverse studies have in common for the issues discussed here is that the families' role in the educational process is largely thought to be encapsulated in pupil characteristics which are linked to social-status background.

In this volume, chapters 3, 4, and 9 are especially informative about the pupil characteristics of some Black students in private schools.   Clearly, however, little is known about such characteristics of Black and other ethnic minority students in the differing types of private school as their achievement performances, aspirations, educational expectations, self-concepts, and life goals and priorities.   In the future, more information--for better curriculum planning in relation to these students--is highly desirable.

Focus on Home Environment

Other researchers have stressed identification and description of those attributes and processes within the home environment which influence children's learning and achievement. Benjamin Bloom, Robert D. Hess, and Virginia Shipman, for example, have stressed that social class is only a proxy variable to home environmental processes indicative of the educational climate of the home and the specific interactions of parents and children that are educationally relevant. The design of many studies in this area, including several by the authors, gives specific attention to parenting processes linked to educationally relevant outcomes in children.[5] What these studies share, however, is (1) little attention to children's families within the context of an identifiable community, and (2) little attention to the in-school experiences of the children.

No studies in this volume address the latter issues. At this time, it appears that little or no research has been conducted which reports how private school students interact in their home environments with their parents. Given that these children are reputed to have special success with school, this is quite surprising. We are in need of research which describes what private school parents do that appears to enhance academic excellence in their children, particularly ethnic minority children.

Focus on Neighborhood and Community

A third important emerging cluster of studies has emphasized community-school relations, frequently focusing on either class or race as broad stratifying dimensions, affecting what occurs inside schools.[6] Though highly diverse, these studies share a focus on how sociocultural forces outside of schools affect in-school social organization and the experiences, behaviors, and attitudes of students.   The researchers implicitly assume that childhood socialization in the family has considerable significance for how students from differing social backgrounds perceive schooling and how they will be perceived by faculty.   Therefore, in-school processes are not solely determined by pupil characteristics. Rather, schools also respond to the dynamics of the communities in which they reside and, of course, communities are composed of families.

The ongoing research of Franklin and McDonald, which is partially reported in chapter 8, takes this approach.[7] The authors of chapters 3-5, 11-12, and 17 do an especially able job of pointing to the many social and historical forces impacting the experiences of Black children and their families with diverse independent and parochial schools. Additionally, Lomotey and Brookins attempt in chapter 12 to relate an identified social context to the organization of in-school life in selected independent neighborhood schools.

Focus on the Family and the School

Finally, there is a tradition of writing in which few actual studies have been conducted. These authors emphasize that schooling has a definite predictable effect on children, particularly when family and school goals are highly similar. Several researchers have found shared values between middle-class White children's families and four schools attended by their children.[8] Two schools were classified as more traditional, and two more modern or progressive. The researchers argued that the schools impacted the values and related personality processes of both children and parents (three schools were public and one was private).

In this same tradition, some authors have emphasized the potential discontinuities between the goals of some families and the schools attended by their children.[9] For example, researchers have contrasted the home learning environments of lower-income Black children to the educational environments of traditional schools and pointed to discontinuities.[10] Although the goals of the two institutions may be highly similar, the exigencies associated with everyday lifestyles result in a discontinuity between what is learned in home and community, and what is to be learned in school.

In this volume, the authors of chapters 10, and 13-16 demonstrate this approach as an attempt is made in each of the studies to interpret Black parent and family data in view of immediate realities in the private school environments.

FAMILY-SCHOOL RELATIONS IN PRIVATE SCHOOLS: SOME IMPLICATIONS FOR BLACK CHILD DEVELOPMENT

Many chapters in this volume suggest that Black communities simultaneously hold three values which have strong implications for children's education: a high value for formal education and academic excellence; a preference for inclusion in mainstream American culture in order to benefit from the high standard of living enjoyed by many, if not most, Americans; and an equally strong desire for maintenance of social and cultural integrity. The actual implementation of any one of these values can lead to parenting behaviors which are conflicting and contradictory relative to the other two values.

In chapter 16, Johnson refers to the delicate balance Black parents create when they juxtapose their child's self-esteem against the parental goal of upward social mobility. To what extent is that balance jeopardized by the private school experience? In chapters 14 and 15, it is shown that these schools generally meet parental expectations and perceptions of the key elements of a school's environment which they feel will promote the life success of their child. That is, parents seem to feel that the school is in fact ensuring upward mobility for their child, insofar as that child will learn to be an effective competitor with majority White, as well as other non-Black, children. However, the potential threats to the healthy social, emotional, and identity development of the child have not been provided for and have often not been considered by Black families choosing these schools. Particularly in desegregated schools, the consequences can include social isolation, a diminished sense of self-efficacy, and the lack of appropriate experiences fostering positive group identity. The full advantage of the private school experience may escape Black children for these reasons. Many of these pitfalls are avoided by Black families who choose predominantly Black independent schools. However, many of these schools model themselves after desegregated private schools and continue to ignore the special needs of Black children and the realities of blocked opportunity while attempting to prepare them for competitive White society.

In chapters 2 and 7, the authors point out that the damage can be great if parent involvement is not at its maximum, and if policies are not developed to address both real and potential problems related to race in the school. In both chapters, the authors reflect on the importance of a curriculum and school support system that go beyond the considerations of the average middle-class and White experience. Although not stated explicitly, both chapters underscore the crucial importance of strengthening the relationship between the home and school for the benefit of the child. As newcomers to private schools, Black families do not always understand or enact their right to challenge the school. In the past, schools were not as pressured to respond to the needs of Black families because the families did not represent a critical mass. This fact is changing very quickly and private schools must respond. The attending Black families are some of their best resources for making the necessary changes in private schools.

The increasing visibility of Blacks in the private school setting is potentially very positive for the social, emotional, and motivational development of Black children. It means that Black parents can command a greater voice in altering the ecologies of private schools, which may directly benefit their children and more subtly benefit all children in these schools. It means that Black children need not feel isolated in these schools or have experiences which eventuate in their marginality in the larger society as Oyemade and Williams have suggested. Finally, it means that Black families do not have to risk exchanging the academic preparedness of their children for the children's racial pride and self-esteem. The willingness of Black families and private institutions to work together can make these schools a place to effect a balance between academic excellence, social mobility, and the full personal development of Black children.

BLACKS AND PRIVATE SCHOOLING: A LOOK TO THE FUTURE

This volume should not conclude without a tribute to those private schools which permitted contributors to gather and report the relevant data from their school communities. Their support will benefit private schooling generally. As is amply demonstrated in chapters 17 and 18, as well as by the reports in several others, the presence of even 10 percent of Black children in nonpublic schools is an open critique of today's public schooling. Given that over 55 percent of Black families have incomes at or below the poverty level, even the most fiscally stable of Black families send children to private school only at costs to themselves and to extended family members. Clearly, Black families are especially desirous of keeping all educational options open for their children. As noted in chapters 8, 9, 11, and 12, we must find ways to support private schools which effectively educate ethnic minority students without simultaneously undermining that which is good about the concept of public education.

We are indebted to Carol Yeakey for positing alternative perspectives on public school reform and alternatives to wholesale and total abandoment by Blacks of this type of formal schooling at the earliest possible opportunity. We are also appreciative of Cathy Royal's important, and unabashedly prescriptive, remarks as to how desegregated private schools can improve upon the academic climates which participating Black children experience. Finally, we are especially grateful to James Comer, Edgar Epps, Thomas Hoffer, Barbara Sizemore, and Edmund Gordon for sharing, given the broader contexts of Black education and American culture, their perspectives on the phenomenon of "Blacks and Private Schooling." Several of our contributors have observed that the education of Black children, whether in public or private schools, desegregated or otherwise, will continue to be problematic as long as our society does not demonstrate true commitment to a pluralistic, egalitarian perspective on human learning and development. Further, as Speede-Franklin so poignantly observes in chapter 3, with increasing numbers of diverse ethnic minorities in private schools anticipated for the next decade and beyond, the problems herein identified in relation to Black Americans will undoubtedly be repeatedly echoed.

NOTES

1. Allison Davis, <u>Social-Class Influences Upon Learning</u> (Cambridge, Mass.: Harvard University Press, 1948).

2. Eleanor Leacock, <u>Teaching and Learning in City Schools</u> (New York: Basic Books, 1969); Ray Rist, <u>The Invisible Children: School Integration in American Society</u> (Cambridge, Mass. Harvard University Press, 1978); and <u>The Urban School: A Factory for Failure</u> (Cambridge, Mass.: MIT Press, 1973); and Janet Schofield, <u>Black and White in School: Trust, Tension, or Tolerance</u> (New York: Praeger, 1982).

3. James Coleman et al., <u>Equality of Educational Opportunity</u> (Washington, D. C.: Government Printing Office, 1966).

4. Benjamin Bloom, "Early Learning in the Home," in Benjamin Bloom, ed. <u>All Our Children Learning</u> (New York: McGraw-Hill, 1980), pp. 67-88; Robert D. Hess and Virginia Shipman, "Early Experience and the Socialization of Cognitive Modes in Children," <u>Child Development</u> 36 (1965): 869-886.

5. See Diana T. Slaughter and Edgar G. Epps, "The Home Environment and Academic Achievement of Black American Children and Youth: An Overview," <u>Journal of Negro Education</u> 56 (1987): 3-20 for references in this area; see also Diana T. Slaughter, "Early Intervention and Its Effects on Maternal and Child Development," <u>Monographs of the Society for Research in Child Development</u>, 48, serial no. 202 (4, 1983).

6. John Ogbu, <u>The Next Generation: An Ethnography of Educa-
    tion in an Urban Neighborhood</u> (New York: Academic Press,
    1974); Thomas Popkewitz, <u>The Myth of Educational Reform</u>
    (Madison: University of Wisconsin Press, 1982).

7. V. P. Franklin, Personal communication, December 4, 1987;
    see also chapter 8, this volume.

8. Patricia Minuchin et al., <u>The Psychological Impact of the
    Schooling Experience</u> (New York: Basic Books, 1969).

9. Jacob Getzels, "Socialization and Education: A Note on
    Discontinuities," in Hope Leichter, ed., <u>The Family as
    Educator</u> (New York: Teachers College Press, 1974), pp.
    44-51; Sara Lightfoot, "Toward Conflict and Resolution:
    Relationships between Families and Schools," <u>Theory Into
    Practice</u>, 20 (1981): 97-104.

10. Shirley Brice-Heath, "Questioning at Home and at School: A
    Comparative Study," in George Spindler, ed., <u>Doing Ethno-
    graphy</u> (New York: Holt, Rinehart, and Winston, 1982), pp.
    96-101; Helen Gouldner, <u>Teachers' Pets,Troublemakers, and
    Nobodies</u> (Westport, Conn.: Greenwood Press, 1978).

Bibliographical Essay
Diana T. Slaughter

The literature which addresses Blacks and private schools has primarily developed since 1959. Between 1959-1976, the emphasis was on the impact of the Brown vs. Board of Education decision in 1954 declaring segregation in public education unconstitutional, a decision intended to positively impact the experiences of Blacks in public schools which had implications for Blacks in non-public schools as well. Concerns were expressed in a number of documents that instead of encouraging integration, exactly the opposite was occurring. Specifically, because of "White flight" from mandated desegregation in the South, there were disturbing trends toward resegregation of public schools. White families and communities were establishing private academies throughout the South to avoid having to send their children to public schools with Black children. See George Cunningham, "Nonpublic school alternatives to busing: Attitudes and characteristics," Urban Education 15 (April 1981): 3-12; George Cunningham and William Husk, "White flight: A closer look at the assumptions," Urban Review 12 (Spring 1980): 23-30; Michael Giles, "Desegregation and private schools," Social Policy 6 (January-February 1976): 46-49; Charles Clofeler, "School desegregation, 'Tipping,' and private school enrollment," Journal of Human Resources 11 (Winter 1976): 28-50; Michael Giles, "The impact of busing on White flight," Social Science Quarterly 55 (September 1974): 493-501; James Palmer, "Resegregation and the private school movement," Integrated Education 9 (May-June 1971): 4-10.

Both Blacks and Whites have been aware of the trend toward creating private schools as vehicles for maintaining segregation. Even today many Blacks are embittered about how Southern Whites attempted to use private schooling to circumvent the law and the will of the highest court in the nation (cf., Yeakey, this volume). Recent research in this tradition includes Crain's study of the impact of Catholic schools upon racial segregation in two cities. He found that the elementary schools in Chicago and Cleveland were highly segregated, but parochial high schools were less segregated than public ones. However, results as to whether private schooling fostered school segregation were inconclusive. See Robert L. Crain, "Private Schools and Black-White Segregation: Evidence from Two Big Cities," Resources in Education (ED 259 430, 1984). Crain's research deemphasizes White attitudes as precipitating "White flight," instead stressing the "de facto" consequences of parochial schooling for the progress of school desegregation.

In contrast to the motivation of administrators in the emerging southern, White, private academies, some private school administrators in established private schools, aware of the mandate for public school desegregation, showed an early and continuing interest in desegregating these schools. See, for example, John B. Coburn, "Independent schools and social issues," Independent School Bulletin 28 (May 1969): 20-27. By 1969, reports were published describing the experiences of Black students in some independent schools: William Link, "Black youth, Black nationalism, and White independent schools," Independent School Bulletin 29 (October 1969): 14-15; Robert Sandoe, "Isn't this what education is all about?" Independent School Bulletin 29 (October 1969): 16-18. See also: David Mallery, "Four Black students talk about school," Independent School Bulletin 30 (December 1970): 11-13; Gregory Witcher, "A journey from Anacostia to the elite White world," Independent School Bulletin 39 (May 1980): 31-33.

By the late 1970s, legislation supported desegregation of private schools. See Leslie Gerstman, "Racial integration in nonpublic schools," NOLPE School Law Journal 8 (1979): 210-220; Eldon D. Wedlock and Cheryl S. McMurry, "Pupils," Resources in Education (ED 145 558, March 1978); "Runyon et ux, DBA Bobbe's School v. McCrary et al. Certiorari to the United States Court of Appeals for the Fourth Circuit: Syllabus. Slip Opinion," Resources in Education (ED 131 176, March 1977); and United States Court of Appeals for the Fourth Circuit No. 73-2348, "Michael C. McCrary and Colin M. Gonzales, Infant by Raymond Gonzales and Margaret R. Gonzales, Appellees, Versus Russell L. Runyon, Katheryne E. Runyon Defendants, Southern Independent School Association, Appellant," Resources in Education (ED 106 395, September 1975).

Educational focus on Blacks and private schools soon included comparisons between public and parochial schools, especially as to benefits to lower income and minority pupils. The focus began around 1967, soon after the timing of the first Coleman report on equal educational opportunity (James S. Coleman, Equality of Educational Opportunity (Washington, D. C.: Government Printing Office, 1966) and continued steadily through 1981, culminating in the production of the more recent and important Coleman study which compared and contrasted public and parochial secondary schools. For an overview of the lively debate stimulated by Coleman's assertion that private schools produce greater cognitive outcomes and are more racially desegregated than public schools, see James S. Coleman, "Public schools, private schools, and the public interest," Public Interest 64 (Summer 1981): 19-30; Ellis Page and Timothy Keith, "Effects of U. S.

private schools: A technical analysis of two recent claims," Educational Researcher 10 (August-September 1981): 7-17; James S. Coleman, "Response to Page and Keith," Educational Researcher 10 (August-September 1981): 18-20; Ellis Page, "The media, technical analysis, and the data feast: A response to Coleman," Educational Researcher 10 (August-September 1981): 21-23. The database in question was a longitudinal study of high school students. Coleman has published two books: (with Thomas Hoffer and Sally Kilgore) High School Achievement: Public, Catholic, and Private Schools Compared (New York: Basic Books, 1982) and (with Thomas Hoffer) Public and Private High Schools (New York: Basic Books, 1987).

Current publications indicate that this comparative perspective continues to be of considerable interest to educators. See Tom James and Henry Levin, eds., Comparing Public and Private Schools, 2 vols. (Philadelphia: Falmer Press, 1988); William Boyd and James G. Cibulka, eds., Private School and Public Policy: International Perspectives, (Philadelphia: Falmer Press, in press). General public dissatisfaction with the achievements of public school students probably contributes most to the increase in comparative studies of the two types of schools. Two articles published by Christopher Jencks in the 1960s foreshadowed this trend: "Is the public school obsolete?" Public Interest 2, no. 2 (1966): 18-27; and "Private Schools for Black Children," New York Times Magazine, sec. 6 (November 3, 1968): 30.

Although initially most attention focused on desegregation issues in relation to Blacks and private schools, later the focus emphasized the educational value of these schools, and the potentially special contributions of predominantly Black independent schools, for Blacks. For reports summarizing the educational value of private schools, in addition to the Coleman and Hoffer report cited above, see: Diana T. Slaughter and Barbara L. Schneider, "Parental goals and Black student achievement in urban private elementary schools," Journal of Intergroup Relations 13 (Spring 1985): 24-33; Diana T. Slaughter and Barbara L. Schneider, Newcomers: Blacks in Private Schools, 2 vols. (Washington, D. C.: Office of Educational Research and Improvement, 1986) (ED 274 768 and ED 274 769); Carol Ascher, "Black students and private schooling," Urban Review 18 (1986): 137-145; Virgil Blum, "Private education in the inner city," Phi Delta Kappan 66 (May 1985): 643-646; John Holmes and Diana Buell, "Parent Expectations of the Christian School," Resources in Education 84 (October 1984) (ED 244 363). For an example of the literature on Black independent schools, see Marva Collins, Marva Collins' Way (New York: J. P. Tarcher Publishers, 1982); Edwin J. Nichols, Teaching Mathematics, Volume I, Culture,

Motivation, History and Classroom Management (Washington, D. C. FGK57295: National Science Foundation, 1986) (ED 283 929); and Joan D. Ratteray, <u>Access to quality: Private schools in Chicago's inner city</u> (Chicago, Ill.: Heartland Policy Study No. 9, 1986) (ED 272 613). This important shift in overall focus as to the relationship between Blacks and private schools is important. Contemporary emphasis is rightfully on the educational experiences of Blacks in private schools, particularly the meaning of the experiences to Black students and their families, thus treating familial socioeconomic status and school racial composition as independent or intervening variables impacting those experiences.

Index

Contributors

NANCY L. ARNEZ is a Professor of Educational Administration and Supervision, School of Education, Howard University, Washington D.C. She received the Ed.D. from Teachers College, Columbia University in 1958, and served as Director of the Center for Inner City Studies, Northeastern Illinois University in Chicago and as Department Chairman, Associate Dean and Acting Dean, School of Education, Howard University. Her research areas include: Black Superintendent-School Board Relations, Racism in Children's Literature, and Desegregation. She recently published with Henry Hankerson and Doris J. Levi two articles on Afro Americans and the U.S. Constitution, Afro-American Black History Month Kit, Associated Publishers (Winter, 1987).

MARY LYNCH BARNDS, M. S., Ed., is a specialist in Parent Education. As Executive Director of the Parent Office for the National Catholic Educational Association (NCEA) in Washington, D. C., she directed the development of "Parent Choice, Parent Involvement and Student Outcomes," a design for a three-year study to fill the gap in knowledge about how different forms of parent involvement affect students in Catholic high schools serving low-income families.

PATRICIA A. BAUCH is an Assistant Professor of Education and holds the Elizabeth Ann Seton Chair at The Catholic University of America. She received her doctorate in curriculum and the study of schooling from The University of California, Los Angeles. She is also a research associate and faculty member at the Youth Research Center in the Interdisciplinary Graduate Research Program in Human Development. She is a Spencer Research Fellow of the National Academy of Education under whose sponsorship she completed this chapter. She teaches and conducts research on Catholic schools, minority families, home-school relations, teacher curriculum beliefs, and the social context of schooling. She is currently editing a volume under contract with Greenwood Press entitled Private Schools and the Public Interest: Research and Policy Issues.

CRAIG C. BROOKINS is a Doctoral Candidate in Ecological/Community Psychology at Michigan State University. His research interests include: independent Black education, Black child development, African personality, social change research and interventions, and the prevention of child abuse and neglect. He is currently the assistant director at the Children's Trust Fund for the Prevention of Child Abuse and Neglect with the State of Michigan.

GERALDINE KEARSE BROOKINS is a Professor of Psychology in the Department of Psychology at Jackson State University. She earned her B.A. degree in History at Oberlin College and Ph.D. in Psychology at Harvard University. Her research interests include work/family interface influences on child development, dual career and dual earner Black families, and adolescent sexuality and parenting. She recently co-edited with Margaret B. Spencer and Walter R. Allen, Beginnings: The Social and Affective Development of Black Children. She is currently involved in a study of coping among dual career Black couples.

JAMES G. CIBULKA is an Associate Professor in the Department of Administrative Leadership, the University of Wisconsin-Milwaukee. He specializes in educational administration and the politics and financing of education, particularly as they pertain to urban issues and problems. He is a past Program Chair of Associates for Research on Private Education (ARPE), a Special Interest Group of the American Educational Research Association.

JAMES P. COMER is a member of the permanent faculty at Yale University where he holds appointments as the Maurice Falk Professor of Child Psychiatry, Yale Child Study Center, Director, School Development Program, Yale Child Study Center, and Associate Dean of the Yale University Medical School. Professor Comer received his B. A. from Indiana University, his M. D. from Howard University College of Medicine, and his M. P. H. degree from the University of Michigan School of Public Health. He completed residences in Child Psychiatry at the Yale Medical School, the Yale Child Study Center, and the Hillcrest Children's Center in Washington, D. C. For many years, Dr. Comer has been committed to elementary school education as a preventive psychiatric focus. He was a major catalyst in the process of stabilizing two inner-city, low income schools, thereby enabling children to achieve both academically and socially. The process, recorded as an intervention program in his book, School Power, has now been extended to 10 schools in New Haven, and other school systems in, Michigan, Maryland, Virginia, Arkansas and Kansas.

EDGAR G. EPPS is the Marshall Field IV Professor of Urban Education at the University of Chicago (since 1970). He has previously held faculty positions at Tuskegee Institute (1967-70); The University of Michigan (1964-67); Florida A & M University (1961-66); and Tennessee State University (1958-61). He was educated at Talladega College, Atlanta University, and Washington State University where he earned the Ph.D. Degree in Sociology. His books include Black Students in White Schools; Race Relations: New Perspectives; Cultural Pluralism; and Black Consciousness, Identity and Achievement. He has authored or co-authored many articles on sociological and psychological factors that influence achievement and motivation. His current research includes a study of educational and occupational aspirations as they relate to educational attainment of Black adolescents and young adults.

V. P. FRANKLIN is currently Associate Professor of History at Arizona State University. He received his Ph.D. from the University of Chicago in 1975 in the History of Education, and is the author of numerous essays and several books in the area of Afro-American History and Education. His most recent work is Black Self-Determination: A Cultural History of the Faith of the Fathers (1984).

EDMUND W. GORDON is a member of the permanent faculty at Yale University, where he holds a primary appointment as the John Musser Professor of Psychology and secondary appointments as Professor of Afro-American Studies and Professor of Child Study in Yale College, the Yale University Graduate School and the Yale University School of Medicine. Professor Gordon completed the bachelor of Science degree in zoology at Howard University. He also earned the bachelor of Divinity degree in social ethics from Howard's Graduate School of Divinity. He earned the Master of Arts degree in social psychology from the American University and the Doctor of Education degree in Child Development and Guidance from Teachers College, Columbia University. Dr. Gordon served for five years as Editor of the American Journal of Orthopsychiatry and for three years as Editor of the Annual Review of Research in Education. In 1978, he was elected to membership in the National Academy of Education. His most recent book, to be published in

Winter 1988, <u>Defiers of Negative Prediction</u>, is concerned with the career development of Black men and women who have overcome enormous odds against success to become high achievers.

JUDITH BERRY GRIFFIN has been President of A Better Chance Inc. (ABC) since 1982. Prior to joining ABC, Mrs. Griffin served as Executive Assistant to a key Assistant Secretary, at the U. S. Department of Education, and then as Director, Division of Teacher Centers, where she led the reformulation of regulatory proposals and the development and direction of technical assistance with strategies for national dissemination. In addition to her distinguished career in education with DOE, and as a teacher and school principal, Mrs. Griffin is the author of three widely acclaimed books for children.

THOMAS B. HOFFER is a Study Director at the Public Opinion Laboratory, Northern Illinois University. He is currently working on a national study of high school and middle school students' attitudes toward and understanding of science and technology. His prior research focussed on national comparisons of public and Catholic school students, work which resulted in the publication of <u>High School Achievement: Public, Catholic, and Private Schools Compared</u> (with James S. Coleman and Sally Kilgore, New York: Basic Books, 1982), and <u>Public and Private High Schools</u> (with James S. Coleman, New York: Basic Books, 1987). Hoffer received a Ph.D. in sociology from the University of Chicago in 1986.

DEBORAH J. JOHNSON is an Assistant Professor of Child and Family Studies at the University of Wisconsin - Madison. Dr. Johnson has been the recipient of several awards and fellowships for her scholarly pursuits and commitment to Black child development. Dr. Johnson was a President's Postdoctoral Fellow at the University of California at Berkeley from 1987 through the beginning of 1989 and a Predoctoral Fellow at the University of California, Santa Barbara's Center for Black Studies. Dr. Johnson was the recipient of the Phi Delta Kappa's Outstanding Dissertation Award at Northwestern University where she received her Ph.D. in the Program of Human Development and Social Policy. In 1988, her dissertation received special commendation from the Board of Ethnic and Minority Affairs, the American Psychological Association.

SYLVIA T. JOHNSON is a Professor of Educational Research Methodology and Statistics, Department of Psychoeducational Studies, School of Education, Howard University. She also serves as Chairman of the Department. She was the principal investigator for the 1984 ABC-Ford Foundation study, Science and Mathematics Career Choice among Talented minority Youth. Dr. Johnson's own educational background includes experiences in public and private education. Her elementary education took place at an independent school, the Francis W. Parker School in Chicago. Following four years at a public high school she completed Howard University with a degree in Mathematics. She took her Master's from Southern Illinois University at Carbondale, and a Ph.D. in Educational Measurement and Statistics from the University of Iowa. She served on state and private college and university faculties in Illinois and New Jersey prior to joining Howard's faculty in 1974. Dr. Johnson serves on the Board of Directors of the National Council on Measurement in Education (NCME), and on the Design and Analyses Committee of the National Assessment of Educational Progress (NAEP). She has written extensively in professional and general publications on the topics of testing, test bias, and minority achievement, and has testified before congressional committees and national commissions on these topics.

FAUSTINE C. JONES-WILSON is a Professor of Social Foundations of Education, School of Education, Howard University, Washington, D. C. She received the Ed.D. from the College of Education, The University of Illinois, Champaign-Urbana, and has for ten years been the Editor-in-Chief of the Journal of Negro Education. Her research areas include: social change, social criticism, successful Black public schools, desegregation, Black family and education. She recently published "Equity in Education: Low Priority in the School Reform Movement," The Urban Review, 18 (1986), 31-39.

KOFI LOMOTEY is an Assistant Professor of Educational Administration at The State University of New York at Buffalo, where his focus is urban schools. He received the Ph.D. from the School of Education, Stanford University in Administration and Policy Analysis. His research interests include elementary school leadership, African American faculty and tenure, African American access to higher education, independent Black institutions and, most recently, ancient Egyptian education. Dr. Lomotey's publications include "Black Principals for Black Students: A Cultural Imperative," and "The Academic Achievement Gap and Black Access to Higher Education." He is a co-founder and former director of two independent Black institutions--Shule Ya Kukitambua in Oberlin, Ohio and Shule Ya Taifa in East Palo Alto, California. He served for eleven years as the National Executive Officer of the Council of Independent Black Institutions (CIBI).

EDWARD B. MCDONALD is currently Social Science Librarian at the University of New Orleans. He received his Masters of Library Science from the University of Illinois at Urbana-Champaign in 1977. He is presently completing a study of Black Catholic Education in New Orleans.

URA JEAN OYEMADE is Associate Professor and Chairperson of the Department of Human Development in the School of Human Ecology at Howard University. She received the Ph.D. in Psychology from Tulane University in New Orleans. With research interests in the ecology of child development, Dr. Oyemade has conducted several major studies on the impact of the family and the environment on the development of Black children. Currently, she is co-principal investigator of studies on the "Effects of Parent Involvement on the Upward Mobility of Head Start Families" and the "Sociocultural and Psychological Factors Affecting the Outcome of Pregnancy." She is also currently Vice-President of the Parents Association of the Sidwell School, where her son is enrolled.

BARBARA PATTERSON is Executive Director of the Black Student Fund in Washington, D. C. In her eight-year tenure with the Fund she has been both a local advocate and nationwide spokesperson for racial and economic diversity in independent schools. Under her Directorship, the Fund has tripled its scholarship offerings, initiated tutorial, counseling, and retention programs for promising Black students; developed a recruitment program for increasing Black faculty representation in independent schools; and published A History Deferred, an educator's guide for teaching Black History. Mrs. Patterson holds a B. A. in Education from Trinity College, Washington, D. C., and is currently pursuing graduate study in counseling. Through her experiences as both teacher and parent in public and private schools, and over 25 years of involvement in the struggle for equal rights, she developed and maintains a commitment to opportunities for academic excellence for Black youngsters.

JOAN DAVIS RATTERAY is President of the Institute for Independent Education, Inc., Washington, D. C. Dr. Ratteray founded the Institute in 1984 to provide technical assistance to independent neighborhood schools and to analyze policies affecting independent education. She has participated on panels of national education policymakers and researchers. Many of her articles on independent schools have been published in journals and newspapers across America. Her presentations to leading groups like Cleveland's City Club Forum have been broadcast widely on public radio and television. A training course for teachers of mathematics that she directed was funded by the National Science Foundation. She received her Ph.D. in Human Development from the University of Maryland in 1973, with prior degrees from Vanderbilt University and the University of Georgia. Before starting the Institute, she was Director of Education Programs at the National Center for Neighborhood Enterprise. She was appointed as an HEW Fellow in 1976 and then served for three years in the office of Secretary Califano as a consultant, and as Special Assistant to the Chairman and Director of Liaison at the White House Conference on Families. Her earlier experience includes positions as Research Associate with The Rand Corporation, Assistant Professor at Howard University, and Education Research Assistant at the National Institute of Education.

CATHY ROYAL has been at Phillips Academy, Andover, MA since 1985. Before Phillips Academy she taught at the Latin School of Chicago. Ms. Royal is an Instructor in English, history and Andover's first Minority Counselor. By her second year at Andover, Mrs. Royal had launched the Dakar Project, a community service center which took 23 students and five faculty to Dakar, Senegal in West Africa to begin a five-year restoration project of a primary school on Goree Island. Ms. Royal has served as a consultant to the National Association of Independent Schools (NAIS) for minority affairs; a member of the NAIS Teachers' Committee; and as part of the original Planning Committee for the N.A.I.S. Understanding and Managing Diversity Summer Institute, 1986. Ms. Royal has also served the Independent School Association Central States (ISACS) as the first chairwoman of their Minority Affairs Committee. While in Chicago Ms. Royal received a congressional award from Rep. Charles Hayes in recognition of her work in the areas of Education and The Women's Task Force

BARBARA L. SCHNEIDER has been an Assistant Professor of Education, in the School of Education and Social Policy, Northwestern University. Her area of specialization is school organizations, and she has written several chapters and articles on private education. Her most recent chapter 'Schooling for minority children: An equity perspective is forthcoming in <u>Private Schools and Public Policy: International Perspectives</u>, edited by William Lowe Boyd and James Cibulka, Falmer Press. She is currently affiliated with the National Opinion Research Center, The University of Chicago.

MWALIMU SHUJAA is a Co-Founder of the Afrikan People's Action School in Trenton, N. J. He co-authored with Dr. Joan Davis Ratteray a U. S. Office of Education study conducted by the Institute for Independent Education entitled <u>Dare to Choose</u> (1987). The study investigated the factors influencing parental decisions to select independent neighborhood schools for their children. He serves on the executive committees of the Council of Independent Black Institutions (CIBI) and the New Jersey Association of Black Educators (NJABE). He is presently a Research Assistant with the Center for Policy Research in Education (CPRE) at Rutgers University.

BARBARA A. SIZEMORE is Associate Professor of Black Studies in the Department of Black Community Education Research and Development at the University of Pittsburgh, Pittsburgh, Pennsylvania. Her research areas include: Black education, Black effective schools, Black superintendents and the Black Family. A former superintendent of the District of Columbia Public Schools, she has written a brook about that experience, <u>The Ruptured Diamond: the Politics of the Decentralization of the District of Columbia Public Schools</u>, University Press of America, 1981. She has done extensive ethnographic research in Black elementary schools in Pittsburgh, Dallas, Texas and Milwaukee, Wisconsin. An account of these studies, The Effective African American Elementary School, appears in <u>Schooling in Social Context: Qualitative Studies</u>, edited by George W. Noblit and William T. Pink, Ablex Publishing Company, 1987. She is currently working on a book with Nancy L. Arnez, <u>Two in the Bush: The African American Struggle for Equality and Excellence in Education</u>, the story of the Black superintendent.

DIANA T. SLAUGHTER is Associate Professor of Education and Social Policy, in the Human Development and Social Policy Program, Northwestern University, where she also has a secondary appointment as Associate Professor in the Department of African American Studies. Dr. Slaughter completed all her formal education in the Committee on Human Development at the University of Chicago. Her research areas include: family influences on academic achievement, Black education and early intervention studies. She recently guest co-edited (with Edgar G. Epps of the University of Chicago) a special issue of the Journal of Negro Education (Winter, 1987) devoted to the Black child's home environment and student achievement. She is currently editing another volume under contract: Black Children and Poverty: A Developmental Perspective (Jossey-Bass), and writing another based upon ethnographic research on Black children in urban private elementary schools. Formerly a member of the Governing Council of the Society for Research in Child Development, Dr. Slaughter is a member of the Board of Ethnic and Minority Affairs of the American Psychological Association, and a member of the Committee on Child Development and Public Policy, National Research Council, National Academy of Sciences.

WANDA SPEEDE-FRANKLIN was Director of Minority Affairs and Director of Information Services for the National Association of Independent Schools from 1982 to 1987. She received a B.A. in political science and a Certificate of Proficiency in Afro-American Studies from Princeton University, and a M.A. in educational administration from Northwestern University. She has been an independent school alumna, trustee and parent. Her civic activities include membership on various boards of directors of educational institutions such as the Metropolitans Council for Educational Opportunity (METCO, Inc.) and Channels for Educational Choices. Her awards include a 1985 citation in Who's Who Among Black Americans. She has recently accepted the position of Director of the METCO Program with the Newton Public Schools, Newton, Mass.

ROBERT D. WILLIAMS is currently Middle School Principal at Sidwell Friends School in Washington, D. C. He is a middle school educator with experience in both public and private schools. Mr. Williams has presented workshops on multicultural - multiethnic education at numerous schools and conferences. He was recently a member of the faculty of the workshop Understanding and Managing Diversity sponsored by The National Association of independent Schools (NAIS).

CAROL CAMP YEAKEY is Professor of Administration and Policy at the University of Virginia where she teaches graduate courses in organizational theory and behavior and educational policy research and analysis. She serves as a consultant and reviewer for funding agencies and national research publications. The recipient of several research fellowships, she has published in major national and international journals. Co-editor of <u>Research and Thought in Administrative Theory</u> and <u>Schools as Conduits: Educational Policymaking During the Reagan Years</u>, she is the author of two forthcoming volumes <u>Of Politics, Ideology and Conservative School Reform: The Formulation of Social Polcy Agendas</u> and <u>Conceptual and Methodological Approaches to Policy Research and Analysis.</u>